THE CRUCIBLE OF WAR

VOLUME I
WAVELL'S COMMAND

Barrie Pitt served in both the European and Middle East theatres in the war, and later edited the enormous partwork *History of the Second World War*. He was also Editor-in-Chief of *Ballantine's Illustrated History of World War 11*. He is the author of *Zeebrugge, St George's Day, 1918, Coronel and Falkland, 1918 - The Last Act, The Battle of the Atlantic, Churchill and the Generals* and a novel, *The Edge of Battle.*

Wavell's Command is the first of the three volumes of *The Crucible of War.* Its companion volumes *Auchinleck's Command* and *Montgomery and Alamein* are published by Cassell in uniform editions.

THE CRUCIBLE OF WAR

VOLUME I
WAVELL'S COMMAND

BARRIE PITT

CASSELL&CO

Cassell & Co
Wellington House, 125 Strand
London WC2R 0BB

The Crucible of War was first published in two volumes by Jonathan
Cape, 1980 and 1982
This three-volume edition published 2001

British Library Cataloguing-in-Publication Data
A catalogue record for this book is available from the British Library

ISBN 0-304-35950-5

Printed and bound in Great Britain by
Creative Print & Design (Wales), Ebbw Vale

To Ann

who makes it all worth while

Contents

Illustrations

PLATES

ILLUSTRATIONS

MAPS

FIGURES

The author and publishers would like to thank Mr John Batchelor for permission to use his line drawings, figures 1–4.

Author's Note

No book such as this can be written without the help of others –
librarians, fellow historians, archivists, survivors of the various
actions – and to attempt to list all who so freely made available to me
their time, their expertise or their memories would add pages to an
already long book. I hope that they will therefore forgive me if I do
not particularise, but accept once again my gratitude for their
contributions.

There are some, however, whose help was either unique or
continuous and to these I would like to express especial thanks.
General Sir Richard O'Connor was kind enough not only to lend me
his own unpublished account of the planning and execution of
Operation Compass (smuggled with great ingenuity out of an Italian
prison-camp in 1941) but also to spend time clarifying various aspects
of the battle which had puzzled me before, as did Field Marshal Lord
Harding of Petherton and the late Major-General Eric Dorman
O'Gowan. To the same extent I am indebted to Colonel C. A. H. M.
Noble, M.C., who lent me the diary he kept, first as adjutant to the
2nd Camerons during *Operation Compass*, and later as a staff officer
with H.Q. 4th Indian Division.

During conversations we had together many years ago, Generale
Giuseppe Mancinelli did much to explain to me the Italian attitudes
to the War in the Desert and especially the psychological problems
besetting Italians fighting with the Germans against the British, while
Generals Walther Nehring and Walter Warlimont helped considerably towards an understanding of the views taken at Panzergruppe
Headquarters and in Berlin.

I would also like to thank Mrs Jane Caunt who completely retyped
the book, Christopher Harrison who drew the maps, Deborah
Shepherd who has so expertly clarified the text, and Anthony Colwell
and Graham Greene for the energy and enthusiasm they have given
to its publication.

Prologue: September 12th, 1882

The advance parties moved out westward at dusk and well before midnight the entire force was on the march – Cameron, Seaforth and Gordon Highlanders plus the men of the Black Watch on the left along the line of the Sweetwater Canal, Royal Irish Fusiliers, Royal Marines and the York and Lancasters on the right with forty-two pieces of artillery trundling between the two divisions. The Household Cavalry and two batteries of the Royal Horse Artillery trotted to the right rear, while to the south of the canal on the left flank and deliberately an hour behind on the march came the Pathan mountaineers, the Baluchis and the Oudh Sepoys with the Sikh Lancers in front. There was no moon but the stars were bright; the night warm, almost velvety.

Along the railway line and between the canal and the Highlanders came the Royal Naval detachment hauling the trolley with padded wheels and the 40-pounder aboard, keeping abreast of the Indian Brigade.

Well in front of the main artillery between the divisions rode the General and his staff while out in front of them marched Lieutenant Rawson of the Royal Navy, piloting the entire force by the stars. Some 11,000 bayonets, 2,000 sabres, 61 guns and six machine-guns were on the move against fortifications manned, it was believed, by 20,000 regular troops supported by 6,000 irregulars, 2,500 cavalry and 60 guns.

Dawn was at 0540 and the North Star and Great Bear, veering very slightly north-west as they set, drew the marching columns some seven degrees off their route so that they were approaching the enemy lines in slight echelon with the Highlanders ahead; but to offset this disadvantage nature had supplied a westerly wind, which took the sounds of the tramping men away back into the desert.

With just over 200 yards still separating the Camerons from the first line of defence, the right wing on the far side of the marching divisions bumped a cavalry picket who fired on them, and as a scattered fusillade followed, a bugle sounded the alarm in front.

The General dismounted and ran forward to peer through the

growing but still dim light, a hostile shell screeched overhead to bury itself between him and his horse, the enemy cavalry picket galloped across in front and then raced off into the morning mist – and with the need for silence at last gone, barked orders and bugle calls rang out all around, followed by a myriad clicks as bayonets slotted home.

To the left the Highlanders and to the right the Irish and the English broke into a run and surged forward towards the sandheaps and the main defensive ditch, ten feet wide and six feet deep, while behind them the Guards – Grenadiers, Coldstream and Scots – tore open their pouches and loaded their rifles, carried empty so far in pursuit of the order for total silence. Solid ranks, crested with steel, swept forward on to the black mounds under a lilac sky. A line of fire sparkled along the top of the mounds, but in their frenzy the defenders fired high, and bullets and balls whined out into the desert to furrow the distant sand-drifts.

The Highlanders were first into the ditch, and first out, cheering and shouting, climbing on one another's shoulders to reach the top and charge the first defence line, gun-butt and bayonet at work in desperate hand-to-hand battle wherever they found the white-clad enemy standing. Enfiladed from redoubts, the Scotsmen still in the ditch rushed or climbed to the loop-holes, thrusting in with bayonet and sword while the first of their comrades to reach the top swung back into the shelters to club or cut the gunners to the ground, thus releasing the main attack.

A hundred yards further on they found another line of entrenchments from which the defenders from the first line who had dropped back and now recovered from the first shock of battle were firing, quite coolly and deliberately, picking off the now-tiring Highlanders. As the front line melted into the ground, the second line wavered – but as they did so their pipers at last got wind into the bags and *The March of the Cameron Men* burst out, to be followed by the skirl of Irish pipes from the north as the right-hand division, held back by the error in navigation, stormed into the attack.

They had further to go but found a comparatively soft spot in the line, and excitement and some degree of desperation was now affecting the Egyptian infantry and gunners (though the Sudanese troops among them fought with an exemplary steadiness) and the shots flew high. With few casualties, Royal Marines and Royal Irish Fusiliers charged down along the line of the second entrenchments and the York and Lancasters mopped up with bayonet and club behind them. The artillery, having found their own separate ways across the main ditch, opened fire, to be joined almost immediately by the batteries of their mounted brothers to the north, while to the south the Indian Brigade, having cleared the southern bank of the canal, crossed it and with their lancers well in front flung themselves against the unprotected Egyptian flank.

And it was at this moment that the Household Brigade, lost for twenty minutes out on the right wing, rode in from the north over the Egyptian guns in a thunderous cascade of heavy horses and gigantic men, to turn what had been until then an orderly and well-fought withdrawal into a disorganised rout.

The Battle of Tel el Kebir was all over in thirty-five minutes. That very model of a modern Major-General, Sir Garnet Wolseley – small, neat and highly professional – had won yet another small, neat and highly professional victory at the end of a well-conducted campaign, and by the following day the first British troops were in Cairo. Arabi Pasha and his chief lieutenant surrendered without further ado, the Egyptian Army quietly dispersed homeward to take up their pathetic, poverty-stricken civilian lives again, and Wolseley and his staff moved into the Abdin Palace. The following day, the General sent a message to London: 'The war in Egypt is over; send no more men from England.'

But in the event, many more men did come out and the British were in Egypt to stay. Although the Liberal Government in general and Mr Gladstone in particular were delighted with General Wolseley's message *in toto*, the second part was to receive little practical application.

The campaign had been fought in order to ensure that the interest on the vast Egyptian national debt of £10,000,000 was paid to the international bondholders, and for that to be possible it quickly became obvious to European eyes that Egypt's administration must be placed upon a far more practical basis. Lord Dufferin arrived as High Commissioner to report upon the entire situation, Sir Evelyn Baring came out as British Agent and Consul-General, Sir Evelyn Wood arrived to organise a new 4,000-strong Egyptian Army, to be officered in the main by British gazetted regulars with himself as Sirdar or Commander-in-Chief. And in order to maintain the good order and discipline considered essential while these reforms were being carried out, a British Army of Occupation of some 14,000 men settled down in barracks between Suez and the Nile.

Long before it could be felt that their presence there was unnecessary the fanatical followers of the Mahdi in the south rose in revolution, and the ensuing assassination of General Gordon in Khartoum in 1885 resulted firstly in the increase of the British forces and then in the launching of relief columns and the general pacification of the Sudan, all of which kept more and more British troops quartered in Egypt during the closing years of the nineteenth century.

After the Sudan was pacified, the regiments stayed because they might be needed in the troubles down in the Transvaal, and when the Boer Wars were over they stayed because the events of the past few decades had demonstrated both the importance and the convenience to Britain of control of the eastern Mediterranean in respect of her communications with India and Australasia. As Lord Palmerston had put it many years before:

> We do not want Egypt or wish it for ourselves any more than any rational man with an estate in the north of England and a residence in the south would have wanted to possess the inns on the North Road. All he would want would have been that the inns should be well-kept, always accessible, and furnishing him, when he came, with mutton chops and post horses.

The possibility that the apparently obsequious, invariably subservient, frequently devious and generally poverty-stricken Egyptians might object to their country being regarded as a hostelry, however convenient and well-managed, seems rarely to have occurred to the inheritors of a solidly Victorian tradition, who shouldered their responsibilities firmly and regarded the growing evidence of their unpopularity with resignation and national phlegm.

And there was always, of course, the matter of the Suez Canal, of which Britain had been a bitter opponent until it was built, but a large shareholder increasingly insistent upon control ever since. If Lord Palmerston had not wanted Egypt, he and his successors were equally clear that no one else should have it, and it was a national axiom that the vital link with India and the southern dominions must always remain under British control.

This became even more evident in 1914 when the passage of the canal became essential for the transport of Australian and Indian troops to France, although in the event fewer Australians or Indians used it to reach the Western Front than British troops sent in the opposite direction to deal with the proliferation of troubles which then ensued (though these were by no means entirely the fault of the Egyptians). By 1918, as a result of the Middle East campaigns, a huge British military base had been built up.

Nevertheless, after prolonged – and often caustic – discussion, the British protectorate of Egypt ended on February 28th, 1922, Egypt being declared an independent sovereign state, with just four matters reserved to the British Government until agreement could be reached upon them: the security of British communications with her Empire, the defence of Egypt itself, the protection of foreign interests and minorities in Egypt, and control of the Sudan.

But as the years between the wars went by, the Royal Air Force grew in size, parts of the British Army became mechanised, and following that astonishing era of maritime revolution inspired by Lord Fisher during the turbulent 1900s, the Royal Navy stopped using coal and relied entirely upon oil-fired turbines. All of this meant that without the products of the Mosul oilfields at the head of the Persian Gulf, Britain would be powerless to wage war.

Egypt thereby became the western shield of an area of vital importance to Britain, especially as her own western border with Libya was demarcated by a 200-mile triple fence supported on five-foot metal stakes embedded in concrete and closely woven with barbed wire, erected by the Italians as security for their Libyan empire. And although Italy had fought alongside Britain in the First World War, it had become evident by the late 1930s that her sympathies would lie initially elsewhere in the event of a second.

Thus, early in September 1939 a British official found himself explaining to King Farouk (younger, slimmer and much better-looking than he is now remembered) that British control of Egypt would now have to be both retained and increased until the Axis had been defeated.

'Oh, all right!' replied the King, moodily. 'But when it's all over, for God's sake *lay down the white man's burden, and Go!*'

1 · The First Adversaries

Upon the outbreak of war, the responsibilities of the Commander-in-Chief, Middle East, had been substantially increased. From the day of his appointment in August 1939, General Sir Archibald Wavell had commanded all British land forces in Egypt, the Sudan, Palestine, Transjordan and Cyprus, but when Britain's ultimatum to Hitler ran out on September 3rd the Army formations in British Somaliland, Aden, Iraq and along the shores of the Persian Gulf also came under his command. The area for which he had thereby accepted military responsibility thus measured some 1,800 miles by 2,000 and included nine different countries in two continents.

Moreover, in the event of actual armed conflict taking place in the area – probably against Italy and possibly against Germany – troops stationed in Kenya would have to be involved in actions under his command, as would South African troops coming up from the other end of the continent – with, of course, the consent and approval of the South African Government.

There were other governments and governmental authorities as well from whom Wavell would have to secure co-operation, if not 'consent and approval'. His instructions were that he must keep in 'close touch and sympathy' with the rulers of Egypt and Iraq; with the High Commissioner for Palestine and Transjordan and the Governor-General of the Sudan; with the Governors of Cyprus, Aden and British Somaliland, the Political Resident in the Persian Gulf, the British Ambassadors in Cairo, Baghdad, Istanbul, and Athens, together with the chief representatives of Britain's allies adjoining his area of command. As at that time France was Britain's chief ally, this meant that he must on all matters of military significance consult the French military commanders in Algeria and Tunisia, in Syria and the Lebanon, in French Somaliland and quite possibly in French Equatorial Africa.

More practically, he had also to work closely with the Royal Naval Commanders-in-Chief in the Mediterranean and the East Indies, and with the Air Officer Commanding-in-Chief, Middle East.

As the general shortage of military equipment with which Great Britain faced the outbreak of war precluded the allocation of a personal aircraft to anyone, however exalted his rank or extensive his responsibilities, it can be seen that whoever fulfilled the duties of General Officer Commanding-in-Chief in the Middle East would need to be a remarkable man. Fortunately for Britain, he was.

General Sir Archibald Percival Wavell was fifty-six years of age when he arrived in Cairo to set up his Headquarters (with a staff of five in addition to his A.D.C.) and he had spent his life in the military world. The only son of an officer in the Norfolk Regiment, he had been commissioned at the age of eighteen into the Black Watch and had seen almost immediate service in South Africa and then on the north-west frontier of India. He had applied to go on the Staff College course at Camberley and after completing it had spent a year in Russia learning the language. He had already passed professional examinations in French, Urdu and Pushtu.

When the First World War broke out, Acting Captain Wavell had managed to evade the pressure to remain safely on the Staff until after the Second Battle of Ypres in 1915, during which he won the Military Cross and lost his left eye doing so. After convalescence, he spent two years shuttling between Russia, where he was sent to report on the probability of continued Russian participation in the conflict, and G.H.Q. France where he spent what he later described as the 'dullest ten months' of his life – before being sent out to the Middle East to join the staff of General Allenby. As a result of this, he took part alongside Colonel T. E. Lawrence in the entry into Jerusalem and the advance to Damascus, ending in 1918 with a brigadier-general's appointment and a clear understanding of the qualities of generalship which had enabled Allenby to win one of the most notable victories of that war. Wavell wrote later:

> In less than six weeks Allenby's army had captured 75,000 prisoners and 360 guns, and had moved its front forward 350 miles. Its own casualty list had been little over 5,000. The most advanced troops, the 5th Cavalry Division, had actually covered some 550 miles in the thirty-eight days from the breaking of the line to the occupation of Aleppo. The greatest exploit in history of horsed cavalry, and possibly their last success on a large scale, had ended within a short distance of the battlefield of Issus (333 B.C.), where Alexander the Great first showed how battles could be won by bold and well-handled horsemen.[1]

Peace brought a year's regimental duty with his beloved Black Watch (as a major) followed almost inexorably by another nine years' progression up the ladder of Staff promotion. The Adjutant-General's Department, the Directorate of Military Operations, the

Headquarters of the 3rd Infantry Division knew him well and appreciated his services, and then in 1930 he had been given command of an experimental infantry brigade at Aldershot. Three years later he had been promoted to Major-General, in 1935 he commanded an infantry division at Aldershot and in 1938 as a Lieutenant-General he was G.O.C.-in-C. Southern Command, United Kingdom. His appointment to the Middle East in August 1939 had been accompanied by promotion to full General.

So much for the bones of his military career. But a man capable of shouldering the enormous burdens which command of Britain's armies in the Middle East would entail required elements of greatness not revealed by a catalogue of appointments. Although he was perfectly prepared to model his outward behaviour along the lines of obdurate taciturnity which had come to be expected of British generals since Haig had set the pattern, Wavell's was a many-faceted character which presented all who knew him with considerable surprises.

Later, during one of the more crucial periods of the war, he astonished Winston Churchill with the casual announcement that during what leisure time he had he was editing a book of poems, and during the second half of the war he organised and judged a poetry competition for men in his command. And this was not, in Wavell's particular pattern of character, anything greatly to be marvelled at. 'Music, mystery and magic are the essence of the highest poetry,' he was to write – and the second and third of these qualities he also considered essential for successful military command.

He took a refreshingly caustic view of his profession, despite his own deep interest in it. In a letter to a fellow officer, he wrote:

The main ethical objection to war for intelligent people is that it is so deplorably dull and usually so inefficiently run. 'I see no reason why the human race, so inefficient in matters of peace, should suddenly become efficient in time of war.' I've forgotten where I saw that but it has always seemed to me that most people seeing the muddles of war forget the muddles of peace and the general inefficiency of the human race in ordering its affairs. War is a wasteful, boring, muddled affair; and people of fine intelligence either resign themselves to it or fret badly, especially if they are near the heart of things and can see matters which ought to be done, or done better, and cannot contrive to get them set right.[2]

Humour, robustness and sound common sense were the qualities which sustained him through life, and they were evident in everything he did – in the solidity of his stance as he watched his troops in training, in the lines which furrowed his brow and the corners of his eyes as he spoke, in the wry iconoclasm of the advice he gave.

I would give you a word of warning on the so-called principles of war, as laid down in Field Service Regulations.

For heaven's sake don't treat those as holy writ, like the Ten Commandments, to be learned by heart, and as having by their repetition some magic, like the incantations of savage priests. They are merely a set of common-sense maxims, like 'cut your coat according to your cloth,' 'a rolling stone gathers no moss,' 'honesty is the best policy,' and so forth. Those in F.S.R. are not necessarily complete or the best. They omit for instance the importance of information in war. Clausewitz has a different set, so has Foch, so have other military writers. They are all simply common sense, and are instinctive to the properly trained soldier . . .

Lastly, I do advise you to study the human side of military history, which is not a matter of cold-blooded formulas or diagrams, or nursery-book principles such as:

Be good and you will be happy.

Be mobile and you will be victorious.

Interior lines at night are the general's delight.

Exterior lines in the morning are the general's warning, and so on.

To learn that Napoleon in 1796 with 20,000 men beat combined forces of 30,000 by something called 'economy of force' or 'operating on interior lines' is a mere waste of time. If you can understand how a young, unknown man inspired a half-starved, ragged, rather Bolshie crowd; how he filled their bellies; how he out-marched, outwitted, out-bluffed and defeated men who had studied war all their lives and waged it according to the textbooks of the time, you will have learnt something worth knowing. But you won't get it from crammers' books . . .

But as a final word, I suggest you put this ideal of an infantryman before you:

Quick-footed, quick-minded and, as far as possible, light-hearted . . .[3]

Here, it was evident, was none of the prodigal habit of mind which had led to the murderous holocausts in France of the First World War, and would again in Russia in the Second. The new Commander-in-Chief, Middle East, was well aware of the value of each human life, and of the shortage of trained soldiers, sailors and airmen with which Britain faced perhaps the greatest trials in her long and arduous history.

This was an aspect of affairs which in any case was daily confront-
ing him, for despite the crucial importance of his own command, he
had hardly enough troops to police it, let alone defend it from
attack. One incomplete and not fully trained armoured formation,
twenty-one infantry battalions, two regiments of horsed cavalry,
four regiments of artillery with sixty-four field guns, forty-eight
anti-tank guns and eight anti-aircraft guns made up the force
immediately under his command, while down in the Sudan there
were three more infantry battalions and twenty companies of the
Sudan Defence Force. In British Somaliland was the Sudan Camel
Corps of 500 men, in Kenya were two brigades of the King's
African Rifles (native troops officered by British regulars) and two
light batteries, while at Aden there were two Indian battalions of
garrison troops.

So far as his allies were concerned, there were apparently some
5,000 native troops in French Somaliland under the experienced
command of Colonel Legentilhomme, an expeditionary force of
three newly raised divisions and some 40,000 troops engaged on
frontier defences and tribal control in Syria and the Lebanon under
the veteran Général Weygand, while to the west in Tunisia under
Général Noguès were eight divisions – six infantry, one fortress
and one light cavalry. But most of these, Wavell considered, might
well be too occupied with their own problems to be able to spare
him much support in time of emergency, despite the politicians'
promises.

As for the forces ranged against him, despite inter-war financial
stringency in intelligence matters and a degree of disapproval of
spying in Italian territories by his political masters (in view of the
danger of upsetting Mussolini), interception of political and military
wireless traffic combined with a quite sophisticated cryptanalytical
organisation had been sufficient to provide him with some relevant
figures.

According to these, there were nine Italian divisions in Tripolitania facing Général Noguès's force, and five divisions in Cyrenaica
in a position to threaten Egypt and the theatre of Wavell's most
immediate attention. In the area encompassing Eritrea, Italian
Somaliland and the recently conquered Ethiopia, there were about
a quarter of a million troops under command of the Duke of Aosta,
equipped with some 400 field and mountain guns, 200 light tanks
and about 100 armoured cars. There were also in both Cyrenaica
and in the Italian East African Empire many thousands of colonists,
a large proportion of whom might well be called to arms if and when
hostilities began.

Thus, the 40,000 British and native troops under his own
command appeared to be rather neatly sandwiched between

250,000 enemy troops on the eastern side and 70,000 on the western, with an extra 122,000 available to join in from the Tunisian border if French attention became engaged elsewhere. Whatever his opinion of the quality of the opposition, against such odds Wavell had no choice but to press as hard as possible for reinforcements – which, to be fair to them, the Government were as anxious to give as he was to receive. But requirements in 1939 and early 1940 were obviously most urgent in France.

None the less, during the winter of 1939/1940, help did arrive. By spring 1940 two brigades of the 4th Indian Division had arrived with much of their artillery, New Zealand provided an infantry brigade, a machine-gun battalion, a field regiment of artillery and the best part of a cavalry regiment, while Australia had sent two infantry brigades, two regiments of field artillery and some divisional troops. From the United Kingdom had come the 1st Cavalry Division complete with most of its horses but with a considerable Territorial Army element, which was hastily training in Palestine to take over the duties of the regular cavalry already stationed there.

Even this increase in numbers, however, made little apparent difference to the enormous disparity between his own forces and those ranged against him; and if he suspected that his own regular and volunteer force might, man for man, possess more military ardour and skill than the conscript Italian and Libyan levies across the frontiers, this was not a factor upon which he might count until it had been demonstrated.

Something else would be required, something which T. E. Lawrence had called 'the irrational tenth . . . like the kingfisher flashing across the pool . . . that is the test of generals.'

Bluff would certainly have to be part of it, as would imagination and audacity.

But even these qualities would be of little avail without a sound base from which to operate, a solid administrative structure from which to draw support for exploitation of success, or protection if things went wrong.

Before Wavell had arrived, the senior officer commanding British troops in Egypt was Lieutenant-General H. Maitland Wilson, a soldier of wide experience, of calm and placid appearance which, however, masked considerable energy and determined attitudes on many matters, and so vast a bulk as to have earned him fairly early in his career the soubriquet 'Jumbo'. He had been appointed in the early summer of 1939, leaving Britain, as he later rather sadly recorded, 'on the day of the Ascot Gold Cup'.

His instructions had been to make an examination of the potential defences of the area under his command, and to do what was necessary to build them up – a task he quickly found comparable to a combination of those allocated to Hercules and the Children of Israel.

There was, for instance, the matter of some important roads which under an Anglo-Egyptian treaty signed in 1936 should by now have been completed. Investigations revealed a twenty-mile gap in the road between Alexandria and the forward advance base of Mersa Matruh (though the rail-track – single line – had been completed during the emergency created by the Italian invasion of Ethiopia in 1935) while those roads intended to link the Canal with Cairo and Alexandria were virtually non-existent. So, also, was the road across the Sinai Desert linking Egypt with the British protectorate of Palestine, which would obviously be needed to carry fast and heavy reinforcement traffic in the event of action on either the southern or the western front.

Another matter was that of co-operation in the event of war between the British and Egyptian Armies, also provided for in the 1936 treaty. Although at first sight much seemed to have been achieved, examination revealed some disturbing aspects. For example, although the Egyptian anti-aircraft artillery and searchlight batteries in the Delta appeared well equipped and of sound if not high morale – as did the infantry and artillery units – those units patrolling the Libyan Frontier or occupying the frontier posts, and thus most likely to meet the enemy at the outset of any hostilities, seemed curiously uninterested in their work.

It did not take long for Wilson to find out why. Serving out in the desert, the Egyptian High Command explained with an air of sweet reasonableness, was less expensive than serving in Cairo or Alexandria – so the Sudanese soldiers and especially the Egyptian officers engaged on border duties were paid less than when serving nearer the delights of home; indeed officers were generally posted to such services as a result of some social or economic misdemeanour. Wilson protested to the somewhat puzzled Army Chief of Staff, Azziz el Mashri Pasha, but six months later heard that yet another young officer unfortunate enough to be overheard making a tactless remark about one of his seniors had been posted to Williams Pass, an important post north-west of Siwa. It was obviously going to take some time for old customs to be changed.

But by no means all the problems facing Wilson were of Egyptian responsibility. Little remained of the huge military bases of 1918, for the 1922 agreement with Egypt had resulted in the reduction of British military presence in the country by over 75 per cent, and since then governmental parsimony on defence matters had reduced the accommodation, the administration and training facilities, even the transport and weaponry for what remained, to an absolute minimum. It all had to be built up again, and at first by in-experienced hands. When the first bulk stores arrived there was very limited storage capacity in which to house and protect them; when transport and trucks arrived they invariably had to be modified for use in the desert as the specifications to which they had been manufactured had been based upon European conditions.

Tank tracks designed for English roads or rough ploughland cracked and split on the desert rubble; dust clogged air-intakes, and in lorry radiators the precious water boiled away under a combina-tion of high temperatures and soft 'going' over sand where the roads petered out; and in the event of sufficient armour and transport to defeat an enemy eventually becoming available, where was the petrol to be stored?

Where were the workshops for repair and maintenance? Where were the skilled men to carry out the maintenance? Where were the barracks for the men to live in, the messes and canteens where they would eat and drink, the stores for them to use, the food for them to eat, the doctors to treat them when they got sick, the hospitals and staff to look after them, the chaplains to bury them if they died? And this was just the base staff.

Where were the replacements for the tanks when they broke up, wore out or were wrecked in battle? Where were the ammunition dumps? Where were the artillery parks? Where was the transport to bring the infantry to the front and sustain it while it was there? Where were the bricks, the cement, the asbestos sheets, the beds, the bedding, the tentage, the oil, the petrol, the gelignite, the tools, the pipes, the plumbing, the roadmaking equipment, the workshop plant, the cargo-handling plant at Port Said, Alexandria and Suez? The cargo-handling plant for unloading bigger and better cargo-handling plant at Port Said, Alexandria and Suez?

And above all, where was water and how could it be brought to where it was needed?

All Egypt's water seemed at first glance to come from the Nile; undrinkable, not even safe to wash in. Water-purification plant was needed; men to run water-purification plant; men to guard men running water-purification plant. Men and equipment to sink wells in the forward areas; surveyors to find the places to sink the wells; equipment for the surveyors to find the wells; pumps to pump the water out when it was found; pipes to pipe the water even further forward when it had been purified.

General Wilson was by no means the first to find that the desert was the tactician's paradise but the quartermaster's hell – but it was while he was coping with and solving many of the consequent problems that war against Germany was declared. Within a week he was instructed by his new Commander-in-Chief first to make preparations to receive into Egypt another six divisions, and secondly to ensure that everyone on his staff worked henceforward on the assumption that the Allies would be at war with Italy within six months.

Thirdly, Wilson was to have plans drawn up for the invasion of Libya, the capture of both Bardia at the northern end of the frontier Wire and Jarabub 200 miles to the south, with a corps consisting of one armoured and two infantry divisions. He was also to look into the possibilities of raising, training and putting to good use a specially chosen body of troops to be transported by air and possibly dropped into action by parachute – for which, of course, he would additionally require aircraft and parachutes.

The practice which 'Jumbo' Wilson had recently acquired in building bricks without straw was apparently to be put to good use.

If the two men with the greatest responsibilities for safeguarding British interests in the Middle East were deeply worried by the realities with which they were faced (and, needless to say, neither gave the slightest outward sign of doubt or hesitation) most of the troops they commanded felt no such qualms. Few in number they might have been and well aware that parsimony on the part of the British public had left them acutely short of up-to-date arms and equipment – but they were professionals, used to soldiering in rough, exacting conditions, and a large proportion of them were quite accustomed to the whine of the sniper's bullet above their heads, the sudden violent explosion of land-mine or bomb.

This was still part of the age when, to use the most apt phrase of a leading American historian, Joseph Lehmann, 'the blood never dried on the British Empire' – and a great deal of it was British blood. Since Easter 1936, British troops in Palestine had been engaged in suppressing the Arab rebellion, policing the roads, searching villages, chasing guerrilla bands and being in turn ambushed, shot at and blown up by them. Many men under General Wilson's command wore campaign ribbons and a number of them had quite recently won decorations for bravery.

And the Arabs were by no means the only enemy against whom some of these men had fought. To the tribes of the north-west frontier of India intermittent warfare against the British (and one another) was part of an accepted way of life, and for a hundred years British battalions had marched and counter-marched, manned pickets, been sniped at by Mahsuds and Afridis, and kept watch and ward from the Khyber Pass to Baluchistan. The 1st Battalion Hampshire Regiment, for instance, had gained the Indian General Service Medal with clasp 'N.W. Frontier 1935', followed by a second with clasp 'N.W. Frontier 1935–1937' – and it was then posted to Palestine where it gained yet another campaign medal; and these were not awarded just for being in the area, they were earned in action by the regiments concerned.

British regular troops of the 1930s signed on for a minimum of seven years 'with the colours' followed by five years on the reserve, but many of them remained with their battalions for much longer, making a lifetime career of soldiering. From these 'long-service' men came the majority of the warrant officers and senior N.C.O.s, and many of these came from regimental families whose names appeared on the rolls of their chosen battalion for periods going back well into the last century. For them, the reason for joining the Army was obvious; for many others in the 1930s it had been the sole alternative to unemployment, and although they may not at first have shown much enthusiasm for the military life, a surprisingly large number remained with the colours even when they might have successfully returned to 'civvy street'.

Yet others had joined the Army because they had believed the recruiting posters, and they stayed in it because the posters had not lied. They 'saw the world', or at least more of it than if they had remained at home, and quite often they had the adventure and excitement that was promised. One young man in the early 1930s who had no wish to become part of his father's hairdressing business ran away and joined a famous cavalry regiment. Within six months he had taken part in a cavalry charge against Afghan tribesmen, wielding a sabre to some effect, and shortly after that he was engaged in the far more humanitarian but just as dangerous task of pulling out survivors of the disastrous Quetta earthquake of 1935. At no time did he feel the slightest regret at his decision to abandon the barber's calling.

Above all, the British Regular Army in the 1930s offered opportunity for sport – football, both soccer and rugger, hockey, cricket, swimming if the station was by the sea, shooting, running, and for the cavalry regiments riding, or perhaps learning to drive a motor vehicle, an accomplishment not, in those days, quite so common as it has since become. Many people have judged that the British Army's dedication to sport was at the expense of professionalism, but any lack of military efficiency in the late 1930s was due as much to lack of equipment as to any other factor. The Army would willingly have trained with tanks and guns had they been available; in 1939, the anti-tank guns of at least one regular battalion in England were still represented on exercises by green and white flags.

In any case, the physical toughness and teamwork engendered by playing rugby football on a sand-covered, rock-hard pitch on the borders of Afghanistan or in the Western Desert were not qualities which would be found useless in the days to come.

And if the life led by the 'other ranks' was strenuous, rarely dull and often exciting, for the officers there was the added bonus of a social life and a degree of luxury varying with the regiment and with the size of private income available to augment their pay. In 1935 a subaltern's pay was £230 a year (and a major-general's £1,100) and the mandatory expenses of a commission necessitated at least a parental allowance to most young officers. As Correlli Barnett put it so pungently, 'Nothing could have suited the British public better than an army in which it did not have to serve, officered by a narrow clique of men of private means who did not demand a living salary.'*

To a great extent the officers came from middle or upper classes (although, as always in the British Army, there were the occasional exceptions who had risen through the ranks) and they had all gone through the mill of Sandhurst or Woolwich; and for the infantry and cavalry officers, Sandhurst had been a great leveller in which the sons of royalty were subject to just the same scarifying and often humiliating treatment at the hands of drill sergeants as the poorest ex-Grammar school boy. Sandhurst may not have taught them a great deal of military law or history – though the opportunities to learn about such matters were there for those who wished to take advantage of them – but it did expose them to the appraising eyes of their coevals with whom, one day, they would be facing battle.

Sandhurst also gave them, though not as part of the academic curriculum, some idea of the violence in which they might find themselves embroiled as a result of their choice of career. The tales of room-wrecking, of tarring and feathering of unpopular cadets, of setting fire to shirt-tails (Field Marshal Montgomery was responsible for one such episode during his time at Sandhurst) are legion, and occasionally news of some particularly flagrant piece of hooliganism would reach the outside world. John Masters has told of one episode in his autobiographical *Bugles and a Tiger*:

> In the previous affair a couple of hundred cadets had battled up and down the corridors that lay between two companies' quarters, for the space of an hour or so. Brass knuckle-dusters, loaded canes, chairlegs, and practically any other weapon that came to hand had been used; two cadets were injured for life, and thousands of pounds' worth of damage was done. News of this episode reached the newspapers, and people asked what the authorities were about to permit such hooliganism.
>
> It was a good question. I do not think any good answer was given in public. The answer, though satisfactory to realists, might not have been thought so by the parents of the injured cadets. That answer was: 'War is a dirty business, and we are training

*The *Sunday Times* magazine (13 December 1970), p. 38.

these young men for war; we are not running a kindergarten; we do not intend to snoop around seeing whether the cadets treat one another like Little Lord Fauntleroys; we have learned that a wild young man can learn wisdom as he grows older – if he survives – but a spiritless young man cannot learn the dash that wins battles. And, finally, we believe that a man's contemporaries are his fairest judges.'[4]

Thus, the officers of the regular British regiments in the Middle East as war came ever nearer during the late 1930s shared in the main one important formatory experience, had all been exposed to influences likely to shape them towards a common attitude of mind, and those who were still with their regiments or battalions after four or five years – for it was quite easy for an officer to resign his commission – were there because they liked the life, 'physically hard and demanding though it often was.

One lesson which they had all learned – and their instructors and senior officers made quite certain that they understood it thoroughly – was that Britain did not possess, as had at one time been believed, an unlimited supply of soldiers' lives upon which they could draw. Not only was the health and well-being of every man committed to their care in peacetime a solemn responsibility, but in any future war there were to be no more holocausts such as the British Army had suffered on the Somme or at Passchendaele. From this it followed that the best way a young officer could ensure that the lives of his men – and his own, come to that – were not wasted, was to see that they were well trained, and no thought of his own social superiority, more expensive education or more patrician antecedents must be allowed to interfere with this aim.

Thus the gap which had divided officers from other ranks right up to the First World War was, by the outbreak of the Second, if not entirely bridged, at least considerably narrowed. Although up to the time of mechanisation of the cavalry units – and some famous regiments did not begin this until 1938 – officers merely oversaw the grooming of the horses, the polishing of the saddlery, the care and maintenance of stable equipment, once they became part of a tank crew they 'mucked in', as the saying went, as able to clean an oil filter or lift a cylinder head as the drivers, their overalls as oil-stained, their hands as filthy. In the field, they were to share guard with their crews, eat with them and if they rarely actually helped prepare the food, this would generally be passed off as because they weren't very good at it.

What a number of them were becoming quite good at, however, was finding their way around the desert, and this was an art which in those days was developed by very few people.

Very little of what was to become known as the Western Desert –
originally just the Egyptian Desert west of the Nile but in due
course usage extended the term to cover an extra 150 miles west
as far as Gazala – bears much relation to the romantic view of the
desert, the Hollywood scenery of wind-formed sand-dunes with
occasional oases fringed with palm. Areas such as these do exist, in
the Nile Valley, along the coastal plain bordering the Mediterranean and in the vast sand seas to the south where the dunes are
sculpted into fantastic shapes, but the greater part of the area is a
plateau standing on average some 500 feet above sea level, barren,
rubble- and boulder-strewn, dark brown in colour, occasionally
dotted with scrub and, at first sight, flat.

It was upon this plateau that, in the summer of 1935 aᶜ a response
to Mussolini's invasion of Abyssinia, a British 'Mobile Force'
formed from the Cairo Cavalry Brigade began its first tentative
attempts at desert manoeuvres, and the fact that its sardonic
participants quickly redubbed it the 'Immobile Farce' was sufficient
reflection upon its need for more realistic training and much more
practice. This, its commanders quickly and systematically organised, and within the limits imposed by the chronic shortage of
equipment and even of petrol or spare parts for the vehicles, soon
achieved remarkable results.

At the beginning of 1935, it had taken three and a half days of
worry, frustration and bad temper for one squadron of the 11th
Hussars to make a 200-mile journey from Cairo to the oasis of
Baharia. Punctures, soft sand in which the lorries buried themselves
to their axles, broken springs and uncertainty of navigation had all
helped to make the trip a nightmare, and they had needed two days
for servicing and reappraisal before they felt confident enough to
begin the trip home. But by the following November they were
driving their Rolls-Royce armoured cars ('1920–24 pattern') quite
confidently from Mersa Matruh across the coastal plain, up the
Escarpment to the plateau, on to the Siwa Oasis and back again,
all within three days.

In the training exercises which from then on became the programme for all the mechanised units of the Cairo Cavalry Brigade,
both officers and men learned to dispense with even the faintly
marked tracks which did exist and to find their way across the
featureless wastes by stars, sun and compass, plus a combination of
keen observation and good memory which made up such a crucial
part of what became known as 'desert sense'. They learned to live in
the desert.

They learned that it is not flat. They learned to find cover for men
and guns in the slightest undulations, they learned to recognise and
take advantage of 'hull-down' positions for tanks behind dunes

from which only their turrets would be visible to the enemy; they learned that the scrub patches gave concealment for machine-gun or observation posts, and from these they learned to judge what constituted reality and what was more likely to be mirage.

A great deal of their training was devoted to movement, and here the techniques of desert driving were paramount. Although the 'going' – a word which was to become of supreme importance during the years to come – was generally good for both wheeled and tracked vehicles on the plateau, there were many traps for the inexperienced or unwary. With a burning sun overhead it was difficult to see a sudden hollow down which the vehicle would drop at the cost of broken springs; sharp rocks would rip tyres, a boulder not seen until too late could buckle a wheel or crack a sump. For the tracked vehicles there were often large and unavoidable areas strewn with rocks and studded with outcrops which strained their springs and ruined their tracks; for the wheeled vehicles, the constant hazard of deep and soft sand in which the wheels quickly became embedded to the axles, necessitating hours of 'unsticking' with spades and sandmats, and often of unloading the stores and equipment carried and reloading when the vehicle was clear.

Above all, the squadrons learned to conserve water, food and petrol in the face of the basic, unalterable fact that everything they needed for existence – or would need for battle – had to be taken with them. The desert supplied nothing but an arena.

However, such training among separate units, even with the friendly rivalry and traditional co-operation which existed between several of them, would not serve to weld them all into a military formation capable of taking the field in anything but a skirmishing role. It took the Munich crisis to begin a process which would bring this about.

Major-General Percy Cleghorn Stanley Hobart, D.S.O., M.C., had been appointed Director of Military Training at the War Office in 1937, a post he had taken up with some reluctance as he was well aware that those with whom he would have to work most closely disapproved of his appointment and distrusted what they knew of his ideas. They believed, with some justification, that he was a 'tank fanatic', and thought this meant that he saw tanks as the only essential weapons, 'tank warfare' as the only course of future battles, and considered tank units capable of winning wars without the assistance of other arms.

His critics were, in fact, mistaken in this suspicion, for Hobart was well aware of the necessity for both infantry and artillery on the field of battle, and he had far more advanced ideas for air co-operation above it than they had; but his was an abrasive, abrupt and occasionally violently argumentative personality, and those senior officers who shared none of his enthusiasms and preferred a quiet life – and there was a large number of them – wished to have as little as possible to do with him. In this they were generally successful, as he did not suffer those who disagreed with him gladly, believing that he had sound precedent for his attitude.

Pat Hobart, as his friends called him (he was also widely known, but rarely addressed in the army, as 'Hobo'), had joined the Army as a Royal Engineer, risen to the rank of Brevet Major by the end of the First World War during which he had served in France both in the trenches and on the Staff, and in Mesopotamia where he had won his D.S.O., been wounded and spent an uncomfortable three days as a prisoner of the Turks. At the time of the Armistice he was G.S.O.2 (General Staff Officer, second grade) to the 53rd Division in Jerusalem, and the despondent subject of a tale which was to dog him through the remainder of his military career and, indeed, in the end find place in his entry in the *Dictionary of National Biography*.

This was to the effect that during September 1918 while acting as Staff Officer with the 8th Brigade, he had taken the blind-eye technique somewhat too far. In the words of his biographer, Kenneth Macksey:

> At one vital moment, when his brigadier wished to make a last-minute change of plan before an attack, Hobart refused to pass the order and made doubly sure it would not be sent by seizing possession of the telephone until the attack had gone successfully ahead to the original plan. It is said that this incident brought his association with 8th Brigade to an end, and the purists will agree, with justification, that for a staff officer to defy his commander is poison to the roots of discipline and confidence.[5]

That there may have been more than a vestige of truth in the tale is supported by advice given to the young Lieutenant Michael Carver many years later. 'The secret of success in the Army', Hobart said, 'is to be sufficiently insubordinate, and the key word is *sufficiently*.'

But whatever his attitude to the conventions of the military world, the lesson which had been burned into his mind throughout the welter of the First World War battlefields had been the values of mobility and of the element of surprise that mobility gives. With these in mind he had transferred in 1923 to the Tank Corps, and during the following years been second-in-command of the 4th Battalion, Royal Tank Corps, and commanding officer of the 2nd Battalion.

In 1933 he became Inspector of the Royal Tank Corps and a year later commanded the Tank Brigade in the annual manoeuvres – a task to which he had looked forward with immense enthusiasm but which, for reasons not unconnected with his personality, ended in near disaster. Kenneth Macksey tells the story:

On its own the Tank Brigade did all that Hobart said could be done, but co-operation with other arms led into deep waters, even when the other arm happened to be the 7th Experimental Infantry Brigade commanded by his fellow armoured enthusiast, Lindsay. A combined exercise in September fell under the control of the G.O.C.-in-C. Southern Command, General Sir John Burnett-Stuart, a forward-looking soldier but one endowed with a destructive sense of humour ('anything for a laugh,' was Hobart's comment), and the chief umpire was Major-General A. P. Wavell.

For the first time mechanised artillery, a mechanised infantry brigade, an armoured car regiment and a tank brigade, were brought together, forming the earliest recognisable shape of an armoured division of the future – all under the command of Lindsay. But the exercise devised by Burnett-Stuart paid scant heed to the future: instead it concentrated on hampering the Tank Brigade as a fillip to the morale of the infantry – the very opposite of the spur of which they were in need. The embryo armoured division was launched on a raid along a circumscribed route towards a limited objective, tied to a schedule that gave insufficient time for the approach to be made at night. Furthermore, Lindsay was told he was not to incur heavy losses during the raid in order that the force might be preserved for use in another more important task later on. In consequence the enemy had only to block one route and the surprise inherent in the mobility of the force was sheered off.

Lindsay tried to solve an almost insuperable conundrum by expedients, not one of which satisfied Hobart or himself. Both were loath to split up the armour, both convinced that speed was essential and that, if possible, the direction of their thrust should be disguised. The sheer speed of their first plan, in which, as it happens, a battalion of tanks was grouped with the infantry, achieved complete success, by taking the 'enemy' and, above all, the umpires, by surprise, catching everybody unprepared and forcing the exercise controllers to adopt bogus measures (by means of an enforced halt for the tanks to allow the enemy infantry to get in position) to restore the situation.

From that moment the umpires under Wavell lost sight of reason in their effort to hamper the mobile force with measures outstripping subterfuge, and as the farce dragged on Hobart got angrier and refused to take part in what appeared to him to be a charade. The knowledge that officers' wives had been employed to guide the 'enemy' into position and that infantry had been told to lie in the road to prevent his tanks passing drove him to fury. This, to him, was a vital experiment upon which the future of armour depended – to make a mockery of it was a senseless waste of time and opportunity.[6]

It is easy to sympathise with Hobart, and easier still to see how his enemies – and these were accumulating rapidly as he hammered his way towards his objectives with no thought or consideration for anything or anyone in his path – made him appear childish and ill-tempered in their subsequent reports. 'Hobart's Tantrums' were the subject of many a barbed comment over cocktails during the months that followed.

Not only was Hobart unpopular, but so was the circle in which he moved and from whom he drew the sparks which set alight his own ideas. Both Captain Liddell Hart and Major-General J. F. C. Fuller had by now been edged by one means or another out of the Army, while within it other tank enthusiasts such as Charles Broad, 'Tim' Pile and G. M. Lindsay were being posted to appointments in which they could have no influence on military development. All three were promoted to major-general and then sent respectively to Administration at Aldershot, command of the 1st Anti-Aircraft Division, and an obscure appointment in Calcutta.

But Hobart was immovable, perhaps because the removing force did not have confidence to match his in their own irresistibility. In the meantime he continued his assaults on some of their more cherished traditions by acidly inquiring why tank soldiers should waste their time on infantry drill when it was their task to acquire the modern techniques needed to fight in machines. He could turn a good phrase, too, when he wished and 'military buffoonery' was an expression first accredited to his inspiration:

> I dislike all this dressing up. This emotional intoxication produced by bagpipes and bearskins, and the hypnotism of rhythmical movement and mechanical drills. The glorification of the false side of war. This is not the gay flaunting of danger that I greatly admire. It is the deliberate inebriation to avoid seeing things as they are.[7]

In 1937 came a sudden upsetting of the conventional military coterie in Whitehall. Mr Leslie Hore-Belisha was appointed Secretary of State for War with a brief from Prime Minister Chamberlain to do what he could to make Britain ready for a confrontation which even Mr Chamberlain could see was a strong possibility, despite his discussion with Herr Hitler; and to the horror of the High Command Mr Hore-Belisha invited Captain Liddell Hart to become his personal adviser on military matters. One result of the ministerial appointment was that before the end of the year General Lord Gort became Chief of the Imperial General Staff in place of the elderly and hidebound Field Marshal Sir Cyril Deverell, and another of the advisory appointment was that Hobart went to the War Office as Director of Military Training with the strict understanding that in the event of war looming he would be given command of a 'Mobile Division'.

The Munich Crisis provided the reason, Gort the instruction – in person. On the afternoon of September 25th, 1938, Hobart was ordered to go to Egypt immediately and form an armoured division to hold off the Italians, who were expected to attack across the Libyan–Egyptian frontier immediately war was declared, if not before.

On September 27th, Hobart arrived at Alexandria in company with the British Ambassador and several senior officers who were to carry out an examination of the entire Middle East situation. They were met by General Wilson's immediate predecessor as G.O.C.-in-C, British Troops in Egypt, Lieutenant-General Sir Robert ('Copper') Gordon-Finlayson, who was considerably taken aback to see Hobart, and greeted him with, 'I don't know what you've come here for, and I don't want you anyway.'

The tone for Hobart's relationship with Cairo Headquarters was thereby set, and it was hardly to vary.

In the field, Hobart's appearance was at first greeted with curiosity mingled with much scepticism, but once the officers and men became accustomed to an unexpected demand for speed in all their activities, they began to appreciate the qualities of the man now in charge of them, and the advantages they might gain from his leadership.

Hobart found that the force from which he was expected to form a modern armoured division consisted entirely of units equipped with old, outdated weapons and equipment, and however enthusiastically trained the personnel they were never up to strength. For instance, the Cavalry Brigade (Hobart soon arranged for it to be renamed 'Light Armoured Brigade') consisted of three Hussar regiments, each of which was over a hundred men short of establishment. The 7th Queen's Own Hussars consisted of two instead of three squadrons and were equipped with light tanks which varied in age and pattern from Marks III to VIB but had no ammunition for their 0·5-inch guns; but they were in better case than the 8th King's Royal Irish Hussars, who practised their light tank manoeuvres in 15-cwt Ford pick-up trucks with Vickers-Berthier guns mounted in them. The 11th Hussars (Prince Albert's Own) still had most of their Rolls-Royce armoured cars of 1920–4 vintage, for which they were very grateful as they were excellent machines, and they were just receiving new models of a Morris car which promised well for reconnaissance work – better than the Rolls in soft sand though the suspension and steering proved not so robust when it came to the rough work among the boulders.

The Tank Group which was intended to form the main striking force – to be called the Heavy Armoured Brigade – consisted of the 1st Battalion Royal Tank Regiment, recently arrived from England with fifty-eight light tanks but with little track mileage left in them and pathetically few track replacements, and the 6th R.T.R. which had both light and medium tanks, though they had to be left behind in Cairo for Hobart's first exercises, for 'internal security' duties. (When Maitland Wilson inspected the tanks of this battalion some time later, he was horrified. They were, he wrote, 'the same medium tanks which one had seen performing at the Aldershot Tattoo for many years and whose armour was questionably proof against anti-tank small arms'.)

As for the 'Pivot Group', whose role was to supply the artillery and infantry support which Hobart considered essential (despite his critics' belief that he professed total independence for tanks), the 3rd Regiment Royal Horse Artillery was almost up to strength even though their 3·7-inch howitzers may not have been ideal weapons for their role (but new anti-tank guns were on their way) but the 1st Battalion King's Royal Rifle Corps were not even in Egypt. They were still in Burma, and would be without any form of transport when they did arrive.

The making of bricks without straw was apparently still considered the local speciality.

Nevertheless, Hobart set to work with his usual application and as his appointment also gave him responsibility for the Garrison Troops at Abbassia Barracks in Cairo, he squeezed and scraped from them enough signals and administrative personnel to put together a divisional headquarters, and a company of Royal Army Service Corps to help with the supply problems. Based on Mersa Matruh, he carried out a series of exercises to test the quality of his new command.

He was not dissatisfied, and as the autumn and winter of 1938 went by without war and more men and equipment arrived, the force – it could hardly yet be called a division – began to take shape. The infantry component arrived, and more light tanks for the Hussars; anti-tank guns and 25-pounders replaced the howitzers of the Royal Horse Artillery and the first ten cruiser tanks (A9s) were taken over by the 6th Royal Tank Regiment, which was also released from its Cairo-bound duties. Hobart wrote:

> I decided to concentrate on dispersion, flexibility and mobility this season: to try and get the Division and formations well extended, really handy, and under quick control. To units unused to the speed and wide frontages made possible by mechanisation these matters present considerable difficulties.
>
> There is the isolation due to the wide intervals necessary in the desert, involving the necessity of being able to keep direction, to navigate a unit, to keep a dead reckoning, to learn to watch for small indications and to use one's eyes in spite of mirage, etc.[8]

Such lessons had of course, to be learned by every unit as it arrived in the desert and this would constitute a problem for every commander-in-chief while the desert war raged; there was always to be a great disparity between the number of troops which arrived in the Delta, and that which could be put into the battle-line. Other problems with which Hobart had to wrestle arose from the recent mechanisation of some of the cavalry units:

> Maintenance in newly mechanised units is not, of course, of a high standard, but great interest is being taken and as knowledge increases the standard of inspection, which is the secret of good maintenance, will improve.
>
> It must be a matter of course for all officers not only to wear overalls but also to take part in the maintenance work on their vehicles.
>
> It has not yet become instinctive for crews and commanders to get down at every halt and look round their vehicles at once. If this were the case many oil leaks, loose bolts etc., would be seen and remedied and many subsequent demands on fitters avoided.
>
> I am certain that we have to encourage in all crews the sense of ownership which makes it a point of honour that they should be able to keep their vehicles running without assistance from outside; even if we have to do it at first at the cost of some damage by unskilled enthusiasts.[9]

Gradually, the separate pieces of the force began to learn their positions and carry out their roles. The 11th Hussars formed a wide screen in front and along the flanks to provide reconnaissance and the first delay to an attacking enemy, the tank group learned to manoeuvre for attack or counter-thrust, the artillery to swing into action to break up a threatened attack before it developed. At all key positions, the infantry dug themselves weapon pits to hold ground won, and to guard the brains and nerve centres which controlled them all.

Thus, if there was still an acute shortage of everything from supply transport and ammunition to radio sets, there was now a growing ability to improvise and a rapidly developing integral spirit. By the middle of 1939 the days of the 'Immobile Farce' were long gone, and by the outbreak of war Hobart's command constituted a force with far greater striking power than any other formation of comparable size in Africa. Certainly the Italian commanders on the other side of the frontier wire had good cause for concern at its rapid development.

As it happened the Italian Command at the outbreak of war had a very exaggerated idea of Allied – and particularly British – strength, and it is interesting to analyse why. Basically, there seems to have been a marked reluctance among the Italian people, with the exception of the ruling Fascist hierarchy, to go to war against the British. This reluctance shows in practically every report on their own readiness for war submitted to Mussolini by the heads of the armed services. Even the Italian Navy, which at that time was undoubtedly the most efficient and up-to-date of the three services and was to score some notable triumphs, especially with its smaller units, decried its own ability. One report from the Chief of the Italian General Staff read:

> The British naval forces (stationed in the Mediterranean) represent an amount of power which compared with ours cannot be described other than 'of crushing superiority'. It is not possible to nourish any hopes of achieving positive results in a struggle with this power since our navy is only a spearhead without any bulk behind it . . . The British battleships, escorted by a considerable number of destroyers, could cruise at will in the Mediterranean inflicting all the damage they wanted on our ill-defended coasts. Nor can we make much use of the air force which finds itself in a state of crisis and whose older material, which is the bulk of it, would be out of action after a few days . . .[10]

It is interesting that there is no mention in this report of the existence of the French Fleet, upon which the Royal Navy was placing great reliance in the coming struggle for naval control of the Mediterranean.

As for the military situation in North Africa, whereas the British saw themselves hemmed in and sandwiched between large military forces in Libya and Eritrea, the Italian Command saw only the dangers to which their Libyan Armies were exposed, of being crushed between the overwhelming powers of the French Army in Tunisia and the '100,000 strong Anglo-Egyptian Army' backed up by an unknown but presumed potent and vigorous force consisting of 'General Wavell's British troops in the Near East'.

It seems likely that the very number of Italian agents, amateur and professional, resident in Egypt added to the confusion, and that one column of tanks leaving Abbassia and reported to Rome by fifty different enthusiasts became a division by the time it arrived at Mersa Matruh. Certainly the powers, both defensive and offensive, of the British forces east of the Libyan frontier were considered great enough to cause Maresciallo d'Armata Balbo to add his voice to that of Mussolini's son-in-law Count Ciano, in late August 1939, entreating Mussolini not to let Hitler drag their country into a war which they were in no condition to fight. Despite his willingness to sign the Pact of Steel in May 1939, Ciano had become thoroughly disenchanted with Hitler and the whole of Nazi Germany during the following three months.

But if the Italians in general and Maresciallo Balbo in particular exaggerated the power against them, they took a realistic attitude to their own military strength. Despite the numbers of men they deployed, despite also their recent military successes in Ethiopia and Albania, the Italian Armies were in no condition to fight a modern war abroad.

Generale di Divisione d'Armata Giuseppe Mancinelli of the Comando Supremo Staff, who had already spent a term as military attaché in Berlin and had seen enough of the Wehrmacht on manoeuvres to recognise military reality when he saw it, found the outlook depressing in the extreme:

At the moment of the declaration of war in 1939, the army consisted of seventy-three divisions, of which twenty-four were deployed in the [Aegean] islands and in the overseas commands. In 1938, the division, through the unhappy initiative of the then Chief of Staff, Generale Pariani, had been transformed from 'ternary' to 'binary': this meant that the infantry component had been reduced from three to two regiments. This was a strange operation which certainly did not do any good to the general efficiency of the army. In the new units, the infantry–artillery ratio had been raised but the result could not be considered satisfactory since the division became too small a unit to be able to undertake and successfully terminate a tactical action of any importance; it was subject to quick deterioration and was incapable of any prolonged effort. Possibly in this decision was involved the more or less conscious aim of 'bluffing' – not so much as regards other countries but for the Duce himself, as a gesture of prestige, an apparently miraculous multiplication of the forces at his disposal.

Modernity in the composition of our army was represented by the 9th Army – the Army of the Po – which with its three armoured divisions, three 'rapid movement' divisions and two motorised divisions was to constitute the 'mass of manoeuvre' for a war of rapid movement. But the tanks of the armoured units were already largely obsolete, little more than pretty mechanical toys from six to ten tons, to be offered as targets to the enemy anti-tank guns. The 'rapid movement' divisions were a romantic and obsolete combination of horsed cavalry and Bersaglieri cyclists, and the so-called motorised divisions did have motor transport of a kind, but were all wheeled vehicles incapable of movement off roads.

In general, the problem of mechanisation, or more appropriately non-mechanisation, of our army represented one of the largest gaps in our organisation, a canker which excluded any capacity for large manoeuvres and which lay at the heart of the very painful losses suffered in the course of the various campaigns, especially those in North Africa . . . For instance, the Italian 'binary' infantry division disposed of one hundred and thirty-five vehicles; the German 'ternary' division had over one thousand.[11]

What of the men who made up the Italian Armies? Except for the Blackshirt Divisions where, as Generale Mancinelli comments acidly, promotion was more likely to be as a result of political enthusiasm than military efficiency, there were now few volunteers joining the Italian Army. By 1939, it had been on a warlike footing for five years, with many units engaged in action or on garrison duties in hostile lands. Ethiopia, Eritrea, Spain, Libya and Italian Somaliland had all called for sacrifices of blood and effort and in all of them the Italian soldier had obeyed his orders, patiently, under a discipline often lax but sometimes harsh, with varying comprehension as to the battle's necessity and rarely with a great deal of enthusiasm. Now he was to be called upon to fight an enemy he did not hate, armed with weapons and equipment which were quickly and effectively demonstrated to be unequal to war against any but a colonial, tribal enemy. In addition, his allies were of a race for whom he felt little affection, however great his admiration for their martial prowess might be.

The Italian private soldier was drawn from traditionally sturdy peasant and worker stock, and so far as it is possible to generalise upon so large a subject, these are hard-working, adaptable, sensible people, with a strong feeling for home and family, a natural gaiety and capacity for happiness, combined with a thoroughly Latin distrust of violent enthusiasms. They respond to friendliness,

recognise natural good manners and, given the slightest encouragement, will be cheerful and co-operative. The world can always do
with such qualities, and in the late 1930s and early 1940s they were
at a premium.

Although the man who commanded the Italian forces in Libya was by
no means of worker or peasant stock, he nevertheless epitomised
their qualities. Italo Balbo was gay, handsome, possessed of great
charm, imagination and courage of a typically Italian brand. He had
served with distinction as an Alpini officer in the First World War,
had joined the Fascist movement soon afterwards and led the
militia in the March on Rome in 1922. He had been promoted
General of Militia in 1923 but then played a leading part in the
building up of the Regia Aeronautica, making many long-distance
flights which gave him an international reputation. But by 1933
when Mussolini promoted him to Marshal and sent him as
Governor-General to Libya, he had incurred considerable unpopularity in Rome as a result of his strongly pro-British views,
coupled with his outspoken criticism of the growing *rapprochement*
between his own country and Germany.

He, like so many of his countrymen who had visited Britain, had
felt at home there, and as so many of them were to find in the years to
come in British company they could relax, chatter, laugh and get on
with their work. Perhaps they sensed a shared fecklessness, a
similar attitude of casual scepticism to the accepted values of
ambition and worthiness.

All this did not, of course, prevent Maresciallo Balbo carrying
out his duties as instructed when war was declared between
Germany and the two western allies, Britain and France. Regroup-
ing and reinforcement of the units under his command duly took
place, all the native troops were re-formed into two divisions, the
three army corps of nine divisions on the Tunisian border were
strengthened and inspected, as were the two army corps of five
divisions facing Egypt. In the Saharan hinterland were posted
special groups at strategic points such as the Kuffra Oasis, Jarabub
150 miles down the frontier Wire south of Sollum, Jalo on the
western edge of the great Libyan Sand Sea, and Murzuk 500 miles
south of Tripoli.

Balbo also conscientiously endeavoured to bring home to the
highest authorities in Rome one basic fact of which they seemed to
be losing sight – that the term 'motorised' as applied to some of his
army corps did not mean that they actually had been motorised. It
meant, as the authorities should remember, that it had been agreed
that 'they had the capacity for motorisation' but that very little had
as yet been done to convert them from their original classification as

infantry corps. As for the request by the High Command for his plans for an invasion of Egypt, he felt that before he could undertake this he should be able to deploy along the frontier at least thirteen divisions – so he would need another eight; of which in his opinion two should be armoured to a degree equating them with the German panzer divisions, and two airborne – with, of course, the necessary adjunctive air support.

With this force, he was quite confident that he could advance through the Wire as far as the edge of the Escarpment running south-east from Sollum. Here, his forces would be able to block any attempted British invasion of Libya, and also to undertake the advance to the Nile and the complete subjugation of Egypt once further reinforcements had arrived, particulars of which would be sent to Rome as soon as they had been worked out.

Oddly enough, Mussolini was neither infuriated nor aggrieved when Balbo's appraisal of the situation in North Africa arrived on his desk, as he was still suffering a sense of outrage at his fellow dictator's totally unilateral activities. Mussolini had had no more warning of the probabilities of the outbreak of war than any other European outside Hitler's immediate entourage, and in view of his own recently well-tried philosophy that it was possible to get everything a reasonable man could want by simply rattling the sabre without actually drawing it, he was perhaps even more taken aback than most.

His immediate reaction was a declaration of non-belligerency, followed by an order to Maresciallo d'Armata Badoglio, the Chief of the Italian General Staff, to take up a defensive attitude on every front, an instruction followed with great alacrity on one front in particular – along the Breonie Alps where the fortifications guarding the Brenner Pass into Austria were strengthened. As for taking the field alongside his partner in the Pact of Steel, he had specifically warned Hitler that Italy would be in no condition to make war against a European power until 1943 at the earliest, and then only with a considerable amount of aid and equipment from Germany.

He thus felt justified in taking a far cooler tone in his communications with Berlin than he had of late, together with an air of detached statesmanship which he was sure would impress the rest of Europe and both Americas, probably leading in due course to everyone soliciting his aid and judgment at some soon-to-be-convened conference table. After all, had this not recently occurred at Munich where both Mr Chamberlain and M. Daladier had been almost fulsome in the attention they had paid him?

The outbreak of war in 1939 was thus followed by something of a diplomatic and military hiatus so far as Italy was concerned, during which it gradually became clear to Il Duce and his immediate circle that perhaps the world was not, after all, hanging on his word. From Berlin came no sign that Hitler was even aware of Mussolini's chagrin (a much worse interpretation of the air of bland friendliness which emanated from Berlin was that Hitler *was* aware, but totally unconcerned about it) and as details of the success of the German Blitzkrieg in Poland began to reach Rome, doubts as to the value of non-belligerency arose. In December, Balbo received from the newly appointed Army Chief of Staff, Maresciallo Graziani, instructions to draw up a more detailed plan for offensives against both Tunisia and Egypt 'to be applied in exceptional circumstances', while during the early part of 1940 Mussolini's pronouncements grew ever more anti-France and Britain who, he informed the Council of Ministers on January 23rd, 'can no longer win the war'.

In February 1940 he forbade sales of any further goods to Britain (much to his Commercial Minister's disgust as the Italian budget was in its usual precarious state and the cancelled deals had been expected to bring in some £20 million worth of much-needed sterling) but insisted that obligations to Germany must be fulfilled. 'Governments, like individuals, must follow a line of morality and honour,' he announced, presumably hoping that Hitler would take the hint and see that the 3,500 tons of copper about to be extorted from the Italian people by the confiscation of their cooking-pots, and sent across the Alps, would be paid for. (They weren't.)

During March, another 80,000 men were sent to North Africa and Mussolini declared 'England will be beaten. Inexorably beaten. That is the sure truth,' while at another Council of Ministers in early April, he claimed that for Italy to remain neutral would 'lose her prestige among the nations of the world for a century as a Great Power and for eternity as a Fascist regime'.

It was, of course, the events of April 1940 which brought the whole situation to a head. As German troops flooded into Denmark and across the Skagerrak to Norway, stamping the Swastika across the face of yet another subjugated country and expelling the hastily committed and ill-organised French and British troops, Mussolini's exasperation grew and his fears that he would not even be invited to sit at a Peace Conference took a harder outline. Then, on May 10th, the panzer columns roared across the frontiers of Belgium and Luxembourg and Il Duce was reduced to a frenzy.

'We Italians are already sufficiently dishonoured,' he declared three days later. 'Any delay is inconceivable. We have no time to lose. Within a month I shall declare war. I shall attack France and Great Britain in the air and on the sea!' And when his military advisers pointed out to him that the lack of almost every sort of military equipment made the carrying out of this declaration virtually impossible, he muttered defiantly but gloomily, 'Then we will do what we can!'

The next day, cheering up, he began manoeuvres to persuade the reluctant King Victor Emmanuel that he, Mussolini, was the best person to assume the Italian Supreme Command, especially as he was even then in communication with his friend Hitler as to the best timing for the Italian declaration of war against the decadent democracies – and by 'best' he meant the timing likely to bring Italy most profit when the French and British empires came to be divided up.

The rest of May passed in a flurry of meetings, conferences and correspondence until at last on the evening of June 10th he read a speech from the balcony of the Palazzo Venezia to a markedly un-enthusiastic crowd, detailing the enormous provocations their country had been subjected to by both England and France, and declaring war on them.

Among his listeners was his son-in-law Count Ciano, who, when he confided the day's events to his diary that night, concluded the entry with 'May God help Italy!'

Whatever Balbo thought of the events of that epochal week, he was sufficiently realistic to know that with the virtual elimination of France from the war, Tunisia would no longer hold threat on the west and he would soon be under pressure from Rome to transfer divisions from there to the east and put matters in train for a march to the Nile.

'It is not the number of men', he wrote to Mussolini in order to damp down too great an excess of martial zeal, 'which causes me anxiety, but their weapons. With two big formations equipped with limited and very old pieces of artillery, lacking in anti-tank and anti-aircraft weapons, I need to be able to depend on the closing of ways of access to Tripolitania, and on the perimeters of Tobruk and Bardia. To have fortified works without adequate weapons is an absurdity. Another urgent necessity is anti-aircraft defences – batteries and organisation. It is useless to send more thousands of men if then we cannot supply them with the indispensable requirements to move and fight.'

But this slightly confused *cri de cœur* did him little good, and quite shortly he received further instructions to proceed with plans for an invasion of Egypt, together with a promise that all the war materials he required would be immediately dispatched. This he countered with a detailed list: a thousand motor vehicles would be the minimum requirement, he claimed, together with a hundred water-tankers, medium tanks for two divisions, a mass of radio equipment and, again, batteries of both anti-tank and anti-aircraft guns.

He was immediately promised all of them, and perhaps a few items arrived quite soon – which he may have had time to regret, for on June 28th, having carried out a reconnaissance flight over Sidi Barrani and Maaten Baggush, he was shot down and killed by one of his own anti-aircraft batteries as he came in to land at Tobruk. The following day, the R.A.F. dropped a note of genuine regret and a wreath on to the landing ground above which Maresciallo Balbo had died. Britain and her allies had lost a good friend in their fight against totalitarian dictatorship.

Appointed in Balbo's place was Maresciallo d'Armata Rodolpho Graziani, who had been responsible for the 'pacification' of Libya between 1930 and 1934 and who enjoyed little local popularity as a result.

2 · Skirmish and Circumspect Advance

Twenty-four hours after Mussolini had concluded his speech from the balcony of the Palazzo Venezia, six troops of the 11th Hussars, each consisting of three armoured cars, left Dar el Hamra, a barren location some thirty miles from the coast and about the same distance east of the frontier, and set out westwards across the plateau for the Wire. They reached it at four different places between Fort Maddalena and Fort Cápuzzo just as the light was fading, and as there was no sign of life on the other side, began the process of 'gapping'.

This was accomplished by a very simple method which they had devised back in the training area around Mersa Matruh. The first armoured car nosed its way up to the nearest picket-post, and in low gear gradually pressed it down until it was almost flat. It then drove over it towards the middle and third posts (there were three lines of upright fencing with barbed wire strung along and also coiled and tangled between them) and repeated the operation, trailing a mass of attached wire behind. Following closely, the second armoured car drove with its wheels actually on the iron picket-posts, pressing them flat to the ground and in some cases snapping them off. It then followed on through, tearing away more of the wire, and the three cars of the troop then drove slowly back and forth across the wire until it gradually disintegrated, while crew members dragged the mass clear with ropes.

It was all much simpler than expected for the wire was older and rustier than that upon which they had practised, the posts more fragile (in one place they were found to be of wood and these just snapped off straight away) and none of the fence was electrified. The rubber-soled shoes which crews of the leading cars had worn thus proved to be unnecessary, though later in the campaign they were to come in useful for foot patrols.

In the north, B Squadron troops fanned out and made for their objectives up around Fort Capuzzo, while the squadron commander, Major Geoffrey Miller, held back a small section of the

Headquarter Troop to guard the gap. It was a cloudless night, warm and with only a light breeze, and the intoxication of this first penetration of enemy territory kept everyone keen and alert. The sounds of the other armoured cars driving off – the gritting of the tyres on sand, the clunk of changing gears – died away and only the murmured conversation of Miller's own section disturbed the taut silence. There was little to do once the immediately surrounding area had been searched.

As the hours passed, there came occasionally to over-anxious ears the sounds of aircraft a long way off – and surely that was the crackle of a Bren-gun? – then shortly before 0200 the northern horizon came dimly alight and in due course the headlamps of a lorry came waveringly into view. Miller and his men watched in silence as a lorry-load of extremely fortunate Italian troops

Map 1   The frontier area

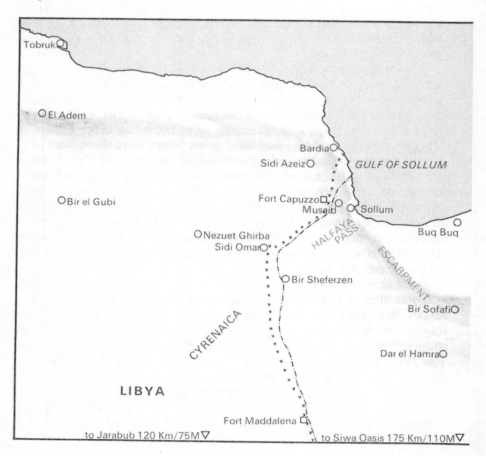

lumbered by, presumably bound for Sidi Omar, revealing to the Hussars the whereabouts of the track normally followed.

With the idea of ambushing the lorry as and if it returned before he and his men withdrew, Miller took his attenuated section across to the track and began disposing them for an attack on a small target approaching from the south; so he was somewhat disturbed when four more lorries appeared from the north and rumbled on down towards them, headlights ablaze. Whether anybody even considered withdrawing in the face of such greater odds is doubtful, and as the lorries came into short range the Hussars opened up with every weapon they had.

There was a babble of outrage, cries of pain and terror, a few wild shots loosed off from the black caverns over the tailboards, and then the unmistakable shouts of officers calling for a cease-fire. Cab

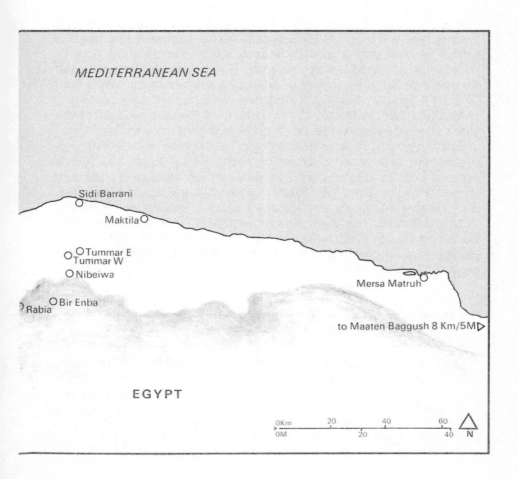

doors burst open and officers and drivers jumped down, dropping their arms as the Hussars rushed out of the darkness with revolvers and sub-machine-guns at the ready; then the tailboards were down and a flood of astonished and frightened Libyans poured out, hands high in the air, rifles left aboard the lorries.

The next few minutes were chaotic as Major Miller and his men rushed from lorry to lorry, herding the prisoners away, quickly searching for small arms any officers or men who looked capable of recovery from shock, and policing the gap between the jettisoned weapons and their now vociferous former owners.

It all made a very tidy haul to be captured by half a section – two officers, fifty N.C.O.s and privates, nine Breda automatics, sixty rifles and several boxes of hand-grenades; but one of the interesting facts which emerged when Miller had time to listen to the indignation of the two officers was that despite Mussolini's proclamation of war to the Italian people at home the night before, no one had bothered to tell the troops along the frontier about it.

But in the meantime, other troops had been at work. At Sidi Omar, No. 2 Troop under Sergeant-Major Howarth had made a useful reconnaissance and exchanged a few random shots with its occupants, at Fort Capuzzo Sergeant Bowyer had had a good look around and lifted a number of land-mines, while to the north-west of Fort Capuzzo, Second Lieutenant Halliday had ambushed and captured a Lancia-Diesel 10-ton lorry with its occupants, all in the same state of exasperated shock as those collected by Miller.

Further south, A Squadron had gapped the wire in three different places, cut a large number of telephone lines, skirmished briefly around Fort Maddalena with an unidentified armoured truck and loosed off a few Bren-gun bursts at a low-flying aircraft; after which they returned through their gaps to Hamra to greet with some envy their exhilarated but slightly awed comrades from B Squadron. By noon on June 12th, seventy disconsolate Italian and Libyan prisoners were making their way back towards Egyptian prison-cages.

It was not to be expected that so simple a success could be repeated, but the next few days were to produce some notable results.

C Squadron went through the Wire the following night and swept around to the south-west of Fort Capuzzo to take a look at Sidi Azeiz, some thirteen miles to the north of the fort. They were greeted with a spectacular cascade of light signals from the defence lines surrounding their target, a fanfare of bugles and then the combined fire of fifteen field guns which became increasingly accurate at each salvo. Altogether, the squadron were lucky to be safely back through the Wire by 0300, with no casualties.

Three troops of A Squadron went in again the following night and drove to Sidi Omar, to find a situation reminiscent of the *Marie Celeste* affair. Everywhere were signs of hasty evacuation – books and documents left lying about, clothing and even arms and ammunition; an unfinished meal was black with a cloud of flies, a sight to confirm Lieutenant Friend in his decision to set fire to the two main posts. They were back through the Wire by dawn with no sign of Italian interference, though their detached troop was having its first experience of a new type of harassment.

Sergeant-Major 'Nobby' Clarke had been sent off with No. 4 Troop to take another look at Fort Maddalena, and with perhaps a little too much confidence drove directly – almost flagrantly – towards the main gate. Machine-guns opened up on the three cars from along the wall, and when this failed to divert the troop, aircraft suddenly appeared and began strafing and bombing them, at which, intelligently, the Hussars turned and fled. In the end, no less than six Caproni bombers and nine Fiat fighters had joined the attack, fortunately without armour-piercing bullets; but their bombs had been a different matter and the cars had had some narrow escapes, only violent swerving on their part and the lack of teamwork between Capronis and Fiats saving them from damage.

On June 14th, the biggest incursion into Libya took place, the capture of both Fort Maddalena and Fort Capuzzo being undertaken by the 4th Armoured Brigade, as Hobart's 'Heavy Armoured Brigade' had now been renamed.

Again, A Squadron of the 11th Hussars attacked Fort Maddalena after a period of 'softening up' by a flight of R.A.F. Blenheims, and with the whole squadron moving together in a wide encircling movement to surround the fort, a sense of great excitement pervaded them all in this, the regiment's first battle-charge of the war. And again, it was all rather a let-down. There was no sign of opposition, a white flag was run up as the cars converged and the Hussars went in without a shot being fired, taking prisoner the five Italians and thirteen native troops who were all that remained of the garrison.

The Hussars found the fort well designed and soundly built, with such luxuries as a refrigerator and an electric-light plant, a radio transmitter and receiver which they wrecked, and a well-stocked store and arsenal (including the twelve machine-guns which had opened up on Sergeant-Major Clarke the day before) which they ransacked, removing the guns for later use against their original owners.

But further north, where the attack on Fort Capuzzo was taking place, the picture was more complicated.

Brigadier J. R. L. Caunter (nicknamed, rather sardonically, 'Blood' Caunter by his troops) had decided that although the main strength of his column should attack Fort Capuzzo itself, a lighter force should capture Sidi Azeiz beyond in order to prevent any reinforcement of the Capuzzo garrison, and then continue northwards to carry out a daylight reconnaissance of the small port of Bardia.

This lighter force consisted of B and C Squadrons of the 11th Hussars, a squadron of light tanks from the 7th Hussars and a battery of 25-pounders from the Royal Horse Artillery, the whole force led by the commanding officer of the 11th Hussars, Lieutenant-Colonel John Combe. As he had further to go, Colonel Combe took his leading elements through the Wire at 0800 on the morning of the 14th, and half an hour later C Squadron was under fire from the same batteries which had chased them away two nights before.

The two 11th Hussar squadrons thereupon diverged to run along the flanks of the position, while between them the light tanks of the 7th Hussars swept in to overrun the infantry defences. At first, this appeared a task as easy as any the Hussars had faced to date, for the Libyan infantry promptly climbed out of their weapon-pits and fled over the ridge behind – but when the tanks pursued them up the slope they found themselves in the middle of a minefield in which three of their tanks blew up and the rest were either stuck or forced to pull back. They then came under fire from Italian artillery skilfully sited on the reverse slope of the ridge, and shells burst all around them occasionally exploding mines alongside. Those crew members who had not jumped or been pulled clear were trapped inside their tanks, praying that the steel was thick enough and thanking God that the Italians were not using armour-piercing shells, while the 11th Hussars raced up and down the flanks, desperately trying to draw fire away from their more unfortunate colleagues, hoping that the flashes of the Italian guns could be pinpointed by the R.H.A. batteries and their observers now in position but with their view masked by the rise.

It was all, however, to little effect. The sun was up, the glare off the desert surface blinding and aswim with mirage, and the 25-pounder crews well aware that not only were they in action and under fire for the first time, but that another battle was going on somewhere behind them. Above all, the Italian artillery was being directed with efficiency and admirable coolness. By noon John Combe was in doubt as to whether he should break off this part of the action and proceed with the second part – the reconnaissance – and it was with considerable relief that at 1500 he heard the news that the main target of the attack, Fort Capuzzo, had surrendered.

(As a result of an R.A.F. attack – in which no bombs had landed inside the target area – followed by a few 2-pounder shells from the guns of the cruiser tanks present, which penetrated the walls. Again, a bloodless victory.)

With his rear therefore safe, Combe divided his force, drew the remaining tanks and guns off and dispatched them back to the Wire, left B Squadron to screen Sidi Azeiz and sent C Squadron northward to descend the Escarpment and take a look at the defences of Bardia.

Three significant episodes filled the rest of the day. Three troops of C Squadron found and negotiated quite easily a pathway up and down the Escarpment, one drove quite unobstructed along the road at the bottom as far as the outskirts of Bardia which they found ringed with well-sited infantry defences, while the others explored towards Sollum and guarded the way back.

Back on the plateau, the first troop approached the wasps' nest of Sidi Azeiz again, only to find it apparently quiet, with the dust of a convoy leading away from it. As they turned to investigate, a white flag was run up – but as the troops deployed to race forward and take over, the flag came down and the guns opened up on them. Whether this event was a deliberate flouting of the rules of war or a misunderstanding overruled by the pugnacity of the Italian gunners was never established, but C Squadron beat a hasty retreat and was extremely lucky to suffer no casualties.

The third event concerned B Squadron. While screening Sidi Azeiz, Halliday's troop had suddenly been attacked by six Italian Fiat-Ansaldo L3 light tanks, and Halliday, with considerable misgivings, opened up on the nearest with a weapon viewed with great scepticism by all familiar with it – a Boyes anti-tank rifle. To the astonishment of all watching, the L3 promptly fell out of the attack, the others scuttled off 'like a lot of little pigs' to quote Halliday's report, while the two-man crew of the disabled tank climbed out and gave themselves up. Closer examination revealed that the L3 was very thinly armoured, carried no wireless and was little but a death-trap for those within. Halliday promptly set this one alight and returned triumphantly through the Wire.

Two days later, between Sidi Omar and the now-deserted Fort Capuzzo, occurred the quite astonishing Battle of Nezuet Ghirba.

Two troops of C Squadron were 'swanning about' on the Libyan side of the Wire north of Sidi Omar when the leader of one troop saw an Italian column of twelve L3 tanks and thirty lorries, apparently full of infantry, moving north along the track towards Capuzzo – presumably to re-garrison the fort. He reported to Squadron H.Q. on the other side of the Wire by radio, but at the same time the leader of the second troop reported another column, east-bound, consisting of forty lorries and seventeen L3s, on a course obviously aimed to converge with the first.

Realising that his men would soon be heavily outnumbered (the first troop had only two cars that morning), Major Miller from his covering position ten miles inside Egyptian territory ordered their withdrawal and asked for some of 4th Armoured Brigade's anti-tank guns to come up in case they should be needed.

But by this time, Second Lieutenant Vyvyan Gape, commanding the first troop to report, had gaily driven up to the first column and opened fire on the thin-skinned lorries and luckless infantry within; and as the twelve supporting L3s – six in front of the column and six at the rear – swung inwards to attack these two incredibly impudent armoured cars, the noise of the battle reached the ears of Second Lieutenant Dier, the other troop commander, who was already withdrawing from his Italian column but who now promptly drove towards the sound of the guns.

By the time Dier arrived, Gape had managed to knock out two of the L3s but was being harried by the rest who between them had managed to puncture a tyre on his second car, thus slowing them both down enough for the L3s to get between the Hussars and their exit through the Wire. Dier now opened fire, knocked out another L3 and frightened the others off (to be fair to the crews, the L3s were probably the most ineffectual fighting vehicles ever put into production), but by this time an Italian field gun hitherto concealed within the column had come into action and both Hussar troops wisely fled to the shelter of a small rise, from which position Gape radioed back the latest developments.

John Combe, who had now come up to take command, mustered all his own reserve troops and alerted the others still on the western side of the Wire. He then set off to meet the support which Brigadier Caunter was sending down, and soon a mixed squadron of light and cruiser tanks, an anti-tank troop of the Royal Horse Artillery and more armoured cars of the 11th Hussars were converging on the gap, while from both north and south beyond it came hastening in other troops of the 11th which had been reconnoitring further afield.

Soon they had concentrated, and Geoffrey Miller led them all forward to the slight rise from which Gape and Dier were watching the Italians below with fascinated disbelief. Soon both Miller and Combe were registering the same stunned astonishment.

Some three miles distant, on a flat plain totally devoid of cover, the Italian column (the second and bigger one never put in an appearance) had marshalled their lorries and infantry into a formed square – a combination of Wellington's infantry at Waterloo and

Figure 1   Rolls-Royce armoured car: weight 4 tons; armour 8mm.; engine
50 h.p.; maximum speed 45 m.p.h.; armament one ·303 Vickers m.g.; crew 3

the prairie laager beloved by Hollywood – which the L3s patrolled
outside but looking towards the British as though the Indians and
Palefaces had joined forces.

Two thoughts crossed John Combe's mind – who do they think
they're fighting, and do they have any concealed artillery?

There was only one way to find the answer to the second and most
immediately important of those questions, and he sent the 7th
Hussars' tanks down to do so with one of his own regiment's Morris
armoured cars to provide a radio link. As the tanks rolled up and
over the crest, they were subjected to a number of near-misses from
the one known piece of Italian artillery, and then valiantly attacked
by seven of the L3s which came forward to defend their infantry.
Knocking these out with one shot each, the advancing tanks then
circled the square, exactly like Red Indians attacking a ring of
covered wagons, pouring fire into the unfortunate and virtually unprotected infantry.

For some reason never disclosed, they were allowed to make two
complete and uninterrupted circuits before the Italians revealed
their hidden punch – field guns at each corner of the square. The
battle now briefly became four separate conflicts between guns and
tanks but the action was really at too close a range for the guns to

exert their power and, despite the desperate gallantry of the crews, they were all mown down by the British machine-gun fire, falling to a man at their guns, surrounded by blazing and exploding ammunition.

At this, the square broke. Some of the infantry threw down their rifles and offered surrender to the nearest tank crew, others ran for the lorries and endeavoured to escape, only to be rounded up by the armoured cars which now raced down to join the fray. The last of the Italian tanks tried unavailing conclusions with one of the 7th Hussars' two cruiser tanks on the field, whose commander merely waited until the Italian had virtually rammed him, then depressed his 2-pounder gun, fired and totally wrecked his gallant but helpless adversary.

In the end, a force of nearly 200 soldiers with 30 lorries, four guns and 12 tanks was wiped out, leaving only 12 lorries and 100 prisoners to make the sad journey across the Wire. Among the dead was Colonello D'Avanso from whose coat pocket an order was taken signed by Generale Sibille, commander of the 1st Libyan Division, ordering him to 'destroy enemy elements which have infiltrated across the frontier, and give the British the impression of our decision, ability and will to resist'.

There were no British casualties, and indeed the day had seen yet another success for the 11th Hussars, further to the north.

The previous night, C Squadron had gone back through the Wire and retraced their steps around Sidi Azeiz to the edge of the Escarpment, this time to the west of Bardia. At dawn two troops descended to the road below and at the bottom set up an ambush, while the remainder watched from the top to provide guard and covering fire if necessary. First the advanced crews cut all telephone and telegraph lines and then, remembering their own experiences in Palestine, they cut down a telegraph pole and manhandled it across the road to form a block. The armoured cars then moved into cover 'where', according to the report, 'the crews settled down to await their first customers'.

They did not have long to wait. A convoy led by a big diesel lorry with a heavy machine-gun mounted on top came up, and at the roadblock the gunner, of all people, dismounted to remove the telegraph pole. As the Hussars opened fire the vehicles behind either crashed into the one in front or were bumped by the one behind, and chaos and confusion followed with panic engulfing the convoy as the true situation became apparent. Another Hussar troop rushed down from the Escarpment to help deal with the prisoners, and as these were being marshalled up the rise 'carrying peculiar suitcases and giving out the overwhelming smell of a Latin army short of water', the original troops worked their way along the road to catch new arrivals. According to the regimental history:

> Altogether they had a splendid morning. Time and again the lorries would come bowling down the road all oblivious of the fate of their forerunners, would stop short of the last one in the queue, and usually dismount the passengers to find out what was holding up the convoy. The sequel was always the same: each in turn found himself confronted by the gun-muzzle of a grinning 11th Hussar, to make the uncomfortable but undeniable discovery that he was 'in the bag'. There was practically no resistance, and the game went on unchecked to the tune of forty vehicles in all.
>
> The chief prize was a Lancia car containing a general and his staff officer – and, to the infinite diversion of the 11th Hussars, two lady friends![1]

One of the lady friends turned out to be pregnant and her baby was eventually safely delivered in Alexandria Hospital, but the general was Generale di Corpo Lastucci, Engineer-in-Chief of the Tenth Army, and he carried with him excellently marked maps of the defences of Bardia. He was also a personal acquaintance of the new commander of the forward troops on the Egyptian side of the Wire, Lieutenant-General Richard O'Connor, for at the time of the Battle of Nezuet Ghirba, Hobart was serving as a lance-corporal in the Gloucestershire Local Defence Volunteers, soon to be renamed the Home Guard, from which exalted position he was grimly reorganising the defence of Chipping Campden.

There had been changes at high level among the British Forces. Hobart had been replaced eight months before, partly as a result of a general lack of communication with and understanding of his superiors, specifically as a result of an undignified row with Maitland Wilson, all the more unfortunate in view of the apparently good relationship established between Hobart and Wilson once Gordon-Finlayson had gone.

In July 1939, almost as soon as Wilson had taken over from Gordon-Finlayson, he visited Mersa Matruh and, in company with Hobart (with whom he had been a fellow-student at Staff College twenty years before) made a journey south into the desert, which he later described:

> The Western desert of Egypt rises gradually from the coast until Quattara depression is reached; the first major rise, in the form of an escarpment varying in height from 100 to 300 feet, runs from south of El Alamein, duplicating itself at times as far

west as Tmimi in Cyrenaica. The distances of these escarpments
from the coast varied from cliffs overhanging the sea, as at
Sollum and Bardia, located inside the Egyptian and Italian
frontiers respectively to in other places some four or five miles
[*sic*] . . .

A force with thorough knowledge of such conditions possessed
a great advantage over an adversary which was new to the
country. We spent two days travelling over the country to the
south, enabling one to get acquainted with desert conditions including navigation and location finding. One was at once struck
with the fascination of those open spaces, devoid of outstanding
landmarks, the only features being low, flat-topped ridges with
striking similarity so that every small object such as a cairn of
stones or an empty tar barrel assumes great importance.[2]

In order to confirm what would seem to have been a good
impression, Wilson then attended the closing phase of an exercise
Hobart held at the end of the month and spoke later to the officers
of the Mobile Force, praising the way in which it had been carried
out and urging further training along the same lines.

Hobart then went on leave to England (leaving on the same day
that Wavell arrived) but an early recall in view of the developing
situation brought him hurrying back to Mersa Matruh and the
deployment of the Mobile Force in case Italy immediately followed
Germany's lead. During the uneasy months which followed, some
patrolling of the frontier took place (but not much, so as not to
annoy Mussolini) and exercises and training continued on the
plateau until it became evident that tracks and vehicles were being
worn out at too rapid a rate in relation to replacement possibilities.

Wilson quite reasonably decided upon a recall to base for at least
the armoured sections of the Mobile Force for rest and refit, but
announced that before they returned he would hold a signals
exercise to test progress. This exercise began with a misunderstanding between Wilson who wanted to test communications and
Hobart who thought it was to try out the whole Mobile Force, progressed through chaos as a result of an important code-key being
retained at the wrong place (for Hobart led his force from the front
instead of the rear, where Wilson assumed he would be) and ended
in consuming ill-temper caused to a very great extent, as one of the
Rear H.Q. Staff was to write, by Wilson's A.D.C. who 'did not
seem to want to understand the instructions given him regarding
map references and compass bearings which were essential to
enable him to guide his General to General Hobart'.[3]

Heat, frustration and confusion all led inexorably to high blood-
pressure, and in the end to a confrontation over the exercise

analysis which became vituperative in the extreme, grossly unfair to all concerned and highly embarrassing to those who witnessed it.

There was a short interval during which Hobart wrote a letter to Wilson rebutting the few purely military criticisms which Wilson had made, but these were no longer of much import. The quarrel had become a personal one and on November 10th, Wilson sent to Wavell a letter which began, 'I regret to report that I have no confidence in the ability of Major-General P. C. S. Hobart, C.B., D.S.O., O.B.E., M.C., to Command the Armoured Division to my satisfaction,' and ended, 'I request therefore that a new Commander be appointed to the Armoured Division . . .'[4]

To what extent Wavell agreed with Wilson is not known – and he could have remembered the 1934 annual manoeuvres at which he had acted as umpire – but one fact was quite clear. Despite the vast size of the area now under his command, there was not room in it for both Lieutenant-General H. Maitland Wilson and Major-General P. C. S. Hobart.

The immediate reaction in the Mobile Force was one of widespread dismay, and two of his staff officers, Horace Birks and 'Strafer' Gott who was later to win great fame in the desert war, urged Hobart to fight the order, but as his biographer put it:

> Nothing of this sort could be of avail, as Hobart knew. Since he could not stay, the best course was to go with dignity. In the event he went in triumph, for as his car drove the mile and a half from his H.Q. to the airstrip it was to find the route lined by the men of his division, gunners, rifle, cavalry and tankmen, all cheering their general in a spontaneous and unforgettable farewell. They none of them knew why he was going – simply that he was and they must pour out to see him off with a demonstration of outright confidence and affection. To the General and his wife came a flood of letters from the C.O.s of all the units expressing their shock and dismay at his departure, and from Major-General Richard O'Connor, commanding the 8th Infantry Division at Matruh, who had found co-operation with Hobart easy and with whom he had worked in close accord, a sorrowful letter saying of the Mobile Division: 'It is the best trained division I have ever seen.'[5]

Fortunately for Britain and the Royal Armoured Corps, Hobart's services were not irretrievably lost as a result of this deplorable affair. Almost exactly a year after Wilson's letter had been written, he was called on Churchill's insistence for an interview with the Chief of the Imperial General Staff (by then Sir John Dill) to discuss his future employment. There was a slight conversational hiatus when Hobart inquired acidly if he should come in the uniform of a lance-corporal in the Home Guard or of a major-general, or even in civilian clothes, but that having been settled the interview took place and in due course Hobart was to raise and train the 11th Armoured Division and then the 79th (Specialised) Armoured Division which drove the 'Funnies' (the Flails which blew paths through minefields, the Crocodiles which scorched out enemy strongpoints with liquid fire, the Buffaloes which swam ashore) on to the Normandy beachhead and acted as 'tin-opener' for the British side of 21st Army Group under General Sir Bernard Montgomery who had, incidentally, been married to Hobart's sister until her tragic death in 1937.

Hobart's place was taken by Major-General Michael O'Moore Creagh, M.C., who had served most of his army career with the 15th and 19th Hussars, and who thoroughly appreciated the good fortune which had come his way. On February 16th, 1940, the Mobile Division – ex 'Mobile Force' and ex 'Immobile Farce' – became the 7th Armoured Division, and under that title was to win renown enough for twenty divisions, to make it the most famous armoured division in the British Army and one of the most famous in the world. But while there were still members of the Mobile Force alive to serve in the division, when problems arose would be heard the words, 'Well, Hobo always used to say . . .'

A much more significant appointment, however, had been that of Lieutenant-General Richard O'Connor to command the entire Western Desert Force. Shortly after the outbreak of war, Maitland Wilson had asked Cairo H.Q. for help in dealing with the growing administration of the forward troops at Mersa Matruh, and O'Connor – who had been in Jerusalem since 1937 – had come over as a major-general on a presumed temporary basis. He had returned to Palestine in early 1940 and three days before Mussolini's declaration from the Palazzo Venezia had been at Sarafan, the Headquarters of the southern district. There he received a cable summoning him to Cairo again and the following day was given orders by Maitland Wilson to go back to Mersa Matruh to assume permanent command of all forces there, and undertake the task of protecting Egypt from Italian attack. He received these instructions, he later recalled, 'with surprise, and of course pride', adding, 'My recollection is that I was given very sketchy instructions as to policy. I did not object, really, as I don't mind being left on my own.'*

The two men made an almost ludicrous contrast – Jumbo Wilson massive, heavy in jowl, deep-voiced, slow and almost majestic in gesture, filling his chair and the space to his desk almost to over-flowing; O'Connor small, bird-like, sitting nervously on the edge of his chair rather like a shy schoolboy at his first interview with his

*First quoted in *The Desert Generals* by Correlli Barnett (London), pp. 19–20.

housemaster. His voice was light and clear, only the ribbons of the D.S.O. and bar, the M.C., the First World War campaign ribbons and, ironically, the Italian Silver Medal for Valour awarded him in 1918 belying this gentle manner and reminding the observer that here was a professional soldier of thirty years' service. After brilliant war service as a junior officer (in addition to his awards he had been mentioned in dispatches nine times), he had recently held very active commands indeed – the Peshawar Brigade 1936–1938, then in Palestine appointments which included the onerous and somewhat exposed post of Military Governor of Jerusalem.

Perhaps in this contrast between manner and achievement lay the key to the man. In the military world an impressive physique is an advantage, the ability to fill a uniform splendidly and gaze levelly over the top of everyone else's head an undoubted help towards promotion – and on occasion those possessed of such attributes have filled high office with great distinction. But quite often the tall, handsome general proves to possess brawn in too great a proportion to brain, and in the years to come large numbers of these, in all armies, were to achieve active command and then pass rapidly to static governorships or even back to civilian life, after a phase of battle in which other men's blood had had to pay the price for their own lack of brain.

This had never been, and would never be, the case with O'Connor. The delicate head held a cool and logical brain which saw to the heart of a problem with a certainty and quickness which could make other quite sound soldiers seem slow-witted; the slight body had already unconcernedly endured battle in Alpine snows, in Ypres mud and the heat of India, and the gentle manner masked a will and determination as firm as Wavell's. Here again was an example of the British regular soldier in the Wolseley mode – small, neat and highly professional.

But there was something else about O'Connor which Correlli Barnett was the first to note – at any rate for the benefit of the non-military world. Although others might draw more immediate attention in a company, 'no-one could talk a quarter of an hour with him without being aware of unusual qualities of character and personality'. Imagination? A more than usually acute perception? A combination of both?

Perhaps here was that 'irrational tenth' that Wavell was seeking.

By the evening of June 8th, 1940, O'Connor had reached his new headquarters at Maaten Baggush thirty miles east of Mersa Matruh, a tented camp though with H.Q. offices well dug in under sand-dunes and thus, it was hoped, bomb-proof. Inland and only a few hundred yards away was the landing-strip and headquarters of the

Desert Air Force under Air Commodore Collishaw, and even nearer, to the north, were two small and pleasant beaches for swimming. It was not so luxurious as Jerusalem had been, but perhaps the coming months would give little opportunity for soft living; in the meantime, the most important things to do would be to get to know the ground, the men under his command (he already knew most of his officers, and they knew him), their state of training and their resultant state of mobility.

Within days of taking command General O'Connor received the best possible indications of the morale of the men under him in the shape of the reports of those first brushes with the enemy, and it was with considerable relish that he greeted his acquaintance Generale Lastucci and sped him on his way towards the prison-camp in which he was to languish for many months; but as the days of June passed, worries arose as a result of the shortages of both men and material, and the strain to which both were being subjected.

On June 19th, the first war-time *khamsin* blew – a hot wind from the heart of Africa like a blast from an opened oven laden with a seemingly unending sandstorm, of which the Arabs maintain that after five days murder is thoroughly excusable. This one caught one troop of the 11th Hussars well behind the Italian lines in the vicinity of El Gubi where it was believed lay the headquarters of the 1st Libyan Division, and another at Jarabub, the oasis at the southern end of the Wire, eighty miles south of Fort Maddalena and on the edge of the Great Sand Sea.

It was here, according to the regimental history, that the effects were felt most horribly:

> On June 25th the *Khamseen* blew its very worst. It was the hottest day the 11th Hussars had yet experienced – and in fact it was probably the hottest one they ever knew. For the time being the weather transcended all considerations – with the possible exception of the growing air attacks which the squadrons were now drawing down each day. Together the two seemed calculated to defeat every attempt they made to carry on: for the heavy armoured cars were scarcely able to move owing to the water shortage, while the unarmoured Rhodesian scout cars which were trying to fulfil their role became an easy prey to the Italian fighter-bombers. In these bare open plains they were desperately vulnerable. 'One had to decide in a second either to stay quite still or to make for a patch of scrub, if available, and hope that one's car would suddenly take on the appearance of a camel-hump,' wrote one of their officers.

Looking back upon it in after years, many of the Regiment maintained that fortnight was the hardest to endure of any they experienced throughout the whole course of the war . . . it is difficult to realize from afar the intensity of the physical strain which it imposed. It was not uncommon for men to collapse unconscious on the floors of their cars . . .

Colonel John Combe, travelling round his scattered squadrons, was horrified to find the men becoming really frightened of their continual thirst under the piercing heat. For the first, and only, time in his life, he said, he saw a hunted look in their faces, as the *khamseen* went on blowing all day long and every day until the armoured cars became too hot to touch. For most of the time the exhausted crews lay sweating underneath them, for now one patrol alone would use more water than the daily allowance for a whole Troop. Bully beef and biscuits was the only fare, and the men's personal water ration had sunk to pitiful proportions. Shaving and washing had long become a rare treat, and even when it was possible pathetic attempts were made to clean used water time and time again by draining it through a perforated petrol tin filled with sand.[6]

A report back to H.Q. to the effect that the capture of Jarabub would require the support of tanks brought down to the troop the second-in-command of 4th Armoured Brigade, who was escorted forward and into the basin which held the oasis.

As they climbed back again in the full blast of the sun, the colonel said he would certainly not hear of bringing his tanks into such a furnace and that he considered the conditions entirely precluded any further operations there. Back at R.H.Q. he was just telling John Combe how he hoped to get the armoured cars withdrawn, when the heat claimed him, too, as a victim and he fell down at John Combe's feet in a dead faint. Soon afterwards General O'Connor himself arrived . . .[7]

and the operation was for the moment abandoned.

But it is interesting to note that two weeks after taking command, O'Connor was 200 miles from his base, and well behind enemy lines. Shortly afterwards, one of the advanced cars of the 11th Hussars already over fifty miles into enemy territory, met the general in his staff car coming towards them from even further west.

When the matter was reported to Brigadier Caunter, supposedly in command of the forward area, he remonstrated with his general; who apologised. But as O'Connor needed to know even more about the ground he wished to make his battle area, neither the brigadier's remonstrance nor his polite acceptance prevented him from going well past the Wire again.

As July passed, two developments became clear: the Italian

forces near the frontier were being strengthened and the British forces were tiring, despite their psychological dominance of the area. Although more men were arriving at the frontier, it took time for them to learn the lessons already absorbed by those who had been there from the beginning and common sense demanded a slackening of pressure, a cool reappraisal of potentialities. The 4th Armoured Brigade were relieved by the 7th; the 11th Hussars – still the only reconnaissance unit available – were ordered to halve their activities so that at least two troops could be resting by the sea at Buq Buq (one of C Squadron's operations had gone wrong and they had lost four men killed and fourteen taken prisoner), and a reinforced Support Group deployed to cover the whole front and act as a delaying force should the Italians attack.

This Support Group, commanded now by Brigadier W. H. E. (Strafer) Gott, consisted of three battalions of motorised infantry – 1st King's Royal Rifle Corps (originally the Royal Americans), 2nd Rifle Brigade and 3rd Coldstream Guards – two 25-pounder batteries of the Royal Horse Artillery, each battery of twelve guns; two anti-tank batteries; a troop of medium artillery; and detachments of engineers and machine-gunners. With an incomplete battalion of cruiser tanks in reserve, this force constituted the shield, and the duty squadron of the 11th Hussars the eyes, of British power in Egypt; behind them the bases were growing, the men training, the tanks and supply vehicles being repaired and maintained, the odds calculated.

These, by any count, were still formidable. Against the known five divisions which Balbo had had facing the Egyptian border plus however many Graziani intended to bring across from the Tunisian front, the Western Desert Force could marshal only the 7th Armoured Division with but 65 of its full complement of 220 cruiser tanks (and these suffered from lack of spare parts and even lack of full armament) and the 4th Indian Division, still short of one complete brigade and of much of its artillery. The Australian and New Zealand troops which had arrived, though full of enthusiasm and courage, were desperately short of all types of equipment, and the only defence against low-flying aircraft was a battery of twelve Bofors guns at Alexandria. As for air cover, there were virtually no modern bombers or fighters anywhere in the area.

With this tatterdemalion collection as his instrument, O'Connor drew up his plans for the defence of Egypt against an Italian attack. Incredibly, he was neither discouraged nor depressed by his conclusions, and quietly confident that if and when an Italian army crossed the frontier and advanced towards the obvious first objective – Mersa Matruh – he would be able to launch out of the desert against its flank a force strong enough to cut through and reach the

sea, thus isolating the main enemy force and perhaps defeating it by
starvation. How long his own force would be able to hold against
attacks which would then almost certainly develop from both
directions, was something in the lap of the Gods; perhaps they
would be kind.

In the meantime, the thing to do would be to continue intensive
training, to use every day that Italian dilatoriness gave him to
strengthen his force qualitatively and hope that Britain or India
would help him quantitatively.

Maresciallo d'Armata Graziani had arrived in North Africa at the
end of June, the recipient of an order intended for his predecessor
Balbo but which, as it had been dispatched the day he was killed,
had never reached him. Mussolini had concluded that the invasion
of Great Britain was imminent, that the first German soldiers would
be ashore on Britain's embattled coasts by July 15th and that Italian
troops must cross the Libyan–Egyptian frontier on the same day.
However, any support Graziani had given this proposal when he
had been Army Chief of Staff in Rome, evaporated during the next
few days as he hurriedly inspected his inheritance in Libya.

His first communication back to Comando Supremo announced
that not only would he require every item on Balbo's list, but that
Balbo had lamentably failed to appreciate the paralysing inadequacy of the Italian air force in Africa. Of the 350 aircraft on
strength on June 10th only 60 were still effective after three weeks
of war, and of these most were obsolescent compared with the
modern, fast, hard-hitting fighters which the enemy would be able
to range against them. (Air Commodore Collishaw would have
been surprised and gratified to read that signal.) Many more
fighters, reconnaissance aircraft and transport planes were essential
before an attack into Egypt could be mounted, and new techniques
along the lines of the German Stuka dive-bombing must be worked
out and practised.

Graziani was probably not particulary surprised at the response
he received from Badoglio – to the effect that the attack *must* begin
on the specified day, that he must if necessary strip the Fifth Army
facing Tunisia of equipment and transport and give it all to the
Tenth Army, and that in the meantime seventy medium tanks had
been dispatched together with other items on Balbo's list which had
become available; but he could not have been very heartened by it
either. The message ended on a note of combined encouragement
and entreaty. 'In Somalia, you overcame very great difficulties; you
will overcome similar ones now. Give me an assurance of this!'

Gloomily, Graziani called a conference with his senior commanders and their staffs and on July 5th he forwarded their con-

clusions and plans for action as requested. It would be taking an enormous risk, his report declared, but in accordance with the wishes of Il Duce as transmitted by the Comando Supremo, Tenth Army would advance through the Wire on July 15th, cross the frontier, descend the Escarpment at its northern end – and occupy Sollum. Here a new base could be set up and, once the expected furious reaction of the enemy had been fought off, the resultant casualties in men and material replaced and reinforcements brought up, a further advance could be considered. Of course, it would be quite impossible to advance much further along the widening coastal belt without the tanks, water-carriers, anti-aircraft and anti-tank batteries plus other miscellaneous equipment which Maresciallo d'Armata Balbo had wisely requested, together with the aircraft which had been the subject of his own latest communication – and now also plus a force of new armoured cars without which any sort of manoeuvring action would be impossible.

What happened during the next ten days is somewhat obscure, but July 15th came and went without either a reply from Rome (though one had been drafted) or, not surprisingly, an advance through the Wire. When Badoglio's letter did at last arrive, it was to the effect that Comando Supremo thought that the trouble and effort of moving forward at all required a greater reward than just the occupation of a small post at the bottom of the hill, and that as it now seemed unlikely that German troops would be fighting on British soil as early as had been expected, it would be better to await the arrival of the required material and then advance in strength upon a more ambitious plan. A convoy carrying 'a great part' of the equipment which Balbo and Graziani had requested should arrive in Tripoli on July 27th, and the advance might be expected to commence in early August.

Two ships duly arrived, and in addition a personal letter to Graziani from Il Duce, spurring him on to greater glories both for his country and himself and ending in a cloud of metaphor: 'I hope and feel sure that having been the anvil for several weeks, it will be possible quickly to become the hammer – which, held in your staunch hands, will deal out resolute blows to the enemy!'

Time, however, had been given to Graziani for consideration of several factors which had perhaps not been quite so clear to him before his arrival in Tripoli. In his reply to Badoglio's letter suggesting a deeper advance into enemy territory than just down to Sollum, there is a note of surprise, tinged with reproof for a lack of understanding of practical realities. 'Such an operation [as was suggested] cannot be considered as other than impossible during this season, given the physical and topographical environment.' The summer heat alone apparently precluded physical effort of the magnitude necessary for such an advance, not to speak of the water shortage – which would now be exacerbated by the enormous number of vehicles which Comando Supremo were promising him, each one of which would require even more water than the men it carried. 'An action of this nature can only be effected, even though still presenting grave difficulties, at the end of the hot season, towards the end of October' – upon which note of sweet reason the letter ended.

The result of this was a curt summons back to Rome where on August 5th occurred an acrimonious exchange of views, ending in a compromise. A 'limited objective' offensive (though presumably not so limited as Sollum) would now be launched in order 'to relieve troublesome British pressure' along the Cyrenaican frontier, to establish a base below the Escarpment and to raise the morale of the Italian troops, now depressed by prolonged inaction.

But a clearer view of the reasons for the proposed advance is revealed in a letter Mussolini sent Graziani on August 10th:

> The invasion of Great Britain has been decided on, its preparations are in the course of completion and it will take place. Concerning the date, it could be within a week or within a month. Well, the day on which the first platoon of German soldiers touches British territory, you will simultaneously attack. Once again, I repeat that there are no territorial objectives, it is not a question of aiming for Alexandria, nor even for Sollum. I am only asking you to attack the British forces facing you. I assume full personal responsibility for this decision of mine.

As a recipe for military disaster, that must rate high in the annals of politico-military incompetence, but it gave some comfort and relief to Graziani who immediately assured Mussolini that his orders would be obeyed. The next day he issued instructions to Generale d'Armata Berti, commanding Tenth Army, to be ready to move on August 27th with as first objective the Sollum Escarpment (top or bottom?), and the final objective, 'should maximum exploitation be achievable', of Sidi Barrani.

As Hitler's invasion of Britain was apparently to be postponed for some time, the date of attack was allowed a little elasticity but, on Mussolini's strict injunction, was not to be later than September 9th. And at dawn on September 13th, it actually did begin – 'with', as one of the generals was later to record, 'much dedication on everyone's part'.

Five days beforehand, an Italian fighter had swooped low over the Advanced Headquarters of 7th Armoured Brigade and dropped a message-bag; it contained the names of all the British soldiers who had been taken prisoner by the Italians to that date (mostly 11th

Hussars) with a report on their health and a letter from the senior
British officer among them, confirming all details, giving surprisingly full explanations of how they had all been taken prisoner, and
assuring their colonel, John Combe, that they were being well
looked after. One sergeant who had died of wounds had been
buried with full military honours.

There were, apparently, to be no hard feelings on either side at
this stage of the desert campaign.

On the Italian side there was also to be a total lack of subtlety or
deception. Graziani's original plan was for an advance along the
coast by the XXI (Metropolitan) Corps, with two divisions in front
and one held back in reserve near Tobruk, while two motorised
Libyan Divisions augmented by a mobile group under command of
Generale di Corpo Maletti (who had won renown in the Ethiopian
Campaign and a reputation as a 'fire-eater') swung across the
Escarpment to the south as a shield for the main infantry.

This was still the plan on September 9th, but during September
10th and 11th, the Maletti Group lost its way to the assembly point
near Sidi Omar and had to be searched for by aircraft diverted from
planned attacks on the British advance posts, while the Libyan
divisions, watched curiously by the ever-present 11th Hussars, had
taken an unconscionable time to rendezvous near Fort Capuzzo.
Moreover, Graziani about this time received word of 'massive
British armoured forces' augmented by the 'excellent and omni-
present Camel Corps' deployed to strike at his southern flank, so he
decided to guard against this threat by giving the lead of the coastal
advance to the Libyan Divisions (62nd Marmarica and 63rd
Cyrene) and instructing Maletti to follow a more northerly course,
thereby sheltering the advancing infantry more closely and perhaps
moving out of reach of the threatening enemy. If battle casualties
among the Libyans at the head of the main advance became too
heavy, then that exposed position could be taken over by 1st Blackshirt (23rd March) Division, while the 4th Blackshirt and the 64th
Catanzaro Divisions could now both remain in reserve near
Tobruk. It was necessary to safeguard the lives of native sons as far
as was possible.

So, at dawn on September 13th the Italian invasion of Egypt
began with a spectacular artillery bombardment of the old
Egyptian barracks at Musaid on the edge of the Escarpment (which
had been empty for some days) followed by their occupation
by a column which entered Egypt through the gaps in the Wire left
obligingly by the 11th Hussars. Once there, the artillery was then
deployed nearby and opened up another barrage on the old
barracks at Sollum and the landing-grounds just below them. When

the dust of this second barrage cleared, the head of the main coastal thrust was revealed, drawn up as though on Sunday parade, lines of motor-cycle troops in front, light tanks and staff cars behind, lorries stretching back into the distance.

With a roar of engines starting up, the whole cavalcade began to move majestically forward to the top of the winding pass which led down to Sollum, while the troops who had occupied Musaid in their turn moved further along eastwards until they came to the top of what was to become one of the most famous and contested passages in Egypt, Halfaya Pass. Meanwhile, the only British troops in the area – a single platoon of the 3rd Coldstream Guards who had been watching all this panoply of war with fascination – closed down the signal net upon which they had been reporting it all, unobtrusively but rapidly left Sollum itself and activated the mines sown along the tracks leading eastwards.

The Italian descent of both passes thereupon became hazardous. As the motor-cyclist advance guards roared around the hairpin bends, rifle shots cracked overhead and an understandable nervous astonishment tweaked their handle-bars to send them shooting over the edge or swerving dangerously in front of their compatriots behind; tank tracks were blown off on mine-fields and at certain bends in the track, lorries would arrive simultaneously with British 25-pounder shells, the guns having been fired as sunlight caught the lorry windscreens on previous bends. (The Royal Horse Artillery had one of the most successful days in its history.)

From above came whistling fragmentation bombs from R.A.F. Blenheims while slow but agile Gladiators zoomed along the routes machine-gunning the stalled lorries and marching troops. High above it all, the few Hurricanes in Egypt fought it out with the Fiats and Macchis, stricken planes wheeling down in flame and smoke to end with a dull thump away in the desert.

And all the time, the marching Italian infantry columns built up behind and began inexorably to overflow down the passes, scrambling around the blocked lorries, over the wrecked tanks, past the scars left along the verges by exploding mines. They were joined by the lorried infantry escaping from the baulked and dangerous caverns of their vehicles, and a khaki-grey flood built up, lapping all the time towards the white-topped stone huts and abandoned dumps of the port area of Sollum.

Here a neat but harmless comedy was being played out. Royal Engineers had mined most of the buildings and dumps, retiring down the coast a short distance with their detonating wires. They had been about to start blowing up the buildings when an Italian artillery observation plane appeared above the port and shortly afterwards a barrage opened up from over the rim of the Escarpment. Appreciating the situation, the sapper officer instructed his men to wait until they heard a gun fire, then, just as the shell was due to land, to blow up one of their charges. Inevitably, the blown charge was not in the same place as the gun-fire had been directed, and the air-observer became obviously more and more confused as too many explosions took place, few of which he could identify as his own. Eventually the British charges were all exploded, the engineers retired, the plane flew off and what remained of Sollum after two armies had tried to destroy it was slowly occupied by weary Libyan infantry. By late afternoon lorries, tanks and more motor-cyclists were arriving and the advance eastward along the coast had begun. As there was no surfaced road at that time between Sollum and Sidi Barrani fifty miles to the east, and British army traffic and now shell-fire had crushed the surface into an even finer dust than before, it was a choking, blinding and tongue-searing experience for all.

Up on the plateau, the Italian troops who had attacked Musaid, together with another division which had come up from Sidi Omar, also spent a tiring and frustrating day, their transport boiling in the hot sun and the enforced slow pace, the thirsty infantry trudging desperately and miserably alongside, the motor-cyclists bumping across rocks or stuck in soft sand, rarely able to show the speed and flair for which they were intended. And all the time they were subjected to machine-gun attacks and occasionally to shelling from the marauding and infuriatingly elusive enemy, cruising always just beyond their grasp with an ease and confidence of movement which appeared magical.

On arrival at the top of Halfaya Pass they found even worse conditions reigning, for enormous traffic jams had built up in the gathering darkness and by nightfall thousands of Italian and Libyan soldiers were crowded into formed leaguer, with lorry headlights and searchlights sweeping the desert approaches to help guard against more enemy onslaughts. These made excellent and rewarding aiming points for the guns of the Support Group detachment, which Brigadier Gott had left up on the plateau.

From the British point of view, despite the undoubted success of their harassing tactics and the boost to their already high morale of this clear demonstration of their superiority, man for man, in desert fighting, one overwhelming and sobering fact emerged. Three battalions of infantry plus assorted artillery, tanks and armoured cars, however well handled, cannot hold up for long a force of five divisions, however lethargic they may be.

Strafer Gott commanding the Support Group and Lieutenant-Colonel Jock Campbell commanding the 25-pounder batteries of the Royal Horse Artillery might have had an exciting and successful day – as had the officers and men of the K.R.R.C., the Rifle Brigade and Coldstream Guards – but to Wavell and O'Connor watching from Headquarters the nagging questions were, 'When would the grey tide stop flowing?' and, 'How many divisions are there still in Libya to back up the five divisions which have now been identified in this first attack?' They were fairly confident that they could hold the first thrust on Mersa Matruh, and the heavier tank units of 7th Armoured Division were now poised to strike northwards from the plateau as soon as the enemy lines of communication were sufficiently exposed – but how long could the tanks and guns of one division hold out against those of at least five divisions, especially in view of the chronic shortage of vehicles and ammunition which plagued them all?

Even now, the gunners of the Support Group were looking anxiously at their ammunition stocks, and although the supply columns had no trouble in racing up when required, the 25-pounders were being fed from ever-diminishing dumps; not that that stopped them on the morrow from repeating and even exceeding their exploits of the previous day, when movement started again and the two Italian columns met and merged (became, in fact, inextricably mixed) at the foot of Halfaya Pass. Batteries of both 3rd and 4th Royal Horse Artillery plastered the concentration as it formed and eddied, spilling out over the plain and re-forming into columns to move forward again to the slight rise where the Coldstream Guards awaited it, to fight the first of that day's series of delaying actions.

All through September 14th, the pattern was the same; the R.H.A. batteries would fire at the plodding mass as it edged forward on wider and wider fronts until the risk of being overrun became real, then they would limber up and move back to the next position. The Coldstream Guards held the line until the guns opened up again, when they in their turn could slip away; by evening, tired and hot but still quite confident, all were back east of the salt-pan by the sea at the miserable location rejoicing in the singular name of Buq Buq. Further east and behind them at Sidi Barrani waited the remainder of the Support Group, with the exception of C Squadron of the 11th Hussars still watching the gap at Bir Shefersen south of Sidi Omar.

And there was no change on September 15th except that in the early afternoon the R.H.A. completely ran out of ammunition and were quickly withdrawn through the supporting infantry, which in turn watched and waited for the moment when they would themselves have to retreat through the line of the 11th's armoured cars, right back to the last defences at Mersa Matruh. Meanwhile, the main weight of the 7th Armoured Division moved a little closer

towards its attack position and girded itself for its first major action
– apparently to be fought on or about September 17th and 18th. All
were quite confident that they would be able to give good account of
themselves.

Then at dusk on the 16th the Italian forward troops reached Sidi
Barrani, probed a little further on as far as Maktila where they
waited for the main mass to settle in behind them, and to the only
British troops still in contact (the 11th Hussars, needless to say) it
gradually became evident that this was where they intended to stay.
The following evening, while the tank crews of 7th Armoured
Division were beginning to relax with some degree of disgust,
Rome radio concluded a long panegyric on the glorious advance of
their Tenth Army in Libya against fanatical but out-manoeuvred
British troops with the announcement that 'All is now quiet in Sidi
Barrani, the shops are open and the trams running again' – which
would have come as a surprise to the inhabitants, most of whom had
never seen a tram in their lives.

A few days later, Sergeant Peacock of the 11th Hussars edged his
way to within 200 yards of an outlying Italian post under cover of
the morning mist, and watched an Italian officer talking to a civilian
dressed in suit and trilby hat, both poring over a civil-engineering
blue-print. Behind them waited a gang of labourers carrying picks
and shovels, and there was curiously little evidence to suggest that
here lay the forward outpost of a thrusting military empire. Solid
fortifications were undoubtedly to be constructed, but it looked as
though a further advance was not for the moment under consideration.

Soon after that, Gladiator pilots reported work commencing on
the construction of a well-surfaced road between Sollum and Sidi
Barrani, the laying of water-pipes and the arrival of tons of supplies
at the end of the Bir Sofafi track, well to the south, where Generale
Maletti's group had also come to rest. Evidently, Graziani's much-
vaunted attack had ground to a halt, and there was for the moment
to be no further thrust towards Mersa Matruh or continuation of the
Drive to the Nile.

'It was all', said General O'Connor as he withdrew the tanks of
the 7th Armoured Division and redeployed the Support Group,
'rather a disappointment.'

3 · The Pace Quickens

'Nobody', wrote Wavell's son many years later, 'would call my father a chatty general' – a delightful comment but one whose truth occasionally makes things difficult for the historian endeavouring to pierce the screen of inscrutability behind which Wavell so often hid his immediate reaction to events.

Because of his Olympian viewpoint of Middle East affairs at this time, his reactions inevitably differed from those of his subordinates, aware only of their own immediate problems. O'Connor and the Western Desert Force were intent only upon events along the Libyan border; Wavell had at least four frontiers to watch – with Libya, East Africa, Syria and Iraq – intricately balanced political situations in the last two to judge, and, ever since hostilities had commenced in Europe, a highly imaginative, demanding and often aggressively argumentative political master in Winston Churchill at home.

The withdrawal of France from the war against the Axis Powers had monumentally increased Wavell's problems. Not only had he now lost any hope of support from Tunis in the battle against Graziani's forces, but by the end of June 1940 it had become obvious that Général Mittelhauser (who had succeeded Weygand in command of the French armies in Syria and the Levant) was prepared to accept the Franco-German Armistice terms, and the announcement to this effect was almost immediately followed by the attack by the Royal Navy upon the French Fleet at Mers el Kebir and Oran.

Whatever the justification for this – and as Churchill said, 'Who in his senses would trust the word of Hitler [that he would not use the French Fleet against their former allies] after his shameful record and the facts of the hour?' – it had the effect of fanning the always latent French Anglophobia into open hatred, and strengthened the hand of the Vichy Government in any anti-British attitudes they cared to adopt. These were quickly indicated by the replacement of Général Mittelhauser by the rabidly anti-British Général Fougère, and then further demonstrated by instructions to the pro-British Général Legentilhomme in French Somaliland to cease all communications with his neighbours to the east, and prepare instead to collaborate with the representatives of the Duke of Aosta away to his west in Addis Ababa. When it became obvious that Legentilhomme had few sympathies with his country's new rulers in Vichy a replacement was sent out who was likely to prove more amenable, and Legentilhomme crossed the narrows from Djibuti to Aden where he received a friendlier welcome than he was likely to get at home.

The hostility from across the Syrian and Levantine frontiers was to pose a problem for some time to come; that from French Somaliland was fairly quickly resolved, though not in the manner Wavell would have preferred.

The Italian forces in East Africa – in Eritrea, Abyssinia and Italian Somaliland, all under command of the Duke of Aosta – had not been entirely inactive, but neither had they exhibited much

Map 2   Italian East Africa

more aggression than had their compatriots in Libya. Caproni bombers had occasionally attacked Port Sudan on the Red Sea coast, Atbara, the inland road junction, Kassala, the small provincial town near the Sudan–Ethiopian border, and Kurmuk further south, but there had been little ground activity. However, on July 4th, somewhat to the surprise of the two companies of the Sudan Defence Force there, Kassala was attacked by three columns of Italian and native troops, consisting of two colonial brigades, four cavalry squadrons with some twenty-four light tanks and armoured cars, together with ten batteries of artillery.

The ensuing action was brisk but shortlived, and the result was inevitable. By evening the defending companies had retired some twenty miles to the next rail-stop at Butana Bridge having suffered ten casualties, while the Italian command was reporting occupation of an important stronghold at a cost of 117 dead and wounded.

This had not been all. Nearly 200 miles south at Gallabat (again, virtually on the Sudan–Ethiopian frontier) an Italian colonial battalion had driven a platoon of No. 3 Company Eastern Arab Corps away, while during the next few days the police posts at Karora and Kurmuk were attacked and occupied, and their Sudanese occupants dispersed, in every case after a spirited defence and well-conducted retreat.

From these successes the Italians made valuable tactical gains, for in Kassala they now possessed a springboard for any further advance into the Sudan, and in Gallabat they had secured a block against any British intentions against Ethiopia.

They had also, inevitably, given hostages to fortune, for they now held outposts which could become targets for that speciality of the British and especially the Indian Army, infantry patrolling – a disadvantage which became only too evident in the weeks that followed.

Then, as July ended and the enormous heat of equatorial Africa in August began to build up, it became evident that in the Duke of Aosta, Britain had a more determined antagonist than the one on the Libyan border. Despite the heat, the Duke intended to rid himself of hostility on at least one border and had concluded that the enclave formed by British Somaliland, now neatly invested on three sides, could be eliminated by the expulsion of the occupying forces out through the fourth side and into the Gulf of Aden.

To Wavell it had always been a cardinal principle that territory should not be given up without a fight, but now, with the acute shortage of men throughout his vast command, he had to compromise and accept the classic dictum to the effect that a soldier saved is a soldier won. He was well aware of the probable size of the force which Aosta was massing along an extremely vulnerable frontier, while his own forces were so exiguous that in July they were still commanded by a lieutenant-colonel of the Royal Marines. Hastily promoting him to brigadier, Wavell endeavoured to amass for him the force of at least five battalions which he would require to put up any worthwhile defence, and by the beginning of August Brigadier A. R. Chater had under his command 1st Battalion North Rhodesia Regiment, 2nd Battalion King's African Rifles, 1st/2nd Punjab Regiment, 3rd/15th Punjab Regiment and the 1st East African Light Battery with four 3·7-inch howitzers. He also had elements of the lightly armed Camel Corps which had recently been augmented by officers and N.C.O.s from the Southern Rhodesia Regiment, while the 2nd Battalion the Black Watch was en route from Aden.

Against this, the Italian Force Commander, Generale di Corpo Nasi, had twenty-six Italian and Colonial battalions, twenty-one batteries of mixed artillery, assorted tanks, armoured cars and air-craft (of which Chater had none at all) and five groups of 'irregu-lars' – who might or might not fight, but who would undoubtedly prove highly dangerous to a defeated or retreating force.

The Italian forces crossed the British Somaliland frontier on August 3rd in the form of a trident, the main force under Generale di Divisione de Simone advancing towards Hargeisa, his left flank guarded by a column under Generale di Corpo Bertoldi moving on to Zeila (and thus masking the frontier with French Somaliland, just in case some of the departed Général Legentilhomme's supporters might wish to help the beleaguered British), his right flank guarded by a similar column under Generale di Brigata Bertello whose first objective was Odweina.

By August 5th, the Camel Corps screens and a company of the Northern Rhodesia Regiment which had been operating with them had withdrawn on all attacked frontages, and the Italian forces had reached their objectives – at which point Bertoldi sent light patrols eastwards along the coast while the other two columns began an amalgamating move on the small town of Adadle. From this area would be launched the main attack across the only natural defence between the Ethiopian frontier and the sea, a range of rugged hills which ran parallel to the coast, about fifty miles from it. A wide gap existed here through which ran the main road from Hargeisa to the capital and only port, Berbera, and here, at the Tug Argan as it was called, would be fought the battle for British Somaliland.

Numbers made the result a foregone conclusion, numbers com-bined with a lack of artillery on the part of the defenders illustrated by the offer from H.M.A.S. *Hobart*, part of the naval contingent standing by to aid the inevitable evacuation, of a 3-pounder saluting gun with thirty rounds of ammunition – an offer which was grateto Nasiyeh

Laferug

Barkasan

Abdal

BLACK HILL
KNOBBLY HILL
MILL HILL
CASTLE HILL
BLOCK HILL

OBSERVATION HILL

JARATO PASS

ASSA HILLS

TUG ARGAN

Adadle

to Odweina
35Km/23M

KARRIM PASS
to Hargeisa 35Km/23M

0Km   10   20
0M   5   10   N

Map 3   The battle of Tug Argan

fully accepted. The only other artillery available were the four light
howitzers mentioned above, although Wavell, once he had realised
that the Italians were invading in strength, had ordered two anti-
tank guns to be sent to Berbera by special convoy, together with
some of the 4th Indian Division's guns from the hardly less
threatened Western Desert. He also requested the Command in
India to dispatch immediately the first convoy of the 5th Indian
Division, already earmarked for the Middle East, and then in view
of the build-up in strength in the area should it all arrive in time to
stem the Italians, he diverted Major-General A. R. Godwin-Austen
from his journey to East Africa where he was about to take
command of the 2nd African Division.

The general arrived on the evening of August 11th and found that
virtually the entire force under his command was already in action.
Five hills in the Tug Argan gap – Black Hill, Knobbly Hill, Mill
Hill, Observation Hill and Castle Hill – had been prepared for
defence with barbed wire and machine-gun posts, and on Observa-

tion Hill stood the *Hobart*'s 3-pounder, mounted on an oildrum and served by a petty officer and two seamen. But it was quite obvious that the posts were too far apart for concerted action between the scanty forces which manned them, and that infiltration was bound to occur once the attackers probed the gaps with sufficient determination.

During August 11th and 12th, the posts came under artillery fire first and then infantry attack, and as the artillery became more accurate the defences were knocked out and the casualties began. It proved almost impossible to evacuate them quickly, and as the day-time heat was intense their plight was dire indeed, especially when, inevitably, the attackers found their way between the posts; as early as the night of the 13th/14th the Italians ambushed a convoy bringing up water and ammunition from the rear, though they failed to halt it.

By the 15th it had become evident to Godwin-Austen that it was time to evacuate his entire force unless it was to be wiped out. There was a brief exchange of signals with Cairo, a final last stand that evening during which Observation Hill with its naval gunners and a desperately defended machine-gun post were overrun, and then the withdrawal began – first through a screen of the Black Watch some ten miles back at Barkasan, then a leap-frog back through a second screen sixteen miles behind the first at Nasiyeh.

In the meantime the evacuation of British civilians had begun from Berbera, and as the ferries moved out, British and Australian naval units moved in to use their guns in the final perimeter battles and to pick up the last of the troops as they reached the coast. By 1400 on August 18th all survivors of the action (together with the civilians they amounted to about 7,000 souls) were safely aboard and away, although H.M.A.S. *Hobart* with Force Headquarters aboard remained until the morning of the 19th in order to be certain that no lone individuals were still arriving. She was also on hand to greet with a final salvo the first Italian troops to approach the port.

The defence of British Somaliland had cost 260 casualties, of which some were later to be recovered, and as the Italians were at that time still broadcasting their losses, the British had the satisfaction of finding out that they had cost their attackers 2,052 in dead and wounded together with a great deal of military equipment. The whole operation had undoubtedly been carried out with great skill and efficiency, under testing conditions, and the co-operation between the Royal Navy, the Army and the Royal Air Force once operations had come within range of the Aden-based bombers had been professional in the extreme.

It was a great pity that this truth was not more evident in White-hall.

Although Wavell was back in Cairo by the time the evacuation from Berbera was complete, he had just spent eight days in London, a substantial portion of them in the company of the Prime Minister. These meetings had not been an unqualified success.

It was hardly likely that they would be, for the two men – both of enormous strength of character – were poles apart in attitude to the common problems and in background and training to overcome them. Churchill, bearing then the enormous burdens of a Prime Minister at the time of his country's greatest danger – and revelling in them – was using his great qualities of courage, imagination and unflinching optimism to sweep his countrymen out of their desperate plight on a tide of emotion and oratory. His attitude to military problems was greatly affected by his tendency to simplify arithmetic by dealing only in round figures – and optimistically rounded at that – allied to a belief that practically any member of any military formation, if issued with a rifle, was perfectly fit and able to take his place in the front line.

To those entrusted with the tasks of actually fighting and winning the battles upon which Britain's existence depended, the Prime Minister's viewpoint therefore posed many problems, though few commanders – and certainly not Wavell – ever forgot the vital impulse which Churchill was contributing to their joint effort or believed that their own part in the war was more important than his.

Even more significant, however, than the differences in technical training between Churchill and the majority of his service advisers – and Wavell was typical of them in this – were their different attitudes to personal behaviour.

Churchill was a politician and parliamentarian – some would claim the greatest parliamentarian of his age – and he had climbed to the peak of power by the use of his great parliamentary gifts. Every facet of the art of verbal persuasion, from sweet reason through flattery, sarcasm, Ciceronian irony, mordant wit, plain verbal bullying and personal abuse, was his to command, and as he was quite rightly convinced of the justice of the great cause upon which he was engaged, he had no hesitation in using all his skills upon every occasion when he felt that his own way was the best. As these occasions were frequent, so were those upon which he used the full range of his talents, and when occurring in the House of Commons or in Cabinet they were accepted by his parliamentary colleagues as part of the day to day cut-and-thrust of the business of government.

But when they occurred in debate with his service advisers, the results were by no means so happy. At this period of the war, the Chief of the Imperial Staff was Sir John Dill, a sensitive and at that time extremely anxious man who was also a great personal friend of

Wavell's; and his sessions with Churchill, which the Prime Minister enjoyed so much, exhausted and sickened Dill.

But at least Dill would answer Churchill's verbal attacks, and endeavour to parry the master's thrusts with some kind of argument. Wavell met them with taciturnity or, even more frustrating for Churchill, with one of his formidable but total silences, followed in due course by a lucid and cogently argued paper in which many of the Prime Minister's most attractively presented verbal points were revealed as impractical and sometimes patently absurd fancies.

Not only did this difference in behaviour create great tension between the two men, but it stirred unfortunate memories in Churchill's mind. Twenty-four years before, Lloyd George had been confronted with just such a façade of impassive silence by General Haig at their meetings, and much later the latter revealed in his diaries a contempt for his political master only equalled by Lloyd George's distrust of the general. As Lloyd George was in many ways Churchill's political model and exemplar, the idea cannot have escaped the Prime Minister that the commander of the only army which Britain had in the field did not hold him in very high esteem. There would also have arisen in the Prime Minister's mind the possibility that Wavell might repeat Haig's performance as a military commander, which in Churchill's opinion would be disastrous.

Nevertheless, the discussions progressed, based to a large extent upon a detailed exposition of the situation in the Middle East given by Wavell on the second day of his visit to the Chief of Staff's Committee, and if there was disagreement between politician and soldier on the distribution and use of military manpower in the area, there was total agreement on the need for further reinforcement and, even more important, for a swift and considerable build-up of supplies and arms of every sort.

Considering the fact that the Battle of Britain was at that very moment reaching its climax and that all over England men were drilling with armbands instead of uniforms, with pikes instead of rifles and still with flags instead of anti-tank guns, Churchill and the War Cabinet showed admirable courage in the decision they took the day after Wavell's dissertation to the Committee – to send to the Middle East a convoy bearing a Cruiser Tank Battalion, a Light Tank Battalion (both of 52 tanks), an Infantry Tank Battalion of 50 tanks, 48 anti-tank guns, 20 Bofors light anti-aircraft guns, 48 25-pounder field guns, 500 Brens, 250 anti-tank rifles and as large a supply of ammunition for all of them as could be assembled in time.

There followed a brisk exchange of memoranda between the Admiralty who held doubts about the wisdom of convoying so valuable a shipment through the Mediterranean, and Churchill who had a keen and justifiable sense of the importance of time in military matters and felt that the risk should be accepted. The argument was not entirely resolved when the time came for Wavell to return to Cairo where he arrived on August 16th, but his reflections upon his meetings with the Prime Minister were perceptive and prophetic:

> I do not think Winston quite knew what to make of me and whether I was fit to command or not. He was determined that something must be done to put the defence of Egypt on a sound basis; and in providing reinforcements of tanks and sending a convoy through the Mediterranean was bold in overriding the views both of those who wished to keep all armoured forces for home defence . . . and of the First Sea Lord . . .
>
> On certain details the P.M. was difficult. He did his best to make me move both South African and West African troops from East Africa to Egypt or the Sudan; and he never realised the necessity for full equipment before committing troops to battle. I remember his arguing that because a comparatively small number of mounted Boers had held up a British division in 1899 or 1900, it was unnecessary for the South African Brigade to have much more equipment than rifles before taking the field in 1940. In fact I found that Winston's tactical ideas had to some extent crystallised at the South African War, just as his ideas on India's political problems . . . had not advanced much from his impressions as a subaltern in the nineties . . .
>
> In the end . . . I succeeded in convincing him that it would not be advantageous or politic to move the African troops from East Africa. At least I convinced him that I wouldn't do it. I am pretty sure that he considered my replacement by someone who was more likely to share his ideas, but could not find any good reason to do so.[1]

Unfortunately, there then followed an incident which deepened the dislike which Wavell felt that Churchill had already conceived for him. As Wavell was leaving Britain there had occurred the exchange of signals between Generals Godwin-Austen and Wilson which had resulted in the evacuation of British Somaliland – a decision to which Wavell gave his full support as soon as he reached his headquarters; but within hours Mussolini was trumpeting loudly his army's victory over British military might in this, their first major encounter, and on August 20th he proclaimed that Italian forces were now exercising a 'total blockade' of all British possessions in the Mediterranean and in Africa.

Although Churchill was well aware of the basic facts of the situation, this propaganda victory by Il Duce annoyed him considerably. At that same moment there arrived on his desk the statistics of the retreat, revealing that British casualties had amounted to a mere 260 dead, wounded and missing, and reverting to a habit of thought of a previous age which had often interpreted a battle's success by the size of the resultant casualty list (on one's own side) he dashed off what Wavell later described as 'a red-hot cable' demanding the suspension of Godwin-Austen from command and the immediate assembly of a court of inquiry into an episode which he clearly regarded as tinged with disgrace.

Wavell replied with a cable refusing both the suspension of a competent general and the holding of an unnecessary inquiry, pointing out that the troops had fought well and hard and, as the Italians had themselves admitted, had inflicted far more casualties than they themselves had suffered. The cable ended with the gravid admonition, 'A big butcher's bill is not necessarily evidence of good tactics.'

For somebody who was used to dealing in the language of both praise and rebuke, Churchill took this very badly; perhaps because it was on paper. The great neck flushed deep red, the baby-blue eyes glowered, and General Dill, who was present, later wrote to Wavell that he had never seen the Prime Minister so angry. It was a reaction which would later exact its toll, but in the meantime Churchill had composed the first of what was to be a long series of directives to the generals in the field. It reached Cairo late on the afternoon of August 23rd as a signal which when deciphered covered three and a half pages of close typing – and as Wavell later wrote, 'It showed clearly that Winston did not trust me to run my own show and was set on his ideas.'

The directive first analysed the military situation in the Middle East as Churchill saw it, then with a series of tables proved that by October 1st Wavell would have under his command a force of thirty-nine battalions altogether totalling 56,000 men with 212 guns, not including any security troops. It was not an analysis with which Wavell agreed, especially as the Prime Minister had again reverted to the suggestion that South and West African troops should be moved up from Kenya, despite Wavell's expressed determination not to carry this out.

The last part of the directive gave detailed and explicit instructions as to how this force of thirty-nine battalions was to be deployed for the defence of the Delta and then went on:

In this posture, then, the Army of the Delta will await the Italian invasion. It must be expected that the enemy will advance in great force, limited only, but severely, by the supply of water and petrol. He will certainly have strong armoured forces on his right hand to contain and drive back our weaker forces, unless these can be reinforced in time by the armoured regiment from Great Britain. He will mask, if he cannot storm, Mersa Matruh. But if the main line of the Delta is diligently fortified and resolutely held he will be forced to deploy an army whose supply of water, petrol, food, and ammunition will be difficult. Once the army is deployed and seriously engaged, the action against his communications, from Mersa Matruh, by bombardment from the sea, by descent at Sollum, or even much further west, would be a deadly blow to him.

All this might be put effectively in train by October 1, *provided we are allowed the time*. If not, we must do what we can. All trained or Regular units, whether fully equipped or not, must be used in defence of the Delta. All armed white men and also Indian or foreign units must be used for internal security. The Egyptian Army must be made to play its part in support of the Delta front, thus leaving only riotous crowds to be dealt with in Egypt proper.[2]

In view of the lack of information of Italian strengths and intentions at this time (for it must be remembered that Graziani had not moved when the directive was written) there is much of truth and value in the overall analysis of the situation as set out in the directive; but it also demonstrated, as perhaps nothing else could, the wide gap between the viewpoint of a political leader – however gifted – looking at the situation from Whitehall, and that of a military technician dealing with practicalities on the spot.

Later, Wavell was to write, 'I carried out such parts of the directive as were practical and useful, and disregarded a good deal of it' – which, in view of the fact that this was obviously the best thing to do, throws an interesting light on the basic tenet of our democracy that the military must always be subordinate to the elected representatives of the people.

Wavell replied to the directive in four cables sent over the next five days, diplomatically sidestepping some issues, avoiding others as best he could, and only entering the difficult arenas of categorical rejection in the matters of demonstrable statistics. Upon Churchill's figures of strength, he commented:

Approximate total of forces excluding Egyptian for defence of Egypt by 8th October is 38 battalions, 156 field guns, 18 medium guns, 90 anti-tank guns, 1,000 anti-tank rifles, 239 Bren-carriers, 40 A.A. guns, 12 light A.A. guns. Above includes reserves. Please note that proper proportion equipment for force of this size should be 380 field guns, 50 medium guns, 320 anti-tank guns, 2,100 anti-tank rifles, 730 carriers universal. Above does not include reserves.[3]

And in a letter to Dill, Wavell echoed the plea which Balbo had made to Mussolini – 'It is material, especially artillery and anti-tank weapons, that is required rather than men. The enemy will not reach the Delta [just] with large forces of infantry, but only if he can bring up superior armoured force.'

But by the time these exchanges had taken place the convoy carrying the promised arms and reinforcements had reached Gibraltar, and as there seemed little sign of immediate Italian aggression across the Libyan border it was decided that the ships should all make the long haul around the Cape, arriving at Suez by the end of September. By then, Graziani *had* moved and Wavell was facing an entirely different situation in the Middle East, acutely aware of the need for the reinforcements up in the battle area but also aware of the time factor. To unload and disperse the equipment, to test the vehicles and adapt them for desert conditions, to train and acclimatise the men to withstand the heat and sand in which they would have to fight, would require a minimum of six weeks.

And he knew that the Italian force must not be left undisturbed for that length of time.

By a quite simple computation, Sergeant Lamb knew that within five minutes he must turn back; otherwise all three cars of the troop would be caught at dawn, still within the arc of Italian camps curving south-westwards from Maktila on the coast down to Sofafi forty miles inland. The question uppermost in his mind was whether he had led his men into a trap – for they seemed to have come a hell of a long way in without seeing anyone, and there was no way of knowing for certain that they were not, themselves, being watched.

The troop – with two Rolls-Royce armoured cars and his own Morris – had been briefed the previous afternoon to patrol north-westwards as far as Bir Enba (which they should not reach before midnight at the earliest) and then to probe as far forward as possible, off the track, retiring immediately any contact with the enemy was made and in any case in time to be clear of the encampments by daylight. It was a cold, clear night, the going had been good all the way – flat and not particularly bumpy – and during the entire time the horizons had remained spectacularly empty. From each side and behind came the creaks, the tyre-gritting, the occasional clunk of metal against metal from the other two cars, the random curse.

They must now be at least ten miles into the gap, and had seen no sign of life whatsoever. No camp, no minefield, no sign of activity except for reflected lights in the sky from the known camps to north-east and south-west, no traffic of any kind – not even the tracks of an Italian patrol. It was slightly uncanny, and had it not been for such similar experiences ever since the 11th Hussars began probing the Italian lines back in June, unbelievable.

Time was up. To grunted orders the cars stopped, closed, the crews muttering between themselves, scanning the empty, faintly luminous darkness around them. Lamb made a last sweep of the horizon, checked his watch again, nodded to the others and the troop swung around and headed back. They passed the lonely pile of stones which marked the bir (a well) about half an hour before dawn, and were far out in the desert before full daylight. They stopped in a shallow gully to brew up tea and eat their meagre breakfast ration, then pressed on, removing layers of clothing as the sun built up strength. By midday they'd be down to shirtsleeves.

They were about twenty miles out when they heard the planes coming, and as the roar grew they scattered – but they had been seen long before they could reach any cover and the whole world was suddenly full of the howl of dive-bombers, the crack of bombs bursting on the hard surface followed by the squeal of splinters through the air, the rattle of their own Brens as they replied. There were twelve dive-bombers up there, swooping down on them as they dodged, and in the short gaps as the Bredas climbed back for height, two Caproni fighters would come in strafing, the machine-gun bullets cutting lines of thrown dust on the desert floor.

The drivers spun the wheels, wrenching the cars around in response to shouts from the gunners fighting the aircraft off, watching for the moment when the bombs swung away from under the bellies. They'd all done it before, they all knew the drill, they all knew the odds; and with fourteen aircraft against them with perhaps others coming to join the fray, these were not very high. It was just a question of who would run out of ammunition first – combined, of course, with who would run out of luck.

Sergeant Lamb's Morris was the first casualty. Two Bredas screamed down on him, and as his driver wheeled to miss the bomb coming down behind, he drove over the one already down in front which went off almost exactly between the axles. As it also went off in what must have been the only patch of soft sand anywhere around, some of the force of the explosion was thus absorbed, and the Morris just bucked violently into the air and crashed down again, its bottom blown out, its engine and chassis wrecked, its crew severely shaken but otherwise unharmed.

And still efficient. As a third Breda, confident now of complete destruction of the smoking and stationary car, screamed in for the kill, Lamb opened up with the Bren at point-blank range and a feeling of some familiarity, for he had done the same only a few days before. He saw the bomb swing away far too early to be dangerous, the dive-bomber flatten out and instead of climbing away, hurtle overhead to crash into the desert only thirty yards away – giving him a personal score of two dive-bombers shot down in just a month.

He reached the wreck seconds before it burst into flames and with his crew pulled the pilot clear – to find the man dead with two bullets through his skull and papers in his pocket revealing that he had been commander of the squadron, which had itself been especially formed to hunt the armoured cars of the 11th. There were other papers, too, which would prove full of interest when they reached headquarters.

And in the meantime, silence had fallen over the battlefield, either because the attackers had run out of ammunition or because they had decided not to interfere with the attempted rescue of their late leader.

It was some hours later that the two remaining armoured cars of Sergeant Lamb's troop reached C Squadron H.Q. and not until the following day that a full report of his exploit reached General O'Connor; but when it did it served to crystallise many conclusions which had been forming in the general's mind.

There were several points to be considered, one of which was that the 11th Hussars were taking far too much of a hammering. Apart from the loss of Lamb's Morris, B Squadron had had two men wounded by shell-fire a few days previously, one of the old Rolls cars had been blown up on a minefield and the sergeant-major who went to get it out killed – the kind of loss which no unit can suffer without some effect on its morale, especially when strain on both men and equipment had been as continual and prolonged as it had been on the Cherrypickers. Even Rolls-Royces cannot be expected to operate properly if they have too little maintenance, and if the 11th's crews were – quite justifiably – taking pride in the fact that they could claim to have seen more action against the enemy than the rest of the Army of the Nile put together, that action was nevertheless taking its toll.

But the 11th were still the only experienced reconnaissance unit in O'Connor's force, and there was still a great deal to find out about Italian dispositions, about Italian movements, about Italian plans. What, for instance, was the significance and extent of those gaps reported by every patrol which went out, stretching between the various fortified camps? How wide were the minefields around each camp? How much artillery was apportioned to each camp and how mobile was it? Were there many tanks within the camp perimeters and – much more important – was there a strong armoured force held in reserve at the back of those tempting gaps, waiting to pounce on those unwary enough to venture too far?

The 11th Hussars just could not be spared from the vital part they were playing in finding answers to these questions, or indeed in the other task which O'Connor deemed essential and for which the Support Group under Strafer Gott had accepted responsibility – the complete and continual domination of the seventy-mile-wide strip of no-man's-land which separated the two armies. In that space, only the men of the Western Desert Force must move; no Italian was to pass the lines of the Support Group except as a prisoner.

Very well – if the 11th Hussars could not be spared at least they could be protected, and at a conference between the various commanders, the tactics were hammered out.

Some of the armoured cars had been lost through shell-fire; then they must have mobile artillery to protect them. Some, like Sergeant Lamb's, had been attacked and damaged by aircraft; as it happened, a few Italian anti-aircraft guns had been captured recently at sea, and these could be put to good use. And as there were undoubtedly Italian tanks in the area which might, one day, come out and offer battle, anti-tank guns must also be made available.

All this artillery would need infantry protection at night, so this too must be an integral part of such a force – and indeed, the same infantry could carry out even closer patrolling than was possible by armoured cars, up to and perhaps through the minefields. As communications would obviously play a vital part in any operations carried out by such a force, signallers would be needed – and sappers as well in case mines had to be lifted.

Such a force of mixed arms would need a single commander accompanied by a staff officer, both of whom would need to combine imagination, a distinct taste for adventure, and a great deal of hard, professional skill. As at the meeting there was one officer who appeared to combine not only all those qualities, but was also still junior enough to command so small a unit, he was given the task of assembling and leading the first column. Thus occurred the first significant step in the career of Lieutenant-Colonel J. C. 'Jock' Campbell, Royal Horse Artillery, towards fame and an enduring devotion among the men he led. The 'Jock Column' had been born.

Two of them were in action by the end of October with artillery and infantry both drawn from Strafer Gott's Support Group, and one or other of them was out most nights probing the Italian defences, lifting the mines, harassing the rear areas and communi-

cation lines. Many of the raids were highly successful, even profit-
able; some were uneventful and a few were totally bewildering. On
October 14th, the armoured cars of the column in the northern
sector were scouting ahead when they saw dust-clouds rising to the
west and reported back that some thirty Italian vehicles and guns
were approaching, apparently the advance spearhead of a much
larger force. Perhaps this was the beginning of another main
advance, so the infantry and artillery component prepared quickly
for a sharp defensive action and the signallers immediately con-
tacted H.Q. But all that happened was that the Italian guns opened
fire and shelled the armoured cars out of their wadi, after which the
spearhead veered off to the south-west and after a couple of hours
of indeterminate activity, retired to Maktila leaving the watchers
wondering what it had all been about.

Not all the actions fought during this period were by Jock
Columns, of course, and not all were successful – except that from
the failures some important lessons were learned.

Quite a heavy raid was planned for the night of October 23rd on
the camp at Maktila, and as the place was believed to contain 'a
battalion or perhaps even a brigade' of Libyan troops, the men of
the Cameron Highlanders and the tank crews of the 8th Hussars
who made up the assault force were quite prepared for a stiff fight.
But café gossip in Cairo had been full of the attack for three days
beforehand, much of the chatter had been unusually accurate, and
as Egypt had been the home of many Italian nationals for years
before the war and still undoubtedly harboured many Italian
sympathisers, if not actual agents, it was hardly surprising that the
entire Marmarica Division who actually comprised the Maktila
garrison were alert, ready and waiting.

Seven minutes after the leading troops had moved across the
start-line there was a shout from a listening-post just in front, a
figure was seen darting back towards the garrison pursued by a
bellicose 'Gie a hold on him!' from one of the Jocks and a burst of
Bren-gun fire, all of which served as a signal to the waiting
defenders, who put down a positive deluge of fire on the unfortunate Highlanders:

> It sounded as though every gun, machine-gun, rifle and re-
> volver in the Camp opened up. Down came their defensive fire,
> and, coupled with mortar bombs exploding, the din was terrific.
> What was most impressive however was the display of tracer,
> which seemed to be attached to every sort of missile. Things like
> 'flaming footballs' floated out across the desert, and the fixed
> lines of the machine-guns were most noticeable.[4]

In the circumstances, it was hardly surprising that the assault company which had run into the listening-post was pinned down and remained so for the rest of the action, or that of the other company only one platoon actually managed to break into the camp. Inside, these took a few prisoners, smashed up some transport and then stole a diesel lorry in which they endeavoured to get back to their own lines, but the lorry attracted a storm of anti-tank fire which wrecked it – fortunately causing no casualties – and in the ensuing mêlée all the prisoners got away. The platoon itself escaped and by 0400 had returned to their start-line, where they found most of their comrades awaiting them, aggrieved but relatively unharmed.

It could not be said that the raid achieved much of significance, but both Wavell and O'Connor knew that the lapse in security which had contributed so much to its failure must not be repeated.

If O'Connor and the men of the Western Desert Force were intent upon embarrassing the Italians on a narrow, tactical front, the Commanders-in-Chief back in Egypt had wider, strategic fields to consider. So, come to that, had their opposite numbers in Rome who had an added disadvantage in the close proximity of their political master, still urging military action for disputable reasons.

During the month of October 1940, Mussolini was becoming more and more frustrated with his military commanders, principally as a result of the comments and actions of his fellow-dictator in Berlin. The tardiness of the advance across the Egyptian border had not passed unnoticed and, following reports to Berlin from the German Military Attaché in Rome, one of the leading German tank experts, Generalleutnant von Thoma, had been sent to tour the desert battle areas and the assistance of a panzer division offered.

But Il Duce was well aware of the atmosphere of patronage in which the offer was made, and also that his request for arms without the men had no chance whatsoever of being met; and although Italy was dreadfully short of aircraft, guns and tanks, she was not sufficiently short in his opinion that she need welcome men of the Wehrmacht into her prospective zones of influence and profit, from which they might prove difficult to eject once they had played their part.

This was a point which had been approached but delicately skirted around when the two dictators had met on the Brenner Pass on October 4th, when Mussolini had the uncomfortable feeling that only a combination of circumstances exceptionally favourable to himself had prevented a bruising and sarcastic tirade from Hitler. As it was, he had been able to dilate upon the glorious victories won by Italian arms in Africa, confident that whatever scepticism his brother-in-arms might feel, he could hardly give much expression to it in the light of the failure of the much-vaunted Luftwaffe to defeat the Royal Air Force, and thus open the way for the promised invasion and conquest of the homeland of the common enemy.

As it was, Hitler had remained somewhat subdued on the subject of the British (though confirming the offer of fully manned and equipped ground and air forces to assist in the drive to the Nile), neutral in his opinion of the possibilities of worthwhile collaboration from either France or Spain and only rising to his more accustomed heights of vituperation on the subject of Bolshevism. It was in Russia, apparently – despite the continuation of the Soviet–German Non-aggression Pact which had been signed in August 1939 to the astonishment of the watching world, including Mussolini – that the real danger for the Axis Powers lay; and if Il Duce had not been so full of Italian triumphs he might have wondered what the Führer intended to do about it.

For not one word of German intentions to the east was mentioned during that meeting on the Brenner Pass, and it was thus with an anger which made him feel physically sick that Mussolini learned, only three days later, that German troops had entered Rumania. The excuse that they had done so 'to reorganise the Rumanian Army' was obviously nothing but cover for actual occupation of the country, as his own observers quickly reported back as soon as he had managed to have them admitted – with Hitler's casual permission – on October 14th.

As a result, Il Duce determined upon at least two courses whereby he might level the score. First of all, Graziani must be goaded to further action in Egypt, with which object a memo was dispatched containing the passage:

> Forty days after the capture of Sidi Barrani, I ask myself the question – to whom has this long halt been of most use? To us or to the enemy? I do not hesitate a minute to answer – it has been of more use, and rather exclusively, to the enemy! Is it not time to ask yourself whether you feel you wish to remain in command?
>
> At the peace table, we shall bring home whatever we shall have conquered militarily. Will it have been worth sixteen months at war to bring home just Sidi Barrani?

Mussolini then turned his gaze immediately eastwards to where, since an onset of aggression eighteen months before, Italian troops had been occupying with varying degrees of success the Adriatic kingdom of Albania.

'Hitler always faces me with a *fait accompli*,' he announced to his immediate entourage. 'This time I am going to pay him back in his own coin. He will find out from the papers that I have occupied Greece. In this way the equilibrium will be re-established.'

It is one of the recurrent ironies of fate that although the sub-sequent advance of Italian troops across the Albanian–Greek border was to result immediately in yet another humiliation for him, in the end his directive to his Commander-in-Chief in Albania was probably the greatest contribution he ever made to the Axis Powers' attempt to achieve world domination.

To the British Commanders-in-Chief in the Mediterranean, Musso-lini's attack into Greece, despite the theoretical drawing-off of enemy attention from the Western Desert Front, despite also the sharp rebuff which Greek forces administered to the invading Italians, was by no means an unmixed blessing. Churchill's reaction was predictable and almost immediate. 'We will give you all the help in our power!' he cabled the Greek Government, and although the Greek dictator, General Metaxas, was of the opinion that unless Britain could send a force of really worthwhile strength – say, six divisions – it would be better if she were to send nothing and so avoid attracting German military attention to the area, the Prime Minister ordered troops to be sent to Crete, airforce units to Greece itself and a Royal Naval presence into Greek waters.

All this could only come, of course, from forces already in the Middle East or en route and eagerly awaited there; and both Wavell and Air Chief Marshal Longmore dutifully scraped the bottoms of their respective barrels and sent units to Crete (particularly for the defence of Suda Bay), and to other Greek islands. As Admiral Cunningham already considered the whole of the Eastern Mediter-ranean his bailiwick, the only extra burdens thrown immediately upon his forces concerned additional convoying of troops and stores, and for these his existing plans could be fairly conveniently adapted. But this further complication of the situation in the Eastern Mediterranean did serve to crystallise in the Admiral's mind certain plans for aggressive action which he had been nurtur-ing for some time.

For weeks past, Royal Naval units had been trailing their coats off Italian ports, trying to draw the Italian battlefleet into action, preferably piecemeal, but the ships of the Italian Navy had re-mained obstinately in port for most of the time, and temptingly out of range whenever they did proceed to sea. Now, large numbers of them were concentrated within the well-protected confines of the harbours at Taranto, offering a splendid target for any plan ingenious enough to provide means for penetrating the very strong defences.

There was obviously no hope of shelling the Italian base in the way that the French Fleet had been attacked at Mers el Kebir, first

because that episode had been observed and lessons drawn from it
by both sides, and secondly because of the presence of Italian air
bases grouped around the port and throughout the length and
breadth of the Italian 'foot' from which units of the Regia Aeronautica had already inflicted damage on British ships, both merchant and naval. Besides, there were strong rumours of a growing
Luftwaffe presence in the area.

A submarine attack was out of the question, too, for once
Gunther Prien in U47 had penetrated Scapa Flow and sunk the
Royal Oak, no navy in the world neglected harbour defences
around their most powerful units. Air reconnaissance revealed
quite clearly that even if a submarine penetrated the Mar Grande at
Taranto, sea walls and torpedo-nets closely screened the only
worthwhile targets.

Attack, therefore, could only come from the air – and Taranto
was far beyond the range of what few bombers the Royal Air Force
had in the Middle East. Cunningham must rely upon the forces
under his own immediate control.

During October and the early days of November there was a
great deal of traffic throughout all the waters of the Mediterranean,
as men and materials were ferried both from the Italian mainland to
Albania and from British bases to British outposts. Generally
speaking the Italian moves were beyond the striking distance of
British forces, but the Royal Navy and its charges were subject to
fairly continuous attention from Italian aircraft and were also well
aware that Ammiraglio Campioni was watching their every move,
waiting to pounce upon any weak detachment which ventured too
close to the Italian mainland. It all made for rather complicated
manoeuvres but perhaps their very complication might provide a
key.

There was no doubt that the garrison on Malta must be strengthened, and by November 7th, some 2,000 infantrymen and gunners
were distributed aboard the battleship *Barham*, the cruisers *Berwick*
and *Glasgow* plus half a dozen destroyers, and en route between
Gibraltar and the embattled island. At the same time, a convoy
carrying stores and weapons from Alexandria for both Crete and
Malta was at sea, closely escorted by cruisers and destroyers, while
the main Mediterranean Fleet consisting of the aircraft-carrier
Illustrious, four battleships, two cruisers and thirteen destroyers
patrolled in the central basin between Crete and Sicily.

By November 9th, the Alexandria convoys had reached Malta
and were being unloaded by an anxious and extremely grateful
populace, while the main fleet went on and rendezvoused with the
Gibraltar force. Swordfish aircraft from the *Ark Royal* carried out a
small raid on Cagliari in Sardinia and during the afternoon the

combined forces were subjected to quite a heavy and concentrated attack by Italian land-based planes which, although they hit nothing, scored a number of unpleasantly near misses, especially alongside the *Barham*. After the reinforcing troops had been landed on Malta, those naval vessels due to return to Gibraltar (where they were later to win fame as Force H) sailed off to the west while the others joined the main fleet from Alexandria, and by dawn this augmented force was steaming north-eastwards towards Taranto.

By late afternoon they were about 200 miles from their target, and aboard *Illustrious* an intent group of officers was studying the latest photographs of the harbour, just delivered from Malta where three R.A.F. Marylands were stationed, one of which had flown over the target area that morning. Overhead, fighter aircraft patrolled and efficiently shot down the two Italian scouting planes which had come within sighting distance of the force below. By early evening, Cunningham knew that six of the most powerful Italian battleships – the *Duilio*, the *Littorio*, the *Cesare*, the *Doria*, the *Vittorio Veneto* and the *Cavour* – were anchored in the Mar Grande together with several assorted cruisers and destroyers, while the Mar Piccolo beyond contained more cruisers and was surrounded by valuable shore installations such as oil storage depots, repair sheds and aircraft hangars.

Ammiraglio Campioni had thus unexpectedly placed all his most valuable eggs in one basket and had also – though Cunningham was not to know this – lost track of the British forces; at that moment the Italian admiral was very close to assuming that the entire Mediterranean Fleet was on its way back to Alexandria.

Shortly before 2100 the first wave of Swordfish – the 'Stringbags' as their crews derisively called them – climbed awkwardly off *Illustrious*'s decks and up towards the clouds which would shelter them for at least part of the way; twelve aircraft, six of them with huge torpedoes slung beneath their bellies, four with six 250-pound bombs, two with four bombs and heavy illuminating flares, all under command of Lieutenant-Commander Kenneth Williamson of 813 Squadron, Fleet Air Arm, each carrying a pilot and an observer. None of the men aboard any of the aircraft could have been buoyed up by much beyond hope and a belief in the luck of the Navy, for their Stringbags were cumbersome, underpowered, years out of date and now some of them were expected to undertake the unlikely role of dive-bombers.

But at least they had been given the range to carry out this extremely hazardous mission, for half of the rear cockpit of each torpedo-carrier was taken up by a sixty-gallon petrol-tank (to the great discomfort of the observers) while similar extra fuel capacity for the bombers was strapped on outside the fuselage. Those among

Map 4   Taranto: November 11th, 1940

the crews with strong imaginations kept them under very tight control.

Williamson led them up into cloud at 4,500 feet and immediately lost all contact with the others, for it was very thick cloud; when he emerged at 7,500 feet into clear moonlight it was to find that one torpedo-plane and three bombers were no longer with him, and as this was in the days before such refinements as radio-telephones, he had no choice but to accept that they would now all make their own separate ways to the target area. This, after another ninety minutes' droning flight, became only too visible, spread out beneath them.

Together, the two anchorages of Mar Grande and Mar Piccolo make up one of the finest harbours in the Mediterranean. The outer one, Mar Grande, is a westward-facing bay embraced by the two arms of Cape Rondinella to the north and Cape San Vito to the south, while two islands between the capes, San Pietro and San Paulo, are joined to each other and to Cape Rondinella by break-waters. A curved mole, the Diga di San Vito, runs out from the south for nearly a mile, and between the end of the Diga and San Paulo is the only entrance to the anchorage – studded at this time with floating anti-aircraft positions.

The main warship anchorage was in the eastern curve of the bay, and here another mole, the Diga di Tarantola, formed a shield a mile and a half long for the vessels behind it. Lines of deep nets between the groups of ships extended the protection of the Diga and added further to the complications facing the attackers, whose torpedoes must either be dropped inside the Diga or the nets – or so far outside the nets that they would pass underneath them in which case they might pass underneath their targets as well, although in theory the Duplex fuses with which the torpedoes were armed would be activated by the change in magnetic field when this happened.

From the northern edge of the bay, a narrow channel led through the town of Taranto itself into the Mar Piccolo – an inner, completely land-locked harbour which sheltered more naval vessels, all armed with anti-aircraft weapons of various calibres and surrounded by dockyard installations similarly protected.

In all, the Swordfish attack was to take place through fire from defences consisting of twenty-one batteries of 4-inch guns and nearly 200 machine-guns, all supported by a thoroughly adequate searchlight system. As the intention was to launch the torpedoes from a height of not more than thirty feet, the machine-guns and the searchlights were likely to be just as distracting as the heavier armament. And to make the manoeuvre even more awkward, lines of barrage balloons were deployed across the most promising axes of attack, making it essential for most of the Swordfish to attempt to fly between the steel cables attaching the balloons to their anchors.

It did not seem to the men flying beside and behind Lieutenant-Commander Williamson, therefore, that there was a very high chance of all of them getting back that night to the *Illustrious*, now waiting anxiously some 180 miles astern like a mother hen worried about her chicks. The only support they had (in addition to nature's built-in comfort that 'it won't happen to me') was the expectation of surprise on their side, an expectation dashed at 2250 when even above the drone of their own engines they heard the shriek of Taranto's air raid warning sirens, followed almost immediately by an eruption of multicoloured fairy lights as the heavy batteries put up a barrage, the machine-guns threw out strings of tracer in every direction and the searchlights swung their beams around the sky like spillikins sticking up from a dark blue tablecloth.

Through it all, the torpedo-bombers must dive.

They were coming in from the south, and just off Cape San Vito the two Stringbags with flares aboard swung away to starboard while Williamson in L4A led the torpedo-bombers away to port to line up for an attack from the south-west. Two followed him directly – L4C piloted by Sub-Lieutenant Peter Sparke and L4R by

Sub-Lieutenant A. S. D. Macauley – and as they curved down
through the ceiling of tracer and swinging light to straighten up for
an attack line across the Diga di Tarantola, the flares dropped by
Sub-Lieutenants Kiggell in L4P and Lamb in L4B burst like candel-
abra in the sky, silhouetting immediately in front and below them
the spectacular outline of the battleship *Cavour*.

They went in line ahead across the first mole jutting out towards
San Paulo, through the line of barrage balloons – incredibly, without noticing them – at thirty feet as they streaked in across the Diga
di Tarantola. Peter Sparke saw the fire of at least two destroyers
converging on Kenneth Williamson's plane ahead and, although he
had also seen and set his heart on the magnificent target of the
Vittorio Veneto just away to port, he held on for the more certain
prize. Williamson's torpedo dropped away, a final burst of fire
caught L4A and she vanished in a pillar of water and then the
Cavour was there, exactly ahead of him and unprotected. As he felt
the Stringbag jump when the weight of his torpedo was released, he
swung away to port, over the unscathed *Vittorio Veneto*, through a
cross-fire of tracer like a three-dimensional mesh and up towards a
moonlit haven – listening as he did so to the honey-sweet voice of
his observer screaming triumphantly that whoever was responsible,
Cavour had been hit at least once abreast her foremost turret.
Behind them Macauley, too, had dropped his torpedo, turned, and
was now braving the curtain of steel cables below the barrage
balloons on his way home.

While those three attacks on *Cavour* had been taking place, both
Littorio and *Vittorio Veneto* had been under attack. Lieutenant
H. I. A. Swayne was piloting the torpedo-bomber which had been
lost in the clouds, but he caught up with the others just as they were
going into their dives, veered to port – as Sparke had intended to
do – as he crossed the Diga di Tarantola, and released his torpedo
about four hundred yards short of the *Littorio*, flying ahead right
over it as a huge explosion ripped a twenty-three-foot hole in the
battleship's port quarter. Just seconds before, Lieutenant N. Kemp
in L4K had swung around the far end of the northern balloon
barrage, skirted the edge of the harbour (where he had seen some
of the shot fired at him from the cruisers and destroyers arching
over and actually exploding amid shore establishments and merchant-ships berthed close in), swooped close down on *Littorio* as
well and launched his torpedo to strike the battleship on her starboard bow. Both Kemp and Swayne cleared the combat area – as
did the others who got away – within five minutes of Williamson's
first attack dive, leaving behind them two badly hit battleships for
the price of one plane shot down. Later, it was learned that both
Williamson and his observer had miraculously escaped unhurt, and,

after some rough handling by the dockyard workers who found them, were treated kindly and chivalrously by the Italian navy.

The last of the first wave to go in was E4F piloted by Lieutenant M. R. Maund, who used both an approach and an escape route all his own. He came in over Cape Rondinella, swung slightly north over Taranto town itself and dived down on the *Vittorio Veneto* – which was to lead a charmed life that night, for Maund's torpedo dived too deep and exploded as it hit the bottom, close to the *Littorio* which seemed to attract all the attention. Curling around hard to starboard, Maund then baffled the machine-gunners frantically trying to get a bead on him by zig-zagging through the masts of the merchant-ships moored along the north shore until he, too, was clear of the area and safely on his way back to *Illustrious*.

But by now the second wave was approaching, fascinated by the cluster of fireworks erupting beneath them and grimly aware that they had now to fly down into it without the slightest element of surprise on their side. Again, two flare-dropping Swordfish detached, swung in over Cape San Vito and behind the main targets, while Lieutenant-Commander 'Ginger' Hale led the five torpedo-bombers in a wide curve over Cape Rondinella to sweep down from 5,000 feet across the neck of land, behind the northern balloon barrage and into a cone of fire coming up at them from the shore-based 4-inch batteries behind, from flak-ships and cruisers to starboard and from the multiple guns of the main battleships ahead of them.

Through it all, the first two Stringbags dived straight on to the doomed *Littorio*, their torpedoes going down straight and cleanly, one to blow yet another hole in the battleship's bow, the other to leave a deep dent in her starboard quarter before sinking to the sea-bed without exploding. Immediately astern of the two leaders, Lieutenant C. S. C. Lea in L5H had swerved slightly to port until he was low over the entrance to the narrow channel leading into Mar Piccolo and he could see the *Duilio* admirably silhouetted against the slowly descending flares. His torpedo thudded home almost exactly amidships, the explosion tearing a hole in the battleship's side some thirty feet by twenty-five and well under water, through which the sea flooded into the main magazines. As the tracers screamed up at him from every angle (each flaming ball with at least three unseen projectiles close behind it), he banked sharply, dodged between two cruisers each erupting fire at him, and fled out across the end of the Diga di Tarantola, between the unseen cables of the balloon barrage into the peace and quiet of the seas beyond San Pietro.

Behind him came frustrating failure and, for the British, the one tragedy of the whole night.

Lieutenant T. W. G. Welham piloting E5H seemed perfectly placed to break the shield which fortune had thrown over the massive flagship of the fleet, the *Vittorio Veneto*. He had come in behind Lea, glimpsed the latter's successful attack on the *Duilio* and then seen, dead ahead and across his path, the huge looming shape of the finest target in the bay; he had steadied on her, let his torpedo go at exactly the right moment, pulled E5H up right over the battleship and was away across the rest of the harbour through the maelstrom of fire with but two machine-gun bullets through the fabric of one wing. But what happened to his torpedo no one ever found out; whether it went too deep or whether it failed entirely to explode is still unknown; *Vittorio Veneto* came through the entire raid unscathed.

But Lieutenant Bayley flying E4H, with Lieutenant Slaughter as his observer and navigator, was last to go in and perhaps by then the incredible luck which had attended the operation so far had run out. They were caught by a concentration of fire as they flew in from the north and crashed in flames in the middle of the Mar Grande, both men dead before the flames were extinguished – a poignant but hardly unexpected price to be paid for such otherwise unqualified success.

At the cost of two elderly and out-of-date aircraft and two young and sadly missed lives, three Italian battleships had been put out of action, *Cavour* permanently, *Littorio* and *Duilio* for many months.

Moreover, that was not the whole of the night's work. In their role of providing distraction and illumination, the Swordfish dropping flares had been highly successful and they had also scored some minor hits with bombs; an aircraft hangar had been left blazing and the cruiser *Trento* had been hit fair and square by a bomb which, like so many dropped in those days, failed to explode though it split decks and did some damage.

Further afield, three cruisers and a pair of destroyers had been detached by Cunningham and sent up through the Straits of Otranto to prey upon Italian traffic crossing the Adriatic. Just about the time that Taranto was recovering from the second wave attack, they turned south and in bright moonlight saw a convoy of four merchant-ships with two escorts making for Brindisi; the action which followed was sharp and conclusive, though the Italian escorts seem to have contributed little. They managed to escape themselves without damage, but all four merchant ships, totalling nearly 17,000 tons, were sunk.

Thus the events of the night of November 11th/12th, 1940, tilted the balance of naval power in the Mediterranean much in favour of Britain, an adjustment which was to be significant for several very important months. The immediate problems of reinforcing the

Middle East were eased, the domination of the Royal Navy at sea confirmed, and the gap between Italian and British morale increased. It was now up to the army to increase it still further.

The idea of an attack against the Italians in the desert had never been far from either Wavell's or O'Connor's minds and even while Graziani was actually advancing, the 7th Armoured Division had been held in a position from which, had the Libyan Division pressed on towards Mersa Matruh, a very heavy counter-attack could have been launched. As time went by and the Western Desert Force grew in both manpower and equipment, the intention to go over on to the offensive hardened, especially in view of the evident domination the Support Group had achieved in the no-man's-land between Mersa Matruh and Maktila on the coast, and in all the country south of Sofafi.

Several plans were discussed in September and October but each was to be abandoned in the light of increased reinforcements arriving in the Delta, and further intelligence of Italian dispositions coming in from the patrols carried out first by the 11th Hussars, and then by the infantry patrols and the Jock Columns. The wide and apparently deep gap between the southernmost Italian posts now proliferating around Sofafi and Rabia, and the next one up at Nibeiwa, held everyone's attention, for a strong force inserted into that gap could strike up to the coast towards the water-point at Buq Buq thus cutting off the main Italian force at Sidi Barrani, and quite possibly isolating all the forward garrisons from their main bases further back, and from the Sofafis in the south. If a force attacking westwards from Matruh succeeded in holding enemy attention to the requisite degree, this raiding force at the rear could well wreak considerable havoc for perhaps as long as five days before withdrawing either through the same gap or directly through the Italian positions to the protection of the holding force.

Because of the need for high security demonstrated on many occasions and highlighted by the failure of the Jock Column raid in early October, this idea of a five-day raid was discussed in very narrow circles – at first, in fact, just by Wavell, Wilson and O'Connor – and with past experience of the Prime Minister's enthusiasm and ebullience in mind, Wavell carefully avoided mention of it in his signals to London. This caution, though understandable, had the unfortunate result of increasing Churchill's dissatisfaction with Wavell's performance as commander of Britain's only army in the field, especially as it was still not deployed as he, Churchill, considered best. Malta was obviously short of troops, there were still in the Prime Minister's opinion far too many inactive soldiers in Kenya, and although reinforcements were arriving in the Delta at an average of a thousand men a day, Wavell seemed to have no plans for using them.

As a result of these factors, the Secretary of State for War, Mr Anthony Eden, arrived in the Middle East on October 4th, had long talks with various Government officials in Cairo, accompanied Wavell to Khartoum on October 28th where he had further discussions with both the South African leader Field Marshal Smuts and the Ethiopian Emperor Haile Selassie, but all the time learned nothing whatsoever of Wavell's intentions in the Western Desert. However, immediately following the Italian invasion of Greece on October 28th came demands from London that Wavell release quantities of men and material – to such an extent that plans for even the smallest raid against Graziani would have been jeopardised. Wavell wrote later:

> All this meant a considerable drain on my resources, and led to my disclosing to Eden my plans for an early attack on the Italians. I had not intended to do so until the plans were further advanced, since I realised Winston's sanguine temperament and desire to have at least one finger in any military pie. I did not want to arouse premature hopes, I did not want Winston to make detailed plans for me, and I knew that absolute secrecy was the only hope of keeping my intentions from the Italians, who had so many tentacles in Cairo. But Eden was proposing to sap my strength in aircraft, A.A. guns, transport, etc., in favour of Greece, thinking I had only a defensive policy in mind, to such an extent that I had to tell him what was in my mind to prevent my being skinned to an extent that would make an offensive impossible.[5]

The reaction when on November 8th Eden was able to tell Churchill of Wavell's plans was far better than had been expected, for if the Prime Minister was put out at first by the revelation of Wavell's secrecy, he 'purred like six cats' as the details of the plan were unfolded, and future events were to demonstrate that there were no security leaks from Whitehall. However, it was too much to expect an entirely passive reaction to the plan, and if Churchill sent no suggestions for different tactics he was quick to insist that, as always, time was of the essence, and that any success achieved should be thoroughly exploited:

> I am having a Staff study made of possibilities open to us, if all goes well, for moving fighting troops and also reserves forward by sea in long hops along the coast, and setting up new supply bases to which pursuing armoured vehicles and units might resort . . .

As we told you the other day, we shall stand by you and Wilson in any well-conceived action irrespective of result, because no one can guarantee success in war, only deserve it.[6]

But other passages in the same cable – and other cables – did reveal one ominous difference in attitudes between the political and military chiefs. Whereas Churchill hoped for a quick success in the desert to release men and material for an approaching confrontation in the Balkans, Wavell wanted one so that he could clean up the situation on his own *eastern* front, in particular down in Somaliland, perhaps leading to a further campaign in Ethiopia. Wavell saw the reduction of all Italian influence in Africa as his immediate and overriding task; Churchill's attitude was summed up in a sentence in his cable which read, 'One may indeed see possibility of centre of gravity in Middle East shifting suddenly from Egypt to the Balkans, and from Cairo to Constantinople . . .

But above all, Churchill wanted as fully exploited a victory as it was possible to achieve, as soon as possible, and his doubts as to Wavell's intentions were exacerbated when he learned the contents of a cable Wavell sent to Sir John Dill on December 6th:

1. If weather permits preliminary move night 7th/8th December, approach march night 8th/9th December, attack morning 9th December.
2. Feel undue hopes being placed on this operation which was designed as raid only. We are greatly outnumbered on ground and in air, have to move over 75 miles of desert and attack enemy who has fortified himself for three months. Please do not encourage optimism.
3. Creagh is in hospital and may not be available which is unfortunate since so much depends on handling of armoured division.[7]

Sir John Dill's explanation of the guarded nature of this message – that Wavell was merely trying 'to write down his intended operation to avoid disappointment' – did nothing to restore Churchill's confidence, but there was by this time little that the Prime Minister could do as the moment for the attack – by now code-named *Operation Compass* – was fast approaching. His reply to Dill's memo was thus blunt and sceptical:

Naturally I am shocked at paragraph 2, and I trust that your explanation of it will be realised. If, with the situation as it is, General Wavell is only playing small, and is not hurling on his whole available force with furious energy, he will have failed to rise to the height of circumstances.[8]

His doubts would have been greatly increased had he known of a meeting held in Cairo four days previously at which had been present Lieutenant-Generals Platt and Cunningham, General Officers Commanding respectively in Sudan and Kenya. At this meeting, plans for at least containing and at best eliminating Italian influence in East Africa had been thoroughly discussed and a decision taken for the early recapture of the railhead at Kassala – for which reinforcements of at least one trained and experienced infantry division would be required from Egypt, together with their transport and artillery. This division, Wavell promised Platt, would begin the move down to the Sudan about the middle of December.

But as there was only one infantry division in Egypt which could possibly be described as 'trained and experienced' – the 4th Indian Division – it would obviously already be playing a vital part in *Compass*; and if *Compass* should succeed to any marked degree, in the light of these new proposals the division would have to be withdrawn at what could well be a crucial point in the exploitation of General O'Connor's attack.

With this fact very much in mind, Wavell enjoined full secrecy upon both Platt and Cunningham before sending them back to their posts, and also upon the only other man in Egypt who was let into the secret, Lieutenant-General H. Maitland Wilson.

4 · The 'Five-day Raid'

It was quite cool in the office at O'Connor's Headquarters at Maaten Baggush on the evening of November 26th, and the men attending the conference were glad of their sweaters, pulled over the khaki drill they had been wearing all summer. There were five of them – the two lieutenant-generals, Wilson and O'Connor himself, and three brigadiers – John Harding, O'Connor's senior staff officer, as small and neat as O'Connor himself, as polite, as determined; 'Sandy' Galloway, Wilson's senior staff officer, lean and hard, quick-tempered, quick-witted and with a caustic tongue; and Eric Dorman-Smith, concealing a fertile and original mind behind the rabbit teeth and soft moustache of the caricaturist's dream of a languid British officer, a man with a cutting wit and an impatience with orthodox doctrine unleavened by imagination and administered by seniority, which had already earned him enemies in high places and would continue to do so.

'Training Exercise No. 1' had just been completed and the troops were now back in their garrison areas, as unconcerned as ever with what it had all been about. Their officers were still engaged with the usual reports and details which always remain to be cleared up after any extensive military movement, and any doubts or conclusions they might wish to draw about the events of the past two days would have to wait until the paperwork was done.

Only the men at the conference knew the whole picture, only they could draw the right conclusions.

The exercise had consisted of attacks upon fortified localities laid out in the desert to the south of Matruh, and although very few knew or even suspected it, the localities had been replicas of the Italian camps at Nibeiwa and Tummar. The attack plans had been based upon perfectly orthodox lines as laid down in the official pamphlet *The Division in Attack*, and the men at the conference knew they would not do.

The two-hour wait after the infantry had arrived at their assembly areas, during which the artillery had registered on the defences, would undoubtedly prove disastrous in the reality of battle, as the troops – keyed up and ready for action – would be completely exposed to inevitable attack from the air, with its consequent casualties, disorganisation and effect on morale. Moreover, the artillery bombardment itself would rob the attack of any chance of surprise – and with the disparity in forces which existed between the two sides, surprise must be a key factor in any British offensive.

According to the information at O'Connor's disposal, the Italian forces in the arc of camps opposite consisted of five divisions – one Blackshirt Division in Sidi Barrani, two Libyan Divisions divided between Maktila on the coast and the two Tummar camps, General Maletti's force at Nibeiwa and a Metropolitan Division in the Sofafi and Rabia camps. One Blackshirt Division was in reserve at Buq Buq while further back at Sollum, Bardia and Tobruk waited the equivalent of four more divisions; and the units of the Regia Aeronautica in the area gave Graziani a superiority in numbers of aircraft over the R.A.F. of about five to one.

O'Connor's own forces in the Western Desert consisted still of just the 7th Armoured Division and the 4th Indian Division, plus 'Corps Troops' and the Matruh garrison. In manpower they amounted to a meagre 36,000 men (against 80,000 enemy in the area of attack) but in addition to their already demonstrated high morale, they did possess some very real advantages.

The 7th Armoured was now up at least to paper strength, with two armoured brigades and the Support Group. The Support Group consisted of one battalion each of the King's Royal Rifle Corps and the Rifle Brigade, with the 1st and 4th Batteries of the Royal Horse Artillery, each with forty 25-pounders – decidedly better guns than the Italian 75mms against which they would be pitted. Working with the group, as always, were the 11th Hussars, now augmented by an extra squadron of ten R.A.F. Rolls-Royce armoured cars and their crews who had spent the previous months, indeed years, pottering up and down the Iraqi pipeline guarding it from the attentions of curious Arab pyromaniacs, or gloomily patrolling the Saudi-Arabian frontier. Now, at last, they were to see some action and bring very welcome aid to the hard-pressed 11th Hussars.

The two armoured brigades – the 4th and the 7th – each of three regiments, made up the main battle strength of the division, and between them could put nearly 200 light tanks into the battle, together with 75 cruiser tanks (A9s, A10s and A13s) which, although many were approaching the end of their track mileage, were more than a match for the Italian M11s or M13s, of which Graziani had a total of about 60. (The remainder of Graziani's 300 tanks were the almost useless L3s.) Normal engineer complements, signals and ambulance sections, recovery and repair organisations and, most importantly, Royal Army Service Corps companies for the supply columns, made up the rest of the divisional strength.

The 4th Indian Division had been made up to a full complement of three infantry brigades each consisting of three infantry battalions, by the attachment to it of the 16th British Infantry Brigade. It would thus put into the field the 5th Indian Brigade – 1st Royal Fusiliers, 4th/6th Rajputana Rifles and the 3rd/1st Punjab Regiment; the 11th Indian Brigade – 2nd Queen's Own Cameron Highlanders, 4th/7th Rajput Regiment and the 1st/6th Rajputana Rifles; and the 16th British Brigade – 2nd Queen's Regiment, 2nd Leicester Regiment and the 1st Argyll and Sutherland Highlanders, plus, of course, its own divisional artillery, field ambulance units, engineers, supply columns and a machine-gun battalion of the Northumberland Fusiliers.

But it was with the 'Corps Troops' that lay the most potent weapon in the arsenal of the Western Desert Force, for in addition to three batteries of 25-pounders, one battery of 6-inch howitzers and one of 4·5s, they included the 7th Royal Tank Regiment which possessed forty-eight heavy 'I' (Infantry) Tanks – the Matildas. The Italians had nothing even faintly comparable and, so O'Connor had every reason to believe, not the slightest inkling of their presence in the Delta.

These unwieldy mastodons were the product of the second line of British tank philosophy between the wars, which had concentrated on trying to produce first a family of cruiser tanks in which armour had been sacrificed to speed and range in order to provide an offensive thrust force, and second an armoured support for the infantry. Armour 78 mm thick rendered the Matildas practically impervious to anything the Italian artillery could fire at them, and their twin 87-horsepower engines gave them in theory a speed of fifteen miles an hour and in practice, by the time they arrived in the desert, about eight miles an hour, which was fast enough for their major tasks of guarding their own infantry and spreading alarm and despondency among the enemy.

But, of course, the Matildas might well prove vulnerable to concentrated attack by dive-bombers, and their tracks could undoubtedly be blown off by mines; and how were they to make their own way across seventy miles of open desert without being seen and having their potentiality for shattering surprise thus dissipated?

The first and third problems could only be solved by the Desert Air Force making sure that enemy aircraft never reached the battle areas, but the Air Officer Commanding-in-Chief, Air Marshal Longmore, was under considerable pressure from Whitehall to send more and more of his units to Greece, and he was by now in some doubt as to whether the R.A.F. would be able to play its part in any attack in the desert. Only by stripping air defences in the rest of his command to an alarming degree could he manage to accept even a portion of the responsibilities which were to be asked of him – and thus for many weeks Aden and the Sudan were without their Blenheim and Gladiator squadrons, and at one time Alexandria was so denuded of its fighter defence that it had to rely completely upon two Sea-Gladiators of the Fleet Air Arm.

By such means a force of 48 fighters – two squadrons of Hurricanes and one of Gladiators – and 116 bombers – three squadrons of Blenheims, three of Wellingtons and one of Bombays – was placed at the disposal of Air Commodore Collishaw, operating from his Headquarters alongside O'Connor's at Maaten Baggush, while a further Army/Air Component was placed directly under O'Connor's command through an air liaison officer. This consisted of two squadrons plus one flight of mixed fighter and reconnaissance aircraft, whose task would be to provide O'Connor with eyes, both before and during the battle. The task of the main R.A.F. contingent, however, would be to blind the eyes of the enemy, to keep the Italian aircraft on the ground or at least away from the area between the two armies, and to ensure that any Italian pilot who did filter through their net and thus catch sight of the converging British forces did not return to base to tell the tale.

But how about the minefields? How could the Matildas get through them?

Even more important, how could 36,000 men, complete with their arms, their armour, their food, their water, their petrol and their ammunition – enough for five days – reach, without being seen, an assembly line close enough to the Italian positions from which to launch a storming attack?

The nights were getting colder now, and the patrol were glad of their balaclavas, their scarves, their thick pullovers, even of the rags wrapped around their boots. As they marched towards the night-glimmer and occasional flares of the Italian camp, they thought of the truck they had just left behind them and the journey up through the Enba Gap to the dropping point behind their objective, and wondered how soon they would be back within the safety of its dark cavern. Despite the number of times they had scouted up to the Italian perimeters, it always felt very naked out here on the desert at night, within the arc of the enemy camps.

There were fourteen in the patrol tonight – quite usual. Two scouts ahead and fifteen yards apart, platoon sergeant between and behind them, officer with compass behind him with a pace-counter alongside, three men in arrowhead formation on each flank and a three-man rearguard. Just like in training – except that the bullets weren't blanks.

After nearly an hour's march the camp perimeter looked just ahead and the pace-counter touched the officer on the shoulder; the whole patrol halted, without a word the formation changed, the officer and the two scouts went forward, and the rest melted into the ground.

So did the officer and the two scouts when they were some 200 yards short of the camp perimeter, now visible as a low wall punctuated every fifty yards or so with sangars in which were mounted machine-gun posts. Some fifty yards nearer them was the line of outer sentry posts – they could see the sentries silhouetted against stars, moving, stopping, occasionally gesturing among themselves, then returning to the posts with the slightly self-conscious, slightly apprehensive, thoroughly bored air of men on stag. Even closer was the anti-tank ditch which led towards tonight's reconnaissance area, and between the ditch and the wall, they already knew, were the minefields.

About half an hour later, crawling northwards in the ditch, they came to a blank end and beyond it stretched a rutted surface covered with the dust of continual traffic. They climbed out on to it, turned right and began to crawl in towards the camp along what seemed very likely to be the approach to the main entrance. But if it were, was it mined – and how and where?

The officer signalled, then went on alone. He could hear sentries ahead and occasionally see their outlined, shadowed forms – but they were moving between dark, vaguely familiar humps randomly distributed along this wide and apparently much used thoroughfare. As he reached the vicinity of the nearest, he realised that the humps were tanks – M11s and M13s with an occasional L3 – stationed out here to cover the main entrance to the camp and to act, in effect, as a roadblock. From this he deduced that the sentries were posted here to check traffic – not that the Italians as a rule travelled much at night – and if mines were sewn in this entrance gap, they must be marked in so clear a manner that the tanks would not drive over them when they were taking up their night positions, or when they withdrew into the camp at daybreak.

He and the two scouts spent the next hour wriggling to and fro along the ruts, keeping the tanks always between themselves and the sentries, finding the edges of the main minefields, searching for indications of mines in the actual approaches to the camp entrance. When eventually they dropped back into the shadows of the ditch, they had good reason to feel satisfied.

They crawled back along to their previous entry point, chose a suitable moment to climb out again and were soon moving back

over their own tracks until, thankfully, they were silently greeted by
the rest of the patrol. Soon, they were jolting back through the
Enba Gap to Battalion H.Q., breakfast, and an hour or so's sleep.

It had been a good patrol. Lieutenant Liddell now knew pretty
certainly the limits of the gap in the minefield through which the
normal supplies reached the garrison, and through which any
attacking force could also make its way. Quite soon the report
would be on the planning desk at Maaten Baggush.

It was, in fact, one of the last pieces of a huge jigsaw to fall into
place, and it served to confirm that only a very indirect approach to
the problems which faced O'Connor and his staff held much chance
of success. The weakest faces of the defences were, not all that
surprisingly, the ones furthest away from the direction of expected
attack – so far as an attack was expected at all; and the essential
thing was to keep that expectation down as low as possible. No
inkling of British offensive plans must reach the Italians and in a
country riddled with their agents, this made security of the utmost
importance. O'Connor's very strict instructions were issued to the
following effect:

1   Only the two Senior Staff Officers at Western Desert Force
H.Q., the two Divisional Commanders and their Senior Staff
Officers (one each), the Brigade Commanders and the Brigade
Majors were to be informed of the plan initially, and others only if
and when some specific action was required of them for which no
acceptable cover story could be devised.

2   Nothing at all was committed to paper until a few days before
the offensive began. (Even Wilson's directive to O'Connor was not
written until four days before the attack went in.)

3   The fighting troops were not to be informed until three days
before the action commenced, and when they were already on the
way to the assembly areas.

4   The formation of the essential forward dumps was explained
as a purely precautionary and defensive move.

5   Leave was not stopped until the move forward had begun.

6   No warning was given to the medical services to expect
anything but the usual run of accident casualties and illness.

To help matters along, Sir Archibald and Lady Wavell embarked
upon a full programme of social events, and were especially looking
forward to a race meeting at the Gezira Sporting Club in Cairo on
the afternoon of December 7th, followed by a dinner party for
fifteen senior officers of his command in the evening.

Bluff, deception and rigid security would all play their parts in
cloaking the intentions and movements of the attack; but what
would succour it? Even given the organisation – and luck – which

would be necessary for the troops to reach their assembly areas un-
detected and launch their attacks, how could they be kept supplied
with water, with petrol and with ammunition for even a five-day
battle, from a railhead seventy-five miles from the enemy front
lines – when they were already behind those enemy lines?

All day and all night long, the lorries churned back and forth across
the desert – those on the northern run from the railhead dump at
Matruh out along the main Sidi Barrani track for some forty miles
until they pulled off into the desert where the military police
waited, into the ever-growing camp, draped with netting until it
resembled nothing so much as a vast, twenty-acre dilapidated
marquee, stacked like a supermarket with giant-sized crates and
cans, and pyramids of what might have been long tins of cold drink
lying on their sides, but weren't. On the side of one of them, some
wag had chalked 'Duck, Duce!'
  But it was the southern route that was real trouble. The drivers
would pick up their loads at the dump just south of Qasaba and
strike out south-westwards across the desert until they reached the
line of the Escarpment, then swing westwards along it, without –
thank God – trying to get to the top. But even the route along the
bottom was fraught with trouble, especially for the newcomers just
out from England who, in trying to avoid the deep dust as the traffic
ground away more and more of the surface, would almost inevitably
run into a pocket of soft sand – and sink to the axles as panic drove
the foot further down on the accelerator, the wheels spun, the tyres
smoked and the sand flew out in a huge spray; while other, more
experienced drivers swung their lorries away and past, laughing; or
sweating in the heat and thinking 'Poor bastard!'
  Then would begin the awful grind of lightening the lorry, digging
out the wheels, backing and filling, sweating and cursing – often for
hours on end until, by one means or another, the lorry came back
on firm ground again.
  'If all the desert's like this,' one newcomer was heard to say
bitterly, 'it's going to be a bloody long war!'
  Then on across the Matruh–Siwa track, still holding the bottom of
the Escarpment (now looming higher and higher like a cliff the
further westward it went) until at last Field Supply Depot No. 4 was
reached, and all the unloading could start again, into dim-lit,
gloomy, canvas- and camouflage-covered caverns until, the lorry
empty, the drive back could start. Back to Qasaba, where it would
all begin again.
  One way and another, the drivers and mates, the loaders and un-
loaders, the storemen and military police and the supply depot
guards, hardly had time or leisure to reflect that the reasons given

Map 5   *Operation Compass*: the opening moves

for forming these dumps – that if the Italians began moving forward
again, these dumps could be drawn upon for the defence – hardly
made sense. If 7th Armoured, who were the only ones out there,
started retreating, they wouldn't have time to use the stuff in the
northern dump (though they'd find the petrol useful) before
Graziani was breathing down their necks and they had to retire to
the main defences at Matruh; which would be a better idea, anyway. As for the southern dump, it was totally exposed if the Italians
made a really forceful drive towards the Nile – and indeed, would
prove extremely valuable to them on their way if it fell undamaged
into their hands.

But who were the likes of them at the bottom to question the
decisions of those at the top? 'We are all', as the drill sergeants at
the depots continually reminded them, 'just tiny little cogs in a
bloody great big machine.'

'Training Exercise No. 2' began for the 4th Indian Division on the
morning of December 6th when they moved out from Gerawla,
heading westwards for Bir el Kenayis on the Matruh–Siwa track. It

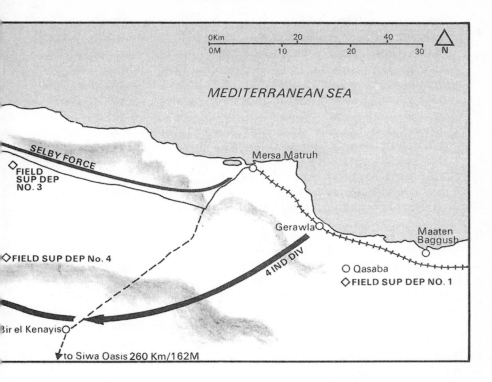

was chilly and overcast, a rising wind whipping the sand first into dancing spirals and then into a continual, infuriating, blinding drift; coat collars were pulled up, the troops huddled together cursing cheerfully and uncomfortable in whatever shelter they could find inside the jolting, heaving lorries. Everything was covered in a fine dust – but 'everything' included the entire movement during the day of 5,000 vehicles which thus arrived at their destination unnoticed by hostile eyes.

The units then scattered out over some thirty or forty square miles giving the impression to all concerned that here was a division about to commence an ordinary training session.

In the meantime, 7th Armoured Division, whose base area had for weeks past been not far from where 4th Indian had just arrived, were now getting ready to play their allotted role in the exercise. One of the young tank commanders in 4th Armoured Brigade was Lieutenant Cyril Joly, who later wrote:

The second exercise started on 7th December. The same routine was to be followed, and we expected to return after three

days and to settle down again to the interminable waiting. I
noticed with no particular interest that the Support Group had
moved out earlier across our front and were now some miles
ahead. Behind us I could see the dust raised by more vehicles.
But soon a mist settled over the desert which shrouded all but the
nearest vehicles and hid the country over which we were moving,
so that I could not even occupy my time by surveying the scenes
around me. The mist was thick enough to prevent any accurate
reading of a sun compass and so, to my annoyance, I could not
follow the course of our move. In wireless silence, shrouded in
mist and resigned to another period of boredom, I spent a lonely
and dispiriting day perched in the cupola of the turret, in discomfort and chilled by the cold winter wind.[1]

But not all had been so completely occupied with the minute-to-
minute routine of remaining unbruised all day in a rocking steel
box. When, that evening after the brigade had leaguered for the
night, Joly crossed over to the command truck, he heard one of his
fellow officers saying, 'You can say what you like but I bet you I'm
right. I followed the route we came and I recognised one or two places
I've seen before. And I tell you we're now just south of Nibeiwa.'
But the brigade received no official information on the subject
then or for some hours to come. Night passed with the usual routine
watches, the few hours of sleep on the desert floor huddled in greatcoats, seeking shelter from the cold and from the drifting wind in
the lee of tanks, or in the scanty protection of grooves in the ground
that only experienced and wary eyes would have seen. But when
daylight came and orders were given that no fires were to be lit that
day and that no one should move about unnecessarily, some
thoughtful glances were exchanged and every move by adjutants or
company commanders was watched by curious eyes.
By now the 4th Indian Division was closing up. They had spent
nearly thirty-six hours around Bir el Kenayis, and on the Saturday
morning, December 7th, one of the brigade padres had held a
communion service. It had been very well attended and when an
Italian aircraft had appeared overhead, no one had moved though a
few lips were seen muttering supplications unconnected with those
in the prayerbooks; and by early afternoon, the orders had come
through. Now everyone knew that this training exercise was likely
to prove more eventful than most.
But they stayed where they were for the moment and passed the
first hours of the bitterly cold night which followed, chilled and
cramped beneath their vehicles or in hastily scraped slits, sometimes sleeping, often lying awake and thinking of what the next
forty-eight hours were likely to bring. Indian sepoy, Scottish

infantryman, fusilier from London, all now waited for the time when their years of professional training would be put to the test, when they too would learn the price of the traditions which their fathers and grandfathers had formed over the years, on so many foreign fields, so many hundreds of miles from their homes.

The division was on the move before dawn. The wind had dropped, the sky was clear and as daylight grew it seemed totally impossible that this vast concourse of over 5,000 vehicles could cover the necessary 60 miles – all directly towards the enemy – without being seen by some prowling reconnaissance plane. Deliberately, they drove slowly to keep down the dust; and every now and then they would see an aircraft – but it was always one of their own Lysanders, sauntering slowly and almost casually up and away, checking on their progress and doubtless assuring the anxious Staff that all was well.

By four o'clock in the afternoon of December 8th, 4th Indian Division was concentrated about fifteen miles south-east of Nibeiwa, five miles east of 4th Armoured Brigade and not quite four miles from the Corps Troops – including forty-five Matildas of 7th Royal Tank Regiment.

As this was long before the days of tank transporters, the Matildas – and indeed all the tanks of the force – had had to make their way from their bases (indeed, some from their points of disembarkation) on their own tracks. In view of the vital part the Matildas had to play, therefore, 7th Royal Tank Regiment had commenced their journey some time before the others, arriving above the southern dump (Field Supply Depot No. 4) as early as December 5th, and spending thirty-six hours there on rest and maintenance of engines and tracks, before moving off again to their rendezvous point for the last evening before the attack. As the whole regiment had only been in Egypt since the end of September, very few officers and even fewer men had been 'up the blue' before and for security as well as mileage reasons their Matildas were also paying their first visits to this lunar landscape in which they were to get their first taste of action.

There was, therefore, a certain amount of apprehension visible in the bearing and expression of many members of the regiment, though humour and ribaldry played their normal part at such times and there was also, of course, a solid underlying confidence in the tanks themselves. All crews were well aware of the thickness of armour which would protect them, and had no reason to doubt the assurances they had been given that the enemy had nothing to throw at them likely to cause much damage.

They all now knew what was expected of them, and were confident of their ability to carry it out.

O'Connor had moved his headquarters from Maaten Baggush (where Wilson had now installed himself) forward to a point quickly to be dubbed Piccadilly Circus, at the top of the Escarpment about fifty miles west of the Matruh–Siwa road, slightly above and behind the concentration of his forces in the plain below. All seemed to be going well. Reports coming in from Collishaw's H.Q. still at Maaten Baggush informed him that no extra activity on the part of forward formations of the enemy had been noticed, that the previous night Wellingtons from Malta had bombed the Italian Air Force base at Castel Benito and destroyed twenty-nine aircraft on the ground, and that a force of his own bombers would shortly be on their way to attack the air base at Benina near Benghasi. More importantly, the remaining bombers and all his fighter aircraft would be over the immediate target area for most of the night, keeping Italian attention in the skies, cloaking the sounds of approaching attack.

As for the one Italian aircraft which had managed to get through over the concentration area about noon that day, either the pilot had seen nothing or he had failed to make an adequate report. (In fact he had conscientiously reported what he had seen, and for his pains was told to 'take more water with it'.)

The Royal Navy were also playing their part. The monitor H.M.S. *Terror* was closing Maktila and about to begin a bombardment with her two 15-inch and eight 4-inch guns in which the comparatively small armament of the gunboat *Aphis* would assist, while further along the coast her sister gunboat *Ladybird* would lob a few shells into Sidi Barrani – an exercise intended not only to cause annoyance inside the target areas but, like the R.A.F. flights over the inland camps, to distract attention from more vital angles. For a third force was moving this evening towards an unsuspecting prey, though its intentions were not quite so aggressive as those of the forces further south.

Part of the garrison had moved out of Mersa Matruh (but only very few of the New Zealand Brigade, to their intense fury) under command of Brigadier A. R. Selby, with some artillery, a machine-gun company of the Northumberland Fusiliers and the 3rd Battalion Coldstream Guards. Their tasks were to engage the attention of the Libyan units at Maktila immediately the attack began and thus to ensure that none of them was available to offer help and reinforcement to their compatriots further south, and then, if matters progressed well, to get behind those units and prevent their retirement into Sidi Barrani. As Selby Force was only some 1,800 men strong this last requirement might seem a little much, but at least the drivers of their transport were determined to get as far along the coast as they could. These drivers, and some others carrying out the same chores for 4th Indian Division, were the only New Zealanders allowed to take part in *Operation Compass*, and they had no intention of allowing anyone to overlook their presence.

As for the 7th Armoured Division, all units were now in place and well aware of their tasks. While 4th Indian Division and the Matildas stormed into the camps north of the Enba Gap from the rear, 7th Armoured would form a shield to guard them from any attempts to interfere by Italian units from further west – from Rabia or the Sofafi camps, from the post along the top of the Escarpment at Halfaya, or from Capuzzo, Buq Buq, Sollum or Bardia. When the attacks went in, 4th Armoured Brigade would move up towards Azziziya and the coast road, the Support Group with its artillery would attack Rabia, and the 7th Armoured Brigade would wait between them as a reserve for emergency or exploitation.

And with regard to that last phrase, General O'Connor now had another problem to consider. In accordance with his orders he had been planning for a five-day raid, but a day or so previously he had been made aware of the contents of a memo received by Wilson from Wavell some ten days before. This read:

> I know that you have in mind and are planning the fullest possible exploitation of any initial success of 'Compass' operation. You and all Commanders in the Western Desert may rest assured that the boldest action, whatever its results, will have the support not only of myself but of the C.I.G.S. and of the War Office at home.
> . . . It is possible that an opportunity may offer for converting the enemy's defeat into an outstanding victory . . .
> I am not entertaining extravagant hopes of this operation, but I do wish to make certain that if a big opportunity occurs we are prepared morally, mentally and administratively to use it to the fullest.[2]

It was a little bit late in the day to let the commander in the field know that he might launch a full-scale campaign aimed at driving the enemy back a considerable distance instead of just conducting an 'in-and-out' raid; but as he had always been of the opinion that something of a more permanent nature could be made out of *Compass*, O'Connor – as soon as he could take his mind off more immediate problems – was quite ready to adapt his thinking towards more satisfying ends. So far as the 'moral' and the 'mental' preparations were concerned there was little problem; he could expand his horizons and so would his staff when pressed. But the administration, like the impossible, might take a little longer.

How far would he really be able to go with just two divisions, even those as well trained and experienced as the 7th Armoured and the 4th Indian? Perhaps their casualties would be light, perhaps they might capture enough petrol and water to keep going, to keep up the essential momentum. Perhaps, too, the Navy would be able to rush supplies along the coast to Sollum, to Bardia or even to Tobruk (stretching imagination and optimism only a little further than reason might allow). But what about weapons and ammunition? Even if the 4th Indian sepoys and gunners could adapt to the use of Italian automatic weapons and artillery quickly enough, the 7th Armoured's losses could not be replaced by the useless Italian M13s and L3s. Where would replacements for the cruiser tanks come from? What about replacement tank tracks for the Matildas? What about the men? One brigade of the 6th Australian Division were apparently the only trained reserve available, whatever happened, and they were already moving up to take the place of the New Zealand Brigade who for political reasons O'Connor was not allowed to put into action. Could one brigade, added to a force of two divisions, give it sufficient impetus to expand a five-day raid into a victorious advance?

Not impossible . . . perhaps. But highly unlikely.

The final moves into the attack positions began very shortly after dusk, when guides from the 7th Armoured arrived at the Advanced Headquarters of both the 4th Indian and the 7th R.T.R to take them forward. By midnight, selected units were moving towards their final assembly positions under a clear sky, the desert gradually silvering as a full, saucer-shaped moon rose to splodge the landscape with dark blue shadows. It was again bitterly cold though this was not so noticeable to the moving men, absorbed in their own private worlds of fear and confidence, of apprehension and eagerness.

Ahead was Nibeiwa camp, and from it came the crump of bombs as the R.A.F. harried the inmates, keeping their attention upwards, cloaking the sounds of the approaching tanks beneath the roar of their own engines. There were flares mushrooming, occasional parabolas of tracer, once or twice the brief glow of an explosion. There were also, inevitably, the much more immediate crises of minor mistake and misunderstanding.

'Where the hell's the Enba track . . . I'm lost!'

'For God's sake, get those damned guns out of our way . . . You're a bigger bloody nuisance than Hitler.'

'If you're the 8th Hussars, old boy, one or both of us is travelling in the wrong direction.'

But they were all quite quickly sorted out – in fact in some ways the slight errors and the distractions they caused were rather comforting – and overall the movements took place in a manner which said much for both the staff work and the troop training. By 0200 the 4th/7th Rajput Regiment were moving up towards the eastern perimeter at Nibeiwa, while the rest of the infantry of the 11th Indian Brigade with their artillery and forty-five Matildas were swinging up through the Enba Gap towards the unmined entrance explored by Lieutenant Liddell and his scouts, and checked again but a few hours previously. They dropped the artillery some five miles short of the entrance, and the infantry and tanks then went on for another mile, settling down for their last wait at about half-past four. The feint by 4th/7th Rajputs had gone in at 0300 and for an hour the rest of the brigade had listened to the continual rattle of rifle and machine-gun fire coming across the desert from the far side of the enemy camp. The R.A.F. light bombers and fighters were still picketing the skies above, the growl of their engines giving both security and comfort, while from far away to the north they had heard the muffled thumps of the naval bombardment. Dawn would be at 0630.

Away to the west, the 7th Armoured Division were also now in position, the riflemen and gunners of the Support Group in an arc around Rabia with the Sofafis further west also masked, the 4th Armoured with (who else?) B and C Squadrons of the 11th Hussars in the lead were high up in the Enba Gap waiting to probe towards the Sidi Barrani–Sollum road, to cut water-pipes and telegraph lines, to establish roadblocks, and also to locate any Italian armour which might be waiting in the desert behind Sidi Barrani. Lower in the gap waited 7th Armoured Brigade with D Squadron of the 11th available as reserve if required, hoping to be allowed to push on to Buq Buq and attack the Italian garrison there.

Selby Force, leaving behind them a complete brigade of dummy tanks spread in the desert to attract the attention of the Italian fighters when events at last forced them into an appearance over the battlefield, had closed up to the south-west of Maktila, listening to the crash of *Terror*'s shells landing in the comparatively confined spaces of the Maktila post. Northumberland Fusiliers talked between themselves in their clipped, northern accents, the Coldstream Guards muttered together in their own highly individual slang, a *lingua guarda* virtually incomprehensible to non-members of the Household Brigade.

Now, for all of Western Desert Force, there was nothing to do but wait.

Back in Tripoli, Maresciallo Graziani had been made aware of the Italian pilot's report of lorries moving just south-west of Nibeiwa and took sufficient notice of it to issue instructions that the matter should be brought again to the attention of Tenth Army H.Q., fifty

miles behind the front at Bardia. But he could not give it a great
deal of thought himself, as he had other problems to consider.

At the end of the previous month, Maresciallo Badoglio had been
forced by pressure of events to resign as Chief of Staff in Rome – a
resignation of which Graziani thoroughly approved. But, of course,
the question of who succeeded Badoglio was just as important to
the commander of the Italian Army in Libya as the fact that he had
gone, and the intrigues of the Fascist court in Rome during the
ensuing few days had been worthy of the days of the Borgias.
However, just two days previously, Generale d'Armata Cavallero
had emerged as victor, and Graziani had at first drawn a breath of
relief for the new Chief of Staff was a man after his own heart.

But now second thoughts were interposing. The news from the
Balkans where, incredibly, the Greeks were showing not only a
resolute defence but also an offensive spirit which bade fair to push
the Italian invaders back behind the Albanian frontier, was so bad
that very soon Mussolini would assuredly be pressing for counter-
balancing good news from somewhere else. And Cavallero, unable
to make much contact with the Duke of Aosta far away in Addis
Ababa, would therefore be turning his eyes towards Tripoli and
exhibiting all the expected characteristics of a new broom. Thus,
Graziani's December offensive towards the Nile, which he had been
hoping to put off at least until after Christmas, would now become
the subject of the same infuriating probing and general interference
which had plagued his life before the last advance, but which had
mercifully eased with the start of the Greek affair.

Fortunately, planning for the offensive was well under way and
he could always point again to the lack of material and the
continued late delivery of reinforcements and stores; but a new man
in a new job would not be placated for very long, and the advance to
the Nile must soon restart.

There were, of course, few solid reasons why it should not. The
British, however much they might like to roam the desert and however many trifling attacks they might care to deliver against his
flanks, were obviously far too weak to put up much resistance –
especially as all the intelligence sources were unanimous in their
opinion that British strength in Egypt was being drained away to
help the Greeks; however little the Greeks might be needing it at
the moment. *Perfide Albion* was at this particular moment
apparently set on honouring her commitments to Greece, and
although it was difficult to see why, it was not a matter upon which
he need waste much thought. The main thing was to exploit British
weakness to his own advantage, and to avoid criticism from Rome,
preferably by forestalling it.

However, the news that Luftwaffe units were now to move in

strength into the Mediterranean area was worth pondering. Perhaps he should put off the advance until they were available to give him air cover? He must talk to Porro about it and find out how the 5th Squadra would feel about flying alongside the Luftwaffe to the Nile. And also about more defences for the airfields; those losses at Castel Benito would be difficult to replace.

He must go forward again, too, and talk to Gariboldi at Bardia and find out how he was getting on while Berti was away ill. It was always a nuisance when generals went sick, but at least Tenth Army was without its commander in a slack period. He would certainly want Berti back before the next phase of the advance began, together, of course, with Pastucci of the 4th Blackshirts who was also in Rome, on leave.

Those camps right at the front must be pretty uncomfortable, despite the fact that he had seen to it that the officers were properly supplied and that the defences were well and logically constructed. But it must be very cold – and very boring. Even that fire-eater Maletti at Nibeiwa would be finding it hard to keep on his toes, with only an occasional pin-prick raid from the enemy to repulse. Something must be done about the officers and men in those camps, otherwise an atmosphere would be generated there of lack of interest and listlessness.

Graziani was quite right. In most of the camps, that night, there was an air of listlessness, coupled with annoyance that the British were again making a thorough nuisance of themselves. Maktila had suffered casualties and damage from the shells of the Royal Navy, the Tummar camps had been briefly disturbed by aircraft overhead and a few ineffective but noisy bombs, and so had the camps right down in the south on the other side of the Enba Gap, Rabia and the Sofafis. Doubtless, the British were again carrying on their interminable patrols up and down the gap and morning would bring yet more reports of sentries shot or lost – presumably into a prison camp – and of more minefields disturbed. And doubtless, tomorrow would be as boring, as uneventful, as thoroughly uncomfortable as all the days which had preceded it.

In Nibeiwa, however, the atmosphere was different in degree, if not in kind. The British were really being a *bloody* nuisance tonight, the R.A.F. especially. Except for an hour or so after three o'clock their planes had been overhead all the time – and during that brief interlude had come an inexplicable attack by some unidentifiable but quite sizeable force of infantry along the south-east face of the camp. What sort of raid was that meant to be, with not even the artillery support that the raiding columns in the gap always had?

The possibility that it might have been a serious attack, as it was on the side that would first receive the full force of any hypothetical British offensive, had of course occurred to some of the senior officers; but when the shooting died away after little more than an hour, it was realised that it had probably all been the result of a part of one of the raiding columns getting lost – which God knows was easy enough out there in that forsaken, featureless wilderness.

With which thought, those not on duty went back to sleep, the sentries resumed their cold and thankless duties, the perimeter machine- and anti-tank gunners huddled back into their sangars with a prayer that dawn and breakfast would come soon, and Generale Maletti and his aide-de-camp – who was also his son – had a quick nip of cognac and also retired to their tents. Breakfast, as usual, would be served to them at 0730.

It was actually in course of preparation when the opening salvoes of the demoralisation fire from the 25-pounders crashed out and shells burst among the tents and vehicles, trenches and foxholes along the southern perimeter; but the scurry of activity down there had hardly begun coping with these problems before the real danger was revealed. Ponderous and irresistible, the lines of Matildas appeared over a crest half a mile from the main entrance to the Nibeiwa camp and proceeded with almost contemptuous accuracy to reduce to smoking rubbish the only defence between them and the camp – the twenty or so M11s and M13s of the roadblock. Only a few of these had even the chance to start up their engines, let alone fire at the approaching hordes – and hordes the attackers now appeared to be to the startled Italian tank and gun crews, shocked out of sleep, in all states of undress, surrounded suddenly by the violence and chaos of battle.

As usual, it was the Italian artillery who reacted fastest and fought most effectively – or rather least ineffectively, for they had nothing which could hurt the Matildas.

These, having brushed aside the Italian tanks, burst through the entrance and fanned out across the camp area like avenging furies. Their 2-pounders had little to fire at once they were in the camp, but their machine-guns chattered interminably cutting down first anyone who moved above ground, then concentrating on the gun crews as these proved the most determined enemies. Often the brave met fearful deaths in that first charge, for as their shells bounced harmlessly off the Matildas' armour the tanks came on and on to crush both gun and crew beneath the awful weight of steel. And all the time British artillery was still pouring high explosive into the camp with occasional smoke to increase the confusion, and huge plumes of sand would vomit upwards to add to blindness and

Figure 2   Infantry tank Mark II (Matilda II): weight 26·5 tons; armour
20mm.–78mm.; engine 174 h.p.; maximum speed 15 m.p.h.; armament one
2-pdr, one 7·92 Besa m.g.; crew 4

dismay, while shards of steel and stone screamed across the wastes
or sliced horribly into yielding flesh.

At first the Libyan infantry, once they realised the dangers on the
surface, stayed in their trenches and cowered away from the storm
above – but when the Matildas had smashed their main enemy, the
guns, they were free to harry the remaining occupants of the camp
and this they did, 'like iron rods probing a wasps' nest' as the 4th
Indian's regimental history puts it. Everywhere the Matildas ranged
they flushed dazed, frightened but often desperate Italians and
Libyans from covered trenches and slits, from open holes in the
ground – some without weapons at all, some with weapons which
they dropped as they put their hands up; some with bombs which
they threw or weapons which they fired before being cut down by
immediate reply from the tanks. One such was Generale Maletti
himself, emerging from his tent with his son just behind him and a
light machine-gun in hand; he was caught by a burst and flung back
across his bed, his son falling badly wounded beside him.

Impervious and implacable, the tanks ground forward, tramp-
ling down every obstacle, leaving death and disorder in their
wake.

Fifteen minutes after the tanks struck the camp, a shout rang
over the radio: 'CAMERONS – GO!' The Highlanders' carrier
platoon shot ahead in screen; the troop-carrying lorries wheeled

in their dust and followed on the trail. Gradually quickening the pace, the carriers flashed through the gap in the perimeter; 500 yards behind them the troop lorries whipped about. The infantry tumbled out and raced in hotfoot with the bayonet; above the noise of battle shrilled the skirl of the pipes as the gravely pacing pipers played in the charge. The Camerons burst upon a scene of indescribable confusion, as masses of demoralised Italians milled about, some seeking to escape, others belatedly endeavouring to organize resistance. Hundreds threw up their hands at the first flicker of the bayonets. 1/6 Rajputana Rifles, riding hard to the hunt, followed in, passed through the Camerons, and began to mop up in the northern and eastern expanses of the camp. Here and there brave or hysterical handfuls refused the summons and fought until shot down, but within an hour resistance was over. Some hundreds of dead and wounded lay among the débris and litter; more than 4,000 prisoners, including 80 officers, huddled in sullen and shaken groups. 23 tanks, together with some scores of lorries and guns, represented material captures. British and Indian losses had been trifling.[3]

The 4th Indian Division had been well and truly blooded, and its historian given a remarkable scene to report.

By now the leading elements of 4th Armoured Brigade were approaching the Sidi Barrani–Sollum road, having seen no sign as yet of Italian armour. No. 3 Troop, B squadron of the 11th Hussars under, coincidentally, Sergeant J. Cameron (the clan were to do very well this morning), reached the road just before 0900, and ten minutes later had captured eight lorries containing fifty men endeavouring to make their way back over the border from what had shown signs of being a thoroughly hostile environment. They gave no trouble to Cameron and his men, but shortly afterwards the troop came under fire from some anti-tank guns on the Escarpment and had to withdraw after three cars had been hit, one of the Hussars killed and two wounded. But they lost none of their prisoners.

Behind the Hussars came the bulk of 4th Armoured Brigade, with Lieutenant Joly in the leading troop on the right flank.

However preoccupied I was with the stark, ominous desert to my right, I could not resist occasionally glancing at the scene on my left. As far as the eye could see, stretching across the horizon to my left front and flank and rear, there were vehicles moving: the tanks of the leading and the other flanking regiment to my

front and left, and behind me the other two squadrons of my own
regiment. Each tank was followed by a plume of sand, lit and
highlighted by the slanting rays of the early sun, as it pitched and
rolled and tossed over the uneven, stony surface of the desert.
Within the three-sided box formed by the tanks were the supply
vehicles, the fitters' lorries, the doctors' trucks, the ambulances.
In the centre of the whole array I could see the few vehicles of the
Brigade Headquarters. In front of them, and behind the centre of
the leading regiment, was the small group of tanks from which I
knew the Brigadier was controlling the whole move and ready to
give instant orders the moment the enemy was met.[4]

They reached the area around Azziziya with hardly an exchange of
shots and no interference at all from the Regia Aeronautica. In
Azziziya itself the garrison of about 400 gave themselves up without
a murmur of protest, so within a very short time the brigade were
firmly across the Sidi Barrani road, collecting prisoners as these
either tried to retreat from Sidi Barrani or came up from the west to
investigate. The news that Nibeiwa had been captured arrived
about 1030 – but then followed a long and uneasy wait, with 4th
Armoured Brigade virtually stationary but acutely aware of the fact
that battles were being fought between themselves and their
base.

Tummar West was proving a tougher nut to crack than Nibeiwa,
for the simple reason that surprise was no longer possible.

As the noise of battle in Nibeiwa died and the Camerons and the
Rajputs of 11th Indian Brigade began the tasks of marshalling their
prisoners and examining their haul, the infantry of the 5th Indian
Brigade were driving past on their way to the main entrance of
Tummar West – again at the north-west point, again unmined –
preceded by all but six of the Matildas which had now pulled out of
Nibeiwa. The missing six had had their tracks blown off as they
drove rather too enthusiastically towards the new battle, over the
edge of a minefield.

Tummar West was of roughly the same size and shape as
Nibeiwa – about two miles long by just over a mile wide, roughly
oyster-shaped – and an anti-tank ditch encircled its low perimeter
wall, studded with machine-gun posts as at Nibeiwa but with many
gaps. Its commander was obviously not so sedulous a soldier as
Generale Maletti had been.

But Tummar West had one protection which Nibeiwa had lacked,
and it was to extend its life for a few extra hours. The wind had now
risen and the haze of battle thickened as a sandstorm developed –
made worse than usual by the violence which was breaking up the
desert surface all the time. Italian aircraft arrived overhead and

added to the confusion by dropping bombs into the murk below; some even attempted dive-bombing attacks and so blinded were they that three of them crashed into the ground as they tried to level off.

All this, of course, caused the British reconnaissance groups considerable difficulty, and when one of them blundered out of the murk to be confronted by a low wall lined with Italian soldiery peering anxiously at them and obviously aware only of general menace but not spécific danger, the officer in charge reacted too late to stop his exasperated driver shouting, 'Are you lot Tummar West or East?'

The answer is not recorded, but doubtless one of the Italians was polite enough to have replied.

But gradually, the attack force was assembled, the targets identified, the guns lined up. At 1330, two hours later than ordered by the commander of the 4th Indian Division, General Beresford-Peirse, the guns crashed out, the Matildas headed in for the entrance shooting up everything before them, the Italian artillery reacted quickly – and just as quickly found out that their guns were virtually useless against the steel carapaces of the irresistible tanks. However, some anti-aircraft crews swung the barrels of their high velocity guns down and when their shells hit the Matildas between turret and hull they jammed the turrets.

Twenty minutes after the tanks went through the entrance, the infantry troop carriers drove up at the unheard-of rate across desert of some thirty miles an hour and to within 150 yards of the perimeter – to the considerable surprise of the men inside, especially of the officers who had ordered the move and who had expected to find themselves with over 500 yards still to go. But this was the transport driven by the New Zealanders of No. 4 Reserve Motor Transport Company, and they had no intention of allowing the Royal Fusiliers they were carrying to go on without them; neither did they see the point of going further on their feet than they had to. Deserting their carriers to a man, they borrowed bayonets from the platoon Bren-gunners and charged alongside the infantry, slightly diluting their swift popularity by their warcries which seemed in a large number of cases to be 'Come on then, you Pommie bastards!'

But the attackers now ran into far more trouble than their comrades at Nibeiwa had experienced. As they hurtled across the perimeter wall, they were met by a fusillade of rifle and machine-gun bullets which cut down the leaders and drove the rest of the first wave to ground. Then the grenades came out and systematic advances with bomb and Bren-gun fire began; the quick rush, the murderous work with bayonet, rifle butt and boot. In the centre of the camp, a line of dug-outs was the scene of several vicious and bitter clashes until the Matildas were brought back to crush their implacable way over the defence – and there were still some of the gallant Italian artillerymen standing and fighting around their wrecked guns.

Then the second wave of infantry – the 3rd/1st Punjabis – swept in to attack through the pinned-down Fusiliers, right across the central areas until at last their Sikh Company penned those Italians who had not surrendered or been killed into the south-east corner of the camp. Shortly afterwards the immaculate form of an Italian general emerged from a concrete dug-out, accompanied by thirteen equally immaculate senior officers, and after a short parley during which it was suggested that the prisoners should be allowed to retain their arms in order to protect themselves against the savage Indian natives, Tummar West surrendered. Another 2,000 prisoners were taken and although the Royal Fusiliers had lost several officers and N.C.O.s in that first rush, the casualties for the attackers had again been unbelievably low.

While Tummar West was being fought over, another battle had been in progress but a short way away. 4th/6th Rajputana Rifles had not been put into the same battle as their comrades from 5th Brigade, but in their troop carriers and Bren-carriers had swept past the embattled entrance and across towards the south-west face of Tummar East. As they did so, two Italian M11 tanks followed by quite a large force of Italian infantry on foot emerged from Tummar East to confront them, while six lorries obviously crammed with infantry began to drive across their front in a well-intentioned attempt to help the Tummar West garrison.

These last had little hope against the Northumberland Fusilier machine-gunners attached to Rajputana Rifles, who had their guns in action pouring bullets into the soft-skinned lorries and their hapless contents long before they could debus – and the lorry drivers reacted understandably but fatally by trying to drive as quickly as possible out of range, thus allowing their infantry no chance to escape the torrent of bullets tearing them apart.

The 4th Indian troop carriers, however, had screeched to a stop the moment the enemy had been seen and identified; the sepoys poured out and flung themselves behind cover or to the ground, and within seconds were directing rapid and accurate fire upon the advancing tanks and their marching support. The M11s had already demonstrated their vulnerability to fire from the Boyes anti-tank rifles with which the Rajputanas were still armed, and so were not much longer in a condition to offer protection to their accompanying infantry; these turned and fled, thus offering an even easier target to the riflemen behind them.

Some 400 killed and wounded were left behind on this particular field of battle, with not even a flesh wound inflicted on the victors – and by this time the British artillery had been released from their tasks on Tummar West and were registering on Tummar East. Moreover, the Matildas had now carried out their main duties in Tummar West and the sixteen runners still left came out to attack Tummar East – but arriving at the assembly line before the delayed infantry, they went straight into the attack without waiting. Again, they wrought havoc through the camp, again there was nothing the unfortunate Italians could do against them; but by this time, the murk of sandstorm and battle had thickened unbearably and the early December dusk was falling. Beresford-Peirse, with every reason to feel pleased with the activities of his division, recalled the Matildas, held back the still eager Rajputana Rifles and ordered everyone into night leaguer between the two Tummar camps.

Unbelievably, this tactic proved to be the cheapest method of achieving victory on that extraordinary day. Probably because of the time allowed them for reflection during that cold and sinister night, the entire garrison of Tummar East surrendered at first light the following morning, without another shot being fired.

In the meantime, the Highlanders and sepoys of 11th Brigade still in Nibeiwa had had time to examine their booty, to take stock of the extraordinary haul which had fallen into their hands.

The Italian garrisons may not have been supplied with very efficient arms with which to defend themselves, but the officers at least lived in splendid style up until the moment of attack. The astonished eyes of the victors were greeted, as they made their way through well-built subterranean tunnels from grotto to grotto, with hanging wardrobes full of superbly cut uniforms, glittering with gold lace and silver epaulettes; with dressing tables covered with silver-mounted toilet sets, each with regimental or Fascist embossed crests; with polished and tasselled jack-boots, with sashes and belts and embroidered caps. There was enough military finery in Nibeiwa camp alone to hold a grand pageant and parade in St Peter's Square, and all the exquisite niceties to set it off – perfume, manicure sets, hair lotions, bootbrushes and polishes, soft cloths and cleaning sets to remove stains from the smooth, pale blue cavalry cloaks which would drape romantically from padded shoulders to gold-spurred heels.

And those on parade would not have been suffering from either lack of sleep or sustenance as they broke all hearts in Rome. Alongside the dressing tables were comfortable beds with clean sheets, obviously made up by servants, the linen replaced each day from the full chest of drawers which made up the last item of apparently regulation equipment with which each officer and many of the warrant and non-commissioned officers were supplied by a generous but unwise command. Italian corporals in Nibeiwa – and in the Tummar and Sofafi camps, too, as was later revealed – lived far more comfortable, indeed luxurious, lives in their front line than had O'Connor at his Western Desert Headquarters.

As for food, Alan Moorehead arrived at Nibeiwa with the first party of journalists and had this to say:

We sat down on the open sand and ate from stores of bottled cherries and greengages; great tins of frozen hams and anchovies; bread that had been baked somehow here in the desert; and wines from Frascati and Falerno and Chianti, red and white, and Lacrimae Christi from the slopes of Vesuvius above Naples. There were wooden casks of a sweet, heady, fruity brandy, and jars of liqueurs of other kinds wrapped carefully in envelopes of straw. For water the Italians took bottles of Recoaro minerals – the very best in Italy – and these, like everything else, had been carted out to them in hundreds of cases across a thousand miles of sea and desert by ship and car and mule team.

The spaghetti was packed in long blue paper packages and stored with great sacks of macaroni and other wheat foods as numerous as they used to be in the shops of Italy before the war. Parmesan cheeses as big as small cart-wheels and nearly a foot thick lay about in neat piles except where some hungry soldier had slashed one open with his sword. Ten-pound tins of Estratto di Pomidoro – the tomato extract vital to so many Italian dishes – formed the bulk of the tinned stuff, which also contained many excellent stews and delicate tinned tongue and tunny fish and small round tins of beef. The vegetables were of every kind. Potatoes, onions, carrots, beans, cabbages, leeks, cauliflowers, pumpkin and many other things had been steamed down into a dry compact that readily expanded to its old volume when soaked in warm water – a fine food for the desert. We sampled one package that seemed at first to contain dry grass, but brewed itself over a stove into a rich minestrone soup.[5]

An Aladdin's cave was opened to the tired, hungry, thirsty but still exhilarated Scots and Indian troops, and one would have thought that discipline would have cracked and an orgy of feasting taken place; but oddly, once immediate thirst and hunger had been satisfied, curiosity, and a rather pitying affection for a race which apparently needed such luxuries even in war, became the prevailing mood. The alcohol had little attraction for the Indian troops who were forbidden it by their religion, and although the Scots could appreciate both the Italian wine and the highly spiced foods, they were for the moment too tired to take the fullest advantage of their good fortune.

But they did appreciate some of the equipment. The small, beautifully made pistols all disappeared quite quickly – though those that weren't sold in the Cairo back streets were thrown away once their ineffectiveness in combat had been demonstrated – and so did the ornamental daggers. The light, aluminium water-bottles were snapped up and remained in use until they split, and many of the leather belts and straps accompanied their finders right through the North African campaign. Cameras and binoculars found at Nibeiwa and the Tummars were still up for sale or barter in Cairo and Alexandria when the war ended, and possibly still are.

The one large beneficence which was admired by all who saw and especially those who needed its ministrations, was that provided by the hospital tent and medical services in each camp. Cool, spacious tents, with stores of bandages, sheets, folding beds and every sort of drug, appliance or instrument for the treatment of wounds or sickness, now provided relief for vanquished and victor alike, both Italian and British doctors working together and on each patient as he needed help, irrespective of rank or nationality. But even this service for the fighting troops was, in reality, impractical for the front line. Such lavish accommodation and equipment should have been located much further back, certainly as far back as Sollum and probably better at Bardia.

Shortly after Beresford-Peirse had given the order to the 5th Indian Brigade to leaguer for the night he was joined by General O'Connor, who, as reports of the last of the day's fighting came in, confessed to being 'very pleased with the excellent progress made'.

He had left the advanced headquarters on the Escarpment as soon as it became obvious that the main action was moving north and away from him, and his first call had been at 7th Armoured Division where 'Blood' Caunter was in temporary command as General Creagh had succumbed to an abscess on the tongue and been forced into hospital in Cairo. There O'Connor had learned of the progress of the 11th Hussars and the 4th Armoured Brigade, that the Support Group had achieved its purpose by totally screening Rabia and the Sofafi camps from which there had been little sign of life – or even curiosity – all day; and that 7th Armoured Brigade, having had virtually nothing to do but wait and listen to the sounds of battle around them, were showing a tendency to chafe at the bit.

To temper their impatience, O'Connor told Caunter to release the 8th Hussars and send them to the west of the Sofafi camps to ensure that the whole of that garrison would be ripe for capture when the time came – and also to send a senior staff officer to

Beresford-Peirse's Headquarters so as to make certain that the
smooth co-operation between the two divisions which had distinguished the battle so far would continue during the more uncertain days ahead. The opening phase of the battle – the only one
which can be planned in detail – was now almost over; from now on
improvisation and exploitation would be the watchwords, flexibility
and co-operation the keys.

Now, in 4th Indian Division's H.Q., he recast the battlefield for
the following day.

The fall of the remaining inland camps – Tummar East and Point
90 – could now be assumed to be but a matter of time and 5th
Indian Brigade could be left in position to deal with them; the
Sofafis in the south would have to wait. Sidi Barrani was obviously
the next target for attack, in many ways the most important of all.
There was no news as yet from Selby Force, but as 4th Armoured
Brigade across the road to the west of Sidi Barrani had not been
subjected to anything heavier than isolated attacks from small and
uncoordinated groups probably dispatched by the garrison merely
in order to find out what was happening, it was reasonable to
assume at least that no spectacular failure had taken place.

And there was still the 16th British Brigade under Beresford-
Peirse's command, uncommitted during the first day's fighting,
waiting alongside 7th Armoured Brigade for the call to action. Sidi
Barrani should be theirs.

During the night they moved north – Argyll and Sutherland
Highlanders in the lead, the Leicesters and the Queen's Regiment
in echelon behind; and behind them those of the 11th Brigade who
could be released from guarding prisoners and counting stores in
Nibeiwa. By dawn they were in position.

Brigadier C. E. N. Lomax, commanding the 16th British Brigade,
was in something of a dilemma. Although his infantry were now
in a position from which to launch the attack, he had little idea of
the whereabouts of his artillery or any of the Matildas which were
supposed to be in support, principally because of the appalling
weather conditions. For British troops who had grown up under the
impression that Egypt was a land of blistering heat, brilliant blue
skies and golden sands, the bitter winds of the morning of
December 10th sharpened by the myriad grains of sand and
pulverised clay which stung their faces and hands and reduced
visibility at times to but fifty yards, were a savage disappointment.

But unfortunately, although the wind remained cold and the sand
stung, the one potentially useful concomitant of the weather – the
fog – was infuriatingly variable. Although it cloaked the artillery
and armour from view on the flanks (they were in fact both within a

thousand yards of Lomax's Headquarters) it had already faded sporadically and given him glimpses of the Italian positions in front, and by the same token would expose his troops to the enemy artillerymen whenever they happened to look in the right direction. There was therefore as much danger in waiting for the arrival of gun and tank support as in going in without it, so just after 0600 he gave the order to move forward and the troop lorries started off. They had covered about half the three and a half miles to the Italian gun-line when the wind slackened again, the fog parted and with the efficiency and accuracy which all had learned to expect, the Italian artillerymen opened fire.

The Argylls poured out of their troop carriers and hit the ground, Leicesters coming up on the flank swung out slightly but then were caught and forced to do the same, anti-tank guns raced up and opened their puny fire on the dug-in enemy guns now firing over open sights, and the whole area was engulfed in the kind of set battle-piece which had characterised the plains of Flanders twenty-five years before. Behind the pinned-down infantry their lorries blazed amid plumes of sand and smoke, alongside them the 2-pounders barked and coughed while all around the dust and smoke thickened, the shells crashed, their own machine-guns chattered.

But on their left flank, the reserve battalion, the 2nd Queen's, were coming up into position and with them – guided solely in the still opaque storm by the sound of guns – were the ten surviving Matildas in one of which was crouched their commanding officer, Lieutenant-Colonel R. Jerram, released from administrative duties by the gradual whittling down of his command and able at last to get into action. Sweeping forward past the line of the Argylls and Leicesters they crashed into the western face of the defences just south of the road – and were immediately enveloped in an even thicker fog as the wind rose again and all the powdered dust of their own activities was whipped upwards.

In it were fought unnumbered small, close, vicious battles. A dozen shadows would rise out of the ground in front of the half-blinded cockneys of the Queen's to be shot or bayoneted before it was known whether they had intended to fight or surrender; a machine-gun would bark, unseen from ten yards away, to cut down half a dozen men before the crash of randomly thrown grenades ended its life and those of its crew; a lumbering Matilda would catch a line of puzzled and frightened Italians trying to give themselves up and chase them away back into the gloom – and then, identifying the crash of an Italian gun nearby, turn like a mastodon and waddle in its direction until it overwhelmed it from flank or rear.

In the meantime, sensing the diversion of Italian attention,

Lieutenant-Colonel R. C. B. Anderson of the pinned-down Argyll and Sutherland Highlanders called for a charge, just as the British artillery wheeled at last through the fog into position, opened up with a barrage intended for the Italian gun-line but – fortunately for the Matildas – crashed down well beyond it. Up from the ground rose the Highlanders, their pipe-major frantically trying to sound the charge through sand-choked pipes, and swept on and on through the murk until, having cleared a series of small hummocks which had been Colonel Anderson's main objective, they found themselves so close under the Italian gun-line that the hostile shells screamed overhead and no attempts at deflection by the gunners could reach them.

Now the Leicesters were on their feet and at some time just after 1000 (no investigation has ever been able to fix exactly when), under a growing weight of artillery support, the whole of 16th Brigade moved forward – Queen's on the left, Argylls in the centre, Leicesters on the right. The crash and thunder of battle rose to sudden fury, the infantry pace quickened along almost the whole line – and the wind and sand dropped to reveal 2,000 Blackshirt troops rising from their trenches just in front, formed up, apparently, for a mass attack.

But as Scot and Englishman launched forward for what looked to be that crisis of infantry fighting, hand-to-hand bayonet work, it was realised that the majority of the foe were unarmed and had their hands in the air. They had had enough. Within two hours all the first objectives for the infantry of 16th Brigade had been taken, a brigade line had been established along the whole of the western side of Sidi Barrani and a part of the southern side, and the outer line of Italian artillery had been overrun. Moreover, the 4th/6th Rajputana Rifles of the 5th Brigade were now closing up on the right of the Leicesters – and the surrender of the Tummar East garrison that morning had also released the 2nd Camerons to join the western flank of the line, north of the Sidi Barrani–Buq Buq road. Everything now turned on the still obscure position of Selby Force.

The Guardsmen and gunners of the Matruh garrison had had a trying and frustrating twenty-four hours. Brigadier Selby had received no word of the progress of the attacks on Nibeiwa and Tummar West until nearly 1530 the previous afternoon, and it was only then that he had felt secure enough to detach a part of his holding force – which had been rather statically engaging the attentions of the men of the 1st Libyan Division in Maktila all day – to advance north-westwards and try to cut the road leading back to Sidi Barrani. But bad going and darkness held up the move until the

following dawn, which broke to reveal columns of Libyan infantry
with their transport and guns marching stolidly westwards to join
their comrades fifteen miles back in Sidi Barrani.

As this was specifically what O'Connor had planned to avoid, it
was now up to Selby Force to close up quickly and hinder the
Libyan retreat and this, to some extent, they achieved. By
advancing as quickly as possible along the flank, they delayed the
rear and middle of the marching Libyans who moved into the sand-
dunes north of the road and took up defensive positions from which
it soon became obvious that they would prove difficult to eject.

It was now that O'Connor's recommendation that a senior liaison
officer from 7th Armoured Division should be attached to
Beresford-Peirse's H.Q. bore excellent fruit, and immediately the
situation became clear, this officer set about its resolution. As 4th
Armoured Brigade's task of shielding the 4th Indian Division's
infantry from attacks from the west was obviously unnecessary in
view of the total lack of any Italian initiative from that direction,
then some at least of its units could be employed actively helping
the infantry attacks – especially as the Matildas were being steadily
reduced in numbers (by the afternoon of the 9th, they were down to
seven runners, though very few were in need of repair work taking
more than four hours). 2nd Royal Tank Regiment could thus be
used to augment the Matildas remaining in 7th R.T.R., while the
cruiser tanks of the 6th R.T.R. could go east and help Selby Force.

As Lieutenant Joly was commanding one of these, we have an
interesting light on the atmosphere and movements. He had just
been helping with first aid to three badly wounded infantrymen, and
then watched the remaining Matildas lead in for another spell of
mopping up:

In the next moment I heard the Colonel's voice again calling
Kinnaird and giving him further orders:

'. . . As the relations have passed through your front you will
lead behind them. As soon as you are through the enemy
defended area, swing right. Take no notice of the relations, as
they are to go left. We are to go east until we have joined up with
other friends about whom you have heard. Off.' . . .

Waiting until the Matildas were about 500 yards ahead,
Kinnaird then gave the order to advance and to follow, as closely
as possible, in the wake of the heavier tanks, so that we could
take the best advantage of the gap they made in the line of guns.
Once through, we swung east, being fired at whenever the sandstorm cleared, by a further line of guns on another ridge to our
left.

It was here that I had my first experience of being hit squarely by a shell, though, luckily for us, it was not armour piercing and did no internal damage to the tank. Nevertheless it was an unpleasant occurrence and served to give me a clear indication of what would happen when the day came when I was unfortunate enough to have my tank penetrated . . . On this morning we were hit by two shells in fairly rapid succession. It was true that these hits jammed the turret so that we could not traverse it, and damaged the gunner's telescope so that, until he had replaced it with the spare one, he was unable to engage any targets. But for the rest, except that the dull metallic thud of the hit and the following crash of the explosion stirred up all the dust in the tank, making it difficult for a few moments for us to see each other, I and the other members of the crew only suffered from headaches for a short while afterwards.[6]

Having completed the switch to the east of Sidi Barrani, still in a blinding sandstorm which necessitated their all keeping very close station, 6th R.T.R. tanks swung north at about 1715, put in a shattering attack on the Libyan defences in the sand-dunes and completely overran them. They then made contact with the Selby Force guardsmen, and just before midnight the combined force went into action again, continuing the pressure and harassment on the unfortunate enemy.

The Italian forces left in the area – the remainder of 4th Black-shirt Division and the 1st and 2nd Libyan Divisions (less one detachment at Point 90, still holding out in Tummar East) – were now penned against the sea in an enclave measuring less than ten miles long and about five miles deep; and neither O'Connor nor Beresford-Peirse had any intention of allowing the escape of a single soldier. Perhaps the inflexibility of this resolve permeated to Generale di Divisione Gallina, commanding the trapped forces, adding considerably to his deep depression and that of his staff.

On the afternoon of the 9th, Gallina had signalled Graziani to the effect that the entire area of his command was 'infested by a mechanised army against which I have no adequate means' – and since then the news of ever-growing disaster to the south had been supplemented by every survivor who staggered in. The rot which set in early in the 4th Blackshirt Division spread quickly and there was obviously no hope of further defiance from them when the British next attacked; and even if the Italian artillery were still prepared to show their gallantry and resolve by throwing back the midnight attack with some success (6th R.T.R. suffered an unexpected bloody nose and were temporarily reduced to seven cruisers and six light tanks), it was quite certain that the Italian infantry had had enough.

And it really was enough. Whether any instructions went out from Gallina's H.Q. that night is not known, but when the British guns opened fire first thing on the morning of December 11th, their advancing infantry were greeted everywhere with white handkerchiefs waved by apathetic soldiers, tired of battle, weary of separation from their homes, no longer interested in the promises of Fascism or its posturing leadership.

Only at Point 90 did a legion of the 2nd Libyan Division still defy their besiegers, occasionally lobbing a few shells towards the positions held by the remainder of the 5th Indian Brigade. According to the 4th Indian Division history:

> Brigadier Lloyd sent a captured Italian officer under a flag of truce with a demand for surrender. The Point 90 commander reiterated his resolve to die fighting. Whereupon 1 and 25 Field Regiments registered and 3/1 Punjabis escorted by 5 'I' tanks moved forward. (By dint of feverish exertions, two crocks from workshop caught up with their hale brethren and seven actually waddled to the attack.) The Punjabis advanced in skirmishing order and closed on Point 90 to find 2,000 Libyans lined up with kitbags and suitcases packed for travel. Honour had been satisfied.[7]

By the evening of December 10th, it had become obvious to O'Connor that his original plans for the 'five-day raid' had succeeded to an unbelievable extent. Now, in accordance with those orders which had come to him so late, he must turn his mind to the enormous problems – and excitements – of that 'fullest possible exploitation' expected of him.

With everything between Sidi Barrani and Nibeiwa in British hands and some basic organisation started for the evacuation of the 20,000 prisoners (British and Indian losses to date had been less than 700, of whom nine officers and 144 other ranks had been from the Argyll and Sutherland Highlanders that morning) the next targets were obviously Rabia and the Sofafi camps, followed by the Italian posts along the top of the Escarpment at such places as Halfway House and Halfaya Pass, and the garrisons at Buq Buq and Sollum on the coast – in other words, the reduction of all enemy forces in Egypt.

The Support Group of 7th Armoured Division could move almost immediately, though if the Hussars from 7th Armoured Brigade had succeeded in bottling up all enemy troops in Rabia and Sofafi, it would be unwise to presume, even in the face of the evidence so far, that all the Italian forces would give up so easily that Gott's riflemen and Campbell's gunners could do the job entirely on their own.

Beresford-Peirse must therefore bring his 5th and 11th Brigades down to just south of Nibeiwa as soon as they could be disengaged, to provide any necessary support, leaving 16th British Brigade and Selby Force to cope with the prisoners in the north – and as soon as they had handed them over to the Australians and any New Zealanders still at Mersa Matruh, they could move forward along the coast road behind the 7th Armoured Brigade.

The 1st Royal Tank Regiment and the 3rd Hussars under Brigadier Russell must move on Buq Buq as quickly as possible, preferably arriving there in time to catch the Italian garrison before it tried to escape back to Sollum; 11th Hussars must try to get around Buq Buq and repeat their old trick of cutting the road, the telegraph and the water pipelines. That would give 4th Armoured Brigade just enough time to reassemble west of the Tummars and then to move up on to the Escarpment and clear the posts along the edge as far as the Wire – and possibly go through it and on to Capuzzo, Maddalena and Sidi Azeiz; though something would have to be done about screening them from the Italians in Sidi Omar or further south along the way to Jarabub. Perhaps by the time those alternatives had to be faced, the Support Group and 4th Indian Division would have cleared up the Sofafis, the road-block of prisoners at Matruh would be clear and the Anzacs could come further forward to take over.

That would release 4th Indian's 5th and 11th Brigades to deal with any threats from the south, so perhaps plans should be drawn up for an attack on Bardia; or even on Tobruk.

With which pleasant, imaginative and exciting prospects in mind, General O'Connor took an hour or so's well-deserved rest.

He was woken before first light on December 11th with a message from General Wavell via General Maitland Wilson to the effect that the two brigades of the 4th Indian Division, plus their transport and divisional artillery, were to be withdrawn from the battle as quickly as possible for dispatch to the Sudan.

'It was a tremendous shock,' he was to write later. '. . . I had had no previous intimation of it and it came to me as a bolt from the blue.'

The fact that the 16th British Brigade attached to the 4th Indian would remain with him was small consolation.

5 · First Battle for Tobruk

However great the immediate shock, it seems that General O'Connor had no intention of allowing it to upset his plans for that day. He left his headquarters as soon as he had swallowed a hasty breakfast, called at Caunter's headquarters and arranged for 7th Armoured Brigade to move as quickly as possible towards Buq Buq and Sollum, hoping to cut off the Italian forces there before they could escape back into Libya, while the Support Group moved against Rabia. Once 4th Armoured Brigade could be disentangled from the Sidi Barrani area, it was to reorganise itself in the Enba Gap and then sweep around to the south to trap the remnants of the Cyrene Division in Sofafi.

He then went on to Beresford-Peirse's headquarters south of Sidi Barrani, to find that solid and imperturbable figure still chain-smoking the cheroots of which he seemed to have an inexhaustible supply, already concerning himself with the problems of with-drawing his two brigades from battle, and transporting them together with their artillery first back to the Delta and then down into Ethiopia. He had apparently been aware of the planned move for rather longer than had O'Connor, and regarded it quite philosophically as just a transfer from one theatre of battle to another; and in the meantime, at least 4th Indian's transport would be moving in a direction which should help with the ever-growing problem of evacuation of the prisoners. When should they go?

It did not take O'Connor long to decide, for the cold facts of administration and supply were unarguable; if 4th Indian were not to continue fighting under his command, then the sooner they were off his ration strength the better. Until they could begin the move, however, would they please do what they could to tidy up the area of the last two days' fighting, help with the wounded and prisoners, and keep their sticky fingers out of the Field Supply Depots.

With which prescient admonition, O'Connor returned to 7th Armoured H.Q. to receive his second disappointment that morn-ing. The efforts of the 8th Hussars to hem in – or at least to give warning of the escape of – the garrisons at Rabia and Sofafi had been neither determined nor continuous enough, and early that morning Sergeant Holland of the King's Royal Rifle Corps had probed forward with his carriers to find Rabia deserted except for two stragglers whom he took prisoner. His reports quickly brought up other carriers and, pressing further forward, they found the main Sofafi camps empty except for about a hundred Libyans totally uninterested in resistance, or indeed anything but sampling the luxuries with which these camps, too, had been stocked, apparently for the sole delight of the Italian N.C.O.s and officers. The rest of the Cyrene Division had stolen out of camp during the night and were now toiling along the top of the Escarpment towards Halfway House and the outpost at the top of Halfaya Pass, with the distant refuge of Fort Capuzzo in mind.

They were harried during the early part of their flight by a squadron of the 11th Hussars who had been posted out south of the Escarpment as a backstop for the proposed drive of 4th Armoured, but the Hussars themselves were caught about noon by two excellently led and conducted flights of 5th Squadra fighters. The second flight were using armour-piercing explosive bullets which effectively put the Hussars out of action for the time being and allowed the Sofafi garrison the rest of the day to continue a virtually uninterrupted retreat.

On the coast, however, matters were proceeding somewhat differently. Early in the morning, 7th Armoured Brigade had been launched towards Buq Buq with B Squadron of the 11th Hussars on its desert flank and C Squadron even further west, patrolling between Buq Buq and Sollum. C Squadron's reports quickly convinced their C.O., John Combe, that the Italians had no intention of making a stand there, and after a delay caused by wireless difficulties and the breakdown of the tank carrying 7th Armoured's commander, Brigadier H. E. Russell, 7th Armoured swept through Buq Buq and eventually found the best part of the 64th Catanzaro Division among the sand-dunes between the coast road and the sea, its guns well placed, its flanks resting on salt-pans and mudflats.

The first charge by a squadron of the 3rd Hussars in light tanks presaged ill for the battle, for in attempting to reach the outer line of guns they tried to cross a dried salt marsh which looked firm enough but broke under their weight, bogged the Hussars down and left them easy targets for the Italian artillerymen – as always both efficient and brave. But the cruiser tanks of the 8th Hussars swung in across firm ground on the seaward flank, the armoured cars of the 11th darted in from further along the coast road and the Italian infantry then broke and fled. Many got away briefly towards

Sollum, but sufficient were rounded up for a report to go in, when the extent of the bag was requested, to the effect that there appeared to be 'twenty acres of officers and about a hundred acres of men'.

By the end of this third day of the battle, there were another 14,000 prisoners, another 68 guns and an uncounted number of lorries to add to the profits of *Operation Compass*. The guns, lorries and other assorted war materials were, of course, extremely welcome to O'Connor who could use every gun and shell, every vehicle, every pint of petrol or water his troops could capture; but the prisoners were an acute embarrassment, even given their native charm, their friendliness and their willingness to help. The second-in-command of 7th Armoured Brigade that day, Colonel Alec Gatehouse, wrote:

> No defeated army has ever co-operated with its opponents to the extent that the Italians did on this day. They assembled their own lorries, refuelled them with their own fuel, and drove them full of their own prisoners to Maktila, and they came back for more – all without escort of any kind.[1]

It was certainly one way of redeeming Mussolini's promise that they would spend Christmas in the Delta.

Even with all this help, however, O'Connor's problems were many and serious, for it would seem that his easiest way out never entered his mind. *Operation Compass* had already vastly exceeded the highest hopes which anyone had placed on it. In three days, Western Desert Force had captured 38,000 Italian and Libyan prisoners, 237 guns, 73 light or medium tanks and over 1,000 vehicles. (The full count of captured vehicles was never made due to an old-fashioned army practice of hanging on to anything which might be useful, and only reporting it to Higher Authority if Higher Authority actually saw it.) Many of the enemy soldiers had been killed, and a high proportion of enemy equipment had been destroyed; all the enemy camps which had been the objectives of the 'five-day raid' had been annihilated in three days – and now half O'Connor's trained fighting strength and more than half of his serviceable transport was to be taken from him.

History would thus hardly have criticised him had he thereupon insisted on reverting to the original plan and withdrawing all his forces to their start positions before the raid began, especially in view of the fact that his Field Supply Depots were now down to two days' stock, and the track mileage left to the armour – his only remaining striking force – was perilously small.

Instead, on December 12th O'Connor was planning not for a retreat, not even for completion of the very acceptable operational target of the expulsion of all hostile forces from Egypt (for that would obviously be attained within days if not hours) – but for an immediate advance into Cyrenaica by the 7th Armoured Division and the investment of the first sizeable enemy stronghold, the port of Bardia. Along the coast road, 7th Armoured Brigade augmented by Rifle Brigade companies from the Support Group must press on into Sollum, while along the top of the Escarpment, 4th Armoured must mop up any Italian resistance which might show itself on the Egyptian side of the Wire, shoulder aside anything across the Wire and cut down the Escarpment and across the Bardia–Tobruk road as quickly as possible.

As 4th Armoured's role in this was obviously the more important, and as Creagh was still in hospital and Caunter thus still commanding the whole division, his second in command, Horace Birks, would have the honour of leading the first invading thrust of British armour into hostile territory. In order to help him, a light striking force was formed consisting of 11th Hussars less two squadrons, two batteries of the Royal Horse Artillery and the 2nd Royal Tank Regiment with light tanks, all under command of the 11th's C.O., Lieutenant-Colonel John Combe. The other two 11th Squadrons remained with Birks.

It was bitterly cold that night along the edge of the Escarpment whether on top or below, with a full moon and a freezing wind. The men were very tired now after three days' continuous fighting, but buoyed up with triumph; there was little comment and no complaint when orders for an advance to the frontier were given which included the words, 'Owing to this change of plan we shall have to be short of food and water so that we can continue to be supplied with the ammunition and petrol we shall need.'

Some of the tanks still carried items from the larders of the Sofafi camps, though the armour had not in fact had much to do with the occupation of any of these and therefore had not done so well as the infantry. Anyway, there was no water with which to cook the soups, which would have been the most welcome form of nourishment in those conditions.

To get forward was the main thing. By the afternoon of December 13th, all of Birks's command were concentrated around Khereigat about twelve miles south of Halfaya, and ready to move. They crossed the frontier shortly after midnight and knifed through between the Italian posts to reach their first rendezvous twenty miles west of Bardia by 0700 on the morning of the 14th. Then Combeforce went forward to find the route down the Escarpment that C Squadron's Sergeant Lamb had used six months before.

It was there that the Italian fighters caught them.

This was the squadron which had been especially formed to find the 11th Hussars, and now they were firing explosive bullets. They came screaming in at just above ground level and in twenty minutes of violent action wrecked five armoured cars, a fitter's lorry and a truck, killed another of the 11th's squadron sergeant-majors, badly wounded an officer and five of the men. Then they were gone again, leaving a scene of smoking desolation, with cars burning, ammunition exploding, blood and oil soaking into the uncaring, absorbent sand. The Cherrypickers were paying the price always exacted of those who choose the sharp end.

But the survivors were ready to move within a quarter of an hour, and there then followed one of the more bizarre incidents in what was to prove a bizarre campaign. One of the Rolls-Royce armoured cars commanded by Sergeant Charles Galpin descended the Escarpment and reached an apparently deserted stretch of the Bardia–Tobruk road along which the sergeant intended to cut the telephone lines. Unfortunately, as he negotiated the ditch which bordered the road, the hump broke the timing gear of his car and totally immobilised it; and at that moment Galpin became acutely conscious of the fact that there was an Italian tank half a mile away along the road, whose crew were watching him with considerable interest.

Very shortly, the Italian tank crew's interest quickened to the extent of their climbing into their vehicle and starting along the road towards him – at which point the sergeant heard the sound of another vehicle, this time an ambulance, approaching in the other direction, from Bardia. He and his crew were therefore sandwiched rather neatly between two hostile units, though as one was probably non-combatant, his danger lay mostly in the immobility of his own vehicle.

Stepping smartly into the middle of the road, he held up the ambulance, highwayman fashion, and within a very short time the astonished driver and his passengers were locked in the back while Galpin and his crew hurriedly fastened a tow-rope between his capture and his car. Three minutes later an onlooker would have been granted the astonishing sight of an Italian ambulance with a British driver at the wheel, towing a British armoured car in the direction of Bardia, pursued by an Italian tank whose crew could apparently do nothing but shout and wave their arms in a positively operatic frenzy.

Unfortunately for Galpin, he had overlooked a small square opening in the partition behind him, through which the driver normally communicated with his passengers – and just as his driving mirror was providing sound evidence that he was drawing away from his pursuer despite the 4-ton weight he was pulling, an arm came through the opening and a hand fastened around his throat. There followed a frantic few minutes while Galpin tried to draw his revolver with one hand and break the grip which was choking him with the other, at the same time keeping the now violently swaying ambulance and its tow on the road. Immediately behind him he could hear at least two of the passengers trying to smash their way through the partition, and he also caught a split-second view in the mirror of the expression of total bewilderment on the face of his driver, struggling with the wheel of the armoured car.

Then his gun came free, he fired immediately back through the opening and felt the grip on his throat relax, put another four shots through the partition until the hammering stopped – and saw immediately ahead of him an approaching convoy.

He and his crew fled into the sand-dunes, watched their late charges being driven back towards Bardia, and eventually reported back to their own squadron headquarters. These, however, had been bombed three more times that morning (in all, the 11th Hussar squadrons were bombed over twenty times that day and were so reduced in strength that they had been withdrawn from the action).

But by now, 2nd R.T.R. had come down the Escarpment and were firmly established across the road. Bardia was cut off from reinforcement, at least from the west.

Needless to say, not all went as well on every front.

When it became evident that 4th Armoured's thrust was likely to meet with success, O'Connor realised that the Italian commander in Bardia, Generale di Corpo d'Armata Bergonzoli, would be very likely to call for the retreat of the Italian garrisons in both Capuzzo and Sollum to Bardia, in order to strengthen his own garrison. O'Connor therefore ordered 7th Armoured Brigade first of all to capture Sollum and then to cross the Wire and get between Capuzzo and the coast, thus holding back Bergonzoli's reinforcement.

But neither of the moves took place in time and both Italian garrisons, travelling at night, safely reached their destinations; and O'Connor was very annoyed, especially when he divined the reasons for the delays and realised that they were also the ones which had allowed the escape of the Sofafi garrison. Admittedly, 7th Armoured Brigade had lost some transport to 4th Armoured by arrangement and was not quite so experienced as 4th, but, O'Connor later wrote:

I feel that this question of preventing the movement of enemy columns at night must be tackled. I think the main difficulty arises from the fact that our training suggests that armoured units

should not be used at night, and I have noted a distinct disinclination of tank units to be used in any [such] capacity. I have a
strong feeling that the real objection is due to a lack of decen-
tralization as regards maintenance and messing – in particular
below a squadron basis. In the case of the 11th Hussars, I have
met no such disinclination. This unit decentralized its messing
arrangements down to single cars, and was constantly employed
at night.[2]

Whether the Italians in Capuzzo actually escaped while 7th
Armoured Brigade were sitting down to dinner or not, it would
seem that the commander of one of the 1st R.T.R. Squadrons felt
unhappy about the situation, for that night he pressed hard on the
heels of the retreating Italians, chased them as far as the outskirts of
Bardia and then, with perhaps too keen a sense of opportunism,
tried to rush the last gap in the defences before it closed.

'I gave the order to advance with all speed,' he wrote afterwards,
'and as my tank was travelling on the road I was soon well in the
lead.'

But again, the Italian artillerymen were on watch, every gun in
the sector opened up and when he was about half a mile from the
entrance, the whole desert exploded about him. Soon his own tank
had been hit repeatedly, the ammunition was blazing and a track
broken, while behind him the rest of his command was turning away
under heavy fire. He and his crew ran for it and got away – but the
defences around Bardia were now closed and as secure as the
garrison could make them.

The defences were, in fact, formidable, and now Bergonzoli had
over 45,000 men and some 400 guns to support them. The eighteen-
mile perimeter defences around Bardia had been planned and
constructed many months before, and kept in good condition since.
Along its entire length ran a thick, double-apron barbed wire fence,
and for most of the way it was accompanied by a sheer-sided
anti-tank ditch four feet deep and as much as twelve feet wide; and
only where natural wadis at the extreme northern and southern
ends of the defences made the approaches totally impossible for
tanks was the anti-tank ditch not continued. Immediately behind
these defences was a line of strongholds, each containing artillery
and machine-gun posts housed in concrete-lined trenches and
shelters, and each protected by a ditch and barbed wire; further
back was a second line of wired posts while between the lines were
six well-dispersed minefields under good artillery cover. Extra
isolated strongholds covered points of especial importance or
vulnerability, and behind the southern arc of the defence line there
was even an extra 'switch line' of duplicated defences, across the

most direct road from the frontier, and here also was the greatest artillery concentration.

By December 16th Generale Bergonzoli had under his command in Bardia the 1st and 2nd Blackshirt Divisions, the 62nd Marmarica Division and parts of the 63rd Cyrene and 64th Catanzaro Divisions, plus the original fortress troops and the frontier guards from the Wire. He had also a dozen M13 tanks held as central reserve and, for what they were worth, a hundred or so L3s scattered about the area behind the main line defences; but it was in the 300 medium and field guns, the 100-plus light guns and especially in the calibre of his artillerymen that the main shield of his command area lay.

The paper comparison between the defending force and those now grouping outside for attack was therefore such that Bergonzoli's reply to one of Mussolini's more supplicatory exhortations would have appeared totally justified. Mussolini had addressed him:

I have given you a difficult task, but one suited to your courage and your experience as an old and intrepid soldier – the task of defending the fortress of Bardia to the last. I am certain that 'Barba Elettrica' and his brave soldiers will stand at whatever cost faithful to the last.

The reference to Bergonzoli's beard recalled his service in the Spanish Civil War during which he had won this apparently acclamatory cognomen, somewhat devalued among the British who had translated it as 'Electric Whiskers'. He, in turn, had replied to his Duce:

I am aware of the honour and I have today repeated to my troops your message – simple and unequivocal. In Bardia we are and here we stay.

The trouble with this splendidly Roman sentiment was that it was not held higher up the line. Maresciallo Graziani was already questioning the advisability of trying to hold Bardia against the hordes of British, Commonwealth and Imperial troops which his overheated intelligence service – aided by a similarly excited imagination on his own part – was conjuring forth. How could the pitiful garrison of tiny little Bardia stand up to the hammering about to fall from skies dominated by the massed air fleets of the R.A.F. – to say nothing of bombardments from the sea by the huge guns of the concentrated and unconquerable Royal Navy?

According to his *cris de cœur* to Rome, the treachery of Badoglio had left Bardia – and perhaps Tobruk and all Cyrenaica – virtually unprotected; so what was Graziani expected to do now? Where was the promised aid from the Luftwaffe? Where were the anti-aircraft batteries he had long been requesting? Where all those promised reinforcements?

In any case, there was only sufficient water in Bardia to withstand a month's siege, so would it not be wise to withdraw all forces at least to Tobruk, thus presenting an even stronger defence to the ravening invaders when they arrived there? In the meantime, he had begun withdrawing the Italian colonists in Cyrenaica back towards Benghasi, and would forward them to Tripoli and the homeland as and when circumstances dictated.

As there exists in all armies a kind of spiritual osmosis whereby lack of confidence seeps inexorably from higher to lower levels, neither the general commanding the garrison in Bardia nor the troops of which it consisted were regarding the solicitations from Rome with much enthusiasm. They knew quite well that from higher up the line and further back in safety, their own situation was regarded as disastrous, their plight unfortunate, and their cause and fate insignificant except in so far as it affected the High Command.

The odds were never really on the side of the defenders of Bardia.

It is doubtful if General O'Connor or the men of the Western Desert Force gave much thought to the odds for or against them during the next few days, for they were all far too busy. With 7th Armoured Brigade obviously for the moment better fitted to undertake the more static role, O'Connor brought them forward to hold the ring around Bardia, while he sent 4th Armoured – now at last again under command of Brigadier 'Blood' Caunter as Creagh had been released from hospital – back towards the Wire where the garrison of Sidi Omar was still holding out.

The camp around Sidi Omar was laid out much as had been the camps further forward, but in this instance the central feature was a picturesque white *Beau Geste*-type fort surrounded, as was normal, with wire, trenches and an unknown area of minefields. As there were no 4th Indian infantry to support the armour, the attack opened with a brisk bombardment from the 25-pounders of the R.H.A. batteries, followed immediately, under the dust-cloud thrown up by the shelling, by a 'glorious gallop' by the tanks of the 2nd R.T.R. and the 7th Hussars. Captain Patrick Hobart – Hobo's nephew – commander of C Squadron, 2nd R.T.R., wrote a vivid description of the charge:

> We drove around to avoid the enemy shelling while the 25-pounders did their bombardment, then formed up in line and

advanced at full speed on the fort in what I imagined to be the best traditions of the *arme blanche*. The enemy must have suffered pretty severely from the attentions of the R.H.A., for in we went unscathed, with every gun and machine-gun firing. My orders to the squadron were to drive straight through the perimeter, doing as much destruction as possible, out the other side, and then to return again and rally back on the near side. I was in the centre of the squadron line, and in an excess of zeal and enthusiasm charged the fort itself. The outer wall was built of solid blocks of stone, and in breaking it I knocked off my near-side idler, so that I found myself inside the courtyard of the two-storey fort, with an immobilised tank . . . There were some hectic minutes, particularly as my second-in-command, David Wilkie, was shelling the fort from outside with his close-support tank. During this time I had inadvertently left my No. 9 set switched to 'send', so that all my frenzied orders and exhortations to my crew were going out over the regimental net – which caused considerable pleasure to my brother officers and later embarrassment to me![3]

The rest of the story is best given by a quotation from the report later written by the driver of David Wilkie's tank, Sergeant Bermingham:

After circling the fort once, my commander gave the urgent order 'sharp left'. This turn placed the tank facing a large breach in the fort. I sailed across it, with all machine-guns blazing, and came to rest beside the squadron commander's tank . . . Looking through the visor, I could see Captain Hobart, with steel helmet on, shooting away over the top of his cupola with a pistol. The sight of a second tank inside the fort must have been too much for the Italians and very soon they were appearing from nooks and crannies everywhere to give themselves up.[4]

It was all over in ten minutes, due in great part to the fact that the Italian guns and crews had been concentrated along the eastern side of the fort facing across into Egypt, and the attack came from behind them. And there had not been time for the lessons taught the Italians at Nibeiwa and the Tummars, even if absorbed, to be put into effect.

The fall of Sidi Omar now cleared the area to the east for O'Connor, and he could concentrate upon his primary – and enormous – problems of supply and reinforcement.

As the New Zealand Government was solidly supporting the attitude of the commander of their troops in Egypt, Major-General Bernard Freyberg, V.C., in his determination that the New Zealand

Division would only go into action as a complete formation, O'Connor could still not call forward the men of the 4th N.Z. Brigade behind Matruh, much to the frustrated fury of the infantrymen, forced now to listen to the patronising tone of their transport drivers telling them how battles were really won.

Fortunately, neither the Australian Government nor the general commanding the 6th Australian Division, Major-General Iven Mackay, took the same attitude, and 16th Australian Brigade had already moved up as far as Sollum and was more than anxious to get even further forward. Moreover, their 17th Brigade was spoiling for a fight and would move up as soon as transport became available to them, while the 19th Brigade made it quite clear that there would be something very close to mutiny if, despite their comparative lack of training and total lack of transport, they were not present when the rest of their division went into action.

But as at every stage in the battle so far, and every stage to come, it was greatly a matter of transport; this was to be the war of the 3-tonners.

O'Connor and Mackay had already met when both were serving in Palestine and had established very friendly relations so there was little to resolve between them but the practical problems. They had a brief conference at Mackay's headquarters at Sidi Barrani during which Mackay took command of the Sollum area and also assumed responsibility for the attack on Bardia. They then planned the necessary moves forward and very shortly 16th Australian Brigade was on its way:

A little before midnight on the 19th–20th the column reached the frontier wire and before dawn the 2/2nd Battalion had taken over positions astride the Capuzzo–Bardia road held by the 1/King's Royal Rifle Corps, one of the two motorised battalions of the armoured division. When dawn came they found themselves deployed on a wide flat dusty plain. Bardia lay ahead over the straight horizon. A bitterly cold wind blew and the infantrymen wore every garment they possessed. The ground was so stony that it was difficult to find places where trenches could be dug even with crowbars; soon the men learnt to look for places where the desert rats had dug their holes because there the soil was likely to be softer and with fewer stones. On the night of the 20th December the 2/3rd Battalion went into position on the left of the 2/2nd.[5]

On 16th Australian Brigade's right were the remnants of the 16th British Brigade, brought up very shortly after the leading elements of 7th Armoured Brigade had taken over from 4th Armoured. The British infantry were still licking their wounds from the Sidi Barrani battles, tired after Herculean efforts to tidy up the battlefield and help in the unending task of bringing forward supplies, and O'Connor wanted them rested and in reserve, for already his eyes were on the next target – Tobruk; but nothing could be moved for a while, so Christmas Day was spent around the besieged town in a manner not untypical of national characteristics. The Italian troops were given many reminders of home – wine, pastas with rich sauces, solemn pageantry in religious services held in the justifiable belief that on this day their civilised enemies would not attack too seriously. The Australian troops each received a Comforts parcel containing plum pudding and tinned cream, cake, fruit and cheese and there was some tinned beer available. The British received another delivery of petrol and ammunition, coupled with warnings to the artillery to hoard their shells for the main attack, and to everyone that shortages of both food and water were likely to continue.

Then on December 27th, 17th Australian Brigade arrived to release the 16th British who went back to Buq Buq, the Support Group of the 7th Armoured Division reclaimed most of their transport which had been given to the Armoured Brigade for the move across the Wire and closed in on the north-western edge of Bardia; and O'Connor, having received word from Colonel Jerram of the 7th R.T.R. that by supreme efforts the fitters had now put twenty-two Matildas back on the road, approved Mackay's plans for the attack and fixed the time for dawn, January 3rd. He also asked Mackay not to use his 19th Brigade unless it was absolutely necessary, as he wanted it in support for the first move on Tobruk by 7th Armoured Brigade two days later.

Nobody could call O'Connor a pessimistic general, even on the diet he was sharing with his men.

If the men of the 6th Australian Division lacked the hard professionalism of the long-service regular soldiers of the 4th Indian, they made up for it in sheer size and physical strength. Far and away the greater part of soldiering, especially infantry soldiering in battle and in preparation for battle, is a matter of sweat and blood – and as military lore has long had it, the more sweat, the less blood. The infantryman, despite motorisation, marches a long way carrying a load often as much as a third of his body weight; before the actual clash of battle, he digs slit trenches for himself and larger chasms for the administration services which will sustain him while away from a more permanent base, and when battle is joined, he is usually called upon to attack before dawn. The battle almost invariably continues throughout the following daylight hours, and even if it slackens at dusk, the second night will be just as short as the first and punctuated frequently by bursts of violence.

Wrenched and aching muscles, fatigue and strain, sweat and thirst make up more of a soldier's life than do fear, anger, blood-lust or death, and the man who can carry most ammunition is often the one with the last, vital shot left at the end of the day.

The Australians were big men. To one startled observer it seemed that those who weren't well over six feet tall made up for it by being three feet wide; and if they were three feet thick as well, it was all bone and muscle. Rifles in their huge hands looked like boys' airguns, they handled light machine-guns as though they were rifles and later in the war would carry anti-tank weapons as easily. A column of marching Australians shook the foundations of the road, and two of them seemed to fill a bar especially if an argument developed.

And these first Australians into action in the Second World War had something else as well; an immense pride in the traditions of military valour set twenty-five years before at Gallipoli and in France, where some of their battalion commanders and senior officers had themselves fought, together with the fathers and uncles of the men who now marched towards Bardia. The battalion numerals reflected this attitude – 2nd/1st, 2nd/2nd, 2nd/3rd, 2nd/8th, the prefix '2nd' indicating that this was the second time the battalion had been formed, the first being the First World War formations. These were the men who, despite an anti-military atmosphere between the wars coupled with the peacetime parsimony towards military matters, had nevertheless joined Australia's citizen army and were now determined to prove they were as good soldiers as their fathers had been.

In France between 1915 and 1918 the men of the Australian Imperial Force had earned for themselves a name for aggressive and continual patrolling, and within twenty-four hours of the arrival of 16th Brigade their sons dominated the no-man's-land opposite (against little opposition it must be admitted) and were feeding back the intelligence upon which their attack would be based. According to their official history:

In the following week patrols went forward each night and, unnoticed by the Italians, continued to measure the ditch and wire at various points along the western side of the enemy's line, or else were detected and drew a deafening fire from the posts. When this occurred the men merely lay still, sometimes for two hours, until the fusillade ceased and then made their way back to their company's area, perhaps 6,000 yards away. Eventually men who went out on patrol wore sandshoes rather than muffled boots and, because they might have to lie motionless for hours at a time, dressed warmly, with sweaters over their jackets, balaclavas under steel helmets, mittens, scarves and long woollen underpants if they had them. From 22nd December onwards two or three engineers would generally accompany each infantry patrol to search for and disarm land mines and to reconnoitre the ditch and the wire through which they would have to make a passage for the infantry when the attack was made.[6]

As the reports came in, the plans were laid. Surprise to the degree achieved at Nibeiwa was of course impossible now, but the timing could be masked and so could the direction of the main thrust. As the Italians had obviously planned their defences with the thought of a direct attack from the Wire at their south-eastern flank in mind, there was no harm in encouraging the idea – so the most blatant patrolling was carried out here by the 2nd/6th Battalion along the line of the Wadi Muatered. Elsewhere, discovery and violence were kept to a minimum, but a ditch of the same dimensions as that running southwards from the Bardia–Tobruk road was dug well back behind the Australian lines, and much effort was spent finding out how long it would take men of the 2nd/1st and 2nd/3rd Battalions to fill it in and which was the best method.

Generale Bergonzoli and his men were allowed little peace during this period, even if they weren't stationed in the outer defences, for O'Connor wished every man in Bardia to know what he was in for. Every night Air Commodore Collishaw's bombers were over the little port, and if most of their bombs fell on the stony desert (for there were very few buildings in Bardia) they made a great deal of noise and their splinters, howling through the night air and smacking against rocks or walls, at least reminded the inhabitants of battle's imminence.

The Royal Navy played her part, too, the monitor H.M.S *Terror* bombarding the port and its defences with her huge 15-inch guns, while on December 17th the gun-boat *Aphis* steamed right into Bardia harbour and for an hour cruised around firing at shore establishments, sinking three small craft and damaging others. But this was a sight unappreciated by the Italian artillerymen, and when *Aphis* tried a repeat performance the next day, she was briskly chased off and along the coast by mobile guns until she was out of range.

With the infantry closing up and the plans developing, O'Connor's next preoccupation was with the materials of war, especially guns and ammunition. His strictures to 4th Indian with regard to the inviolability of the contents of his Field Supply Depots had been observed,

MEDITERRANEAN SEA

0Km 4 8 12 16 20
0M 5 10
N

7 ARMD BDE
ENCIRCLEMENT

to Tobruk & Gambut

2 RTR

SUPP GRP

COMBE FORCE

16 AUS BDE

6 RTR

Wire and
anti-tank ditch

DEFENCE POSTS

Bardia

2/1 BAT
2/3 BAT
2/2 BAT

19 AUS BDE
2/8 BAT

2/7 COY

2/5 COY

SWITCH LINE

Sidi
Azeiz

17 AUS BDE

2/11 BAT

WADI
MUATERED

2/6 BAT

17 AUS BDE

Fort Capuzzo

Sollum

4 ARMD BDE

4 ARMD BDE

THE WIRE

HALFAYA PASS

7 ARMD BDE

Sidi Omar

DEC 1940

Khereigat

Map 6   Bardia: January 3rd, 1941

but he was soon to learn that they had not been wide enough in scope, and with annoyance tinged with reluctant admiration he had had to send bleakly worded orders to Beresford-Peirse to the effect that although his division were entitled to take with them their own field artillery, they were *not* also entitled to take the medium guns and howitzers of the Corps artillery. Would he please instruct his C.R.A. to return them in short order?

It was, as he realised, a piece of quite normal military larceny, though on rather a grand scale; but it had wasted time and used up petrol and vehicle mileage, all in short supply.

The guns were back with him by Christmas Day, bringing his total up to 120 to support two brigades – 96 supporting the main attack into the western border, 24 supporting the feint in the south – and when given these figures, General Mackay made the interesting comment that the 96 guns on an 800-yard front gave only a slightly smaller artillery concentration than that at Messines in 1917, which had been one gun or howitzer every seven yards; but the Messines Front had been six miles long.

Support Group had another forty 25-pounders up in the northern sector.

At the moment when 1940 became 1941, Western Desert Force, in consequence of the rapidly growing build-up of forces in the Middle East, was redubbed XIII Corps (the Roman numerals were an essential part of this new designation) but the weather in which it operated remained the same; vile. Records for the district are hard to come by, but local memory united in agreeing that the winter of 1940/1941 was the worst in recall. Rain fell in unremembered quantities, cold and with traces of sleet, filling the slit trenches with gritty slop and turning the powdered clay which had been mistaken for sand to glue; yet when the rain stopped and the icy wind continued, as it did all the time, it still managed to scrape up genuine sand to sting exposed hands and faces, and at times to turn the greyness into yellow fog. Misery abounded and only a species of confirmed optimists, such as infantry soldiers, could have found any grain of solace in the world at large. 'Who wants Bondi Beach?' one determinedly happy warrior was heard to ask, adding with only a little anatomical exaggeration, 'Sharks and sun-blistered arses!'

But it was very cold in the early morning of January 3rd, and everyone was grateful for the issue of sleeveless leather jerkins made two days before. Some 11,500 of these had been rushed up from Cairo as soon as they had been checked, together with 350 Italian wire-cutters scavenged from the camps in Egypt, mortar sights collected especially by an officer sent back 400 miles for them, 10,000 yards of white tape to mark the boundaries of the attack (too late; they used strips of four-by-two rifle-cleaning flannelette instead) and 300 pairs of gloves for the men who would cut through the wire – issued as the men were actually moving up.

O'Connor was still operating on a knife-edge.

The men of the leading companies of the 2nd/1st Battalion began moving forward just before 0430, almost grotesque in size and shape. Over their tunics they wore the leather jerkins and on top of these their greatcoats, buttoned back from the waist down like old-style Foreign Legionnaires to give freedom of movement. They wore steel helmets, respirators on their chests, and in pouches, haversacks and pockets they each carried 150 rounds of ammunition, grenades, tinned beef and rations for three days; this in addition to their rifles or Bren-guns, and the picks, shovels and Bangalore Torpedoes (twelve-foot-long pipes stuffed with explosive) which the leading patrols would need. Only men built on imposing lines could have stood up under the burden, let alone moved and fought.

From ahead came the sounds of the customary R.A.F. bombardment, for the moment no heavier than on the previous few nights, and around them just the gritting of boots on the desert, the occasional swish as they moved through camel-brush. It was pitch dark, the men following the guides, who in turn watched their compasses, looked out for the white strips of flannelette – and prayed.

Then, as the leading platoons reached the start line just before 0530, the artillery crashed out, shells screamed overhead and an area some 2,500 yards by 500 yards in front of them and just beyond the wire erupted in violence. Immediately, groups of engineers went forward, first to the anti-tank ditch where some began tearing down the almost vertical sides to make passages for the Matildas, while seven groups each of three men went forward with the Bangalore Torpedoes to push them through under the double-apron wire at about sixty-yard intervals. Behind them more engineers were tearing up mines while, with shattering irrelevance, the infantry were singing 'South of the Border'.

There was a slight delay due to the fact that one of the few Italian shells to come back in reply to the assault had knocked out the lieutenant in charge of the blowing party, but his second-in-command gave the order, the torpedoes exploded and as the wire ripped up and away the infantry charged forward, some still singing, some shouting both encouragement to each other and defiance at the enemy.

There was, however, very little sign of the enemy for the moment, for those Italians in the posts who had not been stunned by the artillery bombardment were apparently morally shattered by the sight of these huge figures lumbering up to their posts out of the gloom, cutting their way through the wire as though it didn't exist, firing their Brens from the hip and tossing grenades into trenches and shelters like ping-pong balls. Very soon a stream of shaken prisoners was trotting out through the gaps in the wire towards the ditch where, until an officer arrived who had rather more acquaintance than his men with the provisions of the Geneva Convention, they were employed helping the engineers fill it in.

Behind them, the rest of 2nd/1st Battalion were now through the wire and fanning out to the north up towards the Bardia–Tobruk road, leaving in their wake half a dozen reeking strongpoints and two artillery sangars – the guns wrecked, the shells scattered, the crews to a man shot or bayoneted. Within twenty minutes over 400 prisoners were on their way back, but encountering a new danger as their own artillery put down an accurate barrage along the wire which effectively destroyed all of it that was left, and raised a dust cloud like a London fog.

Through it waddled the Matildas, along six passages made for them across the ditch, on and through the wire to turn south accompanied by the men of the 2nd/2nd Battalion. There then followed a period of close, storming actions which must have put some of the older men in mind of trench warfare in 1918 – prowling, cautious advances followed by a swift rush when the target post was identified, and then a chaos of noise, of cries of anger and fear, of thud of boot or rifle-butt, of crash of bomb and crack of bullet; of sudden silence and whimper of surrender.

Sometimes a tank would roll towards a post and, at the crack of its 2-pounder, men would pour out with their hands up to be roughly directed to the rear; sometimes machine-guns would answer the tank, the bullets ricocheting away on a high note, sometimes to thud into one of the accompanying infantry. Then the charge would go in and the close, set-piece battle would be fought, invariably over in fifteen minutes or less. And as progress continued and the light grew, an excitement gripped the Australians which seemed to transfigure them into total irresistibility, the more adventurous pressing further and even further ahead, quite confident that they could take posts single-handed. One patrol approached a post at a run, lobbed in a grenade and were about to follow it with more when the voice of another patrol's sergeant issued forth from inside bidding them desist in language of which only the gist is given in the *Official History*; but Sergeant Skerrett had been bombing his way along the line in isolated exhilaration for some time.

Behind 2nd/2nd as they swung to the south came 2nd/3rd, pressing forward directly towards the fortified area and the port itself, marching at first through dust so thick that they could hardly see the men around them, while the officers led by compass despite the fact that it was by now broad daylight. A few sangars briefly held their attention, there were three gun positions which were charged, but without casualty for the dust cloud hid the attackers until the last moment – and all the time the prisoners were coming in, to be briefly checked, then escorted by two riflemen back to the Wire. But at two riflemen to a hundred prisoners, the company strengths were dropping too fast for the tasks which might yet face them, for from ahead came the crack of the redoubtable Italian artillery and there was still a long way to go before the port would be reached.

Then another menace appeared, so unexpected that the result had elements of the ludicrous. On the left flank of the line of the 2nd/3rd objective (which had almost been reached by noon) six tanks suddenly arrived, and at first the Australians assumed that they were British. Then Captain Hutchinson noticed that they were painted grey and not khaki, and a moment later came a burst of fire from the leader not more than thirty yards away which killed Hutchinson's runner and shot his own rifle out of his hand. At the same moment one of Hutchinson's lieutenants who had been casually walking towards the rear tank (which he, too, thought was British), realised his mistake, jumped on to the back, emptied his revolver into the open turret and raced away into the shelter of a nearby sangar.

At this, the tanks moved off towards a group consisting of half a dozen Australians guarding about 500 Italian prisoners whom they freed, sending one of the ex-guards to a nearby Australian post with the suggestion that they all surrender. As the reply was a concentrated burst of rifle and machine-gun fire, the tanks moved away (leaving the Italian infantry to be taken prisoner all over again), and a little while later their presence was reported to the crews of two Matildas resting over a rise out of sight. The phenomenon of Italian tanks going into action was so unbelievable, however, that the British crews dismissed the information as a product of Antipodean technical ignorance and the M13s might well have gone on to reach one of the battalion headquarters, had not three 2-pounder truck-mounted anti-tank guns arrived on the scene. One of them, commanded by a Corporal Pickett, opened fire with such lethal accuracy that within minutes four of the tanks were out of action, but the remaining two tanks scored a couple of hits on Pickett's portée (as the truck was called) and put it out of action before the other guns silenced them too.

The end of enterprising Italian tank crews was sad and grisly. The 2-pounder solid shot smashed through the armour with ease – but then lacked the velocity to pass out through the far side of the tank and thus ricocheted around inside until all momentum was lost, with bloodily fatal results.

By midday, the 16th Brigade were thus on their first objectives, holding the perimeter of a deep bridgehead, and 17th Brigade were following in through the gaping entrance along the western flank of the Bardia defences. On their approach to the gap they had been astonished by the apparently unending column marching towards them – and at first some rather uncharitably thought it was 16th Brigade retreating after a savage defeat; but the growing number of prisoners was proving an embarrassment to everybody and the roughly constructed prison-cages were soon overfull. It had been assumed at O'Connor's H.Q. that the entire garrison of Bardia had consisted of about 25,000 men, and the reports by Mackay's Intelligence section by noon on the first day that they had already captured 30,000 brought a swift and ironic query from O'Connor's B.G.S., John Harding – which was soon withdrawn with apology.

The men of the 17th Brigade were to have a tougher time than those of the 16th, for by now surprise had gone again. Nevertheless, they drove south along the fence line taking each strongpost as they came to it, then swung eastwards to take the Switch Line from the rear. By early afternoon they were pushing ever further eastward towards the coast, but several factors were beginning to tell against them.

They had always been chronically short of transport and so had already marched some fifteen miles up from the south, before even passing into the battle area. Moreover, by this time, the Matildas were either out of action through damage, or out of fuel or ammunition or both; only two of them could accompany the men of 17th Brigade, and those only for purposes of morale as their guns were useless. Thus the advances had to take place with only the support of mortar fire and of the heavy machine-guns of a company of Northumberland Fusiliers who had been attached to them – and now the infantry were coming up against the concentration of Italian artillery in the south which had had ample time and warning to make themselves ready for attack.

The result was a bitter battle indeed, during which only the indomitable and highly competitive spirit of the Australians kept them going despite severe losses – including that of many of their most experienced officers and senior N.C.O.s. Time and again they found themselves pinned down in narrow wadis, time and again they found themselves committed to a charge across open country towards Italian guns firing over open sights.

And again, their situation was all the time complicated by the apparently unending accumulation of prisoners. As the Australians

drove further and further in, they began uncovering the same
picture as that found by the Indians below Sidi Barrani. At a turn in
one wadi, they came across an amphitheatre with almost vertical
sides, in which had been carved by man or nature a number of deep
caves. According to the official history –

> At first there were no signs of life but, when Morse fired a shot
> into the pit, about seventy Italians, including twenty-five well-
> dressed officers, began to appear at the openings of a dozen caves
> and dugouts waving white flags. It was the headquarters of an
> artillery group, where the staff had been living in complete
> security against shell fire from the landward side and in consider-
> able luxury. There were enamelled baths, silken garments and
> cosmetics. The notepaper in the offices was embossed and the
> glasses in the messes were engraved.[7]

But this was a lighter moment in 17th Brigade's fight that day;
generally, it was bitter and grim and as the day went by their
casualty figure rose – in one sector, unnecessarily.

The 2nd/6th Battalion had, since the arrival of 17th Brigade,
been carrying out the deliberately exhibitionary patrolling along the
Wadi Muatered down in the south, and their orders for the day
were to bring them to a pitch of noisy activity; but as they were not
really intended to do much but keep Italian attention away from the
areas of the central thrusts to the north, they were not supplied with
armour (which would in any case have been unable to cross the
deep ravine of the wadi) or even with much artillery.

Despite this, and their orders, 2nd/6th were determined to make
a name for themselves that day and when the battle opened, their
leading platoons scaled the sides of the wadis and attempted to
break through the lines of outposts opposite them to attack the
strongholds behind, backed as these were by strong concentrations
of artillery. The results were predictable and tragic. Although some
survivors of the first wave reached the posts, all except four were
badly wounded in the next few minutes and those four were driven
to take shelter in an empty sangar where two hours later they were
taken prisoner.

It was the same all along that sector – not surprisingly, for that
was how it had been foreseen, though apparently the plan had not
been made sufficiently clear to the officers and men of the 2nd/6th.
They had little support and no armour, no plan for the attack which
they carried out – nothing, in fact, but their romantic determination to outshine their fathers' exploits of twenty-five years before,
and those of their brothers now to the north, despite the fact that
they were supposed to attract violence but not instigate it. The

battlefield is a place for ruthlessness, fear, anger and hatred; not for romance.

At the northern end of the arena there was stalemate, too, but only a portion of it was unexpected. Three battleships and four destroyers of the Royal Navy had arrived off the port early in the morning, and for forty-five minutes had poured their thunderous broadsides into the sector to the north of Upper Bardia – more as a demonstration to lower Italian morale than as a practical contribution to the battle. However, an attack was put in on one small sector with six light tanks of the 6th R.T.R., but a party of Free French Marines who had been assigned as supporting infantry declined to follow the tanks, four of which were forced as a result to withdraw, while two pressed on until they ran out of fuel and their crews were taken prisoner.

But the main thrust by the Australians in the centre was proving irresistible and both brigades were advancing all the time, though this was not always evident further back at Headquarters. The reports of the bitterness of the fighting on the 17th Brigade front worried Mackay's staff to such a degree that, despite O'Connor's request, they persuaded Mackay to put in one battalion of the 19th Brigade – the 2nd/8th – which came in on the right of 16th Brigade, releasing some of the 2nd/2nd men to move even further forward.

This move had, apparently, a most impressive effect, and the first one section of the Northumberland Fusiliers knew of it was when their corporal turned around and shouted, 'Christ! Look at this!'

Behind them, silhouetted against the setting sun, was what appeared to be a whole plain full of advancing giants, huge under their flapping greatcoats, their weapons held casually in their hands, their helmets pushed back above their grinning, sand-blurred faces, equipment, bandoliers and shovels hanging apparently unnoticed from their slab-like shoulders as they trotted like friendly Neanderthals past the Fusiliers and on towards the edge of the next wadi.

'Poor bloody Wops!' said one of the machine-gunners, feelingly.

The fighting went on all night in one sector or another, and everywhere the Australians moved forward, the prisoners came in and after a brief inspection were dispatched – generally under their own N.C.O.s when these could be identified – back towards the gap. Their methods of surrender varied from the dropping of arms and the raising of white flags almost as soon as the Australians came in sight, through a brisk exchange of shots before giving in, to the staunch defence, often to the death, of the artillerymen. One extremely foolish infantryman popped up out of a concealed trench, shot an Australian company commander through the chest, threw

down his rifle and climbed out with his hands up and a broad smile
on his face. He was promptly thrown back into the trench and a
Bren-gun was emptied into him – and only the swift action of the
company second-in-command stopped the immediate slaughter by
the incensed Australians of all the other prisoners in the area.

But this appears to have been the single incident of its type, and
by morning well over 30,000 prisoners were herded in and around
the cages outside Bardia perimeter, while inside it the area left in
Italian control was restricted to the town itself and the artillery
concentration in the south.

At 1100 the drive to the town was launched, 2nd/3rd Battalion
driving up across the Bardia–Tobruk road, 2nd/2nd with 2nd/8th on
their right flank driving east towards the lower town and the
headland above the port – and although only six Matildas were now
available in support, the infantry drove forward so fast that the
collapsing Italian defence had no time to destroy the water supply
plant (if, indeed, they ever entertained any idea of doing so) or to
increase the amount of damage in the small harbour over that
already caused by *Aphis*. The attackers were now in what the
official history calls 'the soft centre' of the Italian garrison, and the
results predictable.

> . . . the column of prisoners streaming back to the south was
> soon a mile in length. It was led by dapper officers, wearing
> swords, pith helmets or 'Mussolini caps', and knee boots, and
> shaven and scented. When they were halted for lunch the
> Australians, dusty, unwashed and weary, collected bottles of
> champagne from the dugouts these Italians had abandoned and
> drank it from enamel pannikins.[8]

As one trooper from the Support Group was heard to say as they
closed in from the north:

'What we want is more Wine, Women, and War with the Wops!
——— the bloody songs!'

All defence north of the Switch Line had collapsed by nightfall on
the 4th, and the following morning the 2nd/11th Battalion drove
southwards with another half-dozen hastily repaired Matildas, and
after a brisk battle with the remaining artillery posts were able to
hand over to the weary 17th Brigade who mopped up. By 1300 all
opposition was at an end and the entire area stained with the detritus
of war – abandoned trucks, empty shell-cases, smouldering rubbish,
fly-covered bodies; and paper everywhere. No army in history had
received so many letters as this one and now they were littered
about, blowing in the wind, impaled on the thorn bushes, covering
the floors of trenches, dug-outs and strongposts; and in the buildings
the floors were deep in official forms.

Everywhere roamed the soldiers – disconsolate groups of Italian privates looking for a few of their belongings or something to salvage from the ruins; sometimes a batch of elegant officers trudging along, accompanied by servants carrying their suitcases and occasionally chivvied by a lone Australian, weary, dirty and sardonic, longing to get back to his own sort, and to some sleep.

In three days' fighting, these first Australians into action in the Second World War had taken over 40,000 prisoners, captured over 400 guns and a few serviceable tanks. They had lost 130 officers and men killed and 326 had been wounded; and those few taken prisoner during the action were, of course, released – indeed many of them had exchanged roles with their captors at their captors' request. One of the tank commanders who had been taken prisoner in the north, when he had been isolated without the support of the French Marines, had to look after the whole of the batch who in their turn had surrendered to him as the nearest Australian formation could handle no more; there were, he had rather apologetically explained, about 1,500 of them.

But one of the Italians who got away was Generale di Corpo 'Barba Elettrica' Bergonzoli, who had left on foot for Tobruk on the morning of the last day, accompanied by several of his staff officers. It took them five days to reach Tobruk, and they had to pass through enemy lines to get there – for O'Connor had begun the investment of this major stronghold and port even before Bardia had fallen.

General O'Connor's supply problems were now reaching a pitch of complexity exceeded only by those of maintenance. The country through which his troops were fighting provided nothing – absolutely nothing – except a floor upon which to fight; no food, no fuel, not even water for washing or drinking despite the atrocious weather. A limited amount of warlike materials had been captured from the enemy, but against this slight advantage was the embarrassment of the vast numbers of prisoners; and even had he adopted towards them a totally inhuman attitude (a solution which, it is fairly safe to say, never crossed his mind) he would still have faced enormous problems. Some 40,000 starving and thirst-maddened Italians across his lines of communication would have proved only slightly more hazardous to his enterprise than the disease, corruption and disgust emanating from the same number of corpses.

The problem of prisoners apart, his main preoccupation was with the supply of ammunition, petrol, food and water to keep his men not only in the field, but continually advancing further and further away from their main bases. As he was later to write:

There are always two possible methods of supply which may be adopted in a situation of this sort, depending entirely on the amount of transport available.

(i) Using a number of echelons of transport to carry forward the supplies from the advanced Base to the forward troops. As each echelon has in general a radius of action of not more than 40 miles, the adoption of this method depends on whether there are sufficient echelons to cover the required distance.

(ii) Making dumps or Field Supply Depots with issue sections at stated intervals along the axis of the advance.

As we never had anything like sufficient transport for (i) we were forced to adopt (ii). This method meant that a formation's radius of action was dictated by the position of its most forward F.S.D., which in the case of the Armoured Division was 75 miles . . . in advance.[9]

The day after the Sofafi camps had been occupied, 7th Armoured Division's F.S.D. (No. 4), was already a hundred miles behind the troops it was supplying, and No. 5, set up within two days just east of the Sidi Barrani–Siwa track was another seventy miles behind two days later. By concentrating all 4th Indian Division at Sidi Barrani and putting them to work there forming F.S.D. No. 7, while he used their transport to lift supplies for the armour even further forward to a new F.S.D. at Fort Capuzzo (No. 9), O'Connor gave the arriving Australians a slight degree of security, but it would not have sufficed for the Bardia battle had not 16th British Brigade set up F.S.D. No. 8 at Sollum itself. This depot was fed at first by the Navy bringing supplies up from Alexandria which had to be unloaded by sheer human effort, for the port had only two tiny piers and no heavy-duty facilities whatsoever. Pioneer companies rushed forward from Cyprus and Palestine carried out the bulk unloading and the supplies were then lifted off the beaches by men of No. 4 New Zealand M.T. Company, all within range of heavy guns in Bardia whose shells killed or wounded seventy of them on Christmas Eve.

But now, with 7th Armoured Division and the Australians about to move up to Tobruk, two more Field Supply Depots would be needed – No. 10 half-way between Capuzzo and the Italian airfield at El Adem (which would obviously be 7th Armoured's first objective) and No. 11 for the Australians at Gambut where O'Connor himself was setting up his headquarters. Unfortunately, port facilities at Bardia were soon seen to be virtually useless (as a result, ironically, of the successes of the *Aphis*) so until Tobruk fell, all supplies for any further advance had still to come partly via Sollum from Alexandria but mostly by road from the railhead back at Matruh. What few stocks were left in the Field Supply Depots en route were being quickly eaten down, and some must be left to fuel the transport now engaged on longer and ever-longer hauls.

Moreover, as events had forced upon them all a veritable hand-to-mouth existence, stores had to come forward as they were needed for immediate use, not in accordance either with good storage principles (for there was less and less time for storage) or even with forecasts of needs made a week before; weather conditions and the inexperience of the transport drivers wrecked any system based on forethought, for sandstorms delayed convoys – on one occasion for four days – and only too often exhaustion, inexperience and the plain technical difficulty of finding the way across an unmarked, open, rough-surfaced desert led young drivers far off into wastes, sometimes to be missing for days, on occasion for ever, their ammunition-filled lorries found months later by far-ranging patrols, radiators dry, the bodies of the drivers lying ten yards or ten miles away.

Yet despite conditions of such haphazard chance, O'Connor's men had to have fuel when they needed it, ammunition in time for the attacks, spare tyres when the originals wore through (and on the desert surface, this was every few hundred miles), spare wheels when boulders had been impassable, spare tank tracks after every action; spare carburettors, spare magnetos, spare plugs, spare filters; spare sprockets, spare track pins, spare gun-sights, spare fans, spare fanbelts, spare engines. And water all the time; every ship which sailed into Sollum brought water, even the monitor *Terror* bringing in 200 tons which went straight into water-carts on the beach and off up to the front.

When Capuzzo had been taken it was found that the water in the storage tanks was too salt for use and 12,000 gallons had to be brought forward from Matruh – by road, again, which used up mileage in the battered and now-labouring 3-tonners – but some help was provided by pump-holes at Sidi Barrani and Buq Buq, and a pipeline to the tanks at Capuzzo was run from Sollum so that they could be topped up once the salt water had been cleaned out. Then Bardia fell, and although the water-plant had not been destroyed its product was found to be brackish and almost undrinkable – and there were another 40,000 prisoners to be watered; and fed.

However much the Navy were willing or able to co-operate, Sollum was a bottleneck through which only one-tenth of the necessary supplies could pass, so the vast bulk of everything needed had to come by lorry and truck from the railhead, either along the narrow and increasingly potholed coast road or across the desert above the Escarpment on the southern route. One reserve transport company was fitted out with captured Italian diesel trucks, and fifty lorries and their drivers were brought down from Palestine to join the transport pool – but by the end of December the vehicle wastage in the desert had reached 40 per cent, due in some case to age, in others to inexpert handling by drivers trained on the firm roads of Britain (though they learned quickly), but chiefly to the continual driving in clouds of dust which often thickened into sand-fogs, clogging every moving part and choking every filter and feed-pipe. The journey from railhead to Field Supply Depot and back could now take five days, and just as the exhausted driver would need a rest, so the truck would need a workshop maintenance; and neither would get either.

As for the men who were doing the fighting, the tank crews, gunners and infantrymen of 7th Armoured Division had by January 5th been operating in front line conditions for nearly a month, had advanced nearly 200 miles and played a not inconsiderable part in the destruction of eight Italian divisions – all in vehicles which had been perilously close to the end of their track mileages when they started out. Machines are rarely as efficient as men well trained to handle them, if only because they have no inborn repair and maintenance system; an exhausted tank crew can lie down beside their broken-down vehicle at night and with luck wake up next morning feeling refreshed – but the tank is still just as unusable as when they went to sleep.

In fact, of course, the crews got very little sleep, for no maintenance or repairs could be carried out during the day when action was unremitting, and all servicing and most refuelling and restocking with ammunition had to be done in leaguer at night – generally in almost complete darkness so that enemy attentions would not be attracted, especially those of the artillery. And while such duties were being carried out, guards had always to be mounted and any hot food available to the crews had to be cooked and eaten then. Quite often a choice had to be made whether to use the few snatched moments to assuage the pangs of hunger or to give way to the aching need for sleep, and many a time men were found slumped over congealing plates of bully stew, their one hot meal for twenty-four hours slopped in a glutinous mess into the sand.

But despite the exhaustion, the hunger, the thirst so continuous that life without it became almost beyond recall, despite also the beginnings of boils as a result of lack of fresh vegetables and the continual plague of 'desert sores' caused by the unremitting rubbing of sand-choked serge on sun- or windburnt skin, the men of XIII Corps were buoyed up by a sense of victory. If they sometimes thought of home before sleep claimed them or muttered scathingly of base troops hogging the Cairo fleshpots, few of them would have taken any opportunity to change their lot; they were professionals, this was the life they had chosen and most realised that war had little better to offer its votaries than the confidence of a winning streak.

General O'Connor had hoped, perhaps rather fancifully, to take Tobruk 'on the bounce' but that amount of fortune was not to be his, largely because of lack of transport. Although 7th Armoured Brigade had swept around through El Adem and cut the western approaches to Tobruk by the time the last Italians at Bardia had surrendered, and the 19th Australian Brigade was sealing off the eastern side of the Tobruk perimeter twenty-four hours later, it was not until January 9th that investment of the entire thirty-mile-long defence line was complete and by that time it had become obvious that a deliberate, phased attack would be necessary. Although there were only about 25,000 men in the Tobruk garrison under the command of Generale Petassi Mannella, and they had a longer line to hold than had Bergonzoli's men at Bardia, that line was well conceived and apparently well held. The first patrols both on the west by riflemen of the Support Group and on the east by the Australians had been greeted with accurate and sustained fire, and many casualties had been caused by a new factor in this war – booby traps. The explosion of these, moreover, often brought Italian patrols to the scene and some sharp and bitterly fought skirmishes resulted, complicated for the attackers if they were hampered by the problems of bringing back men wounded by the traps.

But every night the patrols went out and a picture of the defences was built up, including the booby-trap line running some one hundred yards in front of the anti-tank ditch. The engineers also brought back some of these unpleasant weapons – canisters filled with small pieces of metal or ball-bearings which would spray out to about waist height when the canister was detonated by a trip wire – and found a quick and simple way of 'delousing' them; so plans for an attack were laid and the date decided. By which time, of course, General O'Connor's mind was much occupied with what would happen after Tobruk had fallen:

Some time in the second week of January, I flew into Cairo and attended a conference at G.H.Q., General Wavell, the A.O.C.-in-C. [Air Chief Marshal Longmore], and Brigadier Galloway B.G.S., B.T.E. being present. When asked what my proposals were after the fall of Tobruk, I said I considered the occupation of Mechili of great importance, as it immediately caused a threat to the enemy positions in the hilly coastal belt. General Wavell agreed and asked me to come and see him the next day. At this

meeting he discussed with me the possibility of a raid on
Benghazi and asked me to study an 'appreciation' of his on the
subject. I was very much in favour of an advance on Benghazi but
would have liked it to have been on a permanent basis rather than
a raid. However, I was delighted to think that there was the
possibility of an attempt of some sort.[10]

When he returned to his own headquarters, O'Connor had first
to come to grips yet again with his supply problems, which had
unfortunately become even more complicated by the assumption of
all responsibility for his lines of communication by an Advanced
H.Q. set up at Baggush by General Wilson. In theory – and indeed
in intent – this should have relieved O'Connor of much worry and
labour, but in practice the supplies sent forward were those
considered desirable for storage by men 200 miles from the front
line, instead of supplies immediately required by men about to go
into battle; O'Connor very quickly decided that for any future
advance, all control must remain in his own hands. He told General
Wilson of this problem as soon as he returned (for Wilson and he
had exchanged places while O'Connor went back to Cairo) and also
about the plans for an advance to Benghasi; and was thus rather
nonplussed when he received during the days that followed a series
of telegrams from Wilson's Cairo H.Q. to the effect that no advance
towards Benghasi was to be considered, and that not only would no
further transport be made available to XIII Corps for such an
advance but that some might have to be taken from them and sent
to Greece.

As this was completely at variance with what General Wavell
had told me, I wired B.T.E. for an explanation and received an
answer that the Benghazi project was not being proceeded with. I
wrote in and said that I should like to see the C. in C. on the
subject as I found it difficult to carry on with the different policies
and I would like to know how I stood.[11]

Two days later both Wavell and Galloway arrived at Gambut,
and by the time they departed, O'Connor was working directly
under Wavell, Benghasi was confirmed as an objective for permanent occupation and it was clearly established that O'Connor's
authority over all stages of XIII Corps activities was supreme and
unquestioned.

I would like to record here what very great assistance was
always given me by H.Q., B.T.E. and by Brigadier Galloway
. . . throughout the entire operation. General Wilson also was
most helpful whenever I saw him, and I am very grateful to him
for all his sound advice.

This period of working directly under G.H.Q. was the most effective and happiest time of my command[12]

– O'Connor was to write later. But generals are human beings and if the practice of going over the head of one's superiors on occasion gives immediately happy results, it also invariably breeds resentment.

At 0540 on the morning of January 21st, the crash and thunder of the heaviest bombardment the Western Desert had known up to that time rolled out, and a rectangle some 2,500 yards wide and 800 yards deep erupted along the southern stretch of the Tobruk perimeter, about three miles east of the El Adem road. Well in front of the guns, the men of 2nd/3rd Battalion with their attached engineers were already moving forward from their start lines across the flat approaches to the perimeter – so flat, indeed, that they could look back and see the flashes from the gun-muzzles, hear the shells scream overhead and watch the explosions in front.

They reached the ditch – shallow here and unfinished – and while they waited for the moment of the next advance, began filling it in for the Matildas when they came up. In the meantime, the engineers went forward to find and clear the booby-trap line, to delouse the minefields in front and to blow five lanes through the wire with Bangalore Torpedoes. From far ahead came the sounds of a heavy naval bombardment on the town itself, from overhead the roar of R.A.F. bombers engaged in their customary task of distraction of enemy attention and now, inevitably, there came from in front the first barking crashes from the Italian artillery. Away to the east a battery of R.H.A. 25-pounders was putting down a deception barrage on the defence posts on each side of the Bardia road, where waited the 2nd/5th Battalion of the 17th Brigade – allotted the same type of task as that given the 2nd/6th at Bardia, but with stricter instructions limiting their role.

There was an explosion away to the right as one of the flanking platoons, coming up late, veered too far west and kicked a trip wire still connected to a batch of booby-traps. ('It was a quite beautiful sight,' someone reported afterwards with perhaps too keen a sense of the artistic. 'In the flash you could see twenty or more men peeling back like a flower opening.') Then, ludicrously, a bugle sounded from about 400 yards in front across the perimeter. As the wire and front posts were only some fifty yards away, the crouching infantrymen tensed themselves for an immediate counter-attack of some sort, but the last notes of the bugle died away and were followed by an uncanny silence.

Then a red Very light soared into the air, four Bangalore

Map 7   Tobruk: January 21st, 1941

Torpedoes exploded and in the slight pause while the commander waited for the fifth to go, the voice of a young and overkeen lieutenant was heard shouting 'Go on, you bastards!' followed by cheers as the men started climbing out. There then came one of those hints of chaos which dot the course of even the best-run attacks, with the company commander calling them all back and the colonel urging them forward, but eventually the engineers confirmed that there were four clear gaps in the wire, and through these the 2nd/3rd charged – more rapidly than at Bardia for they had left their greatcoats and respirators behind and now carried only their weapons, ammunition and a haversack with the barest rations. They wore their leather jerkins inside out to hide the shine on the leather.

Within minutes they were through the wire and fighting in the first-line posts, and backed by their experience at Bardia they were moving very fast – so fast indeed that only the unmistakable Australian language used by one platoon as it swept towards a second objective saved it from attack by another platoon which had already secured its prime objective and was looking for further prey. As before, resistance varied and some of the platoons had very hard fights, suffering casualties as a result – but by 0645 the projected gap in the perimeter defences was open and eighteen Matildas accompanied by the leading companies of 2nd/1st Battalion were coming through.

Three Matildas turned left and joined the 2nd/3rd fighting their way westwards towards the El Adem road, three turned right and with the 2nd/1st began attacking posts down towards the Bardia road at a steady and apparently irresistible progress of two and a half miles an hour. They had taken twenty-one posts by 0900 – some easily, some only after heavy and sustained attacks mostly with bayonet and grenade; and they had to leave one post, No. 62, which held the Headquarter troops of the Italian Bir Iuned sector, for the attention of the next troops coming up. These were men of the 2nd/6th Battalion (of 17th Brigade which was following in to form and hold the eastern side of the bridgehead) and before they could force this post out of action they had to bring up their Pioneer Platoon to pour a mixture of crude oil and kerosene into the outer trenches and set fire to it.

The Italians manning Post 62 thus held up an important sector of the advance for over three hours and they lost eleven men killed before the other thirty-five gave up in the face of liquid fire. It showed, as one of the attackers pointed out later, what could have happened if all the enemy had been really determined.

The other 16th Brigade battalion, the 2nd/2nd, had come through behind the Matildas and, accompanied by nine of them, pressed forward to cross the Bardia road, wiping out three groups of Italian guns on the way and thus removing the immediate dangers to the flanks of the other two drives. They had been at first blinded by the thick sand-fog stirred up by the battle so far and whipped by a rising breeze, and then helped by it as they approached their first targets; whether the bombardment had severely shaken the Italian gunners or whether they too had been blinded by the sand, this was almost the first occasion when Italian artillery had been easily overrun.

By 0910, 2nd/2nd were on their objective along the Bardia road, 2nd/1st had crossed it well to the east near the perimeter and 2nd/6th, having eliminated the resistance at Post 62, had also crossed the road and held a line between the other two. The 2nd/7th with a company of the 1st Cheshires (machine-gunners) were now following down along the eastern end of the perimeter, mopping up any lingering traces of resistance and engaged upon the now-familiar task of organising the columns of prisoners. The eastern end of the garrison was thus under control and the Bardia road as far as the central crossroads where the Bardia, El Adem and Tobruk main roads joined was strongly held.

To the west, towards the El Adem road, the picture was similar. Despite some firm resistance in places, 2nd/3rd Battalion had fought their way to high ground overlooking the road and now rested there for the moment, sniping at Italian batteries on the other side. To their right were two companies of their old friends from 1st Northumberland Fusiliers, a battery of the Royal Horse Artillery and three troops of the Divisional Cavalry, brought up in their carriers.

Into the gap between the cavalry and the 2nd/2nd came the men of the 19th Brigade, commanded by Brigadier H. C. H. Robertson, a red-haired Digger in the classic mould who had set his mind not only on taking the crossroads against what were known to be well-constructed inner defences, but also on smashing his way through to Forts Pilastrino and Solaro, five miles further on, where he believed he would find the Command Headquarters for the entire garrison.

'If we capture Solaro and Pilastrino tonight, we should have all the Italian generals in the bag,' he told a group of journalists who had at last caught up with the campaign. 'I hope to bring my tally up to six. I captured one major-general in the last war and I've now got two in this campaign.'

19th Brigade had left its start line at 0830, was through the gap well inside the timescale with its three battalions quickly deployed and moving steadily in open order behind a barrage from 78 guns, lifting 200 yards every two minutes. The men of the 2nd/11th Battalion reached their objective beyond the Bardia road to link with the left flank of 2nd/2nd without a single casualty, but the 2nd/4th on their left ran into trouble as they neared a suspected Italian Sector Headquarters just to the north-east of the crossroads. Despite the fact that 2nd/4th had been supported by more elements of the Divisional Cavalry, including one made up of captured and reserviced Italian M13s (each with a gigantic white kangaroo painted on both sides of the turret) their leading company on the left had been caught by heavy machine-gun fire from the defences arced around the crossroads and several men had been hit, including the company commander who suffered two badly smashed legs.

But it was the 2nd/8th Battalion on the left flank of the brigade advance which ran into the fiercest and best-organised resistance, and had no choice but to swing immediately into action and remain committed to it until a considerable local victory had been won. It had been known that a line of defensive posts existed in this area, but the men of C Company soon discovered that the posts actually consisted of dug-in tanks in which were mounted twin machine-guns. At first C Company went to ground to wait for their artillery to open up and give them cover but unfortunately a platoon from D Company had become detached from the main company on their right and, caught in the open, had had no choice but to charge into the defence line without further delay.

There could thus be no artillery cover for C Company who now joined the battle, the platoons taking it in turns to give light covering fire and then to leap-frog ahead. They met spirited resistance from every tank but they had an advantage in the fact that the line of tanks had been formed to meet an attack from the south instead of the east, and as they were thus attacking from the flank, each objective shielded them from the fire beyond. It thus became a series of separate fire-fights in which the Australians soon realised that their winning card was the width of their platoon front. If the men were well strung out abreast, and the last fifty yards of the attack were carried out in a rush, the opposing machine-guns could not possibly sweep from one end to the other with total effect and there would always be some attackers left to finish the fight with rifle, bayonet and bomb; but it was equally certain every time that not all would reach the target. It became, as one of them was heard to remark, 'a bit bloody rough!'

North of this line of attack the other companies of the 2nd/8th, hearing the sounds of battle, had swung west and soon found themselves engaged in another series of close battles, through strongpoints, blockhouses and more tanks, some dug-in but some mobile. One company fought its way out to the right flank of the battle (though it had started in the middle) and its leading element took cover in some apparently empty concrete trenches, only to find that they led down into deep dug-outs where they surprised and took prisoner the artillery commander, Generale di Divisione Umberto Berberis, and his entire staff.

But above ground and in the centre of the battle area, the fighting was still fierce and the casualties on both sides mounting. Three companies of the 2nd/8th were now battling from strongpost to strongpost armed with nothing heavier than their Bren-guns and some Boyes anti-tank guns of doubtful value except at short range and only against thin armour; and if their progress was continual, so were their casualties. Rifles stuck bayonet down into the ground alongside Australian dead and wounded marked their progress like a forest of burnt saplings, stripped, blackened, the smoke of battle drifting between them to heighten the impression. By early after-noon, only one officer, one corporal and nineteen men of C Company were left, and away on their northern flank A and B Companies were losing men at a rate not experienced before.

But at least this phase of the fighting was leading in the right direction – directly towards Fort Pilastrino – though perhaps the first people to realise this were the Italians who hurriedly put together the forces for a counter-attack. Not surprisingly, it caught the Australians off balance, and the first they knew of it was the bursting of shells among them from a barrage put down by Italian artillery as cover. The 2nd/8th Intelligence Officer, Lieutenant Allan Fleming, described it:

We saw several hundred Italians moving towards us from Pilastrino, led by more than a dozen medium tanks covered by a barrage. The barrage lifted – either by design or because our guns got on to theirs. The Italian infantry seemed to waver but the tanks kept moving towards our left company . . . [who took] the first brunt of the attack by seven of the enemy tanks, and for a while they had a sticky time.

Major A. S. Key took up the story:

As the tanks came on we couldn't check them because we had no 2-pounders and most of the men with anti-tank rifles were hit before the tanks got close enough for our weapons to do much damage. The forward platoon was over-run and several men were forced to surrender. The rest of us took cover in sangars and shallow trenches, and fired at the tanks whenever we could. In several cases, men played hide and seek with a tank, sheltering behind sangars, moving as it moved, to keep clear of its fire, and then taking a quick shot with a Boyes rifle. The tanks came up so close that we disabled several – even though they were M13s.[13]

But at last one of the 2nd/8th sergeants arrived dragging a captured anti-tank gun followed by a couple of the R.H.A. 2-pounders, men from one of the flanking companies charged the already hesitant infantry behind the tanks and chased them back and – to clinch the matter – two Matildas came lumbering up from the south, at the sight of which the remaining M13s turned and fled.

At this the surviving Australians rose from the ground and, in Fleming's words:

> With wild yells and fixed bayonets, the troops went for the sangars from which rifles, machine-guns and small mortars were still firing. Some of the enemy were bayoneted; the rest crumbled and so did the counter-attack. [14]

One Italian, however, made an unfortunate mistake. Concealed among a group surrendering with their hands raised, he threw a grenade which killed one of the men walking towards them – and Bren-gun fire cut down the whole group before an officer could hold back the fury of the dead man's friends. Already the Australians were finding it difficult to restrain their anger when, having been pinned to the ground and losing comrades in a fiercely contended scrap, their final charge would be met over the last ten yards by a cessation of fire and the sight of their opponents rising to their feet with their hands in the air and, as often as not, a deprecating smile of welcome on their faces.

With the counter-attack dispersed the close fighting still went on, but as the attackers neared Fort Pilastrino they came under fire from a battery of about twelve guns apparently stationed there as an H.Q. protection. Again the charges went in, again the line of defence was gradually whittled away, but then a group of four heavy anti-aircraft guns began firing shrapnel on them from about half a mile away. Fortunately, F Battery of the R.H.A. came up and when one of their officers inquired what they could do to help, was crisply told to 'Get those bloody guns up there.'

Within ten minutes, to the enormous relief of the infantry, a salvo of R.H.A. shells went over, followed by a terrific explosion which

> sent a column of smoke and debris three hundred feet into the air and dulled all other sounds . . . Later we found our shells had hit a magazine and the guns had been lifted from their concrete emplacements and left twisted wrecks. [15]

There was still some hard fighting to be done by 2nd/8th before they were in the Fort, but it was now just a matter of time. However, when at dusk they eventually broke into the buildings they found them merely a collection of empty barracks – and moreover they were themselves now under fire from a position 600 yards away; but as the enemy were as tired as they were, the firing died as nightfall deepened. The 2nd/8th had advanced twenty miles since they had left their start line at 0430, and since 0900 had been in continuous action against an enemy more determined to resist than any encountered before in this campaign. No wonder the survivors slept.

In the meantime, the other Australian battalions had been moving forward too, against varying opposition. On 2nd/8th's right flank, 2nd/4th had crossed the main road from the crossroads to the port, swept through the fire of some anti-aircraft guns on the airfield (one platoon was detailed off to take them after the divisional artillery had softened them up) and moved on towards Solaro where the leading company commander saw six Italian trucks presumably full of men making off in the direction of the harbour. He and Private F. Wright, both mounted on captured motor-cycles, raced ahead to cut them off but were diverted by machine-gun fire from the nearest building, whereupon Wright rode straight at it and, with astonishing expertise, lobbed a grenade through the window without dismounting. But the next few minutes, as the rest of the battalion arrived at the run, revealed that Fort Solaro, too, was just a collection of barrack huts, empty of anything remotely connected with headquarter functions.

It was now growing dark, and the men of 2nd/4th were almost as tired as their comrades of 2nd/8th – but the barracks they were occupying then came under fire from four machine-gun posts on the edge of the Escarpment where the track leading down from Solaro to Tobruk crossed it. Somewhat wearily, Captain McCarthy led his men out to deal with them (which they did by firing the heavy bullets of the Boyes anti-tank rifles at the edge of the sangars, thus producing a highly dangerous fragmentation of the rocks) only to find that they had been grouped around the entrances to caves dug in the face of the Escarpment. Almost by habit, the Australians drove on in and were soon shepherding prisoners out into the open; eventually, an immaculately dressed Italian major arrived and requested the presence of an officer who, when produced, was first carefully examined for his credentials – for Lieutenant Copland was as dust-begrimed and filthy as any of his men – and then led further into the underground labyrinth until he was confronted by a dignified and quiet old man.

'Officer?' queried the old man.

'Oui, officer,' replied Copland, with the justifiable hope that there would be some strand of common meaning between his own schoolboy French and the general's language. Whereat the old man drew his pistol from its holster and handed it to him, tears streaming from his eyes.

There was a moment of deep embarrassment while the young Australian strove frantically for some commiseration to offer, and in this he was at last aided by luck and memory. The only complete French phrase he remembered would do very nicely.

'C'est la guerre,' he offered gently.

'Oui,' replied Generale Petassi Mannella, 'c'est la guerre.'

The Command Headquarters of the Tobruk garrison had fallen to one of Brigadier Robertson's men just as the day ended.

But not yet the port itself, and whatever Robertson's demands, the old man refused pointblank to issue orders that the whole garrison was to lay down its arms without further opposition. It seemed that another day's battle would be necessary before Tobruk was firmly in Allied hands, but the end was certain. The brigades had become mixed to a small extent, but by the end of that first day Australian formations held a line joining the heads of all the coastal wadis from the eastern end of the perimeter as far as the Wadi Umm es Sciausc four miles to the west, from which point the 19th Brigade battalions controlled everything in a wide arc from Sciausc back through Solaro to Pilastrino and on towards the southern arc of the perimeter where 2nd/3rd Battalion held the El Adem road. According to the official history:

> To most of the weary men in the forward companies it seemed that the battle was won. At Bardia the Italian guns were firing vigorously at the end of the first day; at Tobruk they were now almost silent. Over the harbour black plumes of smoke were rising. Ahead of Solaro and Pilastrino there was no sound except of rumbling explosions as the enemy blew up stores of ammunition and fuel. Along the line of Australian outposts the desert was lit up eerily after darkness fell by the fires that blazed in the west and by intermittent flashes from burning dumps, bright enough to make patrolling difficult. Farther south a cluster of fires showed where some 8,000 Italian prisoners who had been herded along the road to a fenced enclosure three miles north of El Adem were trying to keep themselves warm. Late at night, while the line of battle was still, a squadron of Italian aircraft, in futile response to Tobruk's appeals for help, saw the fires, and dropped their bomb loads on them. The number of prisoners killed was reported at various figures between 50 and 300; the Italians were huddled together and the effect of the bombs was appalling.[16]

The Italians in this campaign had reached that unenviable state which is seen so often on the football pitch, when nothing the losing side tries to do works properly and however fumbling the winners' moves may seem, they always come off.

During the night, General Mackay issued orders for the continuation of the battle. To Brigadier Robertson and his 19th Brigade was allotted the task of clearing the southern edge of Tobruk harbour, taking the town itself and the northern headland, while 17th Brigade on their right cleared the remainder of the eastern half of the garrison area up the edge of the sea. The three battalions of 16th Brigade would be reunited during the night along the line of the El Adem road to continue the drive westward towards the positions of the Support Group of the 7th Armoured Division, still blocking the exits to the west. The 7th's armoured brigades had already left for the next stage of the advance.

There was some desultory patrolling throughout the night, and the approach of dawn was awaited with curiosity; would there still be much fighting to be done? Some indication was given at half-light, when the figures of two Italian officers were seen approaching the positions of 2nd/8th at Pilastrino, waving a piece of white cloth. They announced that Generale della Mura of the 61st Sirte Division was ensconced with his headquarters in a wadi just behind Pilastrino and was prepared to surrender, but when Lieutenant Phelan went forward to assist him in this design, he protested ungraciously that no such junior rank would suffice. He was not particularly pleased even with the production of Major Key to officiate, but by now a brusqueness equalling his own was entering the Australians' attitude and under Key's direction several thousand Italian officers and men trooped away back towards the prison-cages.

In the meantime, 2nd/4th were getting ready to move down into Tobruk itself, and in order to probe the defences two carriers under Lieutenant Hennessy and Sergeant Mills set off along the road leading down the Escarpment. They met no sign of opposition until they were practically in the town, when they came to a roadblock consisting of an iron girder supported on sandbags. Mills and his crew began dismemberment – a task in which they were assisted by two Italian soldiers who ran forward to help – and after a burst from Hennessy's Bren at another Italian who for a brief moment looked as though he might have offered some form of remonstrance at their activities, the carriers pressed on into the town, Hennessy's leading:

> As we drove through, a truck loaded with Italians was moving back into the town. A couple of bursts from my Vickers stopped it and the occupants were taken prisoner. As the carriers moved towards the centre of the town an immaculately clad Italian officer came to meet us and eventually made me understand that he had been sent to lead us to the naval H.Q., where the admiral was waiting to surrender.[17]

Sitting the officer on the front of his carrier as a guarantee of good faith, Hennessy drove on to a large building facing a wide courtyard where, sure enough, Ammiraglio Massimiliano Vietina was waiting to offer him his sword. With an unusually proper respect for protocol, Hennessy declined and the formalities had to wait until Brigadier Robertson himself arrived to accept the last official surrender of the Tobruk garrison. There then followed orders and assurances with regard to mines and booby traps, the sounds of further dumps being blown up away on the far side of the harbour and the occupation of the hulks of three large Italian ships which had been sunk by the R.A.F. in the harbour but which had still been usable as gun-platforms – the *Marco Polo*, the *Liguria* and the cruiser *San Giorgio*.

Perhaps the most satisfactory act of these proceedings, however, was the hoisting to the top of the main flagstaff outside the Admiral's headquarters, by an exuberant Digger, of an Australian slouch hat.

There was still some mopping up to be done during the afternoon, and the battalions of the 16th Brigade continued their wide sweep through the western half of the perimeter, like a bent arm pivoting on Tobruk, until they met the riflemen of the Support Group who had encountered a certain amount of resistance along the western side, mostly from men determined to escape back towards the Jebel Akhdar.

Among the successful escapees had been Generale di Corpo Annibale Bergonzoli.

The port of Tobruk, this first time through, was still a pleasant place of wide streets, white colonial-style buildings, gardens with flamboyants and small green trees. There was an hotel, some shops, well-constructed offices and barracks for the military and naval garrisons, a restaurant and those other staples of Italian service life, garages and at least one brothel.

In the port area itself were found a power station virtually intact, at least one totally undamaged jetty, many large pontoons and a veritable flotilla of schooners, lighters and motor launches. Most important of all were the two water distilleries and the sub-artesian wells which between them could produce nearly 40,000 gallons of water every day and which were completely undamaged; and if the water was brackish, there were thousands of cases of Recoaro mineral water to make a pleasant change for the victors while the supply lasted, though for the first few days champagne slaked a lot of thirsts. There was also enough of the usual high-quality tinned foods to have lasted the garrison of 25,000 men for two months, though a great deal was wasted and very little indeed went to the men for whom it had been originally intended.

Tobruk yielded 27,000 prisoners (in addition to 200 guns and 200 vehicles) and now the accumulation was passing the stage of embarrassment and becoming a major problem for O'Connor's administration. His forces had now captured over 100,000 prisoners (more than three times their own peak strength) in forty-five days, and the distance back to the Delta for this latest batch would be 250 miles, much of it, in view of the acute transport problem, to be travelled on foot. The sight of long crocodiles of weary prisoners trudging from horizon to horizon in interminable zigzags was already only too familiar, and the duty of escorting them (two guards armed just with their rifles to every 500 prisoners) a chore dolefully but philosophically accepted by men much in sympathy with their charges.

But the task of administering the prison-cages at Tobruk and the life inside them until dispatch to the rear could be organised beggared description. All too many of the British and Australians who saw the conditions in the prison-cages at Tobruk were themselves to experience the life of prison camps – from Tunis through Italy to Upper Silesia – but there is some agreement among them that conditions at Tobruk were the worst they ever saw.

At the beginning, over 20,000 Italians were herded into a cage about 800 yards long by 400 yards wide, which they themselves had erected near the crossroads to house prisoners they had expected to take; some of them must have reflected that it was rather a pity that the British had had neither the opportunity nor the foresight to take such precautions themselves. One of the observers wrote:

> There was a terrific dust storm blowing, and the limited area of the enclosure was so full of men that there was hardly room to move. All officers had been removed and 20,000 or more men were a completely unorganised and panic-stricken rabble. Many had not had anything to drink, let alone a meal, for many hours. I found 200 to 300 lying on the ground outside a small building in which an Italian doctor was working. They appeared to be dead but apparently they were acute cases of exhaustion and thirst, and I think nearly all recovered. The first attempt to get water into the cage ended in a wild stampede; I had not thought that a crowd of men could so resemble a stampeding herd of cattle . . . [We] managed to obtain concrete tubs filled with water and, to some extent, to regulate the rush . . . The sanitary conditions were indescribable. After we had fed and watered the prisoners the greatest possible efforts were made to provide trenches and insist on their use. Drastic punishment was meted out to offenders . . . I don't know how we managed to avoid a major epidemic.[18]

It was a problem which the Germans had faced after Dunkirk, with 30,000 British and over 100,000 French, but at least they had been doing so in an environment which offered some facilities, and they had to help them their own superb organisational talents; but in the empty desert, all the British had were their own gifts of improvisation, aided by the sympathy felt by the common soldier for his fellows in distress. The Australians, with something like a stroke of inspiration, organised mass singing in the camp – and to help, they even sang back, though what they sang is unrecorded. One of the first problems facing the men of 2nd/2nd Battalion in the days immediately following the fall of Tobruk was providing each prisoner with a bottle or tin of some sort in which to collect water, and then with a greatcoat or a blanket – and many Diggers spent what spare time they had searching the buildings in Tobruk for such articles for their recent enemies, thereby laying the foundations of the reputation they gained for pillage and looting.

Gradually the numbers in the camp decreased, but by the end of February others began to arrive from points further west; it was going to be quite a long time before O'Connor's lines were cleared of this worrying and vexatious problem. But one point does emerge from every examination of this facet of the first Libyan campaign; O'Connor and his administrators received little help from any of the Italian officers who, according to the records, never protested at being separated from their men and, indeed, would seem in most instances to have climbed aboard their transports and left them with some degree of relief.

Perhaps this explains why their men often lacked enthusiasm in fighting for them.

6 · *Beda Fomm:*
The Narrow Victory

'I could hardly believe my eyes', wrote General O'Connor of the moment when he saw the maps built up by his Intelligence staff of the Italian positions which faced his forces after the fall of Tobruk.

There was not much left of the huge Tenth Army with which he had been faced less than two months before, and what there was seemed so dispersed as to make their destruction in detail, even by the exhausted men of XIII Corps and their worn-out equipment, as easy as possible. Tenth Army Headquarters under Generale d'Armata Tellera was apparently at Cyrene, some sixty miles from any possible battle area, while XX Corps Headquarters – the command for the Italian troops nearest to Tobruk – was at Giovanni Berta, nearly twenty miles behind its main defences. Those defences were anchored on the small port of Derna behind a formidably deep and long wadi, and at Mechili to the south, well out in the desert at the meeting point of a whole network of camel tracks.

Forty miles separated those two points, and if British Intelligence was to be believed, in Derna was concentrated the 60th Sabratha Division less one regiment, while grouped around Mechili was the one detached Sabratha regiment and an armoured brigade consisting of two battalions of medium tanks under command of Generale di Divisione Babini; and there was very little indeed between them. Doubtless there were Sabratha units along the line of the Wadi Derna, and it was known that Babini's force was extended north-wards along the line of a wadi which led from Mechili back into the foothills of the Jebel Akhdar towards Chaulan and Slonta – but at least twenty-five miles separated the right flank of the Derna force from the left flank of the Mechili force, and it should certainly not be beyond average military competence so to engage the attention of one force that it could do nothing to avert the total destruction of the other.

As the armoured brigade at Mechili was obviously the more important of the two, it was equally obviously both the main target and the prey for 7th Armoured Division. General Creagh was summoned for a conference in which O'Connor impressed upon him the necessity for the total destruction of Babini's force, while General Mackay was asked to detach one of his brigades from Tobruk as quickly as possible and to send it along the coast to attack the Italian forces in the approaches to Derna and in the port itself.

Time as always was of the essence but some factors were in XIII Corps's favour, in that even before the fall of Tobruk, 7th Armoured Brigade had moved westwards and come up against some Italian defences at Martuba, while 4th Armoured were already away to the south of Mechili scouring the tracks leading up to it. Needless to say, since mid-January patrols of the 11th Hussars had been probing well to the west of Mechili and up into the Jebel Akhdar past Bomba and between Derna and Chaulan, and indeed it had been largely upon their reports that the Intelligence Summary had been based; some confirmation had also been provided by the R.A.F., whose aircraft now completely dominated the skies, their opponents having been forced off their forward airfields by the army's advance, and heavily battered on their fields around Benghasi and at Barce by bombers from Alexandria and Malta.

It all promised well – and by January 24th, signs abounded that proper progress was being made. Robertson's 19th Brigade, flushed with their victories at Pilastrino and Tobruk, were now fighting their way up towards Derna and totally occupying the attention of all Italian forces in that area, while 4th Armoured Brigade were circling around and making directly for the position O'Connor had urged upon Creagh as the most vital of all – north of Mechili and across the only line of retreat of Babini's forces into the Jebel. Behind them, 7th Armoured Brigade were streaming down from the north to form the southern arm of the pincers closing on Mechili fort and the crossroads.

That night, reports arrived on O'Connor's desk of a brisk tank battle to the north-east of Mechili in which eight medium tanks of Babini's force had been destroyed and one captured for the loss of one of 4th Armoured's cruiser tanks and six light tanks, at the conclusion of which the Italian forces had retired back towards Mechili. Urging 4th Armoured on and detaching immediately two regiments of corps artillery to give them increased holding power in the block across the escape route, O'Connor repeated his instructions to Creagh to see that no part of Babini's force got away, and he then sat back to await events with a justifiable degree of confidence.

Nothing of great import occurred on January 25th or 26th, and as O'Connor's mind was greatly occupied with the unremitting problems of bringing up fuel and ammunition (just showing signs of easement as the harbour at Tobruk came into use) he assumed that the lull was being used to consolidate the block to the north of

Mechili and to prepare for the attack on the southern flank. It was good that the Italians were allowing time for his forces to move into position, for both armoured brigades were severely handicapped by shortages of fuel, ammunition, food and water, not to speak of the condition of their vehicles and the unreliability of their maps, most of which had been acquired during the search of the Italian Headquarters in Tobruk. But doubtless Creagh and his men were fulfilling their tasks admirably.

O'Connor was thus considerably perturbed when on the night of January 26th a report came in from A Squadron of the 11th Hussars that a long column of Italian vehicles had been sighted making for the foothills of the Jebel some twenty-five miles north of Mechili, and even more so when, on the following morning, patrols of the 7th Armoured Brigade went forward and entered Mechili to find it completely empty. And all this with not a shot fired – for 4th Armoured had *not* been sitting across Babini's escape route as Creagh had been instructed, the bulk of the brigade having spent those parts of the night when they had not been on guard soundly asleep.

'General Creagh was also very disappointed,' reads O'Connor's report with marked restraint, and then goes on to list the excuses he was given – bad maps, difficulty of getting the armour across the wadi which ran northwards from Mechili, shortage of fuel. But this section ends with a distinct note of acidity concerning the 'disinclination of armoured forces to take any action at night . . . If the Italians were able to move their tanks away at night, I see no reason why we should not have been able to operate ours.'

He was, he later admitted, very angry indeed.

There was some attempt to make up for the failure the following day when 4th Armoured turned and frantically chased after the withdrawing enemy, but the defiles through which the pursuit had to take place favoured the rearguards, petrol was undoubtedly short and heavy rain descended to turn the ground into red mud. The pursuit was called off on January 29th, 4th Armoured turning back to Mechili and events doubtless justifying O'Connor's cryptic closing remark on this episode: 'I am sure that General Babini must have breathed a sigh of relief on reaching Slonta . . . '

There was better news from the north, however. After the first engagement by the Australian 19th Brigade south of Derna, they had pressed on towards the lip of the Wadi Derna which curled away south and south-westwards from the port and formed a formidable barricade against their attack. It was very deep – 700 feet in places – and as much as a mile wide from lip to lip; and along the coast to the east one side was continued in the form of an escarpment over 400 feet deep which dropped almost vertically to the beach. Derna itself filled the mouth of the wadi and could be approached only by a road which wound snakelike down one escarpment, through the port and up the other.

The fighting along the line of the wadi was extremely tough during the days which followed, not only because of the sheer difficulty of moving men and equipment across such a wide chasm but also because, perhaps heartened by their evident advantages, the Italians fought here more determinedly than elsewhere – and certainly much better than their seniors deserved. Attempts by the Australian Divisional Cavalry to move inland in carriers and turn the end of the wadi were thwarted by well-concealed minefields and well-placed heavy machine-gun posts, and here the Australians lost several of their most promising young officers and N.C.O.s, including Sergeant Mills who had removed the roadblock into Tobruk. The Australian official history gives a moving footnote:

> After the fall of Derna Onslow found the carriers. Ferguson was dead in his seat, Mills dead beside his carrier with a note of farewell scrawled in his diary; Townshend lay dead fifty yards away.[1]

The main object at this stage of the battle was the pinning down of the Sabrathas in the area to prevent their going to the help of Babini's armoured force, and if the core of O'Connor's plan had not gone well, the role played by the men of Robertson's 19th Brigade gave no grounds for criticism. For four grim and heartbreaking days, in cold, wet and appallingly muddy weather, they battled it out with the Italian defenders, at the beginning with nothing much heavier than 3-inch mortars to support them; and even when their guns came up, there were not so many of them as there were of the defenders', and they could not be so well placed.

But if 19th Brigade could not cross the wadi at least they stayed hard up along its nearest lip, and 2nd/11th Battalion took and held the heights overlooking Derna and the sea on the right flank.

Then on the evening of January 29th, which had been on the whole a comparatively quiet day, the Italian artillery along the whole front opened a long and continuous bombardment which, when Robertson's men had moved to positions from which they could watch it in some degree of safety, excited considerable curiosity amongst them. It could not be cover for an Italian attack up the side of a 500 foot wadi (against Australians waiting at the top) and there was certainly no sign of another Australian attack being mounted for the Italian guns to be dispersing. So what was it all in aid of? After a while they began to guess – and a feeling of cheerful certainty overcame the watching men; they grinned at each other and smoked their wet and bedraggled cigarettes with growing enjoyment.

A patrol started down the escarpment when the artillery fire showed signs of slackening; but was seen, fired upon, turned and came back. So was a second which tried to repeat the probe before dawn.

But just after daylight, a party of Libyans climbed the Escarpment with the news that the Italians had gone, and when the 2nd/11th went forward they found the entire town deserted except for a gathering posse of Arabs piling heterogeneous loot – sewing machines, tables, chairs, sideboards full of china and cutlery – on to the backs of diminutive donkeys.

Derna was theirs – and at Derna, the desert ends. From here on, stretching west and south around the Cyrenaican bulge to Soluch, was the country of the Jebel Akhdar, the Green Mountains. Rising in places to over 2,500 feet, these hills were covered with sufficiently fertile soil for olive trees and even some orange and lemon groves to grow; for cultivation and colonisation, for a high degree of comfort and civilisation to attract families from southern Italy to settle there, and to form happy, hard-working farming communities.

In Derna, the Australians found streets of well-designed, single-storey houses standing in green, shady gardens, well-watered from the wadi behind, fragrant with flowers and planted with cauliflowers, radishes and onions – the first fresh vegetables they had seen for months. In the hills to the west were the houses and settlements of 90,000 Italian colonists, and plans existed in Rome for the formation of more settlements to contain double that number. This could indeed be a pleasant place, warm enough in summer to remind the inhabitants that they were in Africa, but with Mediterranean breezes, winter rains to swell their produce and a red soil rich enough to bear it. And until their Duce, who had sent them there in the first place, sent them war as well, the indigenous Arab population could be persuaded by one means or another to help them with the hardest part of the labour.

But through the curtains of rain which at the end of January were turning the fields into bogs of red mud and the roads and tracks into churned up, treacherous quagmires, it did not look particularly attractive to the Australians. Even their physique had taken a hammering during the last few days, especially below the knees; broken ankles were a common cause of hospitalisation, and sprained and bruised ankles, cut and barked shins, blistered feet, broken toes and cut and swollen heels the commonest complaints. The desert might have been dry, gritty and monotonous, but the battles ahead in the Jebel were obviously going to be just as rough for the P.B.I. – and in the Jebel it was certainly going to be an infantry battle, for armour would be virtually useless in attack with only narrow roads upon which to move, and little or no room for dispersal or manoeuvre. On the other hand, it would be excellent for defence.

This was a point which, once he had swallowed his chagrin at the escape of Babini's force, was exercising General O'Connor.

In the Jebel were the armoured formations under Babini, the complete Sabratha Division and, as far as could be judged, elements of two more divisions, the 17th Pavia and the 27th Brescia, around Cyrene and Slonta. There were even rumours that German units had disembarked at Benghasi, although O'Connor felt that, if they existed at all, they would be only anti-aircraft formations.

Well, however hard-worked the 7th Armoured Division might have been since Mussolini declared war eight months before, they had not distinguished themselves recently on two or three rather critical occasions, and if they wished to be considered a military formation of serious worth they had better take full advantage of their next, and greatest, opportunity. Quite obviously the division could not be sent to harry the Italians in the close country of the Jebel, so their most useful move now would be to cut off enemy forces which might attempt to escape out of the Cyrenaican bulge into Tripolitania when the Australians, as O'Connor had every intention they should, chased them out of Benghasi.

Could the 7th Armoured, in their present condition and in spite of their recent failures, cut across the southern limits of the Jebel Akhdar and block the exits leading down southwards from Benghasi, around the Gulf of Sirte and into Tripolitania?

On the face of it – no; and certainly not without the establishment of more of the essential Field Supply Depots. Work on bringing these forward, however, was well advanced, aided not only by growing expertise on everyone's part but also by the unexpectedly rapid opening up of Tobruk harbour by the Royal Navy. F.S.D. Nos 12 and 13 were already in action, one at Tmimi and the other for the armour about twelve miles south, and O'Connor would open No. 14 somewhere south-west of Mechili to service the thrust to the coast as soon as possible. Ten days' supply of food and petrol should be enough, two refills of ammunition and a continual water supply to organise – say 3,000 tons, plus the water; it should take twelve days.

This time-lapse would also give occasion for repairs to 7th Armoured's vehicles of all classes, though the fifty remaining cruiser tanks really required major overhauls. This, however, would not be possible without a return to Abbassia workshops, but some relief other than routine maintenance could be offered. Units of the 2nd Armoured Division had just arrived in the Delta from England and if the C-in-C agreed, two cruiser regiments could come forward in time to join the 7th by February 8th, be given three or four days to become acclimatised and absorbed and then take part in the chase. In the meantime, in order to concentrate what forces he had, O'Connor decided that 4th Armoured Brigade should take over the most reliable of 7th Brigade's tanks and thus be better fitted to lead the advance when it began.

Having discussed these plans with General Creagh, with Brigadier Harding and with Brigadier Dorman-Smith, O'Connor sent the last-named back to Cairo to obtain permission for the move from General Wavell, who immediately granted it with his blessing. As it happened, Wavell had just received a cable from the Chief of the Imperial General Staff inquiring when London might expect news of the fall of Benghasi, and after his talks with Dorman-Smith he was able to reply that this major port should be in British hands by the end of February.

Dorman-Smith returned to Mechili with the good news, arriving back on February 2nd, by which time the Australians in the Jebel had taken Giovanni Berta, while a patrol of the 11th Hussars had entered Chaulan fifteen miles to the south-west to find it un-occupied. This was somewhat unexpected, but the following day the Australians found to their astonishment that they were out of touch with the enemy along their entire front; Graziani had finally lost his nerve and ordered the complete withdrawal of all Italian forces in the Cyrenaican bulge back towards Tripoli.

The immediate result of this is best summed up in the regimental history of the Rifle Brigade. After recounting the part played by one company in the pursuit with 4th Armoured of the Babini force, it continues:

> The rest of the Battalion followed up and concentrated at Mechili on the 3rd of February. It seemed that administration had at last been outrun: it was said that there would be no move before the 15th. The Battalion settled down to rest.
>
> The Battalion had some two hours' rest. Every truck had its bonnet open; for they had most of them already exceeded the useful mileage of their make. Washing operations were every-where in progress as far as one gallon of water a man a day allowed. Hair was being cut; vehicles were being unloaded. Hugo Garmoyle went on leave and Brigadier Gott was due to leave the next day, Colonel Callum Renton having actually taken over command. The Adjutant had already been overtaken by piles of paper. Then General Wilson drove up. The enemy were showing

signs of quitting Benghazi, of giving up Cyrenaica altogether. The plan was to send an armoured force straight across the desert for a good one hundred and fifty miles to cut the road from Benghazi to Tripoli where it ran along the edge of the Gulf of Sirte. The Battalion would take part in this gallop. There was no time to lose.[2]

There was also no time to await the 3,000 tons of stores, the organisation of a better supply of water, the arrival of enough petrol to be sure of getting to the critical point in sufficient strength, or of enough ammunition to be able to enter battle with confidence if they did so; there was quite certainly not enough time to await the arrival of the fresh 2nd Armoured Division regiments and their comparatively unused cruiser tanks. From the reports of Italian withdrawal coming in from every section of the Jebel Akhdar, it was evident that if the formations of the 7th Armoured Division were to block the escape of the enemy forces already beginning to stream south from Benghasi, they would have to move now, and move fast. Administration arrangements would have to comply, improving on the fashionable saying by doing the impossible, as well as the difficult, at once.

The first departures from Mechili shortly after dawn the following day were of A and C Squadrons of the 11th Hussars, augmented by a squadron of the King's Dragoon Guards which had just arrived in the Middle East. Their task was to 'break the trail' for so as not to betray intention it had been decided that reconnaissance of tracks leading westwards, first to Msus and then on towards the coast, would not be carried out until just before the proposed advance, that is, on previous planning, about February 9th or 10th.

Behind the armoured cars came the striking force of 4th Armoured Brigade, its fifty cruisers and ninety-five light tanks stocked with two days' supply of food and water, just enough petrol to complete their journey and as much ammunition as they could find room for. Behind them came the artillery and the 2nd Battalion, Rifle Brigade – the only elements of the Support Group ready in time.

They had been warned by the R.A.F. (who were now down to a flight of Hurricanes and the Lysanders from 208 Army Co-operation Squadron, practically all other fighters having been withdrawn as there were no replacement Merlin engines anywhere in the Middle East) that the going in front of them was rough, but they had certainly never before experienced anything as bad as the first fifty miles or so. Lieutenant Joly, in the leading troop of the leading squadron of the armoured brigade, was, in common with all the tank commanders, desperately worried about the state of his tank tracks and the likelihood of their being disabled before arrival:

For mile after mile I was faced with a vista of huge, forbidding rocks and boulders through which I had to pick my way carefully to avoid the risk of shedding a track. All the time I was being nagged and harried by Kinnaird and the Colonel to speed up and press on. In the mind of every one of us was the vision of the Italians streaming out south of Benghazi, every moment more and more of them eluding the trap which was gradually closing in.

Revived by the short period of rest [about noon], I found that the fever of the chase kept me at a pitch of excitement throughout the day, despite the many frustrations of the incredible country through which we were passing and the uncertainties of the highly inaccurate maps on which we were forced to pin our faith . . . Where the ground improved we accelerated in frantic anxiety to make the best possible time. Where the ground was again cut up by slabs of rock and out-crops of boulders, we learnt to contain ourselves in patience and to pick a slow, laborious route through the obstacles, trying desperately to keep the number of mech-anical failures to a minimum.[3]

But it soon became obvious to General Creagh that other, even more precipitous steps must be taken to ensure the arrival, in time and at the right place, of some form of block to Italian intentions, and he therefore took the decision to split his force. All the wheeled portion – which could travel just that little bit faster than the more cumbersome tracked element – must be released to surge ahead and join the armoured cars, by now nearly a hundred miles in front; so the Royal Horse Artillery batteries and the infantry, all under temporary command of Colonel Jock Campbell, were sent off to catch the Hussars and, in effect, to reconstitute Combeforce.

Meanwhile, by a remarkable feat of driving and navigation, for they had not been spared the daily sandstorm, the forward squadrons of armoured cars had reached Msus by 1500 and by 1530 had chased the very surprised Libyan garrison out of the fort, without, however, managing to capture them. Retaining his own H.Q. Squadron and the King's Dragoon Guards in Msus, John Combe sent A and C Squadrons of 11th Hussars on towards Antelat – for it seemed to him that the lower down he struck the coast road, the greater would be the proportion of escaping Italians cut off. It also meant that he would be attempting with a totally inadequate force to block the escape of an unprecedented number of enemy soldiers, all desperate to get home.

He then sat back to await the arrival of the main force, the first intimations of his new responsibilities being the arrival after

midnight of Jock Campbell in his staff car with headlights ablaze –
a phenomenon he explained as necessary in order to see the
'thermos bombs' which had been scattered across the tracks by
low-flying Italian aircraft just before dusk, and which had effectively
held up the infantry and guns some twenty miles back. These nasty
little devices, resembling Thermos flasks, were a perpetual plague
during the desert war; they were designed to withstand the shock of
hitting the ground, but would then go off at the slightest touch and
maim or blind the curious but uninformed investigator, or blow the
wheel off a lorry or the track from a tank.

They held up not only the wheeled Support Group element but
also the 4th Armoured Brigade tanks, by now out of the really
rough country and at last willing, perhaps with O'Connor's
strictures in mind, to try travelling at night. It was not an experience
which Lieutenant Joly enjoyed, though it had, apparently, some
visual compensations:

> When night fell . . . we continued the advance in the moon-
> light. To me this was a new experience . . . It was bitterly cold,
> so that my face soon became frozen and raw and was painful to
> touch . . . Occasionally I glanced down into the turret to reassure
> myself that I was not dreaming the whole situation. In the eerie
> light cast by the single red warning bulb of the wireless set I could
> see, beyond the glinting metal of the gun-breech, the huddled
> figure of Tilden. At my feet, crouched forward peering through
> the gun telescope – his only view of the outside world – sat
> Holton, on the alert, as he had to be, since we were one of the
> leading tanks of the Division. Beyond, and farther down and
> forward, I could see Sykes' head and shoulders silhouetted
> against the panel and instrument lights on the forward armoured
> bulkhead.[4]

It must have been extremely uncomfortable, with perhaps only
for the tank commanders the full excitement of the chase to offset
it, and it became even more uncomfortable later when, in addition
to the cold, a fierce wind sprang up bringing with it torrential rain.
This, and the growing awareness of the danger from the thermos
bombs, eventually forced a halt – during which the crews had first
of all to carry out their routine maintenance in the bitter weather,
and then prepare their only meal since the previous morning; cold,
of course, for there could be no fires.

General Creagh reached Msus on the morning of February 5th,
hustled the remainder of Combeforce on down to Antelat with
instructions to get across the coast road as quickly as possible; and
then, as reports came in from the R.A.F. that columns of Italian
transport were thickening on the road south from Benghasi through

Map 8 The pursuit: January 24th–February 6th, 1941

Ghemines, decided that his own force had better follow Combe and not try for a block across the road higher up.

One small force he did detach, though – the rump of the Support Group which had now come down from Mechili and the 7th Armoured Brigade with what remained of their tanks – which he sent off due west, first to attack the fort and garrison at Sceleidima, then to press on to Soluch and Ghemines if opportunity and advantage so indicated.

Now all that remained was the practical problem of getting his battered tanks and well-worn guns across the path of the retreating Italians as fast as possible – and then keeping them supplied with ammunition throughout the tough battle which would undoubtedly follow.

As for the northern arm of the pincers up in the Jebel, the Australians were by now in sight of Barce, having found Cyrene, above the beautiful, broken ruins of the old Graeco-Roman city and its port of Apollonia, totally deserted. It had been very rough going for they were in a hurry and just as short of sound transport as the rest of O'Connor's force; in theory the brigades of 6th Division were to leapfrog through each other's positions, the pooled and canni-balised transport switching from one command to the other, but in practice the greater part of the advance was made on the chafed and bleeding feet of weary men who nevertheless would not give up. They found not only their second wind, but third and fourth winds, too.

The physical toughness of the Australians and the tide of victory kept them going. Since leaving Giovanni Berta they had clawed their way along the sides of hills, over wadis, through minefields, across broken bridges, over blown and cratered roads; their forward patrols always in danger of ambush, losing their scouts time and again to the last burst of machine-gun fire as the enemy rearguards slipped away. Wherever they went they were welcomed either by looting Arabs who greeted them as liberators and tried to offer them the hospitality of their own regained lands, or by frightened Italian farmers and their families who were pathetically grateful when they found that the Australians were not going to join or even encourage the looting, and who then pleaded with them to stay and protect them from the vengeance which now surrounded them.

But the Australians had to get on – and by the afternoon of February 5th (while Creagh's armour was moving down from Msus) the men of 2nd/8th Battalion were breasting the last hill before Barce, and elements of the Divisional Cavalry in their carriers were already in the town. Accompanied by the Italian mayor, the officer commanding the detachment was in the process of inspecting this, the last main enemy garrison before Benghasi, and had just left a large ammunition dump in the centre when it exploded with astonishing force, sending a huge opalescent ball of flame into the sky followed by a column of smoke which billowed out until it resembled a vast toadstool – the first recorded time this particular phenomenon was seen.

The infantry moved in at dusk and spent the first few hours driving Arab looters away from their plunder, but there were many random explosions during the night and several stores were found burnt out and wrecked in the morning. Not that the Australians had much time to concern themselves with such matters; Robertson's orders had been issued during that night and as soon as dawn broke, the culminating drive on Benghasi would commence.

The leading cars of C Squadron, 11th Hussars, had reached the coastal road at Sidi Saleh, about ten miles south of Beda Fomm, just after midday, and their reports to John Combe were that only light, administrative traffic appeared to be moving along it. By 1400 one company of the Rifle Brigade was in place across the road with the Hussars on their right flank to guard against any enemy units trying to get around the inside of the block, while two more rifle companies formed protective screens around the gun positions to the rear, where the R.H.A. under the enthusiastic direction of Jock Campbell were preparing for the most concentrated shoot of their careers so far.

Ammunition was stacking up around them, but they were all very conscious of the fact that there would be no more arriving for at least twenty-four hours, possibly for forty-eight; as always, after the first onslaught much would depend upon supply.

The first onslaught was not long in coming. Within half an hour of the riflemen taking up their positions, they saw the head of what proved to be the leading column of the Italian Tenth Army on their way out of Cyrenaica, bowling unconcernedly along the road towards them, apparently oblivious of the presence of hostile forces.

The ensuing action was brief and conclusive for the guns of the Hussars on the right caught the few escorting tanks in the flank and so surprised the crews that they immediately baled out, while the rifle and Bren-gun fire from the infantry scattered the lorries and their bewildered cargo into the sands on each side of the road; from which position they could shortly afterwards watch some 200 of their compatriots, following about ten minutes behind them in thirty lorries, give themselves up practically without firing a shot. Not long afterwards Jock Campbell and his gunners were apprehensively watching the first prisoners making their way towards them (they were occupying, after all, the only 'positions to the rear' in this particular action) and wondering what on earth to do with them; they eventually solved the problem by sending the Italians along the track towards Antelat, assuring them that there they would find someone to look after them.

Then just after 1700 the head of a much larger column came into view and it was obvious that a major action was about to begin. Despite the initial surprise when the R.H.A. batteries opened fire, there were soon signs of a serious attempt being mounted to burst a way through the block – an apparent 'mushrooming' at the head of the column as infantry was dispersed into the sands to the west of the road and towards the sea, followed by a shake-out among the vehicles, evidently in order to bring artillery up to the front.

Fortunately by this time the colonel of the Rifle Brigade, Callum Renton, had appreciated the dangers of the open flank on the left, and filled it with a Support Company on the beach and B Company immediately on A Company's flank; so the Italian infantry soon came under brisk and accurate rifle and machine-gun fire, while the

R.H.A. batteries brought down a discouraging blast on the vehicles at the head of the column and on the artillery coming up alongside.

Moreover, some thirty minutes before, John Combe had sent off a signal to 4th Armoured requesting their presence in the neighbourhood of Beda Fomm, ten miles north of his own position, and 'Blood' Caunter, in command at Antelat and scenting action, had quickly dispatched the 7th Hussars in their light tanks, and six fast A13s from 2nd R.T.R. This force reached the rear of the column forming up to attack Combeforce just before 1800 after a 30 m.p.h. dash over rough tracks, smashed quickly through what proved to be a transport section and in the light of the petrol fires which this brisk *tour de force* produced, caught up and attacked the rear of the artillery concentrating against Combeforce.

This timely arrival relieved Combeforce of increasing pressure, for the sight of the British tanks rampaging up and down alongside the column persuaded many in it to throw down their arms and offer themselves up to anyone willing to take them prisoner. They may have been influenced in this by the large number of civilians in their ranks, but their decision did nothing to help Jock Campbell and the reserve company of the Rifle Brigade who now had over 5,000 prisoners to deal with – and a hard battle to fight on the morrow.

This anticipation was confirmed by the sight of yet another column approaching which, despite the sight of the burning disarray on each side of the road, was pressed forward apparently by the weight of men and vehicles building up behind. Again the tanks of 7th Hussars and 2nd R.T.R. sallied up and down the eastward side of the road, spraying the soft-skinned transport with their machine-guns, saving their shell for the Italian armour when it showed itself; and in this they were helped by a patrol from the Rifle Brigade, sent out by their colonel on the other side of the road, which had with it two anti-tank guns.

Between them, these two groups did a lot of physical damage, but their greatest effect was on Italian morale, giving the hapless survivors of Graziani's Tenth Army a greatly exaggerated idea of the strength ranged against them – which was still, considering the task with which it was faced, positively minuscule. Not that this fact was evident to the majority of British troops present, and the differences in outlook between the two sides at this stage in the battle is fascinatingly illustrated in a letter written afterwards by a tank crew member, Trooper 'Topper' Brown:

My recollections of Beda Fomm start with the thirty-six hour run across the desert to the area. The day before a Hurricane fighter had dropped a message (lead-weighted) slap on the back of

1 Sollum bay, at the northern end of the Wire

2 Jarabub at the southern end

3 11th Hussars in one of their old Rolls-Royce armoured cars, about to go through the Wire

4 The desert: in the foreground, an L.R.D.G. truck

5 Maresciallo Balbo   6 General Wavell   7 Major-General Hobart

8 Lieutenant-Generals O'Connor and Maitland Wilson, and Brigadier Selby

9 O'Connor and Wavell before *Operation Compass*

10 Sollum under Italian bombardment

11 Libyan troops in one of the Sofafi camps

12 *Above*, Matildas on the way up. 13 *Below*, cruisers of 4th Armoured Brigade.

14 Western Desert Force infantry

15 Australian post outside Bardia

16 The interminable crocodiles of disconsolate prisoners

17 Rommel temporarily in amiable mood. Generale Gariboldi on his left.

18 One of Rommel's dummy tanks on the way up towards El Agheila

19 *Left*, soldier in the field: Rommel signals the advance. 20 *Centre*, the theoreticians: Halder poses with von Brauchitsch. 21 *Right*, the defeated: the Duke of Aosta after the surrender at Amba Alagı.

22 Tactical discussion as Rommel's Feiseler Storch waits to whisk him to another part of the battle

our tank. Apparently it was information that the Italians had left Benghazi. I can't remember the exact date; I only know that it was February 1941, and that I had been on patrol and on guard every night since December 8th 1940. I had also been 'Up the Blue' since September and had knocked out three or four M13s at Mechili some time previously. My feelings were ones of complete indifference. I was just utterly fed up, absolutely filthy and badly underfed. The terrain we crossed to cut off the Italians was terribly rocky. As we approached Beda Fomm my commander brought me to my senses by telling me to shoot up an enemy staff car, but the range was too great and the tank was bouncing all over the place – whether I hit it or not I don't know, but some of my tracer certainly surrounded it . . .

It was now quite dark, and after some time my commander told me that we had to go out to spike some deserted enemy guns; this was going to be my job. We mounted and advanced along the convoy of enemy trucks. When we got to the end we saw two Italian M13 tanks stationary, and we approached them from the side until we were about fifteen yards away. The operator, Taff Hughes, was then ordered to get the crews out. I offered to get them out with my 2 pounder, but Lt Plough rejected this, because the flash would have shown up our position.

Taff got out, went over to the tanks and knocked on the outside with his pistol. Seven enemy got out, Hughes took them prisoner and began to walk down the convoy with them. I told my commander that there should be eight and that if he would let me put a shell in the tank where the other man was, he would either get out or stay there permanently, but he again refused my offer. We then followed Hughes and the prisoners down the convoy. As we passed one large truck the driver, who was still in the cab with two others, switched his headlights on us. Lt Plough shouted to me to put the lights out, but I had already started firing: the three of them must have been dead within two seconds of the lights going on. We then returned to the squadron with Hughes, who was later awarded the D.C.M. for this exploit.

It rained very heavily for most of that night – my duty was the second half of the guard and I was soaked, even wearing my greatcoat.[5]

Despite Topper Brown's initial indifference and the discomfort in which he passed the rest of the night, he was not so discouraged as the Italians, again the victims of their own propaganda and convinced that they were surrounded on all sides by overwhelming numbers of heavily armoured, highly efficient and savagely ferocious British and Australian troops.

In fact, of course, although by the morning of February 6th the Italians *were* surrounded, it was by a line so thin as to be in places virtually non-existent. Combeforce still blocked the road to the south, the rest of 4th Armoured Brigade had now moved in from Antelat and was waiting hull-down behind the ridge nearest to the road and on the eastern flank, while the rump of the Support Group was poised to attack Sceleidima and the 7th Armoured Brigade had changed direction and were on their way down to Antelat, for it had become evident that even the most well-worn armour could come in useful down there in the morning. On a map it would look convincing – but Caunter had only twenty-nine cruiser tanks left and events would demonstrate that over a hundred Italian M13s waited in the dip below; and against M13s the light tanks of the 3rd and 7th Hussars could do little but make impudent gestures, and even those only so long as their petrol lasted. Every Italian vehicle captured had already had its petrol siphoned into British tanks, and the fuel situation was so desperate that the artillery was now immobile, its petrol having also been appropriated by the armour. Some fuel came up during the night, but once that was gone, none cared to say when the next would arrive.

What remained of 7th Armoured Division was thus, on the night of February 5th/6th, 1941, at Beda Fomm, in the situation of the hungry boxer; either it must win or starve – and starve to death.

It was still raining hard when daylight came, and the first rush by the head of the Italian column against the roadblock would seem to have been prompted by little more than a fit of early morning pique, exacerbated as much by the gross discomfort of the night as by the desperation of the situation. It was most ineptly mounted, consisting of little but an advance by Bersaglieri units under sparse artillery cover, with a few L3s in attendance and a number of thin-skinned vehicles revving their engines furiously in the background and edging slowly forward, presumably in order to bring up more infantry support if required, or to be ready to spring away towards Tripoli if by any chance the British had disappeared during the night.

But Combeforce was still there (with all their petrol requisitioned they had no choice but to stay), the R.H.A. batteries had had ample time to check the fall of their shot the previous evening and now had a reasonable view of what was happening, despite the weather. Their opening salvo crashed down upon the bunched vehicles at the head of the column, one of their following salvoes completely destroyed an Italian gun and severely shook the rest of the battery (so far as the rather loose collection of artillery the Italians had marshalled could be called a battery) and the Bersaglieri were quickly forced to ground by the cold and bedraggled, but well-dug-in and still expert riflemen in the front line. Another frontal attack on the roadblock fizzled out, and Combeforce could relax and prepare their frugal breakfast.

Seven miles north of the roadblock was a low, round hillock dubbed by the British the 'Pimple', while about a mile to the east was a low ridge topped by a conspicuous white tomb referred to as the 'Mosque'. Nineteen of Caunter's 2nd R.T.R. cruiser tanks were around here, while the 3rd and 7th Hussars, each with a mixture of light tanks and a few cruisers, were away to the north trying to find the tail of the column to continue their harassing tactics of the night before. This, however, as growing daylight revealed, was likely to prove more difficult than expected, for the column of Italian traffic packed three deep on the road and lining the sand on both sides stretched up towards Ghemines and Benghasi as far as the eye could see. Caunter's tactics were therefore dictated by circumstance; in order to keep as much pressure as possible off Combe's light forces to the south, he must form another roadblock here on the Pimple and use every other ounce of power he could muster for attacks along the inviting and virtually unprotected flank – bearing in mind all the time, however, that the very length of the flank might in the end prove the decisive factor. Even if every Italian were prepared to stand where he was and be shot, there would still be a large number left when 7th Armoured had run out of ammunition and the Italians then would win the day.

To Bergonzoli, now in charge of the attempt to break through to Tripolitania, the situation looked much more complicated, primarily because of the usual lack of Italian reconnaissance. He had virtually no air cover (neither had the British for this stage of the battle) and thus no intelligence based on anything seen from above ground level – and since no one had expected the British to appear so far west of Mechili, few ground-level reports either. He therefore subscribed to the general view that large and powerful enemy forces encompassed him on all sides, strengthening a growing conviction that Rome had completely failed either to foresee the problems which would face the Italian Army in the field, or to provide them with adequate equipment with which to overcome them. And in this he was undoubtedly correct; eau-de-Cologne and Parma hams have little protective value against bullets or shells, especially when fired by bloody-minded soldiers after a cold night in the wet.

Bergonzoli was thus half defeated already as dawn broke – tactically blind, desperately worried by his lack of real knowledge of the situation, and resentful at his appointment as the heir to chaos. Although it was obvious that he must somehow organise a hammerhead to smash a way out to the south, he dare not move that part of his command most suitable for this task – the Babini armoured brigade – down from the north where it now constituted the only shield against the menace of the Australians driving for Benghasi. As a result, he gave instructions that whatever armour was available should proceed towards the head of the column, exploring the areas to the east in case there should be a way around the road-block, but holding themselves in readiness to concentrate wherever and whenever he required them once he had obtained sufficient information to make a sound decision.

The first group of ten M13s to move did so from a point about two miles north of the Pimple, edging out into the desert a short way, then running down parallel to the main column with the intention of

Map 9   Beda Fomm: February 6th, 1941

Figure 3   Cruiser tank Mark I (A9): weight 12·5 tons; armour 6mm.–14mm.;
engine 150 h.p.; maximum speed 25 m.p.h.; armament one 2-pdr, three ·303
Vickers m.g.; crew 6

breasting the Pimple in order to see what lay beyond. As they were
moving forward in diamond formation, their drivers and commanders suddenly saw rising purposefully above the crest 600 yards
in front of them the turrets and 2-pounders of over a dozen British
cruiser tanks from which, after the briefest moment for correction
of aim, came the flash of gunfire, followed for only a few of the M13
crews by the whip-crack passage of high-velocity shells; eight M13s
were turned into blazing coffins in an instant, and as the other two
desperately wheeled in order to escape, they too were caught in
flank, and disabled.

Before a single Italian shot could be fired in reply, the cruisers
had reversed back down the slope of the Pimple and disappeared,
never having exposed their main hulls to enemy sight, let alone fire
(the perfect 'hull-down' position, in fact). In response to a curt
order from the Squadron H.Q., they moved quickly across to the
Mosque ridge, from behind which they destroyed another seven
M13s which had moved far out from the road in order to probe to
the east. As this action was concluding, more R.T.R. cruisers came
up on the right, caught another formation of M13s moving un-
guardedly between the crest and the road and then swung across
and down to reoccupy the Pimple from the north. In the meantime,
the cruisers originally on the Pimple had moved rapidly down from
the Mosque ridge to chase after that part of the Italian column
which had crossed the Pimple during their absence and were now
bearing down on Combeforce.

Except for the fact that all these movements were taking place in driving rain across a marsh of churned-up sand – and that they were leaving behind them trails of death, anguish and fire – they could all have been part of the formal movements of an intricate dance. The British tank crews were operating against uncoordinated and ineffective opposition, in country which in its low undulation and openness resembled the Salisbury Plain across which so much of their training had taken place, and almost every crew member was a professional soldier now putting into practice those months of hard work, largely inspired by Hobart.

But now another element of professionalism entered the battle; the Italian artillery was getting itself organised and the Pimple erupted under salvoes of accurately placed shells. Two of the British tanks there were quickly hit, though their situation eased slightly when a battery of R.H.A. 25-pounders attached to Caunter came into action with counter-battery fire, and the cruisers which had gone south completed their task and rejoined those on the Pimple; but now an already difficult problem was becoming crucial, as another part of Topper Brown's letter reveals:

> Practically all morning we never stopped firing, at wagonloads of infantry or tanks. I haven't a clue how many enemy I killed, but it must have run into hundreds. We definitely had a score of twenty M13s at the end of the day . . .
>
> At times we were getting overwhelmed and had to keep withdrawing to the Pimple. One time we came around to the right of the Pimple and stopped. My orders were to traverse left and I then saw at about 600 yards an M13 coming towards me on absolutely flat ground. Just as I was about to fire Taff said, 'There are only two rounds left.' I cursed him soundly, but fortunately hit the tank with both. Taff and I immediately had a good fall-out. We had started out with 112 rounds of 2 pounder, 97 in the racks and 15 extra. Hughes had let us get down to the last two. If I had not been so well trained (I mean this), we could have died . . . I was also nearly out of BESA, so you can understand the amount of firing that I had done.[6]

Topper Brown was by no means the only tank gunner whose racks were empty, and a temporary solution was found by feeding those in front from the H.Q. squadron racks; but how long would that give them and where were the main supply lorries? In an effort to win time, Caunter sent an urgent message north to the 3rd and 7th Hussars that they must increase their harassment of the column wherever they might find themselves and whatever the calibre of the opposition, and received back almost immediately the welcome news that they had at last found the tail and were destroying it piecemeal and rapidly – a relief which proved very short-lived indeed as within a few minutes the Hussars saw over their shoulders the head of yet another enormous column coming up behind them, preceded, unbelievably, by a captured Rolls-Royce armoured car of the 11th's. This was rammed and put out of action in short order – but now other Italian M13s appeared from the north-east, as the result (although this was not realised at the time) of the Support Group's attack on Sceleidima; Bergonzoli, informed of this new threat from a different direction, had ordered the withdrawal of the garrison and its armour and artillery to join the main column of retreat, soon after the first token attack by Strafer Gott's infantry.

With over twenty M13s now moving against the 3rd and 7th Hussars in the gap between the two columns, these had no choice but to retire, and with the cruisers on and around the Pimple both under heavy artillery fire and almost out of ammunition, the situation for the hard-pressed British – however successfully they may have been fighting individually – was, as the R.H.A. battery commander commented, 'decidedly tricky'. There was no point in the 2nd R.T.R. cruisers staying up on the Pimple if they had nothing to fire, and by now they had lost four of their number to the Italian artillery; reluctantly, they came away, holding on as long as possible if only for the sake of morale, until in due course the light tanks of the Hussars which had been chased away from the north came down and they all became aware of an unrealised bonus presented by the weather. It had now become so murky and the visibility so inconsistent that their enemies could no longer distinguish between one British tank and another and so reacted as though every one were a cruiser, and withdrew as quickly as possible.

At 1300 came at last the news that the ammunition lorries had arrived just behind the Mosque.

The next hour was perhaps the most confused and critical of the entire day, as the cruisers made their way in turn back to the Mosque – and three of them broke down, one with a seized engine. Meanwhile the light tanks of the Hussars played an effective but risky game of bluff along the sides of the column, delicately balancing their act so that they wasted none of their ammunition – which itself would run low soon -- and also that their pressure was just enough to hold the Italians without threatening the head of their column to such an extent that it might lunge forward in panic, and thus discover the tenuous nature of the only block now remaining between itself and the haven of Tripolitania.

As for Combeforce themselves, their situation was now slightly ludicrous. Despite the precariousness of their general position and the fact that they had been first in action on both days of the battle so far, the effectiveness of 4th Armoured's tactics to the north meant that they had had little to do but marshal prisoners since the end of the early morning's engagement. Any potentially dangerous concentration of enemy forces in their area had been quickly broken up by Jock Campbell's gunners, and so little serious business had come their way that the commander of the Rifle Brigade H.Q. Company, worthily endeavouring to find work for idle hands, had put some of the men to erecting the Officers' Mess tent a few hundred yards to their rear where, although it provided little sustenance or comfort for the officers, it was to provide a convenient aiming mark for the Italian artillery when action did come close.

For the moment, the battle raged to the north. Although the main force, 2nd R.T.R., were down to ten cruisers, they were at least stocked with ammunition and their fuel tanks were full. But the Pimple had fallen into Italian hands by default and everywhere the British tanks moved between the Mosque ridge and the road, they were in view of the Italian artillery there, which, although showing signs of tiring, was still a force to be reckoned with. Desperately, Caunter sent request after request for the cruisers of 7th Armoured Brigade to hasten from Antelat, but communications were not of the highest standard between the two brigades and 4th Armoured had to battle on alone.

Their luck varied. A perfect example was given when 7th Hussars mounted one of their dashes from behind the Mosque ridge against an apparently vulnerable section of the Italian column, only to see when they were half-way across towards the road that there were several M13s opposite them, though on the western side of the road, together with some guns. They were just about to reassess the situation when the sole cruiser in the squadron broke a track and for twenty-five hair-raising minutes they all milled around creating as much dust as possible and a troop of 25-pounders came up to offer support if necessary, while the crew sweated on the repairs. Nobody dared fire anything lest they should draw attention to themselves – but now their luck returned and the enemy column ignored them completely.

By 1500, it was obvious that the crisis of the battle was approaching. Up to the north, 7th Hussars had now found the tail of the column and were again chewing it up piecemeal; 3rd Hussars had been caught by a concentration of M13s coming down the eastern flank, about mid-column, and had been ordered to remain in contact with the enemy – not to withdraw and let them through but to try to hold them by bluff and manoeuvre; the R.H.A. battery were in trouble as their forward observation post had been hit; the remaining tanks of the 2nd R.T.R. had been foiled in an attempt to get around the front of the column and try to attack the Pimple from the other side, and were grimly assessing their chances of knocking out the now-dominating artillery on it by a frontal charge.

It began to look very much as though, despite all the damage they had done, 4th Armoured's cordon would be burst by the sheer weight of the Italian column which would then lurch on through the Combeforce roadblock and away to the open spaces beyond – leaving 7th Armoured Division to face O'Connor's annoyance yet again. The likelihood of this outcome was increased by the arrival at last of 7th Armoured Brigade's commanding officer at Caunter's H.Q. – in a staff car but with no radio. He was thus unable, even when he eventually appreciated the seriousness of the position, to communicate with his forces, still making their painful way across the broken country from Antelat.

Already Combeforce was in danger. Many Italian units had attempted to bypass the Rifle Brigade lines by crossing westwards through the dunes and slipping past along the edge of the sea, and as the head of the main Italian column closed down towards them, the riflemen's attention was held more and more to their front and away from the flank by which more groups of Italians managed to escape. True, these were only small groups – but it was all too possible that the trickle could become a stream and the stream a torrent. The only place the battle could be won by the British was to the north.

Here, the action was reaching crisis-point. The Hussars had been inevitably driven back towards the Pimple, the 2nd R.T.R. were edging in towards it, drawn by an almost centripetal force in spite of the suicidal effect that a frontal, uphill charge against the Italian guns would have for them; and all around the sound and fury of battle echoed back and forth, the smoke and din and drifting sand confusing the vision, terrifying those on the periphery of the action, infuriating those within it.

Then, at last, two new elements joined. Away to the north, the cruisers and light tanks of 7th Armoured Brigade, having driven to the sound of the guns, came over the last ridge and lumbered down to take the pressure off the Hussars and drive the M13s there westwards back through their own column which, denied the protection of their tanks, was then thoroughly torn apart by the new arrivals and the rejoicing Hussars.

And with their observation post at last back in communication, the gunners on the Mosque ridge were suddenly touched by inspiration and blanketed the Pimple with so accurate a concentration of fire that when a brief lull fell, the overjoyed but rather shaken observers in the British tanks could see that the Italian artillery had been completely wiped out. Within ten minutes, the nearest R.T.R. squadron – now reduced to but four tanks – was in command of the Pimple again, and the battle paused while both sides adjusted to yet another tactical change.

But the overall situation remained the same. Despite the access of power to the British now that the cruisers of 7th Armoured Brigade had come up, they were still facing overwhelming numbers of enemy troops who, however battered they might be, still wanted desperately to get away to the south and had not yet given up hope of doing so. Moreover, the M13s which had been driven by the cruisers through the column to the north had not been destroyed and were now coming down to the Pimple – but on the western side of the road, a direction from which the tired and already over-strained British tank crews were not expecting them.

The Pimple changed hands yet again just before 1800 on the 6th, the three remaining R.T.R. cruisers limping away to the Mosque ridge under cover of the R.H.A.'s fire, again with nearly empty ammunition racks, and leaving one of their number gutted and burnt out. Fortunately, more supply lorries had now arrived and, perhaps even more fortunately, the early desert dusk was upon them. The men of 4th Armoured concentrated around the Mosque, wearily stacked more shells and bullets aboard their battered hulls, the fitters wrestled exhaustedly with vastly overstrained and wrenched tracks, everyone helped with the refuelling of men and machines, and then with the exception of the sentries all fell into varying degrees of coma – while the 7th Armoured Brigade held the ring.

The armour had been holding the ring in the south all day; in the north, the Australians had been closing it. Since well before dawn, with Barce safely in their hands, they had been driving forward against varying opposition. Alan Moorehead was with them during their advance through the Jebel:

A kind of frenzy possessed the Australians now in their utter determination to have Benghazi at once. I cannot conceive that anything would have stopped them from that Wednesday night on. But now hail and rain came that turned the countryside into red mud and slush. Every few kilometres the tracks were blown away by the Italian rearguard, which was fighting only for time and still more time in which to organize and make a stand. Australian engineers slaved at the head of the column until men in their ranks were forced to drop out through sheer exhaustion, while others came forward to take their places. Soon it developed into a contest between the engineers and the squads of Italian minelayers and dynamiters. All that first day after Barce, while the storm still gathered force, the Australians kept flinging boulders into craters along the roads or breaking open new roads along the goat tracks. Kilometre by kilometre – yard by yard sometimes – the troops moved forward. It was a forty-mile-long column of vehicles that crashed over tank-traps and plunged headlong into valleys and across ruined gaps in the railway line. Nowhere could the Italians destroy the way sufficiently to hold them more than an hour or two . . . [7]

Throughout the whole of that day, while 4th Armoured Brigade were hanging on desperately around Beda Fomm, the Australians moved forward. 'Push on! Push on!' was the order everywhere and no one needed further spurring, however exhausted he felt, however hungry or thirsty. Whenever the men paused for a bite or a brew-up of tea, they found themselves surrounded yet again by the incredible disorder of incontinent retreat – the same tangle of gorgeous uniforms, broken swords and abandoned offices and quarters, the same shambles of half-eaten meals, half-emptied wardrobes, rifled cellars; and all the time columns of weary and disheartened prisoners trudged back past them, incredulous at the array of vehicles, however battered, possessed by this enemy they had been so frequently assured was a broken power, old, out-of-date and unprepared for war.

One of their most frequently expressed bewilderments was that anyone should want to fight in such appalling weather, anyway.

El Abiar was entered by the Australians unopposed; then there was a bad hold-up on the icy, treacherous slope of a hill, another detour on a hastily buttressed goat-track, a stretch of road flanked by the chaos of bombed-out railyards; then the brow of another hill and at last a long line of roof-tops by the sea with smoke drifting across from a fire in the middle – Benghasi. It had been a long trip – 500 miles from Cairo, 400 miles from Sidi Barrani – fighting all the way.

Just before dusk, the first Australians drove into the town with an escort of carriers and were greeted by a huge crowd of Greeks, Jews and Arabs (together with what afterwards proved to be a large contingent of Italian soldiers who had judiciously demobilised themselves during the preceding hour), who clapped and cheered and referred to them in the speeches which followed as 'Our Brave Allies' – somewhat to the surprise of those who listened.

Brigadier Robertson had sent a message to the mayor that he intended to enter the town the following morning and that he expected the Italian authorities to keep order until then; and he also issued orders to the commander of the 2nd/11th Battalion to take under his command a squadron of the 6th Cavalry, four armoured cars, a battery of field guns and a troop of anti-tank guns, and get them and his men down towards Ghemines and whatever lay beyond as quickly as possible.

During the night, Combeforce had little to deal with except patrol activity and an attempt by some more M13s to slip by along the seaward flank. Callum Renton's riflemen dealt with these problems efficiently, driving the Italian skirmishers to ground and bagging a brace of M13s when one of their platoon sergeant-majors and a rifleman ran down close on them and fired in through the drivers' slits; but all were aware of the fact that dawn on February 7th would bring their greatest test. They were very cold, thirsty and hungry, but if their morale was reduced from its high peak of a few days before by the evident numerical odds now against them, it also received a solid buttressing from the harsh realities of the situation itself.

There was nowhere for Combeforce to go, for a retreat would sweep them deeper into enemy territory; anyway, with the only petrol which had come their way going to the R.H.A., the infantry still had no choice but to stay where they were and fight it out.

Such practicalities breed resolution and when the Italian artillery opened up on the British lines as soon as the light was strong enough to see the fall of shot, the riflemen huddled deep into their slit trenches and waited, listening to the crash of shell around them and to the scream of sliver and shrapnel above. Then came the roar of engines as some thirty M13s approached, the sharp exchange of fire between the tanks and their own portée'd anti-tank guns, and as the tanks passed through their forward positions, the riflemen rose from their trenches and the infantry battle opened.

Behind them the anti-tank guns were suffering casualties and being pressed further and further back, as the M13s lunged forward and the Italian artillery concentrated against the guns with their customary efficiency. Desperately, the R.H.A. battery commanders to the rear asked for and received permission to fire on the Italian tanks although they were now well into the British lines.

The whole area of Combeforce was now a battlefield with M13s trading shot for shot with the anti-tank guns in this culminating drive towards the escape route, infantry fighting it out in vicious close-quarter mêlées and the artillery on both sides shooting into the growing murk of battle with more hope than certainty that their aim was directed at enemies and not friends. Now, in this cauldron of growing turmoil – almost the perfect illustration of the chaos of battle – the only element which might rescue the result from the random decision of blind fortune was professionalism. As tank after tank was hit, as gun-crew after gun-crew was wiped out, as battery after battery ceased fire in the face of the total obscurity which cloaked the field, it came down to the cold proficiency of the men engulfed in the close confines of the battle itself.

Gradually, the Italian tanks pushed forward, overrunning more rifle platoons huddled in their trenches, seeing the British anti-tank guns overturned, their portées wrecked or blazing, the white mess-tent which had been their target coming closer minute by minute; and although their own numbers were down to five, surely the break-out must be theirs in but a little longer.

The R.H.A. Anti-tank Battery commander, Major Burton, was coming to the same conclusion as he watched the crew of his last gun wiped out by machine-gun fire which, however, left gun and portée undamaged. Collecting his batman and the battery cook, he reached the gun, drove it briefly into the shelter of a dune while he checked the traversing and elevating wheels, the sights and ammunition, and then came out on the flank of the last Italian tanks as they drove for the mess-tent and the centre of the defence positions.

He must have been an extraordinarily good gunner. Within the next few minutes, he and his scratch crew accounted for the last five M13s in a fury of fire which blew one tank turret off its chassis, wrecked the bogey-wheels and tracks of three more and killed the driver of the fifth who had by then driven his tank to within a few yards of the mess-tent; and when Burton looked quickly around to see where danger next threatened, all that met his eyes were Renton's riflemen rising up out of the ground to chase after the rapidly retreating Italian and Libyan infantry who had escorted the M13s on their last gallant charge.

And it *was* the last, for the 7th and 4th Armoured Brigades, refuelled, recuperated and with their ammunition racks full, were again threatening the flanks of Bergonzoli's main column and finding nothing much left to stand against them except the exhausted and now demoralised Italian artillery.

Such was the fact, though not apparently the appearance. Lieutenant Joly had been watching the Combeforce battle:

> For a time there was silence on both sides. For all the efforts of the previous day, the Italian column still looked huge and threatening. I watched with apprehension the movements of the mass of vehicles before me. On either side of me, hidden behind the crests of other dunes and ridges, I knew that there were other eyes just as anxious as mine, surveying the scene before them. In the mind of each one of us was the sure knowledge that we were well outnumbered. Each of us knew by what slim margin we still held dominance over the battlefield. Our threat was but a façade

– behind us there were no more reserves of further troops. Even the supplies of the very sinews which could keep us going had almost run out. If we lost now we were faced with capture or a hopeless retreat into the empty distances of the inner desert. It was a sobering thought. I felt that the day, with all its black, wet dullness, was heavy with ominous foreboding. The scene before me was made gloomy enough to match my mood by the black clouds of acrid smoke which shrouded the battlefield like a brooding pall.

Gradually I became aware of a startling change. First one and then another white flag appeared in the host of vehicles. More and more became visible, until the whole column was a forest of waving white banners.[8]

Not able to believe their eyes, the tank crews for some time thought that it might be a trap; but the Italian Tenth Army had had enough and was laying down its weapons. Groups of Italians of all ranks and of all arms walked out towards the British tanks with their hands in the air, while the British crews, with good reason but an apparent lack of good manners, ignored them and drove quickly through their uncertain ranks towards the main body of vehicles and guns behind them, to disarm and marshal those Italians who had preferred to remain in the column.

The scene which therefore met the eyes of Robertson's Australians, now arriving just south of Ghemines, was that of a film director's battlefield. For a stretch of some fifteen miles the desert bordering the road was littered with the debris of battle – overturned lorries and trucks, abandoned Fiat staff cars and runabouts, field-guns with their barrels splayed out and drooping like banana-skins, or occasionally just left, their barrels pointing nowhere, in perfect condition but usually with broken or empty racks. Dozens of dark green tanks lined the roads, often blackened by fire, sometimes empty but too often still the grim coffins of charred and twisted bodies; rifles, machine-guns, ammunition and grenades were everywhere, boxes of food, torn blankets, bedraggled clothing lay in heaps where it had been thrown by overturned lorries and further disarrayed by disconsolate men providing themselves with some degree of warmth and sustenance for the trials to come.

On every side, the scene was of dank desolation. Rain lanced down in fitful showers, enough to turn the clay to mud but not enough to keep down the sand or put out the smouldering fires which sent black stains of oily smoke drifting along the line of misery and hopelessness. Even the victors were affected, their first surge of relief at the realisation that battle was over for the time being dispersed, their thirst and hunger still with them even if they had found water or food, still desperately tired and now depressed by the dirt, the dead, the dying, the dispossessed.

The immediate taste of victory is very sour.

Generale Tellera, who had commanded the fighting during this last battle, had been wounded during one of the tank skirmishes and died during the day; but scores of colonels and brigadiers were collected and taken to a farmhouse in the drab village of Soluch, together with the captured generals – Generale di Corpo Cona who had taken over when Tellera was wounded; Generale di Divisione Bignani who had commanded at Sceleidima; Generale di Corpo Villanis who at least had some reason to be proud for he had commanded the Italian artillery; Generale di Divisione Negroni; Generale di Divisione Bardini; Generale di Divisione Giuliano; and in the yard outside, Alan Moorehead found a soft-spoken, swarthy little man, wrapped in a blanket for he was ill, his neat, silvery beard parted as usual immaculately in the middle. 'Barba Elettrica' was caught at last.

'You were here too soon, that is all,' he replied to the questions put to him. 'But we gave battle at once . . . And always, here as everywhere else, we were grossly outnumbered. So when our second attack was unable to prevail we had no choice but to make an honourable surrender.'

Two days later, he was flown to Cairo on a stretcher and taken to hospital suffering from suspected appendicitis. He thus had no opportunity then of talking to General O'Connor, who might have disabused him of some of his illusions.

To O'Connor, the moment was obviously one of relief and triumph, and also one of concern and doubt for the future. Where would they go from here?

He and Dorman-Smith had spent the day of the main battle between Corps Headquarters and Msus, aware that all now lay in the hands of the fighting men and that there was nothing, for the moment, for them to do. After breakfasting on a cold sausage each on the morning of February 7th, they drove on to Creagh's head-quarters, arriving at about 0900, just in time to be greeted with the news of the Italian surrender all along the line. After checking the details to an extent which later allowed him to write, 'I think this may be termed a complete victory as none of the enemy escaped,' O'Connor turned to Dorman-Smith and said, 'We'd better send a message to Archie. What shall we say?'*

Between them they concocted a signal, redolent of the close, county-family atmosphere of dogs and horses, of large houses, of trim lawns and open fields in which all three of them, and indeed

*First quoted in *The Desert Generals* by Correlli Barnett (London), p. 56.

the majority of British Army officers, had grown up and to which they hoped to return.

'Fox killed in the open . . . ' it began, and was sent in clear for Mussolini's benefit, though whether Il Duce understood the reference is unlikely.

They then went forward to review the battlefield and were as shaken by the scene as the others who came across it unprepared. Another 25,000 prisoners milled about awaiting collection and organisation; over 100 M13s were counted around Beda Fomm, some of them completely wrecked and burnt out, some totally undamaged and the majority recoverable; no one bothered to take a tally of the light tanks, but there were some 200 guns and over 1,500 wheeled vehicles in various states of serviceability – and as O'Connor would need every one of them if he obtained permission to press on with the advance towards Tripoli, one of the first orders he gave that day was to Strafer Gott to move north and halt the main Australian advance down to the battlefield, in case they felt inclined to help themselves to too much of it.

Another problem which faced O'Connor (but which he quickly passed for solution to one of his subordinates) was presented by a busload of Italian ladies powdering their noses and brewing tea in the middle of the battlefield, protected by a lone priest in a soutane – 'a highly inappropriate figure', as Dorman-Smith commented.

In all, O'Connor's command – first the Western Desert Force and then XIII Corps – had advanced 500 miles in ten weeks, from Sidi Barrani and Nibeiwa to Beda Fomm, during which time it had totally destroyed the Italian Tenth Army, capturing 130,000 prisoners, 180 medium tanks and well over 300 light tanks, 845 pieces of artillery, and killing and destroying uncounted numbers more. As for soft-skinned, wheeled vehicles, the tally will never be known.

But the count of British losses was quickly made. Over 80 per cent of the tracked and wheeled vehicles in which they had ridden to battle had either been destroyed or were now too worn for much further use, and of the remainder only the armoured cars of the King's Dragoon Guards which had joined at Mechili had not grossly exceeded their service mileage – indeed, practically all original Western Desert Force transport was written off when eventually it got back to the workshops. The guns of the R.H.A. batteries, however, remained with them until replacements came out, or the batteries were re-formed.

As for the human casualties, in these ten weeks 500 British and Australians had been killed, 1,373 wounded and 55 were missing, later posted 'believed killed'.

It was certainly a moment for celebration, and as the morning progressed and food and drink became available, a festive note was struck. About mid-morning, O'Connor and Dorman-Smith found their way to the Combeforce area where the Rifle Brigade Officers' Mess was at last in some form of operation, 'like rather badly-organised catering at a point-to-point' as Colonel Renton put it, continuing the strain of sporting metaphor. Later O'Connor visited the farm at Soluch and talked to Italian generals there, his corduroy trousers, leather jerkin, tartan scarf and battered officer's cap in some contrast to the continuing immaculacy (complete with spurs) of his prisoners.

'I'm sorry you are so uncomfortable,' he apologised. 'We haven't had much time to make proper arrangements.'

'Thank you very much,' Generale Cona replied politely. 'We do realise you came here in a very great hurry.'*

Sympathy is catching.

The situation which now faced O'Connor required decisions on both a tactical and a strategic level; the tactical ones he would take himself but the most vital – whether to press on into Tripolitania and perhaps even further to Tunisia, thus ridding the whole of the North African coastline of Axis troops – must be referred to a higher command. Surely Wavell would realise the immense opportunities now open to XIII Corps, and appreciate the wave of enthusiasm and confidence which now swept through them all as rest, relaxation, and the awareness of achievement overcame the effects of battle fatigue? Within thirty-six hours of the surrender of Tenth Army, O'Connor's men were raring to go – no Italian force could hold from Tripoli the men who had stormed into Benghasi.

No Italian force was in fact making much of an effort even to regroup. Scarcely had the noise of battle died down in front of Combeforce before C Squadron of the 11th Hussars was re-forming and driving south along the coast road to Agedabia, where two troops under command of Second Lieutenant Crankshaw took the surrender of the garrison, including the colonel of one of the Italian light tank regiments who had managed to slip past Combeforce during the previous day, but then got his tanks stuck in the salt-pans. He was most affable, spoke perfect English and was anxious for news of friends in the 12th Lancers with whom, apparently, he had spent many enjoyable weeks hunting in Leicestershire.

Hastily handing over the prisoners to the Rifle Brigade company which followed them up (O'Connor had detached the whole of the Support Group as quickly as possible and sent them forward, leaving the rest of 7th Armoured to clear the battlefield and instructing General Mackay to employ his Australians on getting

*First quoted in *The Desert Generals* by Correlli Barnett (London), p. 57.

Benghasi harbour and town ready for use as an advance supply port and base as quickly as possible), the Hussars moved out that afternoon, rendezvoused with B Squadron the following day, and in driving rain moved on to the fort and barracks of El Agheila marking the border between Cyrenaica and Tripolitania.

Wet, cold, weary, but immensely grateful for this almost forgotten luxury of a night in dry bedding under a stout roof upon which the rain was drumming, officers and men were about to turn in when the guard commander announced the approach of two mounted figures who, when challenged, revealed themselves as a Libyan sergeant-major and his orderly. There were, according to the interpreter, some 400 Libyan cavalrymen in the sand-dunes around them complete with weapons and mounts (but minus their officers, for these had departed for Tripoli) and would the Englishmen be so kind as to come out and accept their surrender?

There was a resigned pause while a hundred or so half-undressed Hussars awaited the verdict, distastefully regarding the prospect of sorting out yet another large batch of prisoners in pitch dark and pouring rain. Then, to their enormous relief, they heard John Combe say, 'Tell them to come back again in the morning,' adding sternly, 'and if they don't, they'll all be shot!'

Punctually at ten o'clock the following morning, a strange assortment rode up, some on horses, some on camels. Most of them were Libyan, but there were about twenty Italians including an air force officer and some sailors; there was also an Arab lady of indeterminate status, but by this time it was impossible to surprise the Hussars.

That afternoon, their first patrols drove some ten miles into Tripolitania where the only sign of enemy life was an abandoned remount depot, full of unfed and unwatered horses, some wounded and all showing signs of sad neglect; such was their state that the immediate demands of duty were forgotten and one troop spent the afternoon making up feeds and leading relays of desperately thirsty horses to a nearby well. Many of the Hussars that afternoon lost some of the affection they were beginning to feel for their Italian enemy, and the repeated requests to John Combe for news of when they were going to push on had an extra edge that night.

This was still the question to which General O'Connor urgently required an answer. He and Dorman-Smith had spent much time marshalling their arguments for a further advance. They were both well aware of the existing intentions to call a halt in North Africa and send as many men and as much equipment as could be spared to the Balkans, to succour the Greeks and block any German encroachment towards the eastern Mediterranean; but they were determined not to allow the advantages of their own situation to be lost by default on their part.

They were quite certain that despite the battering and unceasing strain put on their equipment, it could be made to function well enough to get them at least to Tripoli, chiefly because the men would not allow its malfunction to stop them. Tobruk was now in full use as a port and Benghasi soon would be – and if the Luftwaffe's attempts to mine the harbours which started on February 4th were combated with the drive and enthusiasm which enlivened XIII Corps, they could easily handle the supplies neces- sary to keep not only the units already at the front moving, but also 2nd Armoured Division which had been ordered up to help at Mechili, and at least one more Australian brigade which had arrived in the Delta. Perhaps, in view of the promise opening in front of them all, New Zealand would let its 6th Brigade take part in the chase after all without waiting for the rest of the division?

But there was now a reconstructed chain of command for requests for action and orders to travel up and down; Wavell had appointed Maitland Wilson as Governor of Cyrenaica and the latter was already installed at Barce. Dorman-Smith arrived in Barce on February 9th and soon persuaded Wilson of the feasibility and indeed desirability of a further advance; but there were no signalling facilities set up there yet, so Dorman-Smith was faced with another drive to Tobruk in order to send the message on to Cairo. He left Tobruk on the afternoon of February 11th for Cairo in order to be available to buttress the argument in person if necessary, arrived there at 0400 on the morning of the 12th and at 1000 was ushered into Wavell's office.

All the maps of the desert which had previously covered the long wall were gone; in their place was a huge map of Greece.

'You see, Eric,' said Wavell, gesturing towards it, 'I am planning my spring campaign!'

The die had been cast; XIII Corps were to stay where they were in Cyrenaica.

7 · 'In all directions . . .'

The authors of the *Official History*, at one point in their description of the situation facing Wavell and his fellow Commanders-in-Chief during the early months of 1941, write that it must have seemed to them 'that this war was not "one damned thing after another": it was everything in all directions at once'.

One of the great problems, of course, was that so far as material was concerned 'everything' at that moment, despite the Italian booty, did not amount to very much when compared with the tasks to be carried out. Not only had the Greek front already absorbed much of the exiguous R.A.F. strength in the area, together with a great deal of the Middle East anti-aircraft capability and a large part of the captured Italian transport, but Mr Churchill and the War Cabinet were increasingly anxious that a firm Balkan Front against the Axis should be formed which would include not only Greece and Yugoslavia, but Turkey as well; and to this end – as Wavell had good reason to suspect – there were feelings in high places that perhaps some of the forces and equipment now under his command or en route to the area, should be used to fill the evident gaps in Turkey's defences.

In particular, Turkey would need a bolstering of her air defences – and if Air Chief Marshal Longmore's expression when he heard suggestions that yet more of his precious squadrons might leave the Delta for northern destinations was one of bleak incredulity, attempts made to alleviate his sufferings with the announcement that 500 Tomahawk fighters purchased from America would soon be reaching him, probably via the newly opened Takoradi Air Route, did nothing, in fact, to lighten it. Longmore was only too well aware that not only was there no American ammunition to fit the Tomahawks' armament in the Middle East, but there were also no pilots with experience or even theoretical knowledge of the Tomahawks' operational capabilities.

Admiral Cunningham, for his part, had long been pointing out that any attempt to reinforce or supply the Balkan States by sea would encounter enormous difficulties while the Dodecanese

Islands remained in Italian hands – an obstacle which could be rendered well-nigh insuperable if German Luftwaffe units moved into Rhodes as they had already moved into Sicily. A solution suggested by Whitehall was that a Special Service Brigade of newly-trained commando units, earmarked for an assault on the island of Pantelleria in the Sicilian Channel, should instead be diverted around the Cape and into Wavell's command, and these could capture Rhodes and the surrounding islands.

But this idea underlined yet another task which still faced the Commanders-in-Chief. Although the R.A.F. had managed to retain air supremacy over the Red Sea and the approaches to Suez, a third of the Red Sea western coastline – from just south of Port Sudan to the narrows – and the whole of the southern coastline of the Gulf of Aden was in Italian hands, and however ineffective that control might be, in the eyes of President Roosevelt it rendered the entire area a combatant zone. As such, no American shipping was allowed into it to alleviate the desperate shortage of British shipping – in itself a factor adversely affecting supplies.

Indeed, it was in this especial regard that many recent cables from London had been worded; how quickly did the Commander-in-Chief think that he could eliminate the Italian East African Empire? Because once this happened, many more men and much more material could be sent to plug the gaps which would be left in his ranks by the fulfilment of immediate needs – succouring the Greeks, perhaps bolstering the Turks, and certainly demonstrating to the Balkan nations that those who cared to withstand Axis pressure would be assured of British support, *material as well as moral*. This Balkan commitment was, in the light of most of the messages and directives from Whitehall, likely to be given the highest priority, and in order to examine its ramifications in detail and perhaps to advance its course the Foreign Secretary, Mr Eden, and the C.I.G.S., Sir John Dill, would shortly be arriving in the Middle East for discussions and a lightning tour of the relevant capitals. But in the meantime, how about East Africa?

This in fact was the time when, to quote again from the *Official History*, Wavell, Longmore and Cunningham

had to achieve a workable and appropriate balance of forces while doing their best to comply with a rapid succession of instructions and suggestions, such as to part with forces from Kenya, to capture Kismayu quickly, to capture Eritrea quickly, to deter the Japanese by 'liquidating Italian East Africa', to treat as a 'first duty' the air defence of Malta, to be prepared to send ten squadrons to Turkey, to regard the capture of Rhodes as 'of first importance', and to 'let their first thoughts be for Greece'.[1]

All in all, it is therefore hardly surprising that on the morning of February 12th the view across the Cyrenaican border as seen by Wavell differed markedly from the same view as seen by Dorman-Smith. If to the latter it appeared as one of infinite promise, beckoning on into Tripolitania and offering the enticing prospect of clearance from the southern Mediterranean coast of all Axis forces, to the man across the desk from him it appeared instead as little more than a welcome relief from one of his many problems. A welcome and blessed relief, certainly; and indeed from what eight weeks ago had been the most urgent and pressing of his problems, with the added bonus of a display of military expertise which by its superb execution promised well for the future.

But other fronts and other theatres were now demanding attention – and another of the benefits which would accrue from O'Connor's magnificent victory would be the reservoir of experienced fighting troops upon which, after a period of rest and re-equipment, Wavell could draw for dispatch to the other fronts where, for reasons both military and political, their presence was needed. In respect of which, Eric would doubtless be interested to know that the withdrawal of 4th Indian Division from Western Desert Force and its dispatch to the Sudan was already showing benefits and could easily bring fame and honours to that division to equal those already won at Nibeiwa and Sidi Barrani.

The reduction of the Duke of Aosta's fief had, in fact, already commenced. Wavell was later to judge that the development was 'an improvisation after the British fashion of war rather than a set piece in the German manner' but be that as it may, it was promising to develop very satisfactorily.

Its principal blow against the Italians was an uprising in the centre of their empire by Ethiopian patriots, led by Emperor Haile Selassie, fomented by a Colonel D. A. Sandford who had spent some years before the war farming in Ethiopia and whom Wavell had sent back in the previous September for just this purpose, and guided by a young and eccentric English officer who had already made something of a reputation for himself as a guerrilla leader in Palestine, named Orde Wingate. Already Patriot Forces had been assembled, two of the most powerful but hitherto hostile chieftains in the central Gojjam area, Dejesmach Mangasha and Dejesmach Nagash, reconciled sufficiently at least for them to agree to act together for the time being and – most important of all – Emperor Haile Selassie himself had returned to his native country, flown in by the R.A.F. on January 20th.

This central uprising was being assisted and protected by a pincer

Map 10   The East African campaign

Port Sudan

Karora

Mersa Taclai

RED SEA

7 IND
INF BDE

GEN
PLATT
GAZELLE
FORCE

Agordat

Keru

Keren

Massawa

Kassala

Biscia

Asmara

10 IND
BDE
BRIG SLIM

Barentu

Gallabat

Gondar

L TANA

Amba Alagi

Aden

GULF OF ADEN

Djibuti

Dessie

Burye

BRITISH
SOMALILAND

Berbera

Diredawa

Jijiga

Addis Ababa

Shashamanna

ETHIOPIA

Negholli

R. JUBA

ITALIAN

Lugh Ferrandi

SOMALILAND

Isha Baidoa

LAKE RUDOLF

Moyale

Bardera

Mogadishu

KENYA

Modun

CHALBI DESERT

Afmadu

Bulo Erillo

Jumbo

Nairobi 450 Km/270M

Kismayu

0Km 100 200 300 400
0M   80   160   240

N

movement to the north and the south. In Kenya to the south, forces commanded by Lieutenant-General Alan Cunningham – brother of the Admiral – consisting of 1st South African Division and brigades from the Gold Coast, Rhodesia and East Africa, had already established full military control of the area east of Lake Rudolf as far as the borders of Italian Somaliland and were themselves probing up into the southern provinces of Ethiopia. More significantly two days previously – on February 10th – other forces had crossed into Italian Somaliland, and in twenty-four hours one of the East African brigades had reached and occupied Afmadu, nearly seventy miles to the east; already the first main objective, the port of Kismayu, was well within their grasp.

In the north, first with the 5th Indian Division and then with both 5th and 4th, General Platt had already so threatened the Italian garrisons at Kassala and Gallabat that by the end of January both towns were back in British hands, while advanced elements of both divisions were well inside Eritrean frontiers, driving towards the important centres of Barentu and Agordat which guarded the passes through the central highlands barring the way to Keren, the Asmara Plateau and the Red Sea port of Massawa.

What was particularly encouraging about both advances was that they had been successfully carried out across appalling country and in positively terrifying climatic conditions. Cunningham's forces moving up to the Ethiopian border with Kenya had crossed the lava rock and dust of the Chalbi desert where the rocks were so hot that they blistered flesh which touched them, then to encounter the rain, mud and cold of the Ethiopian escarpment – and all this some 400 miles from their operational railhead. It said a great deal for both the administrative ability of Cunningham's staff and also for the morale and determination of the men under his command.

As for the conditions in the north, the historian of the 5th Indian Division, Antony Brett-James, had this to say:

The mirage whose outline faded and then vanished as you drew near, the heat shimmer from which tree-ringed lakes and the likeness of still water might be stared at, were a frequent memorable feature of many a drive over the desert. Wells became important and recognizable by the swarms of flies as well as by the camels, cows, goats and donkeys that watered there in daylight . . . Patches of long *tubbas* grass grew on the sand . . . and camel-thorn bushes studded the ground. Where these bushes flourished . . . men found it difficult to walk any distance without getting caught up in thorns like fish-hooks. The scratches festered into septic sores, and in certain units there was hardly a man without bandages on one or both arms and knees.[2]

There are few less accessible places on earth than the Asmara Plateau, especially from the west. At first the Indian Brigades drove across a rolling plain as desolate as those of the Western Desert but more scarred by water-courses and rock shelving; dust enveloped them, to choke their eyes, their noses and throats, while waves of heat beat up from the arid rock. And when they reached the first foothills they found conditions if anything worse – for now they were in defiles which could be blocked, or which would channel them all into narrow streams of sweating men and overheating machines where they could be bombed by the Regia Aeronautica (2nd Camerons suffered twelve casualties on the first day) – and the heat was intensified by reflection back off the craggy walls.

The actions they were called upon to fight had characteristics all their own, too. One force under command of Colonel F. W. Messervy had reached a small village named Keru, about thirty miles across the Eritrean border, to find it abandoned, the defile beyond it blocked and substantial enemy forces on the crests above. As the force began to organise for the next stage of the advance, a patch of scrub about half a mile away suddenly erupted and a squadron of Eritrean cavalry – Askari natives officered by Italians – charged towards them, their small, shaggy ponies at a furious gallop, the riders standing in their stirrups and hurling in front of them a veritable mist of small percussion grenades.

Once the sheer astonishment at the sight in 1941 of a genuine horsed cavalry charge had evaporated (it didn't take long) the result was foregone. Sepoy riflemen and machine-gunners dropped into the nearest cover of thorn bush or fold in the ground and opened up, and even the light artillery had time to swing and virtually blow the

Map 11   Gazelle Force

horsemen back from the muzzles of their guns; within ten minutes it was all over, dead and wounded men and beasts strewn about, dust clouds covering the survivors as they galloped frantically for the shelter of the scrub from which they had so dramatically appeared.

During the rest of the day, Gazelle Force (as Messervy's command was known) edged its way forward up the seamed and broken slopes towards the defenders at the top, who withstood the artillery harassment stoutheartedly and kept up a heavy though not very accurate fire on those below. The climbing Sikhs spent the daylight hours edging up and over innumerable false crests and suffering quite a few casualties (and the appalling trauma of manhandling wounded down precipitous and open hillsides was to be a feature of this campaign) but by nightfall were still pinned below the final crest. Then a midnight patrol brought back evidence of enemy withdrawal and by morning the heights commanding what had been demonstrably a formidable defensive position were found to be empty.

All next day the Sappers and Miners laboured at clearing rock from the defiles, opening the way forward, fighting off with their Bren-guns the pestiferous attentions of the Regia Aeronautica and on one occasion waving frantically at R.A.F. fighters who were mistakenly making aggressive passes above them. In the late afternoon the 1st/6th Rajputana Rifles who had come up to take the place of the Sikhs broke clear and went on forward, eventually to take the railhead of Biscia during the morning of January 24th. Again, the opposition had melted away.

Almost simultaneously, 10th Indian Brigade which had been attached to the 4th Indian Division from the 5th and was at that time commanded by Brigadier W. J. Slim, later to become famous as the commander of Britain's Fourteenth Army in Burma, had swung across on a line to the south of that driven by Gazelle Force, fought a brisk action with some Italian colonial battalions in which they took some 700 prisoners, and driven the rest northwards into the Gazelle Force net, after which the combined force closed up on Agordat, the first major objective inside Eritrea. Slim's brigade then swung away to cut the road down to Barentu, along which other Italian forces were by now trying to retreat.

Agordat presented 4th Indian Division with its greatest challenge so far in the Second World War. According to the divisional history:

This colonial marketing town lay in the plain a mile south of the Baraka river bed, with bunkers of high ground on all sides. To the south-west the approach was barred by the long steep ridge of Laquetat, with forts on either tip. To the north, across the sandy palm-clad watercourse (itself an obstacle), the terrain rose in a series of jumbled terraces. To the east, four abrupt hillocks stood sentry over the road to Keren. To the south, four miles across the plain, these moderate eminences were dwarfed by Mount Cochen, a steep and involved ridge system which sprang to a height of 1,500 feet, its rugged barrier extending into the east until it ended above a defile four miles long through which the road to Keren passed. From the northern shoulder of Mount Cochen a long tongue of high ground, known as Gibraltar, thrust into the plain. The low ground between Laquetat and Gibraltar was defended by a line of trenches and an anti-tank ditch. The position therefore offered serried obstacles near at hand, while on the southern and eastern horizons the misty outlines of the main Eritrean massif stood into the sky, revealing the Agordat terrain to be the shape of more ominous things to come.[3]

The Italian 4th Colonial Division holding Agordat consisted of three brigades and three additional Blackshirt units, making sixteen battalions in all, and they had ten medium tanks and a scattering of L3s in reserve. Against them the 4th Indian were putting into action two brigades totalling seven battalions – but the last battalion to join had brought the news that four R.T.R. Matildas were making their laborious way forward over the potholed and debris-covered roads.

The action began as all such set-piece battles do, with probing attacks and stealthy attempts to feel for ways around the main defences – and these took until the afternoon of January 28th. By this time Beresford-Peirse knew that there was no passable route for wheeled traffic on either side of the objective and that wherever action was joined, the scene would be dominated by the long straggling outline of Mount Cochen. That night, a company of Sikhs occupied the crest of the Laquetat ridge and held on under heavy fire while 5th Brigade battalions slipped into the re-entrant between the ridge and Mount Cochen where the trench line and anti-tank ditch lay, and waited there the next day.

Meanwhile, 11th Brigade battalions had circled around to the south and east of the mountain. Soon after dark on January 29th, 3rd/14th Punjabis began to climb the rocky slopes and to their surprise encountered no opposition on their first lift to the frontal crest. Up behind and passing through them came the 1st/6th Rajputana Rifles to pad softly on towards the ominous and lowering summit, then suddenly to find themselves in the middle of enemy positions. The night erupted in tracer and rifle fire, the Punjabis came up swiftly to help and from then until dawn bitter and confused fighting rose and fell up and down the mountain side, all

Map 12   The battle of Agordat

the time a matter of countless personal fights between warriors of African and Indian races wielding arms provided by European officers – few of whom took much part in the battle.

But in the morning, the defenders were still in possession of their stronghold and the attackers lay wearily below the first crest, awaiting reinforcement, resupply and the agonising evacuation of their wounded. Above them, they could hear the sounds of Italian reinforcements arriving, and the extension of the enemy line across their front until it overlapped them at both ends, and they were faced with a crescent of enemies who by the afternoon were edging forward and harassing them with grenades and petrol bombs. The Indians clung to the ground and thanked their various deities for the deep clefts around them which had caused them so much anguish on the way up, but which now afforded them shelter.

While 11th Brigade had been fighting dourly on the sides of

Mount Cochen, 5th Brigade, attempting to clear the trenches in the re-entrant, had found to their cost that they were held by large numbers of determined troops. Moreover, every move they made on the plain was under full view of an extremely alert force which held the high tip at the end of the Gibraltar spit, and effectively pinned any major attempt by the Fusiliers (who had been given this particular task) to cross the barren and inhospitable ground.

There was nothing for it but for Beresford-Peirse to mount another indirect attack, which he did by sending the Cameron Highlanders around to infiltrate between the eastern end of the Laquetat ridge and the foothills of Cochen, then to climb under good cover along the spit to take the Gibraltar tip from behind. In this they were aided – as were the Rajputana Riflemen on the mountain itself – by the deep nullahs and cracks in the escarpment sides, but much hindered by the Italian artillery in the forts back on Laquetat; nevertheless, they hung on grimly, beat off two counter-attacks launched against them by enemy forces from both the Gibraltar tip and the nearest slope of Mount Cochen, and during the night of January 30th/31st dug themselves a little deeper into the ground against the sniping and machine-gun fire which was directed at them in sporadic bursts. Both sides then waited for whatever the morning would bring.

It was to a very great extent up to General Beresford-Peirse to decide this, and he quickly made up his mind. During the rest of that night, he carefully and quietly removed the remnants of the Rajputana Rifles from their confined position below the first crest of the southern slope of Mount Cochen, relocated them with their comrades of the 3rd/14th Punjabis and added to their company the 4th Field Company of Sappers and Miners, now about to relearn their basic infantry training. This group sidestepped inconspicuously to their right and by morning were half-way up the south-eastern slope of the hill, behind the apparently unsuspecting left flank of the enemy crescent which had so bedevilled the Rajputanas during the previous afternoon.

Behind Laquetat, he marshalled and briefed his divisional artillery and moved the four 'I' tanks up as close as he could behind the Royal Fusilier positions without breaking their cover. All, then, waited for the dawn.

It came with a quite astonishing explosion of military energy and expertise on the part of the 4th Indian Division. At 0500, while the mountain was still wrapped in mists, the riflemen and sappers on the slopes of Mount Cochen began their ascent to the first crest, reached it without being discovered and charged with terrifying violence along the line of Askaris who had lain there all night, confident that their prey was still penned below them. The sheer speed of the charge, as lines of disciplined infantry swept through the ranks with bayonet and bullet, boot and rifle-butt, chanting their weird and petrifying war-cries, struck terror into the hearts of the astonished enemy, many of whom were skewered to the ground where they had lain all night; as the attackers fought their way to the peak, the surviving defenders broke and fled. It was all over in less than an hour, by which time the mists had cleared and the victors could see the scene spread below them in the plain. It was quite a sight.

The action there had been triggered by the first sounds of battle coming from Mount Cochen at 0520 as the 11th Brigade swept over the false crest in their first charge. Hardly had the chatter of machine-guns and rifles echoed down into the plain than the divisional artillery crashed out in the heaviest concentration they could shoot on to the Gibraltar escarpment and the lower adjacent slopes of the mountain. Under its cover, four companies of Camerons rose from their various concealments along the length of the escarpment and swept along towards the tip, two companies on top and two at the bottom; and despite the undoubted courage of the defenders, they were utterly submerged within a matter of minutes. Highland fury was such, in fact, that having cleared the length of the ridge the Camerons swept down and across the plain to take what their history calls a 'knobbly kopje' standing about 500 yards out on the plain.

At this, two things happened. The artillery abruptly shortened range to blanket the trenches in front of the Fusiliers, and the commander of the Italian forces on the lower slopes of Mount Cochen, overlooking the Gibraltar spit, suddenly became aware of the fact that the summit of the mountain behind him was now in hostile hands. Hurriedly dispatching a masking company to contain them, he was still assembling the rest of his command to move down to the plain to join the battle there, when he was violently assaulted from the rear by the very force which he had ordered to be held.

Under command of a Major Holloway, A Company, 1st/6th Rajputana Rifles together with the attached Sappers and Miners from 4th Field Company had apparently been so fired by their morning's victory – perhaps also by the sight below of the Camerons in action – that they had charged down through the masking company with such force that they had destroyed and scattered it. Carried by their own impetus, they then fell upon the luckless and still unorganised force below them with the bayonet to such effect that after the battle, 104 bodies were found in the path of these avenging furies, none of them showing a single bullet wound. What survivors there were had fled away into the tangled country behind the mountain.

Below, as the smoke and dust of the bombardment of the trenches died away, the four Matildas lumbered around the corner of the Laquetat ridge and escorted by carriers, made directly for the trench lines, with the Fusiliers rising from the ground and following in skirmishing order.

There was a brief moment when the defenders stood and hoped that their parapets might be of some use to them, but nothing could halt the implacable 'I' tanks which turned as they reached the trenches and crunched along the line, followed by the Fusiliers, as expert with bomb and bayonet as the Sepoys on the slopes above. It was all over by 0900, the prisoners being led away, the Fusiliers searching the trenches, the tanks lurching back and forth in the area between the Fusiliers and Gibraltar, and the Camerons on the 'knobbly kopje'. And from the Camerons came the sudden announcement that there was some Italian armour concealed in a defile just behind Mount Cochen.

Brigadier Lloyd, who was the senior officer in the neighbourhood at that moment, quickly recalled the Matildas from what the divisional history delicately calls 'their freebooting behind the trenches on the plain', attached them to the Camerons' carriers and sent them off to winkle out the enemy tanks. It was, as one of the officers present afterwards admitted, rather like taking candy from a child. The carriers went first, rather breezily swanning across the plain, around the corner of the defile and into sight of the M13s and L3s, whereat they abruptly halted and reversed out of sight. They then turned and sped away – followed enthusiastically by the Italian armour past a large and thick clump of thorn bushes at which the crews would have been well advised to take a closer look.

From it emerged the four Matildas to take the Italians from the rear and at virtually point-blank range. Six medium and five light tanks were quickly ablaze, and as the others scuttled back behind the mountain for safety, they were followed by both tanks and carriers who soon discovered the presence of an entire Blackshirt battalion lying in another defile further back, presumably intending to pounce on the flank of any attacking force moving along the road leading from Agordat, thus threatening the principal fortress of Keren.

Lightly armed infantry, except under most unusual circumstances and then only of exceptional quality, cannot stand against heavy armour, and this Blackshirt battalion was no exception. It broke immediately and fled, but unfortunately the first wave of panic led them down on to the plain instead of up and away into the mountains; their scurrying figures proved too much of a temptation to the riflemen and machine-gunners around them, already stirred by the sights and sounds of the morning and the immediate exultation of victory. There were not many Blackshirts left among the prisoners when the final count was made.

The town of Agordat was then occupied, an end put to the looting which had begun as soon as it had become evident that the Italian military would no longer be in control, and plans for the immediate future considered. From the south came news that 5th Indian Division was now firmly in control at Barentu and that survivors of the Italian garrison there had escaped away into the hills to the south-east and would thus present no problems to the commander of 4th Indian Division.

General Beresford-Peirse very soon found that he had quite enough other problems to worry about, so far as that large and phlegmatic man ever worried about anything. Even while the main body of his division was securing the position at Agordat, his reconnaissance units – the chief of which was the romantically named Skinner's Horse – were off probing forward to discover what lay ahead in the general direction of the Eritrean central highlands, and in the particular direction of the only crack in its bleak and forbidding façade, the Dongolaas Gorge leading up to Keren, the key to the Asmara Plateau.

A few miles from Agordat along the Keren road, the highway crossed a four-span steel bridge over the Baraka watercourse – and the Italian retreat had not been carried out in such a hurry that it had not received attentions from their engineers. It took the indefatigable Miners and Sappers eight hours to clear the mines, neutralise the demolition charges and repair the gaps in the trellises, so the leading vehicles of the reconnaissance party covered only twenty miles that day. Let the divisional historian tell what happened next:

> At 1000 hours next morning [February 2nd] the leading troops of Skinner's Horse reached the southering bend in the Ascidera valley, two miles south of the entrance to the Gorge. From the canyon came dull booms; clouds of smoke and dust curled upwards in the still, hot air. The last Italian rearguards had passed through and on a stretch of several hundred yards demolition squads were blowing away the retaining walls which pinned the road to the cliffsides. Two 'I' tanks crossed the valley to reconnoitre and reported the ravine to be blocked by barricades of huge boulders covered by anti-tank and machine guns. The eastern gateway of the Eritrean fortress was bolted and barred.[4]

Even Beresford-Peirse's placidity was ruffled by this event, and his state of mind further disturbed the following day when his Commander-in-Chief's reaction to the capture of Agordat arrived in the shape of a congratulatory cable, ending, 'Now go on and take Keren and Asmara!'

It was not to be as simple as that, and now began an ordeal for the 4th Indian Division, and later for the 5th as well, which was to have no comparison until three years later at Cassino. There was no way for a force large enough to capture Keren and take control of the Asmara Plateau to reach their objectives other than through the Dongolaas Gorge, and in the opening days of February 1941 the obvious tactic was for the nearest troops to try to take the heights commanding the Gorge by storm.

The first battle raged for three days – from February 4th to the 7th, and it bore little similarity to the one being fought at exactly the same time 1,500 miles away at Beda Fomm. By the end of the three days, two peaks had been won and lost, a col taken and lost and only the first objective, a low ridge already known to the division as Cameron Ridge, was still held – and that at tremendous cost. But much had been learned, perhaps the chief lesson being that Italian troops such as the Savoy Grenadiers now facing them, well-officered and adequately supplied, were as grim in defence as the Indians themselves, and just as ready and expert when it came to mounting a counter-attack. The force which had hurled the 3rd/14th Punjabis back from Brig's Peak to Cameron Ridge had earned the grudging respect of their antagonists, and when three nights later the 4th/6th Rajputanas were pinned below the Acqua Col (on a ridge which then took their name) they faced a night of combat reminiscent of the worst battles fought for the Passchendaele Ridge twenty-four years before; and were quite prepared to agree the following day that they had lost it.

Map 13   The approach to Keren

The pattern of the battle was now established. Whatever change in detail the future might show, it was going to be a matter of first storming and then holding, against as fierce counter-attacks as had been mounted to date in the Second World War, the main heights on each side of the gorge – Cameron Ridge, Brig's Peak, Flat Top, Railway Ridge and especially Sanchil on the north; Fort Dolo-gorodoc, Falestoh and Zeban on the south. And some indication of the bitterness of the fighting was already indicated by the names being allocated to some of the vales and hillocks in between – Mole Hill, Pinnacle, Cameron Tunnel, Rajputana Ridge, Bloody Hell Hollow, the Sphinx, Hell Fire Corner (inevitably), and the trapped and exposed basin below Dologorodoc which after only two days became known to the sardonically minded troops as Happy Valley.

A second attack was mounted on the afternoon of February 10th in which the 3rd/1st Punjabis swept upwards from Cameron Ridge, across Brig's Peak and the following morning even across a col to seize the lower slopes of Sanchil. But there the Punjabis found themselves short of men both because of casualties and because as much as a third of the battalion had perforce to be employed as porters, bringing up ammunition and desperately trying to carry away the wounded (no thought was given to such inessentials as food or water). In the early hours of the following morning, a heavy attack fell on the front of the Punjabis' line while another struck them in the flank, sweeping the battalion away from all the ground they had won and back to Cameron Ridge, with a loss of their commanding officer, two company commanders and some 280 others killed. With them went artillery observation crews stationed temporarily on Brig's Peak to direct fire on Acqua Col, the objective of the next planned step in the offensive.

Despite the lack of concentrated gunfire which this loss caused, the next step still went ahead. 5th Brigade swarmed up out of Happy Valley, the Rajputana Rifles again captured their own crest and a few groups of dauntless individuals actually reached the col before being submerged in a sea of enemies, as unconcerned with personal survival as themselves. It was here that Subadar Richpal Ram, a Jat from Patiala State, earned the first of the four Victoria Crosses won by 4th Indian Division during the war, another of which also went to the 4th/6th Rajputana Rifles.

Like the attack on Sanchil and another by the Sikhs on the Sphinx the same day, this attack failed, and that night the troops along the southern side of the pass stole back through Happy Valley under the ominous bulk of Dologorodoc into the main Ascidera Pass, while those on Cameron Ridge were relieved and General Beresford-Peirse and his staff considered the next step – just twenty-four hours after Wavell had told Dorman-Smith that XIII Corps were not to advance further into Tripolitania.

It was quite evident by now that courage and physical toughness were not enough to take the Indians to Keren. Such an attempt must be backed by a well-stocked supply base, launched under cover of massive artillery bombardments, supported by adequate reserves and kept in movement by transport other than weary feet and porterage other than aching backs; one of the enormous advantages enjoyed by the Italian defenders was an efficiently run pack-mule service forward to practically every defence point, and it was particularly galling for the Indian troops carrying everything on their backs to reflect that they had left the best mule transport in the world back at home.

So the main task of building a solid base began and the fighting troops took what rest they could, alternating battalions on Cameron Ridge, while the Central Indian Horse (who had taken the place of Skinner's Horse when Gazelle Force was disbanded and returned to Kassala) guarded the flanks.

During the whole of February, the labour went on. Water holes were bored, disused wells found and cleared; mountain tracks were surveyed, widened and lengthened where considered likely to be useful. Electric generators were brought up, installed and kept going to produce the power for water sterilisation and for ice plants; walls were built out of stone along the approach routes to the pass at night to guard against defilade fire during the day. Wrecked and captured enemy machinery and vehicles were serviced and the railway line which ran back along the Ascidera Valley to Agordat was repaired, rolling stock brought up or dragged out from the tunnels into which the Italians had crashed it during their retreat, the tops sawn off and their platforms blocked to take guns or to bring up equipment. Lorries were fitted with axles long enough for the wheels to run outside the rails and in low gear they could then drag trains of goods vans up the steep gradients; a captured enemy diesel truck was adapted to form a genuine locomotive which then could not only drag water-tanks forward, but could also tow back with some degree of smoothness the trucks carrying the wounded.

While the build-up was proceeding, diversionary threats were made against the objectives by other forces and other arms. A Brigade Group was formed around a 7th Indian Infantry Brigade nucleus under Brigadier H. R. Briggs, consisting of two infantry battalions, a field battery and the Free French Brigade d'Orient of the 14th Battalion of the Foreign Legion and the 3rd Battalion of the Chad Regiment. In January this force had moved from Port Sudan down to Karora on the Eritrean frontier, then down to Mersa Taclai on the coast through which minor port a tenuous line of sea-communication was opened. With this to support them, they now moved south along a thread-like track down towards Keren, their presence sufficient at least to hold the attention of two Italian colonial brigades which might otherwise have been used to buttress the defences above Dongolaas.

And with the capture of both Agordat and Barentu, R.A.F. fighter and bomber squadrons could come forward both to give cover to the troops working in the Gorge and to harass and destroy the Italian rear bases. Eight Wellesleys bombed the Caproni workshops at Mai Edega one night, and two days later a mixed bomber and fighter force struck again, leaving all the main buildings on fire. Asmara airfield was attacked, the railway between Asmara and Keren damaged and even the port installations at Massawa hit – a strike which was repeated a few days later when the aircraft-carrier H.M.S. *Formidable* steamed up the Red Sea towards the Mediterranean to take the place of the damaged *Illustrious*, and flew off two of her Albacore squadrons to attack the harbour workshops.

By March 1st, General Platt had decided on the main form of his next attack – but by this time, there had been startling developments down in the south as well.

General Cunningham had presented his plan for an advance into Italian Somaliland (on a pencilled note, by hand of officer) to Wavell on February 7th and, as has been related, four days later one of his brigades was at Afmadu. The first main objective of the drive was the port of Kismayu, but Cunningham had his eyes firmly fixed on a more valuable prize further east – the provincial capital, Mogadishu. The problem which faced him here was that the river Juba ran into the sea just a few miles east of Kismayu, between two small seaside villages with the unlikely names of Gobwen and Jumbo, and he knew that unless he could cut off the garrison of Kismayu, the river crossings there would be wrecked and the advance on the main objective thus delayed.

With the occupation of Afmadu, therefore, he leap-frogged his second brigade (24th Gold Coast) through the first one (22nd East African) and pitched them forty miles forward to Bulo Erillo, some ten miles short of the river and fifty miles from the estuary. They arrived so quickly that they caught up with the retreating garrison from Afmadu, who then had no choice but to stand and fight. This resistance caused the deaths of eight British officers and N.C.O.s with the men from the Gold Coast as well as over 20 native other ranks, for which price they captured 141 prisoners, four armoured cars and a great deal of fuel and miscellaneous equipment.

Meanwhile, the 1st South African Brigade had also passed through

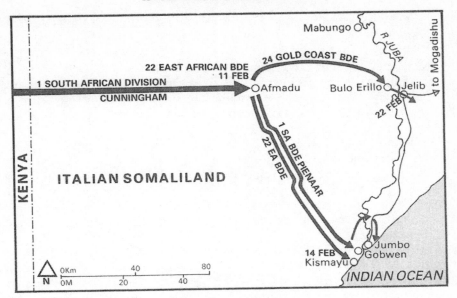

Map 14   Cunningham's advance

Afmadu, turned south and advanced cautiously down towards Gobwen, where it intended to seize the river crossings and take Jumbo on the other side. Brigadier D. H. Pienaar and his men were within striking distance of Gobwen when they heard what sounded suspiciously like the explosions of demolition charges in Kismayu port, but as he was under strict orders to maintain radio silence he continued his advance during the early night of February 13th/14th, his twelve light tanks encountering traffic problems with what were quite obviously streams of evacuees from the main objective. The next morning, Pienaar led his men into Gobwen to find it empty, but the essential pontoon bridge had been destroyed and a strong and evidently determined enemy was entrenched on the opposite bank.

Meanwhile, naval units which had been watching Kismayu had signalled Cunningham on the previous evening of the developments in the port and he had in turn instructed the 22nd East African to get down from Afmadu 'at the double'. They entered the port on the evening of February 14th – six days ahead of schedule – and despite the demolitions carried out twenty-four hours before, the first supply convoys were streaming up from Mombasa within a week.

By this time, the Royal Natal Carbineers of Pienaar's brigade had found a crossing twelve miles upstream and carried it in grand

manner by assault boats. The Transvaal Scottish with them formed
a small bridgehead on the other side from which during February
17th and 18th they beat off determined attempts to wipe them out,
while behind them the brigade engineers threw a second pontoon
bridge across the 200-yard-wide river – under fire all the time; on
February 19th the whole brigade stormed across and down into
Jumbo, capturing most of the garrison with its artillery and another
welcome supply of petrol.

There followed a hasty shuffling of forces to net as many
survivors and evacuees as possible and at the same time to capture
the small town of Jelib, opposite Bulo Erillo and blocking the road
to Mogadishu. By February 22nd it was in South African hands with
evidence of the complete disintegration of local Italian forces all
around. Such was the atmosphere of control in the hastily constituted
headquarters, despite the now thoroughly dilapidated condition of
all vehicles, tanks, guns, and even clothing and footwear (for they
had advanced over 500 miles of appalling country from their
railhead at Nairobi) that groups of armed enemy troops trying to
surrender, some of considerable size, were sent off back into the
bush with orders to come in again in one, two or even three days'
time when arrangements might be made to attend to their wishes.
So far as was ever known, all groups obeyed – thankfully, for the
surrounding country was wild, arid and inhospitable.

In this regard, Cunningham sent a message to Wavell suggesting
that in view of the promise opening before him, could something be
done about retaking the port of Berbera in British Somaliland in
order that his own lines of communication would be shortened if his
momentum took him that far? – a request to which Wavell replied
that a force from Aden *could* be spared to attack the port, but that
Cunningham would have to man the base with his own units if he
wanted it to be operational – a somewhat dampening proposal, as
Cunningham was as short of base units as everyone else.

Moreover, he still had his left or northern flank to guard. There
was no point in jorrocking off on a 250-mile gallop along the coast
to Mogadishu if it left the force there with vulnerable lines of
communication, in danger of investment followed by a highly
embarrassing evacuation by the Navy. One should not take unnecessary chances even with an enemy who showed every sign of
disorganisation – and in any case, it was becoming evident that
other races than the Italian were finding the presence of the
invading forces unwelcome.

The first signs of this had appeared during the attempts to
infiltrate into southern Ethiopia in January when it was found that
the tribal chiefs there had no love at all for the Amharic Christian
Emperor's somewhat feudal rule, and having been left more or less

alone by the Italians saw no reason for the *status quo* to be disturbed. Their somewhat primitive customs with prisoners, too, although useful in influencing Italians to give themselves up when cut off, indicated that it might not be wise to leave lines of communication unguarded, or pickets unsupported or too isolated. It was therefore not until Moyale was taken and a line held along the southern Ethiopian frontier from which a strong advance northwards could be launched if necessary, that Cunningham felt reasonably safe on that front, and even then a holding force installed at Mabungo, ten miles north of Bulo Erillo and on the Juba, had to fight off quite a heavy attack made by a mixed and unidentifiable force on the same evening that Jelib fell.

None the less, he felt confident enough to send off the 22nd East African Brigade the following day on the road to the capital. They reached Modun before encountering any opposition, and this was overcome with the aid of naval units who bombarded the town just before it was entered; then the 23rd Nigerian Brigade passed through them and were in Mogadishu, unopposed, by February 25th. As Cunningham pointed out in his triumphant cable to Wavell, on this latest leap forward, his troops had advanced 235 miles in three days.

But the Commander-in-Chief's thoughts were no longer on East African affairs. Mr Anthony Eden and Sir John Dill had arrived, and Balkan politics were engaging all attentions.

To Mr Eden, just beginning his third and what was to prove his longest term as Britain's Foreign Secretary, it appeared that great changes had taken place in the strategic situation in the Middle East since his previous visit in October. Then he had felt strongly that his task was to curb the Prime Minister's enthusiasm for the Balkan Front, to support the Commanders-in-Chief in their wish to build up their forces in Egypt, and even to abide by General Wavell's concern for secrecy to the extent of giving Mr Churchill no hint of the plans for *Operation Compass* until he got home and could do so in person, despite the tone of the cables he had been receiving from London during the visit.

If his attitude on that occasion had been in any way influenced by his position as Secretary of State for War (elevation to Foreign Secretary had only taken place two days before Christmas) then it had also been backed by the attitude of the Greek Prime Minister, General Ioannis Metaxas, who was quite explicit in his views that he did not want a conspicuous British military presence in his country, unless it was also large enough to repulse the German aggression it was almost certain to provoke. And the three or four regiments of artillery, the anti-tank regiment, the pair of anti-aircraft batteries and the single regiment of cruiser tanks which were all that Britain was offering him as late as mid-January were not, in the General's view, enough to check the force which an incensed Führer might dispatch down through Yugoslavia and/or Bulgaria into Greece for much longer than it would take to organise a hasty retreat. A few squadrons of aircraft to help push the Italians further back into Albania was one thing; an army to confront the Wehrmacht was something entirely different.

But now, suddenly and dramatically, Metaxas was dead – struck down by a heart attack on January 20th, five days after his last meeting with Wavell; and although the new Prime Minister M. Koryzis had at first proclaimed that his attitude in all things was practically indistinguishable from his predecessor's, he had now suggested that perhaps a closer look at the kind of defence line which could be held in Greece by joint Anglo-Greek forces might be desirable.

Mr Eden felt very strongly that this examination should be carried out and, if M. Koryzis asked for it, as much military aid – men, guns, tanks, aircraft – as could be assembled in the Middle East should be sent to him. Britain, in Mr Eden's opinion, had of late broken or at least left unfulfilled far too many promises, had renegued on too many obligations – to the League of Nations over sanctions against Italy during the Abyssinian War, to Czecho-slovakia at the time of Munich, to Poland when the war broke out. Over the first, he had resigned from the position of Foreign Secretary in Mr Chamberlain's government, over the others he had been deeply disturbed; and if M. Koryzis now wished to invoke the terms of the agreement made with Britain on April 13th, 1939, under which Britain would come to Greece's aid if her indepen-dence was in any way threatened, then he, Anthony Eden, would exert all his influence to see that this time his country honoured her obligations, despite the fact that it might be very inconvenient, despite the fact also that the agreement had been made originally by Mr Chamberlain.

There was, indeed, much more than just his own feelings to support his attitude. On February 10th, four days before he and Sir John Dill had left England, there had been a meeting of the Defence Committee at which the whole situation in the Middle East was thrashed out. The advantages of an advance by General O'Connor's forces to Tripoli were obvious – but even if the port were captured at once and at minimum cost, its subsequent defence would make heavy demands on the resources which might be better used in preventing a German encroachment into the Balkans.

In previous discussions on possible developments in the Middle East, the Chiefs of Staff had always argued that Britain's most advantageous first ally in the area would be Turkey – from whose airfields bombers could attack Rumanian oil, and within whose boundaries armies could either block Axis aggression down towards the vital oilfields in Iraq or in the course of time mass for their own aggression 'up' – to use one of Mr Churchill's favourite expressions – 'through the soft underbelly of Europe'.

But M. Koryzis's recent inquiry, backed by his explicit affirmation that whatever support or lack of it was granted his country, Greece would defend her national soil against German aggression even if she had to do so alone, had caused a shift of opinion. Turkey's attitude was still uncertain and so, come to that, was Yugoslavia's; Greece's attitude was a rock upon which plans could be based. As evidence accumulated during January of an ever greater German build-up in Rumania, coupled with reports from agents of the sinister appearance of hordes of German civilians and officials in Bulgaria similar to that which had preceded all previous occupations of neighbouring countries by the Nazis, the question which had to be answered was – what would Turkey's reaction be if, in the face of a German invasion of Greece, Britain did nothing to help?

It was unlikely to be favourable to British interests – certainly not as favourable as if Britain honoured her agreement and demonstrated that when she *could* do so, then she *would* aid those who stood up to the Axis Powers. If an Anglo-Greek defence proved successful, then perhaps Turkey would come in on the Allied side quickly; if it did not prove successful, then Turkey could still become an ally when the tide at last turned against the Axis. The first thing to find out was the most advantageous way for British military capacity in the Middle East to be co-ordinated with Greek defence capabilities, and this was the main purpose of Mr Eden's journey. Talks with Turkish and perhaps with Yugoslav leaders would follow, but Greece was to be the primary and immediate recipient of British attentions.

In the meantime, Middle East Commanders-in-Chief were instructed to initiate such plans – including the collection of shipping – as would enable them to move the maximum forces to Greece at the earliest possible moment. Just before Mr Eden left England, he was given figures which seemed to indicate that General Wavell would be able to supply a force consisting of three infantry divisions and two armoured brigades, while Air Chief Marshal Longmore could promise at least another three bomber squadrons and an army co-operation squadron.

Mr Eden was also given with appropriate solemnity what the Prime Minister referred to as his 'sealed orders', which he opened during a stopover at Gibraltar to find that he had been granted a freedom of action and judgment which few envoys have enjoyed

since the invention of the telephone or the radio, and which was a
gratifying indication of the regard, and indeed affection, in which he
was held. He was to initiate any action he felt desirable with the
Commanders-in-Chief, with the Greek, Yugoslav and Turkish
Governments, to judge himself what was the minimum garrison
necessary to ensure the safety of the western frontier of Cyrenaica
and what were the necessary steps to be taken to make Benghasi a
practical and efficient naval and air base . . . Above all, his main
objective was to provide Greece with speedy and effective help.

The journey from England was delayed by very bad weather
conditions but when they eventually arrived, Wavell was waiting
with the British Ambassador to greet them. He regarded them
briefly with the contemplative expression he sometimes wore,
murmuring, 'You have been a long time coming.'

There was a short explanation, at which Wavell nodded and
continued, 'As you were so long I felt I had to get started, and I have
begun the concentration for the move of troops to Greece.'

Co-operation on all sides could not have been greater.

One simple, immutable fact had to be faced by all in this situation. If
troops, aircraft, tanks, trucks, field-guns, anti-aircraft guns and
signal equipment went to Greece in the quantities required to stem a
German invasion, then the rest of Wavell's command would have to
go short. As his biographer John Connell put it so cogently:

> One soldier could, for a time, do the duty of two; one radar set
> could be overworked till it fell apart; but neither man nor radar set
> could do the same job at the same time in two different theatres
> of operations many hundreds of miles apart.[5]

In order to put the Greek expeditionary force together, Wavell
began by crossing some total impracticabilities off the list of
theoretical possibilities.

For instance, no matter how high the demand for troops in the
Balkans, the 4th and 5th Indian Divisions could not be withdrawn
from East Africa without a prolonged disengagement operation
which would not only throw away their recent gains, but also so
disorganise both formations that they would be virtually useless for
any purpose other than random reinforcement of individual units for
some time to come. In addition, visions of quickly withdrawing the
experienced 7th Armoured Division from the desert and whisking
them away to perform prodigies of valour in the Greek mountains
must also be discarded; the division was, in fact, already back in
Cairo, gazing affectionately after the twelve cruiser and forty light
tanks which were all that was left to them disappearing into the workshops, wondering when and where they would get some replace-

ments. As for the 11th Hussars, they too were back in Abbassia, their last Rolls-Royce cars gone for ever, their Morrises in the repair shops and the few new Marmon-Harringtons which they had received from South Africa being regarded with some scepticism by the old hands, who could spot fundamental insufficiencies a pistol shot away.

All that was left, then, of the formations which had already seen action was the 6th Australian Division which, with the totally unblooded 9th Australian, had been intended to form the 1st Australian Corps under Lieutenant-General T. A. Blamey, to take XIII Corps's place in Cyrenaica. In reserve there was still the New Zealand Division at last up to three brigades, the newly arrived, virtually untrained and poorly equipped 7th Australian Division, a Polish Brigade formed in the Middle East from soldiers who had escaped when their country was overrun, and a British infantry division hastily formed around the nucleus of the British 16th Infantry Brigade by the addition of garrison troops scraped from Mersa Matruh and Palestine. This motley collection had been given the number and name of 6th British Division and earmarked, in the absence of the promised Special Service Brigade, for the attack on Rhodes and the subsequent garrisoning of the rest of the Greek islands.

As for armour, only the untried 2nd Armoured Division had any tanks at all, its cruisers already worn when they arrived in Egypt and now in need of new tank tracks, as a result of training in the desert plus the wear and tear of the journey up into Cyrenaica. No spare tracks had been sent out with them and a supply quickly manu-factured and rushed out from Australia were proving impractical in desert conditions.

The three divisions for Greece must therefore comprise the New Zealand Division plus two of the Australian divisions; the armoured brigades must come from the 2nd Armoured, somehow. But what would this leave to protect the Benghasi flank, the hard-won gains in Cyrenaica?

It would *not* leave General Maitland Wilson and his staff, for one of the earliest decisions taken after the arrival of Mr Eden and Sir John Dill was that in order to convince the Greeks that the British were serious in their wish to support them against aggression, any force sent to their country must be commanded by a senior and preferably well-known general – and except for General Wavell himself, Maitland Wilson was the only military figure known to the public at all. Thus he would go to Greece.

The obvious choice to take over the governorship of Cyrenaica and military control of the area was, of course, General O'Connor, but he had been unwell with stomach trouble during the last days of the Beda Fomm campaign, and had been sent off for a well-deserved rest in Palestine – happily with his wife who was still in the area. Upon his return he would take up Maitland Wilson's old position as Commander, British Troops in Egypt at the Cairo Headquarters, though much to his dismay when he discovered it, his well-trained and experienced staff organisation had already been broken up and its individual members allocated to other formations. Brigadier Harding was to go as B.G.S. to Maitland Wilson (who at least promised O'Connor that he could have him back when next he received a corps command), his chief engineer and transport officers were earmarked for Greece, his chief gunner for Rhodes. Dorman-Smith was back in Palestine. O'Connor was later to write:

A Corps staff is a most complex affair and does not begin to work well, even if the individuals are well trained, until it has been running for some time . . .

A battalion is not put into battle without being trained in its duties, yet the authorities never seem to hesitate to land a campaign with an entirely new staff, who may never have met before and know nothing of each other's peculiarities.[6]

The only senior officer left in the area to take command in Cyrenaica at that moment was Lieutenant-General Philip Neame, V.C., of whom Wavell later wrote:

I did not know him well; he had had the 4th Indian Division and had then gone to Palestine to replace George Giffard. He was a Sapper, and had been an instructor at the Staff College, and was the author of a book on strategy, so I accepted him as a skilful and educated soldier; and his V.C. was a guarantee of his fighting qualities. He was at this time a great friend of Dick O'Connor's for whose judgment I had much respect.[7]

But even a winner of the Victoria Cross cannot be expected to hold a newly conquered province without adequate forces, and as day followed day, General Neame saw more and more of his command being whittled away. The first to go was General Blamey and the Australian Corps Headquarters, followed shortly afterwards by the whole of the experienced 6th Australian Division. Moreover, even the unblooded 9th Australian Division which came up to take its place was not complete, two of its relatively well-equipped brigades changing places with two from the raw 7th Division, thus endowing Neame with an infantry component totally inexperienced and mostly ill-equipped.

As for armour, all he eventually retained was just one of the 2nd Armoured's brigades – the 3rd – and a part of the division's Support Group; and of the 3rd Armoured Brigade's 86 tanks (out of a full complement of 156), those allocated to the 6th Royal Tank Regiment were captured M13s, hastily repaired and adapted at the Abbassia workshops, without radio and therefore unable to carry out the tactics in which the crews had been so painstakingly trained.

At least he was left with the King's Dragoon Guards up in the 11th Hussars' old pitch around El Agheila, with their Marmon-Harringtons.

Mr Eden spent his time in Cairo in earnest conference not only with the Ambassador and Generals Wavell and Wilson, but also with the American Colonel William (Big Bill) Donovan who had been touring the Balkans on behalf of his Government. He had much of interest to tell Mr Eden of local morale and opinion and promised to retail to Mr Roosevelt one special plea. The moves to Greece during the next few weeks would throw an enormous strain on British shipping capabilities in the Mediterranean, and anything the President could do to help would be most gratefully received.

Needless to say, Mr Eden was also the recipient of cables from the Prime Minister during his two days in the Egyptian capital, mainly spurring him on to efforts to bring about the longed-for Balkan Front, but one containing an unexpected passage:

> Do not consider yourselves obligated to a Greek enterprise if in your hearts you feel it will be only another Norwegian fiasco. If no good plan can be made, please say so. But of course you know how valuable success would be.

This strangely hesitant note in the Prime Minister's missive left Eden unmoved. He had already talked over all possible courses of action with practically every senior military figure in the British service, and his diary entry for February 20th reads:

> Met three Commanders-in-Chief and Dill at Wavell's office where we went into a three-hour session. There was agreement upon utmost help to Greece at earliest possible moment. There is grave risk in this course and much must depend on speed and secrecy with which it can be carried out. But to stand idly by and see Germany win a victory over Greece, probably a bloodless one at that, seems the worst of all courses. If we are to act we must do so quickly and we decided at a conference at Embassy later in the day that we would propose ourselves for a secret conference in Greece on Saturday.[8]

But it did seem as though responsibility for the decision to go to Greece had subtly shifted from London to Cairo.

They flew to Athens on February 2nd – Eden, Dill, Wavell,

Longmore and a Captain Dick, R.N., as Cunningham's representative. There they were met by senior Greek generals all muffled in civilian clothes and motored discreetly to the Royal Palace at Tatoi, where it was considered that their conferences could be held in appropriate comfort and security. The first meeting was between Eden and M. Koryzis alone, at which the Greek Prime Minister handed over a note which stated again, quite unequivocally, Greece's determination to continue the war at Britain's side until final victory and that she would defend her native soil against any invasion, if necessary alone. The King wished the British Government to know of this resolution before any conversations took place, and before he or his Government knew whether any British help would be available or not.

With so clear an affirmation of purpose as foundation, it only remained to examine the military situation and make plans to integrate the British and Greek armies to their greatest mutual benefit – and the first note of complete accord was struck by the pleasure and appreciation shown by the Greek Commander-in-Chief, General Papagos, when Mr Eden announced that Maitland Wilson would command the British and Commonwealth force.

From then on it was almost a matter of simple mathematics. The bitterly cold winter had caused enormous suffering and casualties among the Greek troops fighting in Albania, where the evident build-up of Italian forces had drawn troops away from the Bulgarian frontier. There were thus far too few troops left in the eastern sector to hold back a German invasion force driving south down through eastern Macedonia or Thrace towards Salonica, especially if a large-scale Italian drive out of Albania was mounted at the same time, while if the Germans instead came down through a compliant Yugoslavia, then there would be nothing in the middle to stem the tide except the British – if they arrived in time. And every indication was that time was of the essence.

What forces did the Greeks have? What forces could the British send?

The sum was not encouraging. Grasping the nettle, General Papagos admitted that his forces along the Bulgarian frontier were a waste of strength as they could never hope to defend Salonica against any worthwhile attack, in view of the lack of depth between the enemy frontier and the sea, plus the extremely vulnerable east–west communications running along the coast. Work on defence lines along the valleys of both the Nestos and the Struma had commenced, but these would be completely outflanked and useless unless the Yugoslavs successfully stemmed any German advance down through their country – and as Yugoslavia's attitude was uncertain, the wise course would be to assume the worst, abandon the Nestos and Struma lines and build another one down from the Yugoslav frontier through Edessa and along the Vermion Mountains, south across the valley of the Aliakmon and then on to the sea across the northern face of the Pieria-Olympus range.

Into this line, Papagos could put thirty-five battalions, mostly withdrawn from eastern Macedonia and Thrace, but some from the Albanian front which he was prepared to shorten. He could hold one division back in reserve, perhaps two if the Greek hospitals could clear enough rested and recovered casualties, and with the British and Commonwealth forces this defensive position would prove quite formidable, even against Generalfeldmarschall List's Twelfth Army and General Freiherr von Richthofen's Fliegerkorps VIII which, according to Allied intelligence, was massing against them.

General Papagos would need twenty days to withdraw his forces to that line; how quickly could the British forces close up, realising that they would now have to be landed at Piraeus and Volos as Salonica would be far too vulnerable to German air attack?

As the answer to this question would depend upon shipping factors which had not yet been worked out, no firm response could be given then – but as some consolation it was pointed out that when the British did arrive their mobile units would be able to act in front of the Aliakmon Line as a delaying force. And they would come!

In the meantime, could work start immediately upon improving communications so that the British armour could move up as quickly as possible once it had landed?

At a final plenary session late on February 22nd, total agreement was reached upon the military plans, and as far as the political side was concerned, Mr Eden would approach Prince Paul, Regent of Yugoslavia, and endeavour to persuade him to harden his attitude to the dictators. If he would, all well and good, but preparations should at once be made and put into execution to withdraw the Greek advanced troops in Thrace and Macedonia to the line the allied force would be obliged to hold if the Yugoslavs did not come in.

The conference ended with expressions of trust and the utmost goodwill between all parties, and pledges of mutual co-operation until victory was secured. Mr Eden and his party returned to Cairo the next day, deeply impressed by the courageous attitude of the Greek leaders, and after a brief exchange of signals the War Cabinet in London approved the scheme – subject to agreement with the Governments of Australia and New Zealand. Mr Churchill's final exhortation on the subject read, 'Therefore while being under no illusions we all send you the order "Full steam ahead".'

It is always easy to be wise after the event, and no explanation has ever been given of the fact that no written version of the agreements reached between the British and Greek military leaders was drawn up and signed by both parties. Mr Eden made the agreed approach to Prince Paul, then on February 26th went to Ankara where he had friendly discussions with the Turkish leaders at which it was decided that, as things stood, it would be better for Turkey to remain out of the war unless she was herself deliberately attacked – at least until her many military deficiencies were made good. She guaranteed, however, to remain loyal to her alliance with Britain.

On the evening of February 27th, while still at Ankara, Mr Eden received a reply to his inquiry to Prince Paul, which was friendly – but uncertain enough in tone to make it quite clear that neither Greece nor Britain would be wise to depend upon Yugoslavia offering much resistance to an invading force; in the circumstances, all felt they had been wise to plan the retreat to the Aliakmon Line as a matter of urgency.

The events of the next few days seemed to confirm this feeling, for on March 1st, German troops crossed the Danube and moved in large numbers to positions around Sofia and Varna – with the agreement of the Bulgarian Government which at the same time announced itself wholeheartedly on the side of the Axis Powers. The danger to Greece was apparent to all; but for the moment there was nothing that Mr Eden could do, for appalling weather conditions marooned his party at Ismid on the Sea of Marmara.

They did not arrive in Athens until the afternoon of March 2nd – there to be told to their horror that no orders had yet been given for the transfer of Greek troops back from Thrace or Macedonia, apparently because General Papagos was under the impression that it had been agreed that such moves would not be made until a reply had been received from Yugoslavia to Mr Eden's approach. Moreover, in view of the German advance into Bulgaria, it was now too late for such manoeuvres, for not only would they have a disastrous effect on the morale of the Macedonian people, but they would lay the whole force open to the danger of destruction en route by German armies catching them in the flank.

The next few days were spent in talks sadly much less agreeable than the ones of two weeks previously, and no one would claim that the compromise finally achieved was in any way satisfactory in form – and certainly not in outcome. No one was happy, least of all the Commanders-in-Chief, Middle East.

But as it happened, when eventually Wavell did return to Cairo he was greeted by one piece of excellent news, and although it came from the same direction as all the best news had come of late – from Libya – it concerned a location of great importance over 400 miles from Beda Fomm, and it also concerned a special force which Wavell had sponsored since the previous July, and which promised to be of exceptional value.

Despite the recent birth of this force, its roots lay in the past – in the fighting which had taken place in the Western Desert twenty-four years before.

In the First World War, Italy had been an ally of Great Britain while the Senussi Arabs of Marmarica were, via the Turks, allied to the Central Powers. During 1915 the border areas between Libya and Egypt had been the scene of several minor skirmishes, and at the end of that year the Senussi, aided by Turkish money and German efficiency, had invaded Egyptian territory as far as Mersa Matruh. Quite a large number of British and Australian horsed cavalry units were engaged in holding back this incursion, but – like their successors in 1940 – had soon found their theatre of action limited to the coastal strip by problems of supply, especially of forage and water. The use of camels went only a little way towards solving the problems, for the Senussi were not only far more knowledgeable than their adversaries in the ways of the beasts, but they also knew far more about the terrain – virtually unmapped – away from the coastal belt.

It was in order to neutralise both these enemy advantages that Yeomanry Light Car Patrols had been set up in 1916. Using Model T Fords with 'oversize three and a half inch tyres' these patrols ranged well down into the desert, learning the basic techniques of existence there, inventing methods of both navigation and movement for wheeled transport in such conditions, carrying out surveys and map-making, eventually clearing the frontiers and nearer oases of the enemy presence, and then keeping them clear.

In 1917 that phase of the war ended and the following year the Light Car Patrols were disbanded, the men returned to their various more conventional units, the desert to its 10,000-year-old calm.

But it was not to remain undisturbed for very long.

Egypt was the overseas station for several British regiments including those of the Household Brigade, and not all of their officers were content with a social circle limited to the polite confines of Embassy, Officers' Mess and Gezira Sporting Club, varied occasionally by uncharacteristic forays into the Levantine worlds of Greek business or Alexandrine sophistication. Moreover, there was other employment in the Middle East between the wars for the adventurous or curious-minded – with the Sudan Forest Commission or the Egyptian Desert Survey for instance, or with one or other of the archaeological expeditions at work in Egypt, or further afield in the deserts of Sinai and beyond the Jordan.

From among the men and women who thus found themselves in the area had grown up a body of enthusiasts who, learning of the activities of the Light Car Patrols, had ventured out themselves along uncharted ways and into unmapped spaces to acquire again the techniques which the Yeomanry had pioneered, to refine them and to invent new ones – and in so doing had fallen under the spell of that empty, harsh, desolate landscape, which demands so much of its devotees and whose rewards are so fleeting; but unforgettable.

The acknowledged leader of this group was Major R. A. Bagnold of the Royal Corps of Signals, and between the late 1920s and the outbreak of war he organised and led many small parties thousands of miles across the lunar landscape between the Mediterranean and the Sudan, between the Red Sea and the Tibesti Mountains. What began as weekend trips from Cairo to Siwa and back in the 1920s, had by 1938 grown into safaris lasting three weeks and covering a thousand miles or more in trips to Kuffra, 'Uweinat or Wadi Halfa.

When war broke out, Bagnold had been on leave in England and in October had been on his way back to East Africa to a new and unexceptional posting. En route through the Mediterranean (still controlled by the French and British navies and with Italy still neutral) his ship was involved in a collision so the captain put into Alexandria for repairs. During the delay, Bagnold travelled to Cairo to visit old friends. Gossip flew as rapidly as only in the Middle East it can and within a few hours Wavell had learned of his presence; within twenty-four the East African appointment had been cancelled and Bagnold was on the staff at H.Q. Cairo – simply as a communications officer, however, for the political injunction against activity which might offend Mussolini's sense of Mediterranean proprieties was still in force and Bagnold's first suggestion for the formation of a unit capable of carrying out reconnaissance deep into Libyan territory was firmly pigeon-holed.

The Italian declaration of war on June 10th, 1940, quickly put an end to this situation.

On June 19th Bagnold submitted another, and even more deeply considered scheme, four days later it had been approved and by the end of the month he was collecting together the most immediately available of his pre-war collaborators. Their objective was to create a formation which could penetrate deep into the deserts of both Egypt and Libya – to carry out, in fact, the kind of journeys for which they had each lately been paying some £20 per head per thousand miles of their own hard-earned money; now they would be encouraged to do so at Government expense. No one turned the offer down, though some were prevented from joining by superior edict for as long as it took to circumvent it.

W. B. Kennedy Shaw resigned from the Colonial Service in Palestine (where, despite his intimate knowledge of Egypt and the Sudan and his repeated pleas to be allowed to return there, he had been retained since the outbreak of war on the stultifying duties of censoring newspapers) and joined Bagnold in Cairo within a fortnight; P. A. Clayton, one of the few men who had been to Kuffra in the course of duty (with the Egyptian Government Survey Department) came up from Tanganyika, and Captain E. C. Mitford who had also been to Kuffra was posted in from the 6th Royal Tank Regiment, somewhat to his surprise as he had been expecting fairly early action as one of the 4th Armoured Brigade's officers under 'Blood' Caunter.

As they began planning the composition of the force, it quickly became clear what its first assignment would be. Just because the enemy were Italian, it was not enough to assume that they were doing nothing. Italians had already colonised Cyrenaica and Eritrea, had kept in subservience the indigenous though sparse population of Libya for twenty years and had apparently done the same in Ethiopia for four. This could not have been achieved without martial talents and administrative abilities of some order, and if the leadership in the north appeared somewhat hesitant for the moment (and this was still at the time when Balbo was in command) it did not necessarily ensure that the same applied in the south.

The Italians controlled Kuffra and it was known that they had a garrison and landing grounds near Jebel 'Uweinat, the 6,000-foot massif marking the junction point of Egypt, the Sudan and Libya. From Kuffra, they might be planning for an advance down into Chad Province which would influence the French there, still hesitant between Vichy and de Gaulle; from 'Uweinat they could launch a raid across to Wadi Halfa where they could wreck the dockyard and railway workshops, sink the river and lake steamers and thus cut the inner link between Cairo and Khartoum. If at the same time the Italian Navy in the Red Sea – perhaps aided by Italian submarines which would have made the journey around the Cape – could block the narrows north of Djibuti, then there would be no way in which South Africa, Rhodesia, Kenya or the Sudan could send up aid to the Middle East command if and when an Italian advance towards the Delta took place.

These were the possibilities; was the Comando Supremo about to exploit them?

Answers to that and similar questions would obviously be required quickly, and Bagnold and his assistants were spurred to utmost effort – to which end Wavell, who took a close and personal interest in them from the beginning, ordered that the needs of the new force were to be met with the minimum of fuss, opposition or red tape.

The first requirement was for men – and men of a certain type. The British soldier is, almost by definition, a man of infinite adaptability but the necessity for speed dictated that the first teams should be formed from men born and bred to country life as opposed to urban, to the outback as opposed to English pastoral. Australian formations were not immediately available in the summer of 1940 but the first New Zealanders had arrived in the Middle East and from them came the men for the first patrols, possibly – in view of their Government's later attitude – because of the comparative smallness of the numbers required. About a hundred men, mostly from the New Zealand Divisional Cavalry and in civilian life farmers or otherwise independently minded professionals, made up the first patrols – to be followed fairly soon afterwards by Rhodesians and in due course by men from the British Yeomanry Regiments comprising the Territorial Division which had arrived in Palestine. Eventually, too, there would be patrols made up of men from the Guards Brigade.

While the recruitment was proceeding, the problems of transport and supply were also being tackled. Trucks of somewhat greater engine-power and capacity than those used in peacetime would obviously be needed if only to carry the extra weight of weapons and ammunition, of explosives, signal sets and an allocation of medical equipment rather in advance of a motorist's first aid kit. Fords were unavailable, but there were Chevrolet 30-cwt trucks capable of adaptation to take a load of at least two tons with extra leaves fitted to the springs, and doors, windshields and main body tops stripped off. Racks were then fitted for radio sets, water containers, jerricans (when they became available) and mountings welded on for light and heavy machine-guns. All these adaptations and a couple of dozen others had to be carried out not only rapidly, but also with some degree of secrecy. It was fortunate that the American and Greek technicians at Chevrolet in Alexandria and at Fords in Cairo were not only well disposed towards the British, but discreet as well.

One of the most valuable additions to each truck was a radiator condenser, usually in the form of a steel tank bolted to the step. Sealed and half-filled with water, it was connected by tube to the top of the radiator which was itself sealed, the overflow blocked off. When the radiator boiled – which it did with monotonous regularity several times during every day of a patrol – the steam would be condensed in the water of the condenser tank and when the radiator cooled the vacuum thus formed would suck water back until the original balance was regained. If all seals were perfect (which by the nature of things they rarely were) there would be no need to top the radiator up from the beginning of the patrol to the end.

Problems of desert navigation had also to be solved, and techniques mastered. From the English Schools in Cairo and Alexandria logarithm tables were scavenged; theodolites were borrowed from Egyptian Survey or bought in obscure second-hand shops in half-forgotten back-streets of Khartoum, binoculars cadged from the Gezira Sporting Club membership. From the Egyptian Army came the essential 'sun-compasses' with which direction could be maintained despite the magnetism of the metal truck chassis, which could throw an ordinary compass ten degrees out. And a ten-degree error on a 500-mile journey would mean missing the objective by 87 miles; even a two-degree error would miss it by 17 miles, which at daybreak behind enemy lines might be serious.

Desert navigation was not just a matter of map-reading, for maps of the major part of the region either did not exist or were hopelessly inaccurate. A small part of the Egyptian desert was well mapped (often as a result of the work of the Light Car Patrols or of members of the pre-war Bagnold parties), a large proportion of it was indicated on maps by vacant white spaces marked 'Unknown' – and far too much of the Libyan Desert was splattered on captured maps with considerable detail which proved on investigation to have but a tenuous connection with geography. Kennedy Shaw, who as Intelligence Officer for the newly born formation had to deal with such problems, later wrote of these Italian creations:

There was no nonsense about the petty details of topography on these sheets. Many of them were obviously based on air observation (but not on air survey), and after a few flights across the country the cartographer had roughed in a range of mountains here and a sand sea or two there. The mountains were all high as became the dignity of Fascist Italy. Making our way anxiously towards an obviously impassable range of hills, we would find that we had driven over it without feeling the bump. But I have a certain grudging admiration for Captain Marchesi of the Istituto Geografico Militare, the equivalent of our Ordnance Survey, who made the 1/100,000 map of Jalo. Marchesi, I am sure, was a realist. Jalo, he felt, was a one-eyed hole of which no map was really needed. The sand was soft and the day hot, so why worry? Marchesi put his feet up on the mess table shouted for another drink, and drew his map. It is just possible that the absurd inaccuracies were a deep plot to mislead our attacking forces, but it seems hardly likely that the Italians had thought of that as long ago as 1931.[9]

Eventually, the formation was joined by a professional survey officer, Captain K. H. Lazarus, who would disappear for weeks on end with two or three trucks and reappear with sheaves of pencilled notes and drawings from which, in due course, detailed maps of yet another thousand square miles of enemy territory could be printed. The present rulers of Libya owe a great, though unacknowledged, debt to Captain Lazarus and his assistants in the Long Range Desert Group.

This was the title assumed by the formation gradually taking shape under Major Bagnold's expert guidance. It is possible that only he possessed both the practical knowledge of the problems which the new unit would have to overcome, and the understanding of British Army practice and regulation into which the unit would have to fit. In all corporation life, it is a great advantage to know which is the right form to fill in.

Clayton was the first of the group to venture out, taking six trucks borrowed from the Egyptian Frontier Administration complete with Sudanese crews (the L.R.D.G. trucks and men were still in the process of adaptation and assembly). During the first days of August 1940, he pushed his way south across the Great Sand Sea along a line parallel with the Libyan border to a location known as Two Hills, then westwards and across the border over a gravel plain of excellent going until he reached another sand sea, later to be identified as the Kalansho but at that moment marked on no maps and completely unknown to anyone in Cairo. For two days, they laboured to cross this new obstacle, over range after range of high and convoluted dunes, eventually to reach the Serir of Kalansho along the edge of which ran the main Jalo–Kuffra route.

This he watched for three days – unavailingly, for it had broken up under regular traffic and the Italians had abandoned it in favour of a new track some twenty miles to the west – but by the time he returned, he had learned some valuable new facts and relearned some old ones. Among the first was the discovery of the level plain to the north of Kuffra within the horseshoe of sand seas, and among the second was the desirability of examining footwear for scorpions and other night visitors before trying to put them on in the morning. It is incredible how easily and quickly such habits are forgotten in the cushioned luxury of town life.

In the meantime training was continuing, and as a part of it a vital preliminary chore was carried out. The main routes south-westwards out of Cairo and down past Baharia, either to 'Ain Dalla and across the Sand Sea to Two Hills, or down even further to Pottery Hill and around to the Gilf Kebir, were safe routes still in Egyptian territory and secure except for an occasional marauding enemy aircraft. It was thus possible for dumps to be formed along them and emergency posts set up between the main dumps with supplies of water and food, boots, clothing and medical supplies for victims of accident or attack. In the establishment of such posts much valuable experience was gained in navigation, driving, unsticking trucks and lorries from soft sand, keeping in wireless touch with headquarters despite the vagaries of the radio sets, the problems of 'skip distances' and the infuriating obscurity of ciphers which would not come out.

By the end of August 1940, hundreds of gallons of petrol and water had been cached between Baharia and the western edge of the Great Sand Sea, and an investigation carried out into Italian activities at 'Uweinat. As this revealed that the Italians were doing nothing – nothing offensive, that is – Bagnold decided it was time for his men to venture further afield and tackle the job of crossing the Sand Sea. Kennedy Shaw's description of the obstacle and the task can hardly be bettered:

> There is nothing like these sand seas anywhere else in the world. Take an area the size of Ireland and cover it with sand. Go on pouring sand on to it till it is two, three or four hundred feet deep. Then with a giant's rake score the sand into ridges and valleys running north-north-west and south-south-east, and with the ridges, at their highest, five hundred feet from trough to crest.
>
> Late in the evening when the sands cool quickly and the dunes throw long shadows the Sand Sea is one of the most lovely things in the world; no words can properly describe the beauty of those sweeping curves of sand. At a summer midday when the sun beats down all its shapes to one flat glare of sand and the sand-drift blows off the dune crests like the snow-plume off Everest, it is as good an imitation of Hell as one could devise. It was across 150 miles of this dead world that Bagnold was proposing to take for the first time a force of heavily loaded trucks.[10]

It took them two days to cross from opposite 'Ain Dalla to Big Cairn, two days of excruciating physical effort in a world full of heat and blown sand, of continual hunting for gaps in the dune ranges, of labouring trucks fighting their way up to uncertain summits, there to be greeted at worst by an unacceptably steep drop in front, at best by a mile-long plough down a treacherous slope spotted with patches of soft sand. Then it all had to start again . . . and for the trail-breaking leading trucks the stops and starts were endless. At one moment you would be steadily forging ahead to the encouraging hum of tyres on hard sand and the thump of gear-changes, the next stopped dead with the back wheels spinning and the truck quickly down to the differential in soft and apparently bottomless dust.

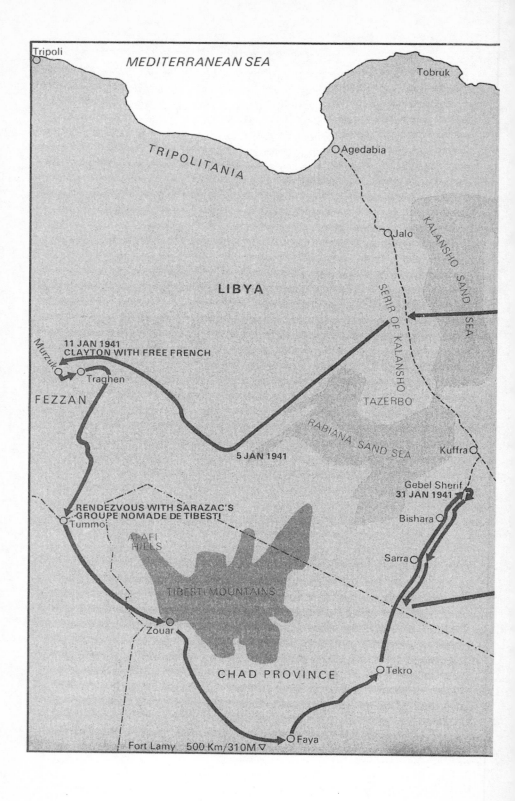

Tripoli

MEDITERRANEAN SEA

Tobruk

TRIPOLITANIA

Agedabia

LIBYA

Jalo

KALANSHO SAND SEA

SERIR OF KALANSHO

11 JAN 1941
CLAYTON WITH FREE FRENCH

Murzuk

Traghen

FEZZAN

TAZERBO

RABIANA SAND SEA

5 JAN 1941

Kuffra

Gebel Sherif
31 JAN 1941

RENDEZVOUS WITH SARAZAC'S
GROUPE NOMADE DE TIBESTI

Tummo

AFAFI
HILLS

Bishara

Sarra

TIBESTI MOUNTAINS

Zouar

CHAD PROVINCE

Tekro

Fort Lamy   500 Km/310M ▽

Faya

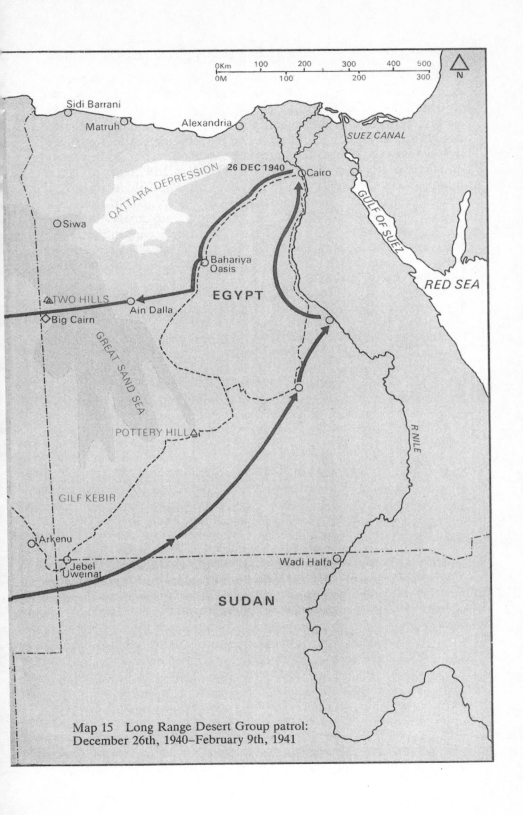

Map 15   Long Range Desert Group patrol:
December 26th, 1940–February 9th, 1941

Then would come the decision whether to try to go forward to firm ground or to cut an immediate loss and back out of it; and then the hard, sweating graft of digging out under the wheels to get sand-channels or canvas strips under the tyres, the gentle and ever-hopeful letting in of the clutch to see if the wheels would grip and not just tear the channels or strip back under the tyres, while twenty cursing men tugged and shoved and rocked the truck to get it moving back just the two-yard length of the mat; then to start all over again. After a day of such labour, every inch of flesh was clogged with sand caked into mud with sweat, and chafed further in by shirt and trousers, collar and belt, all equally impregnated with sand. And it was not helped by the fact that at times the metal of the trucks was too hot to touch with bare hands, at least until they became covered with calluses.

At Big Cairn, virtually on the Libyan border, they unloaded stores and began marking out a landing ground, while one group went back to 'Ain Dalla to bring forward another load . . . and because they could follow the tracks and avoid the pitfalls, the return journey took only six and a quarter hours!

Then the patrols split, Clayton circling Kuffra and driving down the track leading south to the French post at Tekro in Chad Province where he was to investigate possibilities of co-operation with the pro-De Gaulle troops there, while another patrol with Mitford and Kennedy Shaw searched the tracks north of Kuffra and a third made yet another trip back across the Sand Sea to bring forward yet another load of supplies.

At first Mitford's patrol made excellent going across the gravel plain but they hit the edge of the newly discovered Kalansho Sand Sea at the same time as a Libyan *gibli*, the transborder equivalent of the Egyptian *khamsin*, but as it was further south it was also fiercer and even more dehydrating:

> You don't merely feel hot, you don't merely feel tired, you feel as if every bit of energy had left you, as if your brain was thrusting its way through the top of your head and you want to lie in a stupor till the accursed sun has gone down.[11]

All day they fought their way through the Kalansho, emerging in the evening near the Jalo–Kuffra track where the *gibli* developed into a sandstorm which stung their hands and faces unbearably and forced them to button up their clothes and thus secure no relief from the heat. But at least no enemy would be abroad in such revolting weather, so they visited two of the Italian landing grounds along the track and wrecked the petrol pumps and fuel tanks.

The next day they moved even further west in heat which brought men to the edge of delirium, one of the navigators afterwards confessing that for over twenty miles following behind the leading truck he had found himself repeating endlessly to the rhythm of the tyres, 'If he doesn't stop I shall go mad. If he doesn't stop I shall go mad. If he doesn't . . .'

Conditions improved the next day, and three days later the L.R.D.G. went into action for the first time, capturing two six-ton lorries belonging to the firm of Trucci and Monti with their civilian drivers under contract to supply stores and mail to the garrison at Kuffra. A few days afterwards the patrol joined up with Bagnold again in the Gilf Kebir east of Kuffra, hid the lorries in a cave where as far as is known they remain to this day, kept rendezvous with the returning Clayton who brought excellent news from Chad Province and then moved south to take a closer look at the Italians around Jebel 'Uweinat. There was nothing of note to delay them there, and by October 1st all were back at base to receive Wavell's congratulations as soon as their reports, and the contents of the captured mail-bag, had been thoroughly examined.

Other, less tangible but equally important results from the trip had been the impressions brought back from Tekro by Clayton, for the French were enthusiastically for De Gaulle and against Vichy, and uncomfortably anxious to recover the military prestige which had been lost by the sorry misadventures at home four months before. Since the outbreak of war there had been French plans for raids up into the Fezzan if ever Italy showed herself more aggressively committed to the Pact of Steel than she did at the beginning, and French eyes had been fixed upon Kuffra as an objective for attack well before British Headquarters in Cairo had been made particularly aware of its existence.

It was this potential for French co-operation which took Bagnold down to Fort Lamy in November 1940 (when O'Connor was setting up his first Field Supply Depots between Matruh and Sidi Barrani) to explore possibilities, the most significant of which was help with supplies – especially petrol – for an L.R.D.G. raid to the far side of Libya below Tripolitania, culminating in an attack on the town of Murzuk. And if the French wished to send troops to take part in the attack they would be most welcome, as would aid and refuge in French territory for the patrols on their way home.

Colonel Jacques Leclerc, who had assumed command of the French troops in Chad as soon as the governor, M. Eboué, had declared unequivocally for De Gaulle, was more than anxious to collaborate, and indeed suggested that this could well be the time for the attack on Kuffra, with the L.R.D.G. patrols on their way home helping the French in comradely exchange for the French help received on their way out.

This was obviously a situation full of promise, and while it was being thoroughly explored the now-thriving L.R.D.G. grew in both size and experience. Both Rhodesian and New Zealand patrols, each consisting of two officers and about thirty men, were trained and active and two Guards patrols had been formed, one from the 3rd Coldstream Guards and one from the 2nd Scots Guards. During October and November they were all out on separate forays, mining roads leading up from Jalo to Agedabia in the north and between 'Uweinat and Arkenu in the south, attacking isolated garrisons, blowing up explosive and fuel dumps, on one occasion destroying a Savoia bomber caught on a distant landing ground; but chiefly they were learning the duties of reconnaissance – penetration, observation, communication and, above all, survival. No one, inside or outside the Long Range Desert Group, ever gained the impression that it was a suicide squad.

On December 26th, 1940 – while the Australians outside Bardia were recovering from their Christmas dinners and the British were still waiting for supplies – G (Guards) and T (New Zealand) patrols, consisting of seventy-six men travelling in twenty-three vehicles, left Cairo under overall command of Captain P. A. Clayton. On the way past Mena, they picked up Sheikh 'Abd el Galil Seif en Nasr, of the family of paramount chiefs of the Awlad Suleiman nomad tribe who had fought against Italian occupation of Tripolitania since its beginning, and who was himself the veteran of many desert battles. Not only would he act as guide at the crucial junctures of the expedition, but he would also lend an air of Arabic respectability to what might otherwise be seen as a piece of marauding brigandage, by one foreign race against another. Which is what it was . . . but then the sheikh himself was no pillar of polite society, being majestic in girth, fierce in temperament, crippled in arm and leg in some long-forgotten desert skirmish and much given to chewing tobacco and spitting, which could be unfortunate for his travelling companions if the wind was in the wrong direction.

They reached 'Ain Dalla, crossed the Great Sand Sea and the Kalansho beyond, and ten days after leaving Cairo were at the rendezvous point 150 miles north of the Tibesti Mountains. Clayton drove off south to meet the French and collect the essential petrol which had come by camel across from Bardai, while Kennedy Shaw, that indefatigable explorer, tried to ferret out a hitherto unknown route from the west to Kuffra through a rumoured but unidentifiable pass across the Eghei Hills; he was unsuccessful this time, but the route did exist and was to prove useful.

Meanwhile, Clayton had collected the French party consisting of the commander of the French troops at Fort Lamy, Lieutenant-Colonel d'Ornano, a monocled figure, tall, hawk-featured and clad in turban and burnous; Capitaine Massu and an Alsatian lieutenant with two French sergeants and five native troops. There was no doubt that these French meant to fight.

Two days later, on the morning of January 11th (by which time the Australians were moving up to complete the investment of Tobruk) they were ten miles north of Murzuk and from a nearby ridge could see the white roofs, the palms, the radio masts above the fort and the roof of a hangar. It was quite evident that total security had blanketed their 1,500-mile journey throughout its entire eighteen days and that no one in the enemy camp ahead had the slightest inkling of their presence.

They drove into Murzuk after lunch, being greeted by natives around a well with casual 'Buon Giorno's and kidnapping the post-master to act as guide to the fort; then half the trucks peeled off to attack and pin down the garrison, while the rest swung away towards the airfield which constituted the main objective. By the time the second party was in sight of the main hangar the sounds of mortar and machine-gun fire from the fort had alerted the airfield troops, and it became a race towards the machine-gun posts between guards and trucks.

The result was mixed. Kennedy Shaw and Bruce Ballantyne with one group won their race and took prisoner the crews of the nearest machine-gun posts, but Clayton's truck, screaming round a corner of the hangar, ran full tilt into a post as the crew opened up, and as Clayton frantically threw the gears into reverse, the Vickers gun alongside him jammed. There was a short intensive burst of firing, the truck shuddered as Breda bullets ripped along the sides, and then Clayton was back in the shelter of the hangar with d'Ornano dead behind him with blood streaming from a gaping throat wound, and beside him the body of an Italian Air Force sergeant who had also been forcibly co-opted as a guide.

Then the truck with the patrol Bofors came up and quickly put out of action the responsible post and its courageous crew, then turned its heavier metal on to the hangar itself, whose inhabitants were thus caught between Shaw and Ballantyne's machine-gun fire and the Bofors. They quickly surrendered. Inside, Shaw found three Ghibli Bombers which he soaked with petrol, sluicing more over the floor and walls of the hangar and then laying a petrol trail out and across the airfield. The patrol vehicles drew clear, a match was applied and the results were practically instantaneous and dramatic in the extreme. The hangar erupted like a giant torch and, as the L.R.D.G. men watched, the roof collapsed on to the aircraft below while bombs and ammunition exploded in a highly satis-factory display of pyrotechnics. And with the smoke and flame as a background, a string of old African women with bundles of firewood on their heads shuffled with half-bent knees across the airfield exhibiting not the slightest interest in the happenings around them.

Meanwhile, the Guards patrol attack on the fort had set the main tower and flagstaff alight and successfully penned the majority of the garrison inside, as was intended. The exception was the Italian commander who had been out to lunch, apparently with a lady friend and her child; they drove up to the main gate in the middle of the battle and the Guards Bofors was unfortunately turned on the car before it was realised what its cargo was.

Within two hours of the beginning of the attack the patrols were clear of the town again on the route by which they had come in, leaving behind them a burning fort, an airfield with all installations totally wrecked, and some twenty dead bodies. They had also caused such a state of panic and confusion among the Italian command throughout Tripolitania that from then on all garrisons on this unimportant front were to be strengthened, and all vehicle movement along the thousands of miles of desert tracks would be in convoys, guarded by extra armed patrols and as much air cover as could be spared. Italian soldiers and aircraft of the Tripolitania command were henceforth to wear out their boots and engines on sentry go.

The attackers, however, had by no means got off scot free. In addition to d'Ornano, one of the New Zealand sergeants had been killed and four men had been wounded, one of them seriously. (It was later discovered that Capitaine Massu had also been wounded by a bullet through the calf; but he had merely cauterised both entrance and exit wounds with the end of a lighted cigarette and not bothered to mention it to anyone. When questioned as to what he had done with the cigarette end, he replied gravely that he had thrown it away, 'but of course, I had practically finished it beforehand . . . ') In the light of such an episode, his later career is hardly surprising.

They were not pursued by any force from Murzuk, and their fears of air attack proved empty. Moreover, when they approached the small post of Traghen about thirty miles from Murzuk it was evident that nothing was known there of earlier events, and there was no sign of opposition from the garrison who trailed sheepishly out to surrender almost as soon as demands were made. At the next post, however, this pusillanimity was not repeated – and as the fort was of stone construction and the defence resolute, Clayton decided that it was not worth the risk of further casualties. Moreover, it was time to move back into friendly country so he led them south to a rendezvous with a French Camel Corps unit – Sarazac's Groupe Nomade de Tibesti – at Tummo on the border of Libya and French West Africa.

There is a widespread though somewhat insular belief that love affairs with deserts are an English prerogative, and that the only European feet to leave footprints in the burning sand belong to people with names like Doughty, Shakespear, Gertrude Bell, Lawrence, Thesiger and, more lately, Hillaby. This is not so. One of the first and greatest of the camel explorers at the end of the last century was the German Gerhard Rohlfs, and both the Spanish and the Italians have produced notable travellers into the empty, arid wastes of the world. As for the French, after their first incursion into the African continent, they practised desert travel to such an extent as to make it almost an accepted and even unremarkable profession.

Kennedy Shaw was most impressed:

> At times in L.R.D.G. we used to consider ourselves tough, but the life of those French Méhariste officers made one think again. With nothing more than a roll of bedding to spread on the ground they were away for months on end even from the small comforts of their desert posts. We knew that in a few weeks we would be back in the civilisation of Cairo. But the life of the Groupe Nomade is the life of its camels. Camels must follow the changing grazing and the men must follow them, and Sarazac, having finished his operations, would move at once to the scanty pasturage of the Afafi Hills. Added to this – Pétain and Laval being what they were – these men were outlaws from their own country, lost after years of service in the most desolate area of the Central Sahara, having had no home leave for years and with no prospect of leave for years to come. And, perhaps worst of all, with never a word of news from their families in France. Mail day roused no interest in Tibesti.[12]

These were the men who now escorted Clayton's men back through Zouar to Faya, where plans were discussed with Colonel Leclerc, an officer completely in the mould of d'Ornano and Massu, for a joint attack on Kuffra.

It was not until January 26th (the night on which to O'Connor's fury, Babini's armour escaped from Mechili) that Clayton's two patrols left Faya to act as advance guard for the attack, for a great deal of preparation was necessary, especially in view of the distances to be covered. Chad Province main base at Fort Lamy lay 450 miles back behind Faya, while the first stage towards Kuffra would be to Tekro, 200 miles ahead. Moreover, Tekro was the nearest water supply to Kuffra, for both intermediate wells – at Sarra 165 miles and Bishara 270 miles on – had been filled in by the Italians. Water, and indeed everything else, for the 365 miles between Tekro and Kuffra must therefore be carried in the trucks and the ration reduced considerably below the six pints per man per day upon which the trip so far had existed.

Unfortunately, if French military enthusiasm and desertworthiness was admirable, the same did not apply to their security. 'Vers Koufra' had been the toast in the messes and the gossip in the streets for some time, and too much loose chatter on the wireless had taken place for the enemy in the target area to be as unaware of their situation as those at Murzuk had been.

The result was that when, on January 31st, Clayton with T patrol reached Jebel Sherif, sixty miles south of Kuffra, he found himself neatly ambushed in a narrow valley by men of an Italian Auto-Saharan Company, supported by four 20mm. Breda guns and three aircraft. The action which followed was short, sharp and decisive; at the end of it, three of the L.R.D.G. trucks had been burnt out, a New Zealand corporal and two of the Italian prisoners were dead, Clayton and two others taken prisoner (Clayton had been wounded), four men were missing and the remainder of the patrol was in rapid retreat to Sarra where, fortunately, the Guards patrol had been left in reserve. They joined up later that day, and after a brief conference and rest, fell back towards the main French force at Tekro. What none of them realised was that the four men 'missing' had decided not to give themselves up and were following them out on foot.

Trooper Moore from New Zealand, Guardsmen Easton and Winchester and an R.A.O.C. fitter named Tighe had run for cover as soon as their truck had erupted in flame, and had spent the rest of the afternoon crouching among the rocks of Jebel Sherif (accompanied by the remaining Italian prisoner) in a situation aptly described as 'far from pleasant'.

They watched the end of the action, the departure of their surviving comrades, the collection of Clayton and the other two prisoners by the victors, and the Italians' return towards Kuffra without any attempt either to search or to clear up the battlefield. During the extremely cold night which followed the four discussed what to do, and despite the fact that Easton had been wounded in the throat and Moore in the foot, that they had no food and only one and three-quarter gallons of water contained in a two-gallon tin with a bullet-hole through it (fortunately near the top), they overrode the opinion of the Italian prisoner and decided not to surrender. Thus began the first of the series of epic desert walks with which the story of the North African campaign is punctuated.

Three days later, on February 4th, they had reached and passed Bishara, but Tighe was feeling the effects of an old operation and beginning to lag. (Not surprisingly, the Italian prisoner had disappeared during the first day, and eventually made his way to

Kuffra.) On the fourth day the men found some lentils which had been thrown away during a meal on the way up which gave them back a little strength, but next day they decided that they must press ahead leaving Tighe to follow at his own, slower pace. They left him with his share of water in a bottle they had found.

On February 6th, a sandstorm blew up and virtually obliterated the car tracks they were following, but they forced their way on until they reached the mud huts around the blocked well at Sarra. Here the three spent their first night in shelter (the previous ones had been freezing and it had been very difficult to get any sleep in the open, clad only in thin khaki drill), and they found some waste motor oil in which they soaked their feet.

On February 7th, they walked on, and behind them during the evening Tighe arrived at Sarra, took refuge in one of the huts and decided to rest there the whole of the next day. During that day and February 9th the first three slogged on, but the pace had slowed and the gaps between the staggering figures were widening, with Moore always out in front despite the wound in his foot, and Easton now gradually dropping behind. Then during that day, they were seen by a French aircraft which circled around and dropped some food and water; they never found the food and the cork burst out of the bottle as it hit the ground and only a mouthful remained. But late that night a French patrol, sent up to carry out a reconnaissance for another attempt on Kuffra, called at Sarra and found Tighe.

The patrol set out after Moore and his companions at first light on the 10th, found Easton still just alive about fifty miles south of Sarra, Winchester ten miles further on, delirious but just able to struggle to his feet as he heard the trucks – and Moore ahead of him, having walked 210 miles from Jebel Sherif in ten days, on a wounded foot with virtually no food and half a gallon of water. He was quite confident that he could have covered the eighty miles to Tekro in another three days, and according to the Frenchmen who picked him up, seemed rather put out that they had prevented him. He was awarded the Distinguished Conduct Medal – the first won by the L.R.D.G. – but Easton died the evening he was found.

Back in Tekro, Leclerc decided that the conditions for the attack on Kuffra had changed irrevocably, for it would now obviously lack any element of surprise. Moreover, the L.R.D.G. contingent had lost too many trucks and what were left were showing signs almost of disintegration after the battering they had received since leaving Cairo – so except for the best truck and its crew which remained behind to help the French with their navigation, he released the rest. Led now by Captain Bruce Ballantyne after the loss of Clayton, the L.R.D.G. men arrived back at base on February 9th, two days after Beda Fomm, having travelled 4,300 miles in forty-five days, mostly behind Italian lines.

Leclerc wasted little time. He assembled a force consisting of 100 Europeans and about 300 natives, 30 machine-guns, two 37mms, four mortars and a portée 75mm. cannon. They left Sarra on February 17th and during the next two days fought what must have been the first mobile battle of the desert war – between Bedford lorries and Lancia diesel trucks crewed by infantry firing rifles and machine-guns. They were taut, close-fought battles of manoeuvre and counter, of swift pounce and covered retreat – and at the end of the second day, an impartial observer would have been hard put to say whether the French or the Italians were winning.

But as had happened before and was to happen again, when Leclerc's men drove out on the morning of February 20th to renew the action, they found that the Auto-Saharan Company had departed for Tazerbo and left the field to them. By that evening, the French had fully invested the fort at Kuffra, and the 75mm. was lobbing shells into its courtyard while offensive patrols were roaming at will over the entire oasis – for without their mobile screen the garrison were virtually helpless.

During the next week, a curious pattern developed whereby the native inhabitants would leave their homes each morning and spend the day watching the battle, then return home through the investing lines each evening to prepare the evening meal. On February 28th the Italians suggested that the wounded on both sides be placed in an agreed area out of the firing line, but during the consultations which then took place, one of the Italians inquired as to what the surrender terms were likely to be.

Realising that the end was therefore near, Leclerc stepped up the shelling and increased the patrolling and at dawn on March 1st, a white flag was flying from the tower. The Italian rule over Kuffra was at an end.

8 · Enter Rommel

Unfortunately for Wavell – and indeed for the British Army in the Middle East as a whole – as he was reading the cheering reports of the events of March 1st down in Kuffra, other reports, this time on the situation along the most southerly curve of the Gulf of Sirte, were being assessed by a new arrival on the desert scene – one, moreover, who was to stamp his imprint upon the North African campaign to such an extent that no mention of it can fail to evoke his name.

Generalleutnant Erwin Johannes Eugen Rommel had arrived at Castel Benito airfield south of Tripoli on the morning of February 12th and spent the intervening time giving all who came into contact with him an exhibition of the extraordinary mental and physical energy which was to be the hallmark of his command. At this time, Rommel was just nine months short of his fiftieth birthday, a stocky, compact man with no excess flesh, lean features and grey-blue eyes which generally sparkled with both humour and friendliness but which could crackle into blazing fury in an instant.

He had been informed of his new appointment by the Führer himself on the afternoon of February 6th (thus making that week one of the most significant in the history of the campaign) and despite the strict limitations placed upon his activities by the Commander-in-Chief of the Army, Generalfeldmarschall von Brauchitsch, during a subsequent interview, he was quite determined not only that the British advance must be held, but that it must also be thrown back at least as far as the Egyptian border, and preferably further.

Moreover, in view of what he quickly discerned as 'the sluggishness of the Italian command' he had also decided 'to depart from my instructions to confine myself to a reconnaissance and to take the command at the front into my own hands as soon as possible' – a decision which he had imparted to Generalleutnant von Rintelen in Rome, who earnestly advised against it. That was the way, von Rintelen warned, to lose both reputation and honour; but it was a risk Rommel was prepared to take.

Another warning he received within an hour of his arrival in North Africa was from Generale d'Armata Italo Gariboldi, who had taken over command from Graziani upon the latter's not unexpected resignation a few days previously and who now, after listening unenthusiastically to Rommel's plan for the immediate establishment of a strong defence line in the Sirte area – some 200 miles in advance of the lines around Tripoli which Gariboldi had envisaged – gloomily pointed out that Rommel lacked any vestige of experience of desert warfare and had no idea of the difficulties presented by the terrain. To this, Rommel replied crisply that he had every intention of repairing any gaps in his knowledge as quickly as possible, and suiting the action to the word, took off in a Heinkel 111 that same afternoon to fly over the soil of Africa for the first time.

He was by no means discouraged, appreciating immediately the truth behind the remark that the desert was fit for nothing except war. There was a long stretch of undoubtedly difficult country immediately east of Tripoli which would help the defence if and when the British reached that far, but beyond that there was a level plain in which he would be able to deploy his mobile forces, when they arrived, to best effect; while beyond Buerat as far as Sirte lay a stretch of salt marshes which could again provide sound defences if held by stolid infantry. And as Rommel was a great believer in Napoleon's maxim that there are no bad men, only bad officers, he was not unduly concerned at the fact that the only infantry immediately available were Italian, as he intended to command them himself.

When he returned to Tripoli that first evening, he had already made up his mind upon a number of subjects – and his road to success had been smoothed by the arrival of the Chief of Staff of the Italian Army, Generale d'Armata Roatta, bearing with him a directive from Il Duce instructing Gariboldi to place all Italian motorised units in the area at Rommel's disposal. As Rommel was both liberal in his interpretation of the adjective 'motorised', and forceful in argument, the Italian X Corps, consisting of the Brescia and Pavia Divisions, were soon moving up towards Sirte to reinforce the scanty defences already there, while the tanks of the Ariete (only sixty of them, mixed M13s and L3s) were following in its wake.

Moreover, Rommel's first explosion of anger in the Mediterranean theatre was already taking effect. On the day before his arrival in North Africa, Rommel had visited the Commander of the X Luftwaffe Korps at Catania in Sicily, General der Flieger Geissler, and asked him to concentrate his bombing attacks upon Benghasi and the British columns to the south – a request which Geissler had turned down with some force. He was, he explained, virtually a visitor to Italy and a none too popular one at that; and he had recently received strong representations from his hosts to the effect that he should not bomb Benghasi, as so many high military and civilian officials owned houses there.

'I had no patience with this,' Rommel later reported with some understatement, and messages flowed between Rome and the Führer's Headquarters on the subject. The bombing of Benghasi started that night and when, six days later, the first British supply convoy for O'Connor's forces arrived, it found the port under such strong attack that it had to return to Tobruk with its cargoes still in the holds.

Rommel's main concern in those first few days was, of course, to get German formations ashore and up into the forward areas and it was with considerable relief that he learned that the first convoy had arrived in Tripoli on the afternoon of February 14th. His immediate instructions that unloading was to continue throughout the night by lamplight, despite the dangers of attack by the R.A.F., were accepted with resignation by the port authorities and the following afternoon the first contingent of the Afrika Korps, glistening with self-confidence, paraded through the streets of Tripoli before their dispatch to the front.

One of the observers was Leutnant Heinz W. Schmidt, newly arrived in Libya from Eritrea where he had been commanding a small unit of Germans stranded in the area by the outbreak of war, and even more newly appointed as Rommel's aide-de-camp. His account reveals some interesting facets of the Italo-German alliance:

It was a bright sunny day, but the Italian population did not seem to show a great deal of interest in this display of might. The only dense group of civilian spectators was round the platform, where Rommel, who was accompanied by several Italian generals, took the salute. I stood close to my new chief.

Singly and at regular intervals the Panzers clattered and rattled by. They made a devil of a noise on the macadamized streets. Not far past the saluting base the column turned into a side-street with mighty squeaks and creaks. I began to wonder at the extraordinary number of Panzers passing, and to regret that I had not counted them from the beginning. After a quarter of an hour I noticed a fault in one of the chains of a heavy Mark IV Panzer, which somehow looked familiar to me although I had not previously seen its driver. Only then did the penny drop, as the Tommies say, and I could not help grinning. Still more Panzers passed, squeaking and creaking round that bend. The road surface was beginning to show serious signs of damage from the caterpillar tracks. The Italians stared with wide-open eyes, but otherwise were dumb. Where, I wondered, was their proverbial animation and enthusiasm? But I soon understood.

After the Panzers had passed – really passed – the saluting base there was a gap in the column. Then followed, not quite so fast, not quite so noisily, a long line of Italian tanks. The tank commanders showed themselves as conspicuously as they could. Their expressions were bold, daring, audacious. There was an immediate cheer from all sides. The crowd waved and chattered wildly. There were cries of 'Viva Italia!'

With my Staff comrades I pondered over the cool reception of the German troops who had come, after all, as allies to assist in the defence of the city. It seemed that we were tolerated rather than popular.[1]

By the following day, the 3rd Reconnaissance Battalion was at Sirte to be quickly joined by 39th Anti-tank Battalion, while behind them a stream of Volkswagen cars, mocked up to resemble panzers from the air, trundled along the Via Balbia; and if the last element was bluff, the first two were highly efficient, well-equipped and battle-toughened formations. Moreover, they were to be well supplied. Despite more warnings from the Italian command (despite also the difficulties experienced by the Royal Navy in supplying O'Connor's forces by sea), Rommel's quartermaster, Major Otto, successfully organised a flotilla of small cargo boats which carried fuel and ammunition along the coast between Tripoli and Sirte, and later between Sirte and Ras el Ali, greatly easing the pressure on the Via Balbia, not to speak of the lorry columns of which Rommel was suffering from the same shortage as was plaguing his opponents.

Not that Rommel concerned himself greatly with matters of supply. When, much later, he proposed that his command in Africa be augmented by another two divisions in order to allow him to conquer Egypt and then sweep down to East Africa, the Army Chief of Staff Oberstgeneral Halder acidly inquired how, even if he could be spared the divisions, he would supply and feed them, Rommel replied, 'That's quite immaterial to me; that's your problem!' Supply problems in his opinion were the concern of the Staff and the Staff were the servitors of the soldiers in the field; how else did they justify the comfort in which they lived, the regard in which they were held?

It was an attitude at which the Staff-trained purist might well purse his lips and the quartermaster raise his fists to heaven in vain supplication to the insensate gods; but the uncharted capacities of humanity under stress could often make it work, especially when fired by some extra quality of spirit such as loyalty to an inspiring commander.

Every day, as the men and supplies were found and ferried forward, Rommel would follow the hours spent encouraging, persuading, bullying, with more hours in the air above the scene of action, studying the lie of the ground, the capacity of the routes to the front, the areas most advantageous for defence – and more especially, the potential assembly points for the launch of an offensive. For no matter what his orders said or his masters in Rome or Berlin believed possible, Rommel's thoughts were for ever directed towards the attack.

In such a mood, he observed extra British activity between El Agheila and Ras el Ali on February 17th, and the following day the movement of a sizeable British force down from Agedabia towards El Agheila – and to discourage any thoughts which Wavell or his subordinates might have (but hadn't) about a further advance towards Tripoli, he moved his German troops and one Italian battalion under command of Maggiore Santa Maria who had already much impressed him by his aggressive attitude, forward to a new defence line past Nofilia.

These troops were then instructed to move even further forward and let the enemy know of their presence, with the result that during the morning of February 20th two patrols drove past each other along the Via Balbia, only one of which was in any way expectant of the meeting. Both skidded to an abrupt halt and the eight-wheeler armoured car of the 3rd Reconnaissance Battalion promptly swung across the road to block it. On the British side, there was a long moment of question and incredulity ('My God! Weren't those Germans?') and after the briefest exchange of shots the armoured cars of the K.D.G.s, mindful of their chief duty to get back with information, circled around to the south and hastened back to report.

Four days later, at dawn, seven panzers, three armoured cars and a section of motor-cycle grenadiers were waiting by the abandoned fort at Agheila for the early morning British patrols, and as these probed forward across the frontier opened fire on the leading armoured car, badly wounding one of the crew and taking two others prisoner. The second K.D.G. troop swung around to report and an Australian anti-tank troop came up at the same time – and in the general confusion, the anti-tank officer received the impression that it was German prisoners who were being taken and climbed out of his car to assist. Ten minutes later the Germans were roaring back towards Nofilia with their three prisoners, towing one damaged Marmon-Harrington and leaving another in flames behind them, plus a burnt-out lorry and the officer's wrecked staff car. And a number of very red and anxious faces.

On March 4th, Generalleutnant Streich, commanding the 5th Light Division – of which the bulk was still in transit – took immediate command at the front, and on Rommel's prompting moved a mixed force of engineers and infantry up as far as Mugtaa where they sowed the defile with mines – and as salt marshes here extended almost twenty miles south from the coast and across the road, this meant that there now existed a firm block against any British advance at a point already 500 miles east of Tripoli. Three weeks beforehand there had been little or nothing to stop an aggressive task force reaching the outskirts of the port, had they attempted to do so.

One of the most attractive facets of Rommel's character was his total devotion to his wife and son. He had first met Lucie Maria Mollin in 1911, they had become engaged in 1915 and married a year later – and it seems likely that he had cast no significant glances at any other girl or woman before or since. The years which he later claimed to have been his happiest were spent with her and their son, born in 1928, and when they were separated – even by the exigencies of battle – he endeavoured to write to her every day, sometimes twice or even three times. These letters are a valuable barometer of the daily strains and stresses to which he was to be subject:

5 March 1941

Dearest Lu,

Just back from a two-day journey – or rather flight – to the front, which is now 450 miles away to the east. Everything going fine.

A lot to do. Can't leave here for the moment as I couldn't be answerable for my absence. Too much depends on my own person and my driving power. I hope you've had some post from me.

My troops are on their way. Speed is the one thing that matters here. The climate suits me down to the ground. I even 'overslept' this morning until after 6 . . . [2]

At last, the main bulk of the first division of the Deutsche Afrika Korps was well on its way, and although even this was but an offshoot of a complete armoured division – the 3rd Panzer – it nevertheless constituted a solid and hard-hitting force. The 5th Light Division, as it was called, consisted of 3rd Reconnaissance Battalion (already at the front), a 12-gun battery of field artillery, two anti-tank battalions amongst whose weapons were numbered a few 88mm. guns of the class which had already made a name for themselves in Spain and were to emerge from the war as one of the most famous pieces of artillery of all time; and two motorised machine-gun battalions.

These were the ancillary troops; the main striking power of the division lay in its two panzer battalions comprising the 5th Panzer Regiment, with 120 tanks of which half were Marks III and IV, which were certainly the equal in armour and gun-power to everything the British had except the Matilda, whose speed they exceeded by nearly ten miles per hour. But the main advantage 5th Light Division would hold against anything facing it in March 1941 was its practical experience of mechanised warfare, its doctrine of total co-operation between all arms, and its well-developed and intensively practised battle-drill.

There were inevitably some adaptations to be made in view of the unfamiliar conditions the division was now facing – extra air and oil filters to be fitted, carburettors adjusted to take Italian lower-grade petrol, clothing redesigned and rations modified to include more fresh vegetables – but the heart of the division was sound and its attitude young, eager and willing to learn. Rommel's spirits bounded as he watched it move forward along the Via Balbia towards the front where both the division's name and his own would become famous.

Just as valuable from the point of view of an attacking general was the arrival of the first units of Fliegerkorps X under command of Generalleutnant Fröhlich who had been appointed Fliegerführer Afrika. By the time the Reconnaissance Battalion was at Nofilia, Fröhlich had nearly fifty dive-bombers and twenty fighters based on North African airfields and thus available to cover ground operations, and he could also call upon longer-range aircraft based in Sicily. Already they had inflicted casualties on the British troops around El Agheila, who were learning that air attack nowadays could no longer be greeted with sardonic comment or fought off if it came too close with a few bursts from a Bren-gun. The 11th Hussars had lost one of their old armoured cars and its crew to an attack by twenty Junkers 87s, on the day before they moved back to Cairo.

Reports from Fröhlich's pilots were also confirming Rommel's growing conviction that the British were not only devoid of intention for the moment to advance further, but were actually in some disarray, possibly owing to their need to find troops for Greece – a factor of which German Intelligence had kept Rommel quite well informed – but possibly also for another reason, which was beginning to look uncommonly like unimaginative or even unrealistic leadership at a high level.

The more information that came in, the more inviting the

situation appeared; but there were a few minor matters to be dealt with before he could take the necessary steps to exploit it to the full.

On March 15th, at the request of the Italians and with the added intention of both gaining experience and testing equipment in desert conditions, he dispatched a mixed German and Italian column under command of Oberst Graf von Schwerin south towards Murzuk where, it was reported, some of De Gaulle's troops had been making nuisances of themselves; and he also sent young Schmidt, his aide-de-camp, off down to the oasis of Marada with instructions that if he found it unoccupied, he should then make his way some 150 miles further eastwards and discover if the oasis at Jalo was similarly devoid of enemy troops. About this time, he also moved his own headquarters forward to Sirte and in doing so underwent a thoroughly chastening experience:

> My original intention was to fly to Sirte in a Ghibli aircraft with my Chief of Staff. After taking off, however, we ran into sand-storms near Tauorga, whereat the pilot, ignoring my abuse and attempts to get him to fly on, turned back, compelling me to continue the journey by car from the airfield at Misurata. Now we realised what little idea we had had of the tremendous force of such a storm. Immense clouds of reddish dust obscured all visibility and forced the car's speed down to a crawl. Often the wind was so strong that it was impossible to drive along the Via Balbia. Sand streamed down the windscreen like water. We gasped in breath painfully through handkerchiefs held over our faces and sweat poured off our bodies in the unbearable heat. So this was the Ghibli [wind]. Silently I breathed my apologies to the pilot. A Luftwaffe officer crashed in a sandstorm that day.[3]

He also gave General Streich instructions to prepare an attack to be carried out by all available elements of the 5th Light Division against British positions at El Agheila, with the object of capturing both airfield and fort and establishing the front line for the Afrika Korps hard up against the entrance to Cyrenaica; the attack to be ready for launching on the morning of March 24th.

Then, on March 19th, after taking another hard look at the British dispositions facing his troops, he flew off to Berlin to obtain permission to take more offensive action, and to ask for sufficient reinforcement to ensure its success.

Rommel was not the only person to be surprised by the state of the British defences along the western flank of Cyrenaica. Wavell paid his first visit to the area on March 16th and was appalled by what he found.

Since the conclusion of O'Connor's offensive, Wavell's hands had been full. Not only had there been the offensive in East Africa to watch and nurture, but also growing evidence of Nazi infiltrations into Iraq, and schemes for Free French activities in Syria – both of which would significantly affect the eastern border of his command. Most demanding of all, however, was the developing situation in the Balkans, the stream of instructions from Whitehall to direct his fullest attention towards every sector on the northern flank from Malta to Turkey, and especially the Eden mission and its decision to send the greater part of his military strength to Greece.

He had had little time to spare for purely tactical matters and had been content to leave these to his subordinate generals. He now discovered this to have been a mistake. From Maitland Wilson he had obtained a totally false picture of the escarpment running south from Benghasi and parallel to the coast, believing it to be similar to the land-cliff running westwards from Sollum and thus impassable except at a few easily guarded points. Had this been so, then mobile forces could have held the passes and flooded down to take any enemy advance on Benghasi in flank, while artillery shelled it from above.

But the escarpment south of Benghasi is in fact not so much a cliff as a line of sloping hills, and a strong enemy force could ascend them almost anywhere and then sweep along the top to wipe out any less efficient or powerful force in its path. And the British armoured force now left in the area lacked both the training and the experience to qualify for the adjective efficient, and it was certainly not powerful.

The core of the defence was the fifty-two cruiser tanks of the 2nd Armoured Division (of which there was only one brigade as the other had been sent to Greece) and of these fifty-two, half were already in the workshops and the rest liable to break down at regular intervals having already grossly exceeded both their track and engine mileages. Some idea of the state of the armour is given by the fact that the 6th R.T.R. men who crewed the captured Italian M13s were comparatively satisfied with their vehicles, which at least kept moving.

Ill luck had contributed yet another deplorable feature to the condition of the 2nd Armoured Division for it had come out from England under command of Major-General J. C. Tilley, but he had died suddenly in January to be succeeded by Major-General M. D. Gambier-Parry, who was thus trying to fit an incomplete force which he did not know at all well into a defence system which was unrealistic to say the least.

General Neame was not living up to Wavell's hopes – perhaps grown too exorbitant on O'Connor's excellences. Wavell later wrote:

I found Neame pessimistic and asking for all kinds of reinforcements which I hadn't got. And his tactical dispositions were just crazy; he had put a brigade of Morshead's 9th Australian Division out into the middle of the plain between Agheila and Benghazi, with both flanks exposed, immobile with no transport, completely useless and an obvious prey to any armoured vehicles that broke through at Agheila. I ordered it to be moved back to the heights above (east of) Benghazi, where there was at least a defensible position . . . I told Neame that if his advanced troops were driven back, he was not to attempt the direct defence of Benghazi, but to pull his Armoured Brigade back on to the left flank of the Australians . . .

I was also appalled at the size and unwieldiness of the 2nd Armoured Division headquarters. Gambier-Parry, though he had only one brigade to handle, had brought forward the whole of his headquarters, with the idea of getting them exercised in the field. All right if they were not attacked but a dangerous encumbrance if they were.

I came back anxious and depressed from this visit, but there was nothing much I could do about it. The movement to Greece was in full swing and I had nothing left in the bag. But I had forebodings and my confidence in Neame was shaken.[4]

One factor which depressed Wavell more than any other was the realisation of the strength of the defensive position in the salt marshes west of Agheila at Mugtaa, which Neame had felt beyond the supply capabilities from Tobruk 300 miles back, but which Rommel apparently considered well within the supply capabilities for his troops from Tripoli 400 miles back; and the Afrika Korps was now immovably entrenched there. Certainly the Via Balbia was a much smoother run for supplies than the Mechili–Antelat tracks or the Trig el Abd – but in March 1941 a touch of Rommel's ruthless attitude towards supply officers would not have come amiss on the Allied side of the border.

However, there was no point in an excess of despondency, and there was always some comfort to be extracted from consideration of the enemy's problems, together with plans to increase them. As Wavell wrote in a directive to Neame:

The enemy's supply and maintenance problem will be a most difficult and precarious one, and do everything in your power to render it more so. Forward dumps of stores are likely to be the surest indication of the offensive intentions of the enemy and should be attacked by air action as far as possible. Similarly, during the advance, attack on his maintenance system will be one of the best methods of bringing him to a standstill . . . Time is pressing and you must put all necessary moves and work in hand without the least delay.[5]

These instructions Neame endeavoured to carry out but, ever mindful of his own supply difficulties and knowing the crucial value which his friend O'Connor had placed upon the Field Supply Depots during his great advance, Neame used what transport he had available firstly to build these up, especially the forward ones at Barce, Benghasi and El Magrun. The problems of troop movement must await their turn, as must those of clearing the battlefield and scavenging the vast quantities of abandoned Italian equipment and supplies.

Back in Cairo, Wavell pondered the situation which would be facing this new opponent, Generalleutnant Rommel, of whom reports were so uniformly flattering, but in view of detailed information now arriving from England in ever-increasing volume, he concluded that Neame and his troops still had some time in hand. Station X, the highly secret decoding organisation at Bletchley Park in Buckinghamshire, was now producing its 'Ultra' intelligence by almost daily reading of Axis wireless traffic, and G.H.Q. Cairo had been warned not only of Rommel's arrival and of the formations already in North Africa, but also of the acceleration of plans for the dispatch forward to Nofilia of the 5th Light Motorised Division, to be followed by the 15th Panzer Division when it arrived in May.

The motorised division was apparently intended to be at the front by March 24th, but as its support would be the Italian Ariete Division with only half its allotted number of tanks and at the most four Italian infantry divisions whose morale would still be suffering from the recent setbacks during *Compass*, Wavell considered that no real threat as yet existed beyond El Agheila. Even the warnings he received from his chief intelligence officer, Brigadier John Shearer, to the effect that an enemy commander of the first rank prepared to take risks and display imagination could already wreak havoc among Neame's dispersed and inexperienced force, were discounted by Wavell as nothing more than the pessimistic presentation by a conscientious staff officer of a 'worst possible situation' report, of the type he had himself occasionally prepared.

It would take at least thirty days to dump into the forward areas the supplies necessary to maintain any forward movement even for the force now available to Rommel, so Neame must have at least until April 16th to make his defences ready for an attack on a comparatively small scale . . . and as Rommel's main reinforcement – the panzer division for which he would surely wait – would not be

arriving until May, after which it would need time for acclimatisation and absorption into the existing force at the front, was it not
more likely that Neame's men would have in fact until June to make
themselves ready to throw back an attack on Cyrenaica?

It would be a serious attack of course, delivered by a mainly
German striking force of almost two divisions, but by that time not
only should Neame and Gambier-Parry have welded their present
command into a strong defensive nucleus, but Keren should have
fallen and Wavell would have one and perhaps two Indian divisions
available as reinforcement, and perhaps a South African division as
well.

Time, for the moment, appeared to be on the British side;
however imaginative, aggressive or daring the enemy commander
might be, he could not ignore the iron laws of logistics.

But Wavell did not yet know Rommel.

Neither, come to that, did his own Commander-in-Chief, von
Brauchitsch, nor even Hitler.

Rommel's brief stay in Berlin was not a particularly satisfactory
one from anybody's point of view. True, the Führer received him
kindly, pressed upon him the Oakleaves to the Knight's Cross in
recognition of his outstanding performance as commander of the
7th Panzer Division during the Blitzkrieg through France, briefly
discussed his report on the situation in Africa and then passed him
rapidly on to the General Staff.

First von Brauchitsch and then Halder listened coldly to his plans
and requests, then made it quite clear that he could expect no extra
reinforcements, no larger scale of supplies than already indicated,
and also that despite the marks of the Führer's favour which
Rommel had in the past received, his command in Africa was not
one of overwhelming importance in the eyes of the High Command.

They did not go as far as to say that the campaign in Africa was
little to them but an unimportant sideshow, for this might have
necessitated revealing their nascent plans: first, for an attack down
through Yugoslavia and Greece to the eastern Mediterranean to be
launched almost immediately; and even more important and thus
secret, those for the Reich's most ambitious and indeed awe-
inspiring project, *Operation Barbarossa*, the invasion of Russia.
But they were quite firm in their declarations that Rommel could
expect no increase in the establishment of the force under his
command, pointing out that its only *raison d'être* was to sustain
Italian morale and to protect their Libyan empire from further
incursions by the British.

Agreed – the best defence might well be to attack the British
forces around El Agheila and push them back perhaps as far as

Agedabia; even Benghasi might be taken. But no further advance should be considered, and obviously even so limited an operation could not be undertaken until the rest of the 5th Light Division and the whole of the 15th Panzer Division had arrived in Africa, and had been given time for acclimatisation. Had they known of it, they might have buttressed their position by pointing out that the opinion of so eminent a soldier as General Wavell almost exactly coincided with their own.

Rommel's protestations that it would be impossible just to advance as far as Benghasi and then stop there were listened to without comment, for both Brauchitsch and Halder were sufficiently realistic to see when it was pointed out to them that geographic factors dictated either the total occupation of Cyrenaica, or its total abandonment; it could not be held by either side *in part*. And their silence indicated that in such circumstances, perhaps Rommel would do best to leave well alone and commit his forces to nothing more than a defensive role.

Certainly, he must not attempt to re-enact his spectacular feat of arms with the 7th Panzer Division in France, which had spear-headed the breakthrough to the Channel coast, earned the division the questionable nickname of the Ghost Division, and brought the High Command to a state of extreme nervous tension. There must be no repetition of that sort of escapade; the Afrika Korps was intended basically as a blocking force, a *Sperrverband*, and its commander – bearer of the Oakleaves to the Knight's Cross though he might be – must obey orders and restrict himself and his troops to the duties which had been allocated to them.

According to Rommel's first biographer, Brigadier Desmond Young, Rommel once called Halder a bloody fool and asked him what he had ever done in war except sit on his backside in an office chair – but it is not recorded if this was the occasion. Whether it was or not, explicit instructions handed to Rommel on March 21st made it quite clear that he was not to consider moving forward until after the arrival of the 15th Panzer Division in May, that Agedabia must be the limit of the first advance and only when the result of that offensive had been carefully analysed would any further action be sanctioned. And he had better report back again in a month's time, in case his superiors should decide that even that first advance was inadvisable or unnecessary.

Rommel arrived back in Africa on March 23rd, and proceeded to disobey his orders with a diligence which compels the admiration of all who have ever cocked a snook at Authority.

The attack on the fort and landing ground at El Agheila which he had ordered for the 5th Light Division before his departure for

Berlin duly took place the following morning, the few British and Australian troops there withdrawing in the face of obviously superior strength. Last to leave was the duty troop of the King's Dragoon Guards, the troop leader only getting out of the fort by the skin of his teeth.

Rommel's description of what then faced him is as transparent a piece of special pleading as one is likely to come across among the literary outpourings of the military commanders of the Second World War, the only difference between it and the vast majority of them being that this is an excuse for action – action moreover which was to prove successful:

> The defile at Mersa el Brega was the first objective for the attack which we were due to launch in May on the enemy forces around Agedabia. After the British had been driven out of El Agheila, they established themselves on the commanding heights at Mersa el Brega and south of the salt marsh at Bir es Suera, and began to build up their position. It was with some misgivings that we watched their activities, because if they had once been allowed time to build up, wire and mine these naturally strong positions, they would then have possessed the counterpart of our position at Mugtaa, which was difficult either to assault or to outflank round the south. The country south of the Wadi Faregh, some 20 or 30 miles south of Mersa el Brega, was extremely sandy and almost impassable for vehicles. I was therefore faced with the choice of either waiting for the rest of my troops to arrive at the end of May – which would have given the British time to construct such strong defences that it would have been difficult for our attack to achieve the desired result – or of going ahead with our existing small forces to attack and take the Mersa el Brega position in its present undeveloped state. I decided for the latter.[6]

An extra reason he gave for the decision to move even further forward was the availability of a better water supply at Mersa el Brega – and another was that Mersa el Brega would give his forces just as suitable a forming-up area 'for the May attack' as the one they already occupied at Mugtaa, an opinion with which both Wavell and Neame would have disagreed had they known of it.

The first probing attacks by 3rd Reconnaissance against the forward British posts at Mersa el Brega began about 0800 on the morning of March 31st, and by 1015 they had driven them back to the main infantry defence positions which were then dive-bombed. The leading tanks of 5th Panzer Regiment then moved up and the rest of the morning was occupied by a brisk tank versus 25-pounder battle, each side feeling out the other's strength, the panzer crews sweating it out for the first time in the close confines of battened-down tanks in the desert at noon. During the early afternoon, the panzers withdrew behind a low rise called by the British Cemetery Hill, which had in the meantime been occupied by some of the 5th Light Division's infantry and artillery, who thus dominated the British infantry positions below. As these were new Territorials (1st Battalion Tower Hamlets Rifles) in their first battle, their position was by no means enviable.

Just after 1400, another wave of dive-bombers struck the British infantry positions and then at about 1630 Generalleutnant Streich, commanding 5th Light, put in an infantry attack through the sand-hills along the coast, backed by more panzers and a machine-gun company, which by dusk had won through to a position completely outflanking the British infantry and threatening their artillery as well. More panzers rolled down from Cemetery Hill towards the main defences, overrunning some forward sections, setting alight some of the British carriers, and through the flame and smoke their gunners sent a few derisory shots after the rapidly retreating British infantry and guns. No British armour had been seen, for when the unfortunate commander of this forward section of 2nd Armoured Support Group appealed for protection, Gambier-Parry withheld it on the grounds that insufficient daylight was left for tank deploy-ment; in view of the reluctance that the far more experienced 7th Armoured Division had always shown to operate in darkness, he was probably right to do so – but it meant that from now on he danced to Rommel's tune.

Rommel, needless to say, had spent the day at the front and in fact, accompanied by his personal aide Oberleutnant Hermann Aldinger and his Chief of Staff Oberstleutnant von dem Borne, he had personally reconnoitred the route through the sandhills along which Streich later sent the infantry attack. He had also kept a close eye on the speed and efficiency with which his panzers and vehicles had been refuelled and restocked, and a far-ranging eye on what lay beyond.

Nothing, he quickly concluded, lay beyond for at least twenty-five miles – and very little there. And as both air and ground reconnais-sance next day (April 1st) revealed little but emptiness back as far almost as Agedabia, he immediately gave orders for all forces to close up to Mersa el Brega and Maaten Giofer, while 5th Light were to be ready to advance and take Agedabia sixty miles ahead the following morning. So much for the value attached to the area around Mersa el Brega as a 'forming-up area for the May attack'.

General Streich had no doubts or hesitations about the advance on April 2nd. The reconnaissance units on their motor-cycle combinations (three men and a machine-gun plus personal arms) rode well forward abreast the Via Balbia, while the panzers and infantry carriers followed on each side, in well-balanced and flexible battle formations capable of rapid switch towards any recognised danger. Those on the southern flank ran into some British armour – and unexpectedly, for these suddenly emerged from under the curious but innocent-looking black folds of some bedouin tents – but the British cruisers were either inexpertly handled or broke down, for seven of them were left blazing in as many minutes; and by evening, somewhat to their surprise, the main body of the Afrika Korps were in and around Agedabia with their advanced units twelve miles further on, and the small port of Zuetina already in their hands.

The following day, April 3rd, Rommel moved his own head-quarters up to Agedabia and then gave perhaps his most classic demonstration of the advantage to be reaped from the occasional disregard of established principles. Faced by an as yet unbroken enemy, he should by all orthodoxy have kept his own forces concentrated; Rommel split his three ways, thereby bewildering his opponents and thoroughly astonishing his Italian superior, Generale Gariboldi.

Divining the disarray which was already loosening control among the British, Rommel sent the Santa Maria Battalion with some German anti-tank units, all under command of Graf von Schwerin who had returned from the expedition to Murzuk, off eastwards first of all to Giof el Matar and then to Ben Gania, with orders to penetrate even further up through Tengeder towards Mechili – thus swinging in a semicircle even wider than that of 7th Armoured's in the opposite direction two months before – to find out if the British really were evacuating Cyrenaica, as appeared possible, and to trap as many of them as they could.

At the same time, he took the armoured cars and motor-cycle troops of 3rd Reconnaissance under his own immediate command and sent them off up to Soluch and Ghemines, and ordered the main bulk of 5th Light to improve their positions forward of Agedabia for an advance to Antelat and Msus. General Streich voiced doubts that morning about the serviceability of some of his panzers, and after brushing aside these objections ('I could not allow this to affect the issue. One cannot permit unique oppor-tunities to slip by for the sake of trifles,') Rommel then dealt in his own fashion with yet another dire prediction by another Italian general.

Warned by Generale di Divisione Zamboni that the track to Giof el Matar along which he had just dispatched the Schwerin Force was a 'death-trap', Rommel, accompanied by Aldinger and Schmidt, set off and within a comparatively short time had overtaken the head of the column and thoroughly satisfied himself that the Italians were trying to place non-existent obstacles in his path. In such a mood he returned to Agedabia about 1600 hours to be confronted by Streich maintaining that 5th Light – who had given up some of their petrol to 3rd Reconnaissance for the probe northwards – were now so short of fuel that it would be another four days before they would be able to move forward.

> This seemed to me to be utterly excessive and I immediately gave orders for the division to unload all its vehicles and send them off at once to the divisional dump at Arco dei Fileni, whence they were to bring up sufficient petrol, rations and ammunition for the advance through Cyrenaica inside 24 hours.[7]

This would undoubtedly mean that the enemy would remain unmolested on the central front for the following day, so Rommel went north to investigate possibilities up there. There he found that 3rd Reconnaissance had made no contact with the British during that day but had been informed by an Italian priest that they had evacuated Benghasi, whereat Rommel ordered Oberstleutnant Freiherr von Wechmar to drive straight into the port – which he did, to receive a delirious welcome from the inhabitants who could not offer their gallant allies too warm a hospitality.

3 April 1941

> Dearest Lu,
> We've been attacking since the 31st with dazzling success. There'll be consternation amongst our masters in Tripoli and Rome, perhaps in Berlin too. I took the risk against all orders and instructions because the opportunity seemed favourable . . . We've already reached our first objective, which we weren't supposed to get to until the end of May. The British are falling over each other to get away . . . You will understand that I can't sleep for happiness . . . [8]

Rommel was certainly right about the consternation in Tripoli, for Generale Gariboldi had already protested once over the advance beyond the first agreed objectives at Agheila, had then been thoroughly outraged by the day's dispersion of effort along three distinct and divergent paths and now, upon Rommel's return to Agedabia on the evening of April 3rd, was waiting to bring the full weight of his superior rank and more ebullient personality to bear upon his errant subordinate.

It was not a successful venture. Rommel secure in achieved success might have been amenable to gentle reproof about his

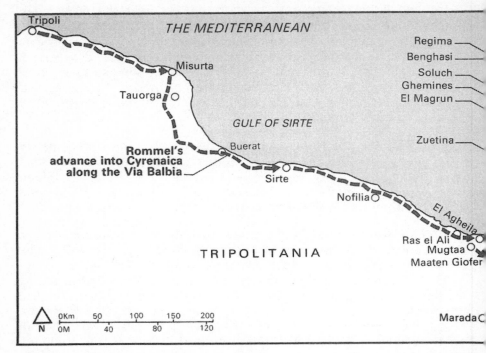

Map 16   Rommel's first advance

methods; Rommel on the flood tide of potential success and clearly perceiving it within his grasp was uncontrollable. He swept aside Gariboldi's warning about the insecurity of his flanks and his supply situation, he totally rejected Gariboldi's claim that as his superior officer he had the authority to forbid any further aggressive operations, and as for the Italian's amended demand that permission for any further advances must at least be obtained from Rome, it was demolished in language which, to quote one observer, 'only generals would use to each other!'

Into the climactic atmosphere thus generated walked, like Mercury, one of the headquarters communications staff bearing a signal from the German High Command. Whatever Halder's reaction to the latest news from the North African front might be, Hitler's had been immediate and enthusiastic; Rommel was granted the fullest freedom of action to exploit the situation which faced him, and there was no room for doubt in the wording of the message that Mussolini's agreement would be forthcoming, should anyone be interested in obtaining it.

It would seem that there may be some truth in the belief that during periods of success, people make their own luck.

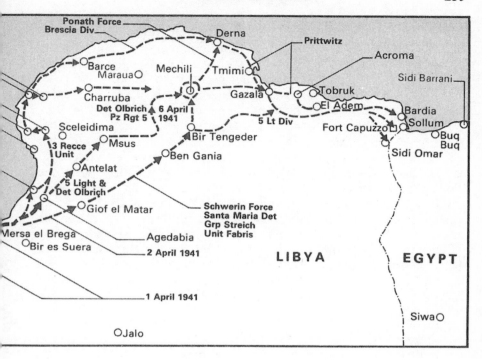

Freed now from all restraint, Rommel became a positive fount of
energy. He spent the first few hours of April 4th harrying the 5th
Light transport to ensure the division's mobility the following day,
then pushed the Brescia Division up and into Benghasi to release
3rd Reconnaissance, whom he then ordered to make their way
eastwards through Regima and Charruba towards Mechili, where
he had decided that the crucial battle would be fought. He then
instructed General Streich, still at Agedabia, that once his division
was refuelled – at the latest by that evening – he should split his
forces, himself taking the more mobile section along the track used
by von Schwerin towards Ben Gania and eventually Tmimi, the
remainder consisting of 5th Panzer Regiment and some forty Italian
tanks under command of Oberstleutnant Friedrich Olbrich to drive
up to Msus and then across to Mechili along the tracks made by 7th
Armoured. The main Italian forces – the Santa Maria Battalion,
followed by the rest of the Ariete Division in two sections, one
commanded by a Colonello Fabris and consisting of motor-cyclists
and light guns in advance, and the main bulk coming up behind –
were to follow the Streich Group as far as Tengeder, after which
they could either join the battle at Mechili or cut across towards El

Adem and Tobruk if the Mechili garrison had escaped. He then met Generalmajor Heinrich Kirchheim (who was merely paying a visit to North Africa), shanghaied him into command of the Brescia Division and instructed him to get it across from Benghasi to Derna along the coastal route as soon as it was safe to do so.

That afternoon Rommel commandeered a Junkers, his Storch being unavailable, and flew over the whole of the battle area checking on the positions of his troops and looking even more closely for indications of enemy movements. It seemed to him that the British armour was slowly marooning itself between the prongs of his own advance and that the Australian infantry along the escarpment east of Benghasi, although it had at first administered an abrupt check to 3rd Reconnaissance at Regima, must shortly pull back if it was not to find itself outflanked. With which reflection, he returned to Agedabia, ordered his Kampfstaffel (Headquarters Company) to be ready to follow the Ariete on the Ben Gania track by 0400 hours the following morning, and after a brief sleep, set out to join the battle himself. Before he did so, he wrote the daily letter:

5 April 1941

Dearest Lu,
    Off at 4 this morning. Things are happening in Africa. Let's hope the great stroke we've now launched is successful. I'm keeping very fit. The simple life here suits me better than the fleshpots of France. How are things with you both?[9]

He was over Ben Gania in the Storch during the morning, at noon on the ground again sending Olbrich away northwards towards Msus, and back at Ben Gania in early afternoon. Here he received information that Mechili appeared empty, so von Schwerin, who was the nearest, was instructed to drive hard for the fort while all other forward troops were ordered to close up towards it. Rommel took off again to fly over the area and check where all his forces were (they were getting badly strung out and would undoubtedly have been in danger had there been any coherent British force in the area to threaten them), then returned to Ben Gania to drive forward in what became known as his 'Mammoth' – a captured British headquarters vehicle reputedly originally used by O'Connor – to find out what conditions on the ground were like. Two and a half hours later, he learned that his chief Intelligence officer had been shot down and taken prisoner, that Mechili, far from being evacuated, was full of British forces, and that Streich's force having reached Tengeder had therefore been switched towards Mechili by his Chief of Operations, Major Ehlert, acting independently:

It was now night and too late to fly back to Agedabia. In view of the new and rather less favourable situation, I decided to drive up to the 5th Light Division and take over command of the operation myself.[10]

They drove forward through the night at first with headlights on until they were attacked by British aircraft, and then without – picking their way along the edges of minefields by the light of burning vehicles which had not been so fortunate as themselves – until at about three o'clock in the morning they found the head of the 5th Light Division column, together with the uncomfortable knowledge that they were lost.

But luck had not deserted him. Shortly after dawn on April 6th he was discovered by two aircraft which had been out on a special mission, and given not only his own position but the latest report on Mechili as well. By 0730 two columns had been sent off to block escape routes to the east of the fort and another under Oberst-leutnant Ponath dispatched even further north to do the same across the Via Balbia east of Derna, while Rommel now waited impatiently for the Fabris and Olbrich forces to arrive and close the ring around Mechili.

He had some time to wait, and his account of the next few days offers some comfort for a chauvinistic British reader. Everybody was running out of petrol; Olbrich's force had run into sandstorms stirred up from the surface of the desert, ground to dust by innumerable tank tracks, every time the wind rose; and people got lost, including Rommel again. On one occasion he ran into the rear of a British outpost consisting of several Bren-carriers, but escaped by driving hard at it in three cars and enormous clouds of dust, which so deceived the enemy as to his strength that they hurriedly decamped – allowing him to reach the Fabris column with the only petrol reserve in the area (thirty-five cans stowed in staff cars), enough to bring them up into position but certainly not enough to get them out again.

But there was still no sign of Olbrich, so Rommel set off in the Storch to find him and very nearly landed alongside a British column which had cannily laid out a landing cross to entice him down; but alas for them, he recognised their helmets in time. He found the 3rd Reconnaissance Battalion south of their route and set them on their way, then found a stray section of the Streich Force which had been misled by a mirage and which caught the rough edge of his tongue as a result . . . but still not the 5th Panzer Regiment which would be necessary for any powerful attack on the British at Mechili.

Rommel did not in fact locate them until after dark on the

evening of April 7th, because the same appalling ground which had held up Lieutenant Joly and his companions of 4th Armoured Brigade now proved just as difficult to the panzers – not that this soothed Rommel's temper or saved the hapless Olbrich from a tongue-lashing. Not until 5th Panzer were rerouted and well on their way did Rommel leave them to fly back to his advanced air base, where he found that the R.A.F. had delivered a low-level attack and shot up several of his Junkers.

April 7th had not been a good day for Rommel.

But it had been an even worse one for the British.

Wavell had flown up to Barce on April 2nd, as soon as he realised the seriousness of Rommel's intentions, but his first intervention in the battle had not been of the happiest. Neame had ordered Gambier-Parry to move to the agreed deployment area near Antelat from whence he could cover either the routes to Benghasi or those across the desert to Mechili, but Wavell countermanded this instruction, still convinced that Rommel could not possibly have organised, in the short time in which he had been in North Africa, a force capable of occupying the whole of Cyrenaica. Benghasi itself must surely be the objective for so hastily organised a force, so all of Gambier-Parry's armour could be deployed to block it.

But although this countermanding order was issued at nine o'clock on the evening of April 2nd, signals were being so badly delayed by the increasing chaos that Gambier-Parry did not receive it until half-past two the following morning, by which time his armour was scattered, running very short of petrol and breaking down at the rate of about one tank every ten miles. As the Support Group infantry were also down to half strength through casualties and sheer loss of direction, he felt that he had little option but to disobey this order and collect whatever force remained to him around Sceleidima, setting the first example of a habit which was to grow among British divisional commanders in the desert over the next eighteen months, bitterly described by one aggrieved senior officer as regarding orders from above more as subjects for discussion than as instructions to be obeyed.

But now Wavell made what was to prove the most unfortunate move in his long military career. Feeling the need for stronger and more experienced direction in control, and already somewhat disillusioned with Neame, he sent for O'Connor to come up and take command; and the latter arrived obediently early the following morning, accompanied by John Combe who only hours before had handed over the 11th Hussars upon his appointment to take command of the 6th Cavalry Brigade in Palestine.

O'Connor quickly persuaded Wavell to leave Neame in charge –
for he felt most unhappy about taking over in the middle of any
battle, let alone one which promised as dismally as this one – but he
agreed that he should stay at Neame's headquarters to offer his
advice when asked; upon which note Wavell left for Cairo to
organise further reinforcements, and to put an immediate stop to
the dispatch of troops and equipment to Greece.

It soon became obvious that O'Connor could best occupy his time
by organising rear positions upon which the troops could fall back if
necessary while Neame direct the battle being fought, but already
what one observer has called 'the *danse macabre* of military reverse
– changes of command, role and deployment, planned by commanders and staffs frantic to plug gaps, which never in the event
take place' was in process. And with it went, hand in hand, the bad
luck of defeat which was the obverse of Rommel's fortune at that
moment.

Some extra reinforcement had already made its way to the
various scenes of action. An Indian motorised brigade (without its
armoured vehicles, artillery or anti-tank weapons; but with its
rifles) had arrived at Mechili and was rapidly organising its defence,
and a squadron of the Long Range Desert Group was sent up from
Siwa to play any useful role which could be found for it. It was this
unit, unorthodox in establishment and virtually unknown at that
time in its career, accompanied by some light tanks which had
become lost and now attached themselves to someone who seemed
to have both form and purpose, which on the morning of April 3rd
was seen approaching Msus, the main supply base of 3rd Armoured
Brigade's fuel, and was presumed in the panic to be hostile.

Reports of supposed enemy armour so close to a focal supply
point spread ripples of alarm and confusion across the whole area,
but long before detachments from 3rd Armoured Brigade could get
across to investigate the threat, a Free French motor battalion
which had also come up as reinforcement and had been stationed at
Msus had hastily revictualled their own vehicles, burnt all the
remaining petrol and a substantial amount of other stores, and
smartly withdrawn. From then on, 3rd Armoured's tanks dropped
out of the battle at an ever-increasing rate as their fuel ran out.

Neame and O'Connor moved the headquarters from Barce to
Maraua, tried with but mediocre success to remain in contact with
their troops in the ever-growing chaos, and watched with dismay
the disintegration of 2nd Armoured Division, its isolation and
defeat in detail. The only solid achievement during those days was
by the Australian infantry who had the advantage of being commanded by a resolute and highly intelligent commander, Major-
General Leslie J. Morshead, and despite their inexperience they

twice flung back solid attacks by 3rd Reconnaissance and later by Ponath's force.

But nothing would halt the grotesque palsy of the *danse macabre*. After two days trying to organise 3rd Armoured Brigade to stem the advance, O'Connor and Neame decided that it should instead be fed into Mechili to reinforce the Indians and thus to hold as a solid bastion the fort which had already achieved the cognomen of the 'heart of Cyrenaica' – but this was frustrated by what O'Connor later referred to as the 'complete disobedience of orders on the part of the [2nd] Armoured Division' which became 'absolutely incomprehensible'. Instead of acting as additional protection to the Australian Division, and later as a much needed reinforcement to the Indian Motorised Brigade at Mechili, it had apparently sought its own safety by relinquishing its tanks and joining in the route by which the main withdrawal was to take place.

Such are the consequences of hasty training, inadequate equipment and uncertain command. Worse was to follow, for unalloyed misfortune was now to overtake the British.

During April 6th, Neame had spent most of the day searching fruitlessly for Gambier-Parry in the Got Derva area east of Charruba (Gambier-Parry had already retired to Mechili but had been unable to inform Neame) and he returned to H.Q. at Maraua in the evening. With all lines falling back to the east, it was evident that the time had come for H.Q. to go as well, but O'Connor, still without official appointment and position, was also still without transport. Neame therefore offered to take both him and John Combe in his own staff car and they set out following the main flow of traffic, with Neame at the wheel as his driver was exhausted.

Shortly before dusk it became obvious that they had missed the way and were on one of the northern tracks, but as this seemed anyway a safer route, Neame handed over to his driver and told him to carry on towards Derna. Well after midnight, O'Connor and Combe, who had been asleep in the back of the car, were woken to find the car stationary and voices shouting in front. Combe got out to investigate, quickly realised that the voices were not British and on asking the driver what was happening, received the classic answer: 'I expect it's some of them bloody Cypriot drivers, sir!"

But it wasn't. It was part of the Ponath Force, which had made its way with commendable speed and unerring accuracy north to the Derna road, and now collected as its reward the most valuable car-load of booty to fall to the Afrika Korps during its entire existence.

It is typical of General O'Connor that the only regret he ever recorded was of the abrupt curtailment of the promising career of John Combe who, he wrote, would quickly have won fame as a great cavalry leader had he not been taken prisoner so early in the war. It is at least arguable that a lot of other young men were to suffer curtailment of their careers, and indeed of their lives, by the loss to Britain of so talented a commander as Sir Richard O'Connor.

One person whom the Afrika Korps were not to capture (and they were to bag quite a collection of generals, brigadiers and colonels in this first offensive) was Brigadier John Harding, who had after all remained behind as Neame's B.G.S. when Wilson went to Greece, and who had been travelling with Neame's A.D.C. a few hundred yards ahead of the car carrying O'Connor and Combe. Such is the confusion and random chance of battle that he arrived at Tmimi in the early morning of April 7th without a hint of what had happened behind him, and it was not until 0630 that he became worried enough about the dearth of generals to communicate his fears to Wavell.

He did not, however, hesitate to take on the responsibilities of the senior officer in the area, encouraged by the continuous and well-organised stream of dour and sardonic Australians pouring back along the coast road under Morshead's firm direction. Together, Harding and Morshead formed a line with the Australians stretching from Gazala back to Acroma, with a small force detached to El Adem for observation of the southern approaches to Tobruk, and in the Fortress itself, the 18th and 24th Brigades hard at work on the defences.

Back through this line and into the base were at first to trickle, and later to flood, platoons, sections, half-companies, isolated and random groups of British and Indian soldiers – exhausted, bewildered, parched with thirst, still resolute but often very angry. It was a phenomenon to be observed on two or three later occasions in the desert campaign, and sprang apparently from a deep-rooted objection on their part to being beaten, even by men for whom they later developed the greatest respect.

Mechili fell to the Afrika Korps on the morning of April 8th and Rommel very nearly fell with it.

He had taken off in the Storch early in the morning to ensure that all escape routes to the east were blocked, and in doing so flew low over a Bersaglieri battalion with the Ariete, who failed to recognise the aircraft as friendly; and Rommel's annoyance over the episode was substantially increased by the fact that although they were only some 300 feet above the frantically firing Italians, the Storch wasn't hit even once.

From 3,000 feet, to which height they had rapidly ascended,

Rommel could see that the attack from the east of the fort was going well, but also that quite a large force of British was moving out to the west, obviously intent upon circling around and either catching his own force in flank or escaping altogether. Here Olbrich's panzers should have been waiting, but despite his efforts of the previous night, there was still no sign of them – though on flying off in that direction, he did spot a stationary 88mm. gun about two miles in front of the advancing British.

Thinking that the rest of Olbrich's force must be somewhere near – for the morning wind was raising its usual sandscreen – Rommel ordered the pilot to put down by the gun, which he managed to do extremely efficiently considering the conditions; but as the Storch taxied towards the gun it ploughed into a sandhill and smashed its propeller. It was then that Rommel discovered that the gun had been put out of action the previous day, that it could not even fire from its isolated position as the firing-pin had been taken by the crew member sent to bring aid, and that the British columns were driving closer every minute.

Fortunately for him, the gun crew had retained a lorry and in it they all drove off at great speed, arriving back at H.Q. to find that there was still no sign of Olbrich but that more and more of the Ariete were arriving to be fed into the battle. Within an hour, Rommel was on his way again, but now he and his party ran into a violent sandstorm which delayed their arrival in Mechili until noon, where they found that Gambier-Parry, having authorised the early morning breakout, had then concluded that the smoke and sand to the east denoted an overwhelming force against him and that the Mechili garrison should surrender.

Olbrich's force had arrived at about the same time, and neither Rommel nor Streich was particularly impressed by his presence at the subsequent capitulation ceremony. He was quickly ordered to refuel his panzers and take them off after von Schwerin's light forces towards Derna, while Streich and the Italians held Mechili and looked after the prisoners. These were already proving an encumbrance.

At Derna himself by 1800, Rommel first congratulated Ponath upon his recent exploits, thanked Kirchheim who had brought the Brescia Division up from Benghasi, then welcomed Generalmajor Heinrich von Prittwitz und Gaffron, commander of 15th Panzer Division, the advanced party of which had landed at Tripoli a few days previously. Handing command of the 3rd Reconnaissance Battalion, the 8th Machine-gun Battalion and the 605th Anti-tank Battalion to Prittwitz, he instructed him to follow the Australians along the coast road and take part in the operation designed to 'bounce them out' of Tobruk, the other details of which Rommel would now organise. There was no room for idle hands, of whatever rank, in Rommel's theatre of operations.

It took two days to bring up the forces for the first attack on Tobruk, two days during which Rommel hardly rested for an hour, and during which he had to inform the commander of 5th Light Division coldly that when he gave orders for the division to move immediately, it did not imply that they had two days for rest and vehicle maintenance. They must be in position to the south of Tobruk within twenty-four hours, their advanced units were to push on east and then north, to reach the coast, cut the Bardia road and seal in the Tobruk garrison by the morning of April 11th – Good Friday – at the latest. Move now!

In the meantime, Prittwitz was to send 3rd Reconnaissance away to the south through Acroma to take El Adem, then launch his main attack straight up alongside the main Derna–Tobruk road, driving through the perimeter and into the town from the west. This attack was to start in the early hours of April 10th, and by 0900 the crash of artillery – rather heavier than had been expected – told Rommel that battle had been joined. The machine-gun and anti-tank battalions were obviously having a rough time, but speed was of the essence and Rommel was soon at the front urging them on, then away after the 3rd Reconnaissance to check their progress; and with news at last that the Ariete were moving from Tengeder towards El Adem he could harry 5th Light to move even further around towards the Bardia road. Then, at about 1030, a sinister shimmer came to the air, the daily sandstorm blew up, visibility was abruptly reduced to twenty feet and news came through that General Prittwitz, driving forward to control the battle more closely, had been killed by a shot from an anti-tank gun.

It was a portent. For the first time the Afrika Korps was meeting a resistance which had had time to organise, in a defensive position which was not to be given up. Although by April 11th the encirclement was complete and the country to the south, west, and as far east as the Egyptian border (where the 11th Hussars had resumed their old watch) was clear of British troops, Tobruk was fast hardening into a rock-solid enclave, based on the well-conceived defences built by the Italians (who were apologetically unable to provide Rommel with a map of them for some time) but manned now in great part by Australians of the 9th Division, grimly determined that no one would be able to call them the division which lost all that the 6th had won.

That afternoon the first attack was delivered from the west by the Brescia Division and from the south-east by the panzers of the 5th Light, in a blinding sandstorm which should have given them some protection from the enemy artillery, but which instead so robbed the attack of impetus that it stalled along the perimeter wire and anti-tank ditch until, reluctantly, Rommel broke it off. Again, the British artillery had proved more concentrated and more accurate than had been expected, and so hammered the panzers that their commanders were beginning to lose confidence and raise objections to their battle orders – 'which I had to brush aside', as Rommel was to write rather tetchily. He was becoming as angry with some of his own troops as he had previously been with the Italian generals.

By noon on April 14th, he was even more angry. The previous evening 8th Machine-gun Battalion with ancillary troops, all under command of the excellent Oberst Ponath, had crossed the anti-tank ditch just west of the El Adem track and filled part of it in, then crossed the wire and formed a bridgehead under a well-coordinated artillery cover. Just after midnight, the panzers of 5th Light formed up to move forward and by daybreak Ponath was reporting excellent progress though to Rommel it seemed that flank support for the penetration was weak; so he drove away to find and bring up the Ariete in support. But when he returned to the focal point of the battle he found that the advance had come to a stop under murderous British artillery and Australian rifle fire about two and a half miles from Tobruk itself, and that the panzers had withdrawn leaving the infantry exposed – and probably lost. In the violent outburst which followed this news, both Streich and Olbrich were given clearly to understand that they were to go in and get the infantry out, and Rommel went off again to harry the Ariete into position – only to return to find that the panzers were still immobile under the hail of British shelling.

Rommel then decided to bring the Ariete up himself to a position on the left of 5th Light, had got them up just south-east of Gasr el Gleicha when a salvo of shells came over from beyond the perimeter – and total confusion ensued, the division turning tail and fleeing off in streams back towards Derna and Mechili. As it was by now almost dark, the divisional commander could do little to regain control and Rommel had to organise a small assault force from his own troops to try to break through and release the now encircled Ponath force.

They were too late. Although they broke through into the area which the machine-gunners had occupied, they found that most of the battalion had been wiped out, including their commander – who had just been awarded the Knight's Cross by Rommel.

A further attack by Ariete on April 16th and 17th also failed, accompanied by the humiliating sight of troops under heavy artillery fire throwing down their arms and running en masse *towards* the British and Australian lines in order to give themselves up. In addition the Italian armoured force was reduced from over a hundred tanks to less than ten in the matter of a few days and two of the remainder were wrecked in error by German anti-tank guns. This brought about the final acceptance by Rommel that nothing could be done to reduce the Fortress before the arrival of a substantial number of reinforcements, preferably German, and of replacements for destroyed panzers; and that those panzers which remained were in dire need of maintenance. He also required some more senior officers as he had decided to dispense with the services of both Generalmajor Streich and Oberst Olbrich.

In the meantime, there was the rest of the front to clear up.

The front line east of Tobruk was by this time an indeterminate area between the line held by the Germans from Bardia down through Fort Capuzzo towards Sidi Omar, and the positions held by the only force Wavell could move up in a hurry from the Delta, basically the 7th Armoured Division's Support Group, still commanded by Brigadier Strafer Gott and with Colonel Jock Campbell as second in command.

Gott had been sent up to El Adem after the collapse at Mechili to form some sort of screen to the south and east of Tobruk, and one of the first units to join him there had been the 11th Hussars who found themselves at one time desperately trying to hold a fifty-mile semi-circle around Tobruk on their own. They were inexorably thrown back as first Prittwitz's and then Streich's forces came up, but they kept Gott informed of enemy movements and delivered some sharp, mosquito-like attacks.

But by April 19th, Gott and his men were back behind the frontier with the main force consisting of 22nd Guards Brigade on and around Halfaya Pass, and four Jock Columns, each with a company of infantry (the 2nd Rifle Brigade had also been rushed up from Ismailia), one or more troops of 25-pounders and a few armoured cars or light tanks. These columns operated from Halfaya, Sofafi, Buq Buq and Sidi Barrani, and there was also a Free French motor battalion at Halfway House on top of the Escarpment; between them they endeavoured both to keep their new overall commander – Lieutenant-General Sir Noel Beresford-Peirse, who had been promoted, knighted and appointed G.O.C. Western Desert Force upon O'Connor's disappearance from the scene – fully acquainted with the situation at the frontier, and at the same time to make it as uncomfortable as possible for the new occupants.

Perhaps they tried too hard. During the last week in April, three troops of the 11th Hussars staged a raid on Fort Capuzzo in which they attacked it from three sides and so disrupted traffic back to Sidi Azeiz that the local commander, Oberst von Herff, reported to

Rommel that his forces in the area were in danger of being cut off. Two days later, a strong force under the Oberst swept along the Escarpment as far as Halfaya, drove in the advance posts there and at Halfway House, and effectively pushed the Mobile Force back to the Buq Buq–Sofafi line. In addition, a flight of Messerschmitt 110s caught two Hussar troops in the open and virtually destroyed them, while in Halfaya Pass itself, a German eight-wheeled armoured car caught two more of the 11th's cars and in the resulting skirmish, Vyvyan Gape was killed – the first 11th officer to fall in the Second World War.

The whole pattern of war in the Western Desert had changed.

From Wavell's point of view, the pattern of war in the whole of the Middle East had changed too, and only on one front had the change been anything but disastrous.

During March, matters had at first promised well. The transporting of British and Australian troops was proceeding expeditiously by the end of the first week, while in East Africa Cunningham had advanced 600 miles north of Mogadishu by March 10th, Berbera had been reoccupied by a force from Aden on March 16th and eight days later (on the day that Rommel took El Agheila) the whole of British Somaliland was regained. On March 25th Wavell himself had gone down to pay a visit to General Platt in front of Keren, had agreed the method for the final assault and had not been at all surprised to learn upon his return to Cairo two days later, that success had at last crowned the efforts of 4th and 5th Indian Divisions and the gateway through to the central plateau had been stormed and taken.

What had come as a surprise – though quite a happy one – was the news that a *coup d'état* had taken place in Yugoslavia that very morning and the pro-British King Peter had taken over from his pacific-minded Prime Minister and appointed, to the evident delight of his subjects, a Cabinet of patriots who promptly rejected the Tripartite Pact signed between Yugoslavia and Germany only two days before. This obviously portended a resumption of Mr Eden's attempts to form that Balkan Front about which he was so keen, and Wavell soon learned that both Eden and Dill were returning as quickly as possible (they were still at Malta when the news from Yugoslavia broke) and would be with him tomorrow.

Any lack of warmth which Wavell may by now have been feeling towards the idea of another series of conferences with a senior politician, was dispelled during March 28th as the news came in of the resounding defeat administered by the Royal Navy to Admiral Iachino's fleet off Cape Matapan, thus lessening the threats to the Greek convoys – and the following day, he felt sufficiently secure to be able to end a passage in the directive to Neame quoted earlier with the words, 'But I do not believe that he [Rommel] can make any big effort for at least another month.'

From then on practically everything went wrong.

Eden and Dill went off to Athens on March 31st – and Rommel captured Mers el Brega; then 2nd Armoured Division retreated to Agedabia, and although 5th Indian Division captured Asmara the same day, another cloud the size of a man's hand appeared upon an entirely different horizon, when the pro-British Regent of Iraq, Amir Abdul Illah, was forced to flee from Baghdad, and it became fairly evident that power would fall into the hands of one Raschid Ali el Gailani, whose political stance was well indicated by his friendship for Haj Amin el Husseini, the violently anti-British Mufti of Jerusalem, long a refugee from Palestine.

But Wavell's closest attention was at that moment obviously focused on events in Cyrenaica, and on April 2nd he had gone to Barce where, as has been related, he amended Neame's plans for defence and called O'Connor forward to join him. By the time he returned to Cairo, Benghasi had been abandoned and Raschid Ali was indeed Premier of Iraq.

Three days later, German forces invaded both Yugoslavia and Greece and by the evening Belgrade was in flames and an ammunition ship had been hit by a Luftwaffe bomb in Piraeus harbour, blowing up and almost totally wrecking all the port installations. Moreover, news from Yugoslavia indicated that however hardy in physique and independent in mind the population might be, their army was proving no match for the fourteen infantry and mountain divisions and six panzer divisions which were pouring down through their country; thus it could not be many hours before the flank of the Greek defence was torn open.

During the afternoon of April 6th, there was a conference of the three Commanders-in-Chief in Cairo attended by both Dill and Eden (who had at last abandoned the dream of a Balkan Front), but the best hope to come out of this was a unanimous determination that, however far Rommel might advance towards or even into Egypt, Tobruk must be held; and the following day Eden and Dill left for London, the Yugoslav southern front was broken and Neame and O'Connor were captured.

On April 8th (the day that Mechili fell and the Germans also captured Salonica) Wavell took a very bumpy and uncomfortable flight up to Tobruk, accompanied by the commander of the 7th Australian Division, Major-General J. D. Lavarack, in order to talk to General Morshead and John Harding about the possibilities open to them. As both thought that Tobruk could be held, Wavell confirmed them in their tasks – with, apparently, the memorable comment, 'Well, if you think you can, you'd better get on and do it!' – appointed Lavarack for the time being commander of all troops in Cyrenaica and Libya and Morshead commander of the main force in Tobruk, then wrote out a six-paragraph directive for Lavarack which could serve as a model of brevity and lucidity – and perhaps optimism – for any Staff College course.

It was late afternoon before he was free to leave and a storm was blowing. As the aircraft was about to take off, a wheel brake seized up imposing a delay of about an hour, and then about a quarter of an hour after take-off, oil pressure failed on one engine. The pilot returned to El Adem airfield – by now abandoned by the British and about to be occupied by the Germans – effected a hasty repair and took off again. Twenty minutes later, the oil pressure failed again and the attempt by the pilot to complete the journey with a single and fast overheating engine ended in a forced landing, a shattered port wing and a disintegrated tail.

Fortunately no one was hurt, but the only certainty about their position was that they were still far west of the Egyptian border and thus in imminent danger of capture. A fire was lit, tea was brewed – and just before anyone could enjoy a cup, some vehicles approached out of the murk, halted some fifty yards from the wrecked aircraft and from the first emerged a gigantic figure carrying a rifle, challenging them in a distinctly foreign tongue.

He proved, however, to be a friendly Sudanese and the party were soon bowling happily along towards Sollum from where, about midnight, Wavell was able to contact the Cairo Headquarters – by then distraught with worry at his disappearance. One of the pieces of news they were able to give him was that the British armour in front of the Aliakmon Line was already under attack and that the line itself appeared in considerable danger of being outflanked by German troops moving down towards the Monastir Gap.

Another day to remember was April 11th. To the eventual and enormous relief of the Middle East Command, President Roosevelt that day declared the Red Sea a non-combatant zone and thus open to American shipping, but for Wavell this good news was offset first by reports of the breaking of the Aliakmon Line, and then by the sealing in of his forces in Tobruk. This was followed by a request from Whitehall that he make instant arrangements for the dispatch from Palestine of 'a sizeable force' to Habbaniya, the R.A.F. station some 40 miles from Baghdad (and thus 500 miles from Jerusalem) which with the advent of Raschid Ali to power was presumed – rightly – to be in danger. There was no practical suggestion as to where either the men or the equipment for such a force could be found in Wavell's command (obviously if he had men for such a task they would already be in employment) or recognition of the fact that never in history had Baghdad been captured along any other routes but those of the valleys of the Euphrates or Tigris, neither of which was available to Wavell.

He went back to Athens the following day at Maitland Wilson's request to discuss withdrawal of the British and Australian forces to what was optimistically referred to as the 'Olympus line' and which in fact hardly existed, and upon his return (April 13th) learned of the attack on Tobruk and the occupation of Belgrade by the Germans. He was able to remain in Cairo for the next five days (during which he proposed to Whitehall that approaches should be made to the Italian Government to exchange O'Connor for any six captured Italian generals; a serious suggestion which Whitehall took two weeks to turn down on the egalitarian grounds that exceptions couldn't be made for senior officers!) but on April 16th, with the troops in Greece now pushed back almost as far as Thermopylae, General Papagos put a request through Wilson that the British should be withdrawn as quickly as possible from his country in order to 'save it from devastation' – a request which took Wavell back to Athens for the last time.

On April 17th, the Yugoslav Army laid down its arms, and Wavell issued a warning to the forces on the island of Crete to expect a rapid influx of troops evacuated from Greece followed soon afterwards by a sea and airborne invasion by Germans; and in Athens, he received a cable from Churchill which demanded in imperious language that London be kept in much closer touch with affairs on the Greek front than hithertofore. As neither Wavell nor indeed Wilson had been able to obtain from the Greeks any accurate, up-to-date pictures of events along their portions of the front, and thus had had but a sketchy idea of what was happening on their flanks, there was undoubtedly some cause for concern in London, but a mistaken idea of where the fault lay. The cable marked the beginning of a breakdown in understanding between Churchill and Wavell which had probably been inevitable from the start, although relations had in fact improved lately as a result of Churchill's remarkable sympathy over the reverse in Cyrenaica.

The Greek Government capitulated to the German forces on April 24th and the evacuation of the British and Australian survivors began on the same day – preceded by the virtual destruction of the remaining R.A.F. units in Greece by overwhelming Luftwaffe attacks. Three days later – on the day that von Herff's troops took Halfaya Pass from the Guards Brigade – the Germans were in Athens and evacuation could then only take place from small and isolated ports in the Peloponnese, but it continued until April 30th, by which time Wavell was in Crete discussing its defence with the famous New Zealander Major-General Bernard Freyberg, V.C. Here he learned that on the previous afternoon 350 British subjects had taken refuge in the British Embassy in Baghdad, another 150 in the American Embassy – and that 240 women and children had been given safe conduct to the R.A.F. station at Habbaniya by Raschid Ali, who then ordered the Iraqi Army to invest and attack it.

Somehow, and from somewhere, Wavell had to find the troops to rescue them.

On the same day, Rommel mounted his biggest attack so far on the western face of Tobruk and in a determined action lasting two days carried out by German troops under General Kirchheim, drove in a salient two miles deep towards Fort Pilastrino which then became so well entrenched, despite every Australian attempt to eliminate it, that it remained there like an abscess threatening the heart of the Fortress until the end of the siege.

So much for April.

May was dominated for Wavell by three main events – the first British counter-attack against Rommel, the German airborne invasion of Crete, and the elimination of Raschid Ali with, as a consequence, the end of German influence in Iraq and later in Syria.

Of these, *Operation Brevity* on the Egyptian borders at first bulked largest in Wavell's eyes. Although it was obvious to all that the sooner the Afrika Korps were pushed back at least beyond Tobruk the better, two factors introduced by personalities outside the Middle East theatre determined its timing.

Not altogether surprisingly, one of these personalities was Churchill's. His reaction to the reverse in Cyrenaica had been magnificent. The nagging ceased, there were no recriminations – only sympathy, understanding and an immediate concern to help; and one of the most practical aids which the Prime Minister felt that he could give to his hard-pressed commander in the field was to override the natural apprehensions of his senior Army and Navy advisers in England, strip the Home Defence of every tank and aeroplane that could be spared (and this at the time when the industrial heart of Britain was under heavy attack; Coventry had been virtually destroyed during two nights in early April) and send them by the fastest means possible through the Mediterranean to Alexandria. By April 28th Wavell had been informed that he might expect some 300 new tanks and over 50 Hurricane fighters by mid-May; and generosity was a quality to which Wavell responded far more readily than to truculence.

The second personality concerned was Halder's. Like many another theoretician risen to eminence in a vast organisation, he invariably exhibited signs of outrage when success was achieved by means other than those enshrined in his own dogma; and the fact that they had been thus achieved by a man who had had the temerity to call him a bloody fool did nothing to ease his chagrin. His diary entries covering the period immediately following Rommel's advance contain such passages as:

> Rommel has not sent in a single clear report, and I have a feeling that things are in a mess . . .
> All day long he rushes about between his widely scattered units and stages reconnaissance raids in which he fritters away his strength . . .
> Air transport cannot meet his senseless demands, primarily because of lack of fuel . . .
> It is essential to have the situation cleared up without delay . . .

To this end he dispatched to Africa 'perhaps the only man with enough influence to head off this soldier gone stark mad' – Generalleutnant Friedrich Paulus, as yet supremely unaware of the fate which was to overtake him at Stalingrad.

Paulus arrived at Rommel's H.Q. on April 27th and at first refused permission for the attack on Tobruk planned for April 30th, but two days later relented and remained at the front to watch it. Perhaps because he had himself some responsibility for the action taking place at all, he reported it as 'an important success' – but then went on to state that the Afrika Korps was in a tactically difficult and unbalanced situation, logistically unsupportable and from a strategic point of view (for he knew of *Operation Barbarossa* whereas Rommel still did not) grossly over-extended. No further attempt should be made against Tobruk, he felt, unless the garrison evacuated it voluntarily; and indeed, the principal task for the Afrika Korps should be restricted to the holding of Cyrenaica, irrespective of who held Sollum, Bardia or even Tobruk.

These views he communicated to Berlin by cable and within hours the Bletchley Park organisation were reading them. Churchill's reaction when they arrived on his desk, and Wavell's in the light of Churchill's recent benevolence, were predictable. If the German Command already felt that their forward troops should not be further east than, say, Tmimi or Gazala, then the lightest push might be enough to send them back there and thus relieve not only the Tobruk garrison, but also the hard-pressed Royal Navy from the onerous and increasingly dangerous task of supplying them. Such a move would also cheer up the home population in their tribulations and so ease Churchill's gigantic burden a little.

Operation Brevity began at dawn on May 15th, lasted some thirty-six hours and was from the British point of view a complete failure – compounded later by wrong conclusions drawn from the fighting at almost all levels of command.

Brigadier Gott, who commanded the operation in the field, had planned for a three-pronged advance. Along the coast road the 2nd Rifle Brigade supported by artillery were to take the post at the bottom of Halfaya Pass, and then to push on into Sollum to occupy the village, force their way up the pass there and take the barracks at the top. Parallel with them the infantry of 22nd Guards Brigade plus two squadrons of 4th Royal Tank Regiment in twenty-four Matildas would drive along the lip of the Escarpment, taking the post at the top of Halfaya, then capturing Fort Capuzzo and exploiting northwards, with luck as far as Bardia. Away to the south an Armoured Brigade Group, considerably under strength and consisting of the Support Group with two squadrons of cruiser tanks (twenty-nine in all) were to provide a screen for the slower-moving forces inside them, and also a means of exploitation should all

Map 17　*Operation Brevity*: May 15th–17th, 1941

hopes be realised and the Afrika Korps in the area retreat in haste.

In the light of conclusions to be drawn from Paulus's cable, it was not a wildly impracticable scheme – but perhaps unfortunately, neither Rommel nor his local commander Oberst von Herff were as fully aware of the thoughts of the emissary from Berlin as were Whitehall and Cairo. They certainly showed little inclination to abandon their positions and hurriedly decamp towards Gazala, and although the Armoured Brigade did reach around as far as Sidi Azeiz in their screening endeavour, it took the coast group practically all day to capture their first objective at the bottom of Halfaya Pass, and the battle which developed around Fort Capuzzo reached a pitch of intensity new in that particular area.

By 2100 that evening Brigadier Gott was sufficiently worried by the stalemate to signal Beresford-Peirse suggesting a withdrawal to the Halfaya Pass line, and after five hours without a reply ordered the Guards Brigade and their remaining Matildas to fall back – just three-quarters of an hour before receiving Beresford-Peirse's instructions to hang on until morning in the positions attained. By that time, the British infantry who had reached Fort Capuzzo (1st Durham Light Infantry) had been driven back as far as Musaid with heavy loss, and Gott was well aware of the vulnerability of the rest of the Guards Brigade on the top of the Escarpment should von Herff receive armoured reinforcement.

This appeared at Sidi Azeiz in the early morning of May 16th and although it was stranded there through lack of petrol for most of the day, its mere presence was enough to cause the withdrawal of the Armoured Brigade Group, for many of their cruiser tanks had broken down on the way up – and more were to break down on the way back.

By the morning of May 17th, the Afrika Korps stood on the line Sollum–Sidi Suleiman–Sidi Omar, and although the British now held Halfaya Pass, they had bought it at the cost of 160 dead and wounded, five Matildas destroyed and 13 damaged, and extra wear and tear on the already over-worn engines and tracks of their cruisers.

Ten days later, von Herff sent panzers and infantry forces from Capuzzo and Sollum and retook the top and bottom of Halfaya Pass, which he then turned into the anchor point of a strong defensive line swinging back in an arc crossing Hafid Ridge at Point 208 and ending at Sidi Azeiz. The main strong-points in the arc consisted of 88mm. anti-tank guns sunk so deep into the ground that little was visible from the front except the barrels, but each of which commanded a wide field of fire.

'I had great hopes of the effectiveness of this arrangement,' wrote Rommel later, with all the smug security of hindsight.

Few people really expected the defence of Crete to succeed, probably because the pattern of advance, confrontation and early retreat for the British seemed set, and no recent portent in the sky had given hope for a reversal of fortune. Yet it was in Wellington's famous phrase, 'a damned nice thing – the nearest-run thing you ever saw in your life!' Despite the lack of arms and especially of air cover, despite the hastily assembled staffs and scratch formations which were all that could be scavenged from the evacuation from Greece, there were many extended periods when the German Fallschirmjäger – in many ways an elite force – felt that they were facing defeat; and it would have been the first for German arms in the Second World War. Rarely has the difference between defeat and victory apparently been balanced for so long on such a fine knife-edge, when in fact a comparatively minor decision had already decided the issue within hours of the first landing.

In a corner of Maleme airfield the commander of a New Zealand battalion, wise, experienced, brave enough to have won the Victoria Cross during the First World War but in receipt of faulty information and so anxious for the lives of his men, ordered a withdrawal on to supporting battalions. A lodgment in one corner of the airfield was thus given to the German paratroops who, before the significance of the loss was appreciated by Freyberg, widened their area of control until troop-carrying aircraft could bring in reinforcements. From that moment the invader could be regularly supplied and augmented while the defenders' strength was inexorably whittled away. Like the fall of a grain of sand which starts a landslide, the withdrawal of 22nd New Zealand Battalion from that single point eventually gave Crete to the Germans.

Ironically enough, this violent and protracted battle, which left a strategically valuable position in German hands, proved a Pyrrhic victory for the practitioners of the new and apparently successful military technique which had brought it about. General Student, who had raised, trained and commanded the German airborne troops, later wrote, 'Crete was the grave-yard of the German parachutists', and they were never used in an airborne role again.

This, however, was a judgment of the future and no comfort at all to Wavell, watching on the last day of May the Homeric conflict fought out among the orange groves, the scented gardens and across the terraced hills, to reach its dusty and depressing conclusion on the tiny south coast beach of Sphakia; followed by yet another evacuation, another tale of unavailing gallantry, of abandoned equipment and of brave and valuable men killed and taken prisoner. Of the 32,000 British and Commonwealth soldiers on Crete when the battle opened, only 18,000 got back to Egypt and of these over 1,000 would never fight again. Very few could bring back even their rifles, let alone some of the heavier armament which had been sent across the Mediterranean from the theatre which now needed it so desperately.

But at least the whole Greek entanglement was now over, and could no longer drain men and material from the main battlefront in the desert, or distract the Commander-in-Chief's attention from the crucial area.

The bare outlines of the Raschid Ali revolt are quickly told.

At Habbaniya was an R.A.F. flying school and upon investment by the Iraqi Army, the instructors and pupils first dispersed and then armed their aircraft as best they could. Some idea of the problems which faced them in this operation can be gained from the list of aircraft at their disposal – thirty-two Audaxes, eight Gordons, twenty-nine Oxfords, three Gladiators, one Blenheim and five Hart trainers; in the many hundreds of books dealing with the Second World War which the present writer has read, he has only come across mention of two of those types of aircraft in any other context. Nevertheless, they were able to carry out reconnaissance flights and to provide information that the surrounding forces comprised at least two infantry battalions with supporting artillery; and at dawn on May 2nd, augmented by eight Wellingtons which had flown up from Shaiba they were out bombing and strafing the enemy positions.

This action attracted first some scattered rifle and machine-gun fire against them and then sporadic shelling of the cantonment, followed by the arrival over the area of planes of the Iraqi Air Force. By the end of the day, five of the assorted Habbaniya aircraft had been destroyed and their desperately inexperienced pilots killed, several had been damaged and seventeen people inside the camp had been killed by shellfire. The investment force had been increased to brigade strength.

The next two days were spent in similar pattern, but at night patrols carried out by men of the King's Own Royal Regiment who had been flown up from Basra ranged well out on to the surrounding plateau, and their encounters with the Iraqi Army were not marked by any high degree of aggression on the part of those surprised. At dawn on May 6th, a large proportion of the investing army had disappeared, leaving the ground dotted with abandoned equipment which the besieged quickly dragged into the confines of Habbaniya and put to some use.

That afternoon, two brisk actions were fought with Iraqi columns on the road back from Habbaniya towards Baghdad in both of which the enemy was thoroughly routed, for their troops seemed both unwilling to fight and unable to stand. The siege was thus lifted within six days.

However, Habbaniya was an isolated garrison at least 200 miles inside the borders of a potentially hostile country, and British men and women were still penned within the embassies in Baghdad; a flying column was hastily cobbled together from the 1st Cavalry Division in Palestine (still in the process of exchanging its horses for vehicles) and set out under command of Brigadier J. J. Kingstone on its 500-mile dash, crossing the Iraqi frontier on May 13th.

Its size was limited by the extreme shortage of lorries available, and some indication of the lengths to which Wavell had been driven to form it at all is given by the fact that its one experienced formation consisted of eight cars of the R.A.F. Armoured Car Company, withdrawn from the vital co-operation with the 11th Hussars on the Egyptian Frontier.

The column was attacked by German fighters, diverted by floods caused by destruction of bunds as they approached their objective, and much hindered by the problems of digging heavy lorries out of soft sand in temperatures of 120 degrees with inexperienced hands; but they swung around to the south of Lake Habbaniya and reached the road to Baghdad by May 19th (by which time two infantry brigades of 10th Indian Division had reached Basra) and during the next few days all forces in the immediate area were reorganised. During this phase also, rumours reached the Iraqi capital grossly exaggerating the British forces, which in the end were reported to be advancing with an unknown but vast number of tanks – at which Raschid Ali's nerve broke and when the advance did begin on May 28th, he and his supporters fled to Persia.

The armistice was signed on May 31st, the British troops moved into Baghdad the same day and on June 1st the pro-British Regent flew back and was reinstated. On the surface, the episode was over.

But from Wavell's personal point of view, there was far more to it than that.

'I always disliked Iraq – ' Wavell was later to write, 'the country, the people and the military commitment . . . It blew up at the worst possible time for me, when I had the Western Desert, Crete, East Africa and Syria on my hands, and no troops.'

His basic psychological allergy to the country had found expression in early March when he had arranged with the Chiefs of Staff in London that the entire area should come under the India Command, and that any trouble in it should be dealt with by the new Commander-in-Chief there, General Sir Claude Auchinleck – a suggestion with which the Chiefs of Staff then agreed, as did General Auchinleck. To both generals it seemed that hostile control of Iraq would not greatly jeopardise Wavell's defence of Egypt and Palestine whereas, via Iran and Afghanistan, it would affect the entire defence system of the Indian Empire.

Moreover, India could and indeed did supply troops during April as soon as trouble threatened, shipping two trained Indian infantry brigades to Basra at Auchinleck's suggestion, at precisely the time that Wavell was resisting the demands from London that he dispatch the 'sizeable force' to Habbaniya from Palestine on the not unreasonable grounds that with Tobruk just sealed in, Rommel's forces at Bardia and threatening Capuzzo, and the Aliakmon Line breaking, the agreement that India should deal with troubles in Iraq should surely stand. And General Quinan, commanding the Indian troops at Basra, brought with him a directive from Auchinleck beginning, 'You will command all British Empire land forces in Iraq from the time of your arrival. You will be under my orders,' – a sentiment with which Wavell was in complete agreement.

But both Churchill and the Chiefs of Staff now changed their minds again, for reasons partly geographical and partly historical. Baghdad might be 500 miles from Jerusalem but it was 1,500 from Bombay, and although men could and should be rushed up from the vast reservoir of the Indian Army, it seemed obvious and logical that supplies – vehicles, fuel, equipment and ammunition – should come from the Middle East Command, a view which took note of the realities on the map but not on the quartermaster's store-sheet.

The result was a plethora of signals passing between London and Cairo containing such phrases as:

Chiefs of Staff to A. P. Wavell   2nd May, 1941
. . . operational command should now pass temporarily to Mid-east whence alone immediate assistance can be given. This will take place forthwith . . .

A. P. Wavell to Chiefs of Staff   3rd May, 1941
I have consistently warned you that no assistance could be given to Iraq from Palestine . . . commitment in Iraq should be avoided.
There are no guns or A.F.V.s in Palestine . . . merely asking for further trouble.
My forces are stretched to limit everywhere . . .
I do not see how I can possibly accept military responsibility.[11]

In this last cable he suggested that the Iraq problem must be solved by diplomatic action and later that either Turkey or the U.S.A. be asked to mediate, courses of action which raised hackles in the Foreign Office and caused a noticeable increase in Churchill's blood-pressure. It also resulted in another long cable from the

Chiefs of Staff to Wavell on May 4th which, while regretting the
extra burdens now thrown on Wavell's shoulders, firmly rejected
the ideas of diplomatic negotiation for mediation by neutrals and
equally firmly ordered him to take specific action – a cable which
elicited a reply whose opening sentence read:

A. P. Wavell to Chiefs of Staff   5th May, 1941
Your 88 takes little account of realities. You must face facts.[12]

The cable went on again to list the difficulties facing him, the consequent weakness of any force which he could assemble for dispatch
into Iraq, the desirability for mediation and for military operational
control of the theatre to reside with India.

As this cable arrived in London at the same time as one from
Auchinleck – who was deeply sympathetic with Wavell's problems
and anxious to help him – offering to send five complete infantry
brigades plus ancillary troops to Basra if London could find ships to
carry them, Wavell's stock in London sank and Auchinleck's rose;
but the gist of the reply sent to Cairo was to the effect that Wavell
should stop bellyaching and get on with it.

A. P. Wavell to C.I.G.S.   5th May, 1941
Nice baby you have handed me on my fifty-eighth birthday. Have
always hated babies and Iraqis but will do my best for the little
blighter. Am hatching minor offensive in Western Desert but not
sure yet can bring it off.[13]

But this last cable was to his old friend Sir John Dill, who had
himself been trying to argue Wavell's case and thus found himself
becoming increasingly unpopular. On the following day, the Chiefs
of Staff sent another cold and formal cable to Wavell, dismissing his
objections, informing him that they would take responsibility for
the dispatch of the force from Palestine, but nevertheless hedging
their bets at the end with the equivocal instruction

Subject to security of Egypt being maintained, maximum air
support possible should be given to operation in Iraq . . . [14]

At the same time, they sent a cable to Auchinleck:

C.o.S. to C.-in-C. in India   6th May, 1941
Your bold and generous offer greatly appreciated. Please prepare
forces as a matter of urgency. Notify dates by which they will be
ready to sail and we will confirm before despatch.[15]

And what the Chiefs of Staff gave expression to, the Prime
Minister was at the same time feeling. He had greeted Wavell's
statement that there was no worthwhile force in Palestine to send to
Habbaniya with the acid comment, 'Fancy having kept the Cavalry

Division in Palestine all this time without having the rudiments of a
mobile column organised!' – which was grossly unfair, for if the
equipment had been available, that and even more could have been
organised, and employed on the most immediately threatened
fronts in Egypt or Greece. On the morning of those last cables, Sir
John Dill told one of his confrères that he felt that Churchill had
now lost all confidence in the Middle East Command.

Churchill's disenchantment with Wavell now seems to have been
so great that it was not to be readjusted even by the news of the
successful conclusion of at least one campaign in the area – for by
the middle of May, Italy's East African Empire had totally
collapsed.

As has been mentioned, the two Indian divisions stormed up
through the Dongolaas Gorge to take Keren on March 27th, 5th
Indian advanced to Asmara four days later and by April 8th the
Red Sea port at Massawa was in British hands. To the south,
Cunningham's forces had swept up through Harar Province reaching Jijiga by March 17th where they joined the Aden force which
had taken Berbera and regained Somaliland, the combined forces
then pressing on to take Addis Ababa on April 5th. Emperor Haile
Selassie was back in his capital a month later, after an absence of
almost exactly five years.

The position of the Duke of Aosta, Viceroy of Ethiopia, was now
critical. The large majority of the forces he had commanded
consisted of native levies, and as Platt in the north and Cunningham
in the south advanced into the heart of their country, these melted
away and the Duke found himelf by mid-April penned with his
remaining forces into the mountain fortress of Amba Alagi where,
although they could undoubtedly repel for some time any attacking
force, they could not themselves break out nor, in the circumstances, expect relief from the home country so many miles away
across the Mediterranean.

The end was inevitable and began on May 16th with armistice
negotiations, to be solemnised three days later by a parade of 5,000
Italian survivors marching past a Guard of Honour, after which
they were disarmed and the Duke of Aosta formally surrendered.
He was then taken to the villa near Nairobi, his chosen place of
incarceration as a prisoner of war where, on the morning of March
3rd, 1942, he died of tuberculosis – mourned by all, for he had been
a charming, generous and extremely civilised man. But alas, these
are not the qualities of which victorious soldiers are made.

By the end of May, then, three of the major problems which had
been facing the Commanders-in-Chief, Middle East, had been
resolved, and two of them satisfactorily. True, the incipient

animosity against the British which had flared into open hostility in Iraq seemed about to erupt again even nearer, in Syria – but the East African front was now completely closed down and would remain so. As for the northern front, although there the battle had ended in defeat, at least it was no longer a drain on valuable supplies.

On paper the overall situation was more favourable than it had appeared six weeks before, and Britain had demonstrated that against at least one of the Axis partners her armies were invincible. Whether they would be so against the partner who showed strong indications of making up in martial prowess for whatever might be lacking in Latin charm, remained to be seen.

9 · *Battleaxe*

Rommel's problems during May were perhaps not as disparate as those facing Wavell, but they were just as acute; and they all sprang either from the inadequacies of his subordinates or the unconcern of his superiors.

The attack on the western perimeter of Tobruk at the end of April, however deep the salient it had driven towards the port, had revealed a lack of expertise in plain infantry fighting among his own German troops, more unacceptable even than the evident lack of enthusiasm for the battle exhibited by some of the Italians:

> The high casualties suffered by my assault forces were primarily caused by their lack of training. Even in the smallest action, there are always tactical tricks which can be used to save casualties, and these must be made known to the men. It frequently happened that dash was used where caution was really needed, with, of course, casualties as a result. On the next occasion, when boldness really was required, the men would be over-cautious.[1]

The main problem for the German troops, especially the panzer crews, was that it had suddenly become an entirely different sort of war. Their fame, their confidence, their expertise were all concerned with the mystique of Blitzkrieg – the rapid movements, the sharp clash of armour followed quickly by either parry and disengagement or (and more often for them so far) by breakthrough and victory. Their first serious attack on Tobruk had been their first experience of a hard, slogging infantry fight against solid defences which could not be outflanked, and apparently would not be over-run.

There was another aspect of the battle, too, which came as a shock to a large number of Rommel's troops, and awoke unpleasant memories amongst the rest. The most searing experience which comes to a soldier, and the one to which the majority of his early training is directed to help him overcome, is the first moment when he realises that out there is another man intent on killing him – not a far-distant artilleryman blindly firing his huge missiles at random into a target area, but another infantryman like himself, who knows where he is, has his sights on the immediate position and will fire to wound or kill at the first false move. Infantry fighting in such circumstances is a very serious and personal business, and such exhilarating factors as speed and excitement have nothing to do with it. It is cold, destructive and dreadfully exhausting, and an additional shock to the morale of the German troops who found themselves in the Ras el Madauer salient was the realisation that the Australians were for the moment better at it than they were. Rommel, who probably had more first-hand experience of this type of fighting than the rest of his command put together, was most impressed:

> A batch of some fifty or sixty Australian prisoners was marched off close beside us – immensely big and powerful men, who without question represented an elite formation of the British empire, a fact that was also evident in battle. Enemy resistance was as stubborn as ever and violent actions were being fought at many points.[2]

These violent actions were being fought by the Afrika Korps troops from slit trenches so shallow in the rocky ground that they often had to lie there pinned down all day, defenceless, under the onslaught of thousands of flies attracted to the site by the awful detritus of war now exaggerated by the effects of the dysentery from which so many of them were suffering. Their days were aeons of agony and the relief of night was punctuated by the shock of battle with Australian patrols – sharp, vicious and invariably bloody.

In such work, the Italian ally was of little account, both for lack of training and total inadequacy of weapons or equipment, and also because, as Rommel wrote, 'Many Italian officers had thought of war as little more than a pleasant adventure and were, perforce, having to suffer a bitter disillusionment.'[3]

Another problem with which Rommel had to grapple was his lack of authority over the Luftwaffe in Africa. Although Fröhlich was amenable to suggestion it was *his* choice whether his aircraft acted in close tactical support of Rommel's troops, or in more wide-ranging tasks of enemy harassment – and his choice did not always coincide with Rommel's. And there was always the basic problem of supply, for the Italians still preferred to sail their convoys into Tripoli, declaring Benghasi far too close to R.A.F. bases to risk either ships or cargoes, which were anyway both in short supply. Even the voyage to Tripoli was proving costly, for British submarines and light naval forces operating from Malta took toll of almost every convoy, and during April two destroyer flotillas, one under command of Captain Lord Louis Mountbatten aboard

H.M.S. *Kelly*, had operated from Grand Harbour with disastrous effect, on one occasion sinking all five ships of a convoy together with its escort. It was thus proving exceedingly difficult to bring in the 1,500 tons of supplies needed every day at the front, let alone enough to build up a reserve against the time when a further advance could be made.

As for the Italian colonists of Cyrenaica, grown used over the years to a certain minimum of sustenance from the homeland, there was little or nothing to spare for them and they were faced with increasingly overt hostility from the indigenous Arabs – by now well aware of the fact that whoever was in control in the area, it was not the previous and much-resented occupants of their land. A number of Italian troops had been found murdered in the rear areas, and punitive expeditions against tribal villages had been fought off with arms evidently salvaged from the recent battle-fields.

But above and beyond all this was the total lack of appreciation exhibited by Berlin for the achievement of the Afrika Korps and their commander. This was not only wounding but also incomprehensible, for Rommel and his troops were still kept in ignorance of the gigantic operation being planned for mid-June in the east, not least because it was shrewdly suspected that had he known of it, he might have attempted to return hotfoot to Berlin to secure a place in *Operation Barbarossa* for himself. Compared with the invasion of Russia, the Desert War to his political and military masters would be an unimportant skirmish, and this attitude was illustrated by the arrival of Generalmajor Alfred Gause with a large staff of appointees from the Oberkommando der Wehrmacht. They were charged officially with a number of liaison duties, but sent out in reality to act as a bureaucratic curb on what Halder considered intransigence bordering on gross insubordination on the part of 'this particularly disagreeable character'.

One significant fact that Rommel quickly elicited was that Gause had received explicit instructions not to place himself under Rommel's command – instructions which did not stand long in the face of Rommel's anger when he heard of them. Cables, orders and counter-orders flew apace, and Gause soon found himself taking von dem Borne's place as Rommel's Chief of Staff, a role he filled for many months with exemplary efficiency; but the circumstances surrounding his arrival could not easily be brushed aside, and they were accompanied by others:

Dearest Lu,   26 May 1941

    Yesterday evening I received a considerable rocket from Brauchitsch, the reason for which completely passes my comprehension. Apparently the reports I send back, stating the conditions as they exist, don't suit their book.

Dearest Lu, 29 May 1941

Von dem Borne is to take this letter with him to-morrow and I hope it will reach you earlier than usual. I've had a major rocket from the OKH – to my mind unjustified – in gratitude for our previous achievements . . . I'm not going to take it lying down, and a letter is already on its way to von Brauchitsch.

For your peace of mind, I've kept very well so far . . .

Dearest Lu, 2 June 1941

It was 107° here yesterday, and that's quite some heat. Tanks standing in the sun go up to as much as 160°, which is too hot to touch.

My affair with the OKH is under way. Either they've got confidence in me or they haven't. If not, then I'm asking them to draw their own conclusions. I'm very intrigued to know what will come of it. It's easy enough to bellyache when you aren't sweating it out here.[4]

There were a few reasons for satisfaction, though, the first being that by the end of May, the bulk of 15th Panzer Division had become available for deployment at the front and its new commander, Generalleutnant Walther Neumann-Sylkow, was able to take over command in the Capuzzo area in early June. This meant that the majority of troops immediately facing any British threat would be German except along the line Sollum–Musaid–Capuzzo where there were three battalions of the Trento Infantry Division and one regiment of the excellent Italian artillery, with two more Italian artillery regiments back in Bardia.

The German element at the frontier consisted of two battalions of the 8th Panzer Regiment, the 33rd Reconnaissance Battalion, a battalion of lorried infantry and a motor-cycle battalion, an anti-tank battalion with twenty-one 37mm. guns and twelve 50mms – and an anti-aircraft battery with thirteen of the superb 88mm. guns, mostly built into dug-outs to serve in their most effective role as anti-tank guns; and one battery of field artillery. The static elements were concentrated along the Hafid ridge, at Point 206 and Qalala, with the most forward positions at Halfaya well fortified and under command of an extraordinary soldier and clergyman, Major the Reverend Wilhelm Bach, of whose military ability Rommel had the highest opinion.

The 5th Light Division by the end of May had been largely withdrawn for rest and maintenance to the south of Tobruk, while around the perimeter were the tanks of the Ariete Division and the

Figure 4 88mm. flak gun: weight in action 5 tons; travelling weight 7·5 tons; traverse 360°; horizontal range 16,200 yards; vertical range 35,100 feet; weight of projectile H.E. 20 lbs, A.P. 21 lbs; rate of fire 15/20 per min.; crew 10

infantry of the Brescia and Pavia Divisions, buttressed by German Rifle Companies, especially in the salient.

One other vitally important unit operating between both battle-fronts was Rommel's signal intercept service, which kept him very well informed indeed about both British and Australian intentions, for neither the Imperial nor Commonwealth formations, from individual tank crews to Headquarter Staffs, had yet learned to curb their inclination to chatter, using on most occasions the simplest codes or the most transparent jargon.

So far as vehicles and artillery were concerned, too, the position was better than Rommel had expected, for from the acres of equipment abandoned by the Italians and left almost undisturbed by the British, the industrious Germans salvaged and repaired a great deal. Italian guns appeared in German positions (with their correct ammunition efficiently stacked alongside), Italian lorries, cars and motor-cycles, all newly adorned with the Afrika Korps insignia of palm tree and swastika, patrolled the roads and tracks with German drivers at the wheels; so it was not long before Rommel was in receipt of a diatribe from Generale Gariboldi to the effect that such equipment was Italian property and must only be put to use by Italians – an instruction which elicited only an extremely acid comment from the Afrika Korps commander.

If, then, prospects for the distant future appeared vague and unsatisfactory as a result of equivocation in both Rome and Berlin, those for the immediate future were much more clear. It was quite evident from a number of indications, including the signal intercepts, that the British opposite were intending soon to launch a heavy attack along the frontier, possibly in conjunction with an attempted break-out from Tobruk. The task for the Afrika Korps – and its allies, however unwilling – was to strengthen their fortifications and train hard for something new to them, a defensive role.

Whatever Rommel's distractions from Rome and Berlin, at least he could concentrate his military skills on one front; Wavell had still to conduct two separate and distinct campaigns, for the revolt in Iraq had exacerbated the dangerous political situation in Syria, and directed Churchill's attention towards an area where he believed his old (and decidedly un-English) love affair with France could be satisfactorily pursued.

Under the terms of the Armistice with France, an Italo-German Commission had arrived in Syria at the end of August 1940 charged with the task of progressively disarming, demobilising and repatriating the 120,000-strong Army of the Levant, which in the early days of the war Wavell had regarded as his strongest bulwark against German aggression in the Middle East, and its commander, Général Weygand, as his staunchest ally. By early 1941, it had been reduced to 35,000 officers and men retained to ensure internal order and security – but these were all hard-core professional soldiers, equipped with a considerable proportion of the war supplies originally sent to Syria for the entire Army of the Levant, and they were commanded by Général Henri Dentz, a soldier who buttressed his pro-Vichy patriotism with a strong personal Anglophobia.

Of this situation Wavell was well aware, but Churchill was not – and the Prime Minister's illusions were fostered and encouraged by the ambitions of Général de Gaulle, together with the glowing optimism of the latter's representative in the Middle East, Général Georges Catroux, aided and abetted by Churchill's old friend and liaison officer with the Free French, Major-General Edward Spears. The situation was thus fraught with possibilities for misunderstanding and resultant friction.

The official British position regarding Syria was quite clear. Britain was not at war with Vichy France, but she could not allow Syria or the Lebanon (both provinces ruled by the French under a mandate granted by the League of Nations after the First World War) to be occupied by any hostile power, or to be used as a base for attacks on neighbouring countries in which Britain had interest; neither could she allow Syria or the Lebanon to become the scene of disorders which might threaten in any way the internal security of such countries.

Unfortunately for Wavell, towards the end of 1940 Général Catroux became convinced that conditions in Syria were ripe for a *coup d'état* in which, so he and his supporters believed, the rump of the Army of the Levant would rise in support of Général de Gaulle, throw off the shameful mantle of Vichy and join the fight against Nazi oppression.

To this opinion Wavell did not subscribe, remembering that during the hiatus immediately after the collapse of France, the only worthwhile body of men to decamp from Syria to Palestine in order to continue the fight had been a brigade of Poles who had escaped from Europe after the tragic defeat of their own country. They had been accompanied by less than a thousand individual Frenchmen, though a Colonel Collet had managed to bring over with him his own picturesque regiment of Circassian Cavalry. Wavell was far closer to the truth of the matter than either the leaders of the Free French or Churchill, appreciating that in the eyes of many Frenchmen – and especially in the eyes of the French professional officers – De Gaulle and his followers represented nothing but a traitorous and dissident faction which, by breaking away from the decisions of the official government of France and by maintaining what was still regarded as a hopeless struggle alongside the pig-headed British, were jeopardising France's prospects of obtaining tolerable peace terms from the eminently reasonable and scrupulously well-behaved Germans.

Général de Gaulle paid a visit to the Middle East in April and one result was that in early May a feverish exchange of cables took place between Wavell and the Chiefs of Staff, the British Ambassador in Egypt and the Foreign Office, Général de Gaulle (who had gone on to French Equatorial Africa) and Général Catroux, General Spears and Mr Churchill. The main burden of the messages from the French was that on the one hand their propaganda bombardment of the Vichy French Forces had now rendered Syria ripe for invasion (later events demonstrated that it had merely irritated both French and Syrian opinion) and on the other hand, the Germans were on the point of invading Syria themselves, so Général Dentz would welcome assistance against them from any source, especially the Free French.

On May 18th, Général Catroux went so far as to announce that secret intelligence sources had informed him that Général Dentz was about to withdraw all Vichy French forces into the Lebanon and present the rest of Syria without battle or even argument to an advancing German occupation force – so as the road to Damascus was now open, would General Wavell please give orders for an immediate advance? General Wavell declined to move – much to Général de Gaulle's indignation – so Catroux then requested permission for the five battalions of Free French troops in the Middle East to go at least as far as the Syrian border in order to test reaction on the other side, pointing out that all he would need from the British would be 300 lorries and a minimum of air support; this at a time when Wavell had to cut down the size of the force he had been ordered to send into Iraq precisely because of lack of lorries. It was also the day after *Operation Brevity* ended and two days before the launching of the German airborne invasion of Crete.

With a restraint which had marked all his actions since his appointment as Commander-in-Chief but which was now showing signs of wearing thin, Wavell cabled Whitehall with his own cogently expressed objections both to the entire scheme and to this harassment by the Free French, and rather pointedly asked if London expected him to accept the French suggestions despite his own objections; to which he immediately received a reply telling him to do as Général Catroux wished!

The heated exchange which then followed culminated in a cable sent direct from Churchill, which ended:

> For this decision we of course take full responsibility, and should you find yourself unwilling to give full effect to it arrangements will be made to meet any wish you may express to be relieved of your command.[5]

The writing was on the wall, plain to read, but as it happened, on the day Wavell received it, Général Catroux discovered that he had been misled by his secret sources, that the information about French withdrawal to the Lebanon was untrue, and that, far from withdrawing, Vichy French forces had in fact moved to key positions in which they could effectively block any attempt to enter Syria from the south or east.

The storm died down but there is no trace of any signal to Wavell apologising for the doubt which had been cast on his judgment, or even for the trouble he had been caused; but then these were the days when the German battleship *Bismarck* was loose in the Atlantic, and Wavell was not alone in having to fight the war on many fronts. It is surprising that more sympathy did not exist between sets of people grappling with similar sets of problems, but the sad fact remains that the impression left in London – especially in Churchill's heart – was not that Wavell had been right, but that he had been obstructive.

So strong was this feeling that despite the collapse of Catroux's case for the invasion of Syria, despite also the myriad tasks with which Wavell and his forces in the Middle East were grappling, he was instructed to make ready the largest force possible – without, of course, endangering the security of the Cyrenaican front or interfering with the launching of an offensive against Rommel at the earliest opportunity – and dispatch it northwards into Syria in order to capture the important airfields from which, undoubtedly, several Luftwaffe squadrons had been operating against Habforce, and from which they might in the future launch operations against Egypt and especially the Suez Canal.

Operation Exporter began on June 8th when elements of the 7th Australian Division, a brigade of the 4th Indian Division (hastily rushed back from Eritrea), two regiments of 1st Cavalry division (one still on horses), a battalion of the Special Service Brigade now stationed in Cyprus, and a weak Free French Force under Legentil-homme, now promoted Général, crossed the frontier in three drives, one directed towards Damascus through Deraa, one in the centre towards Rayak through Merjayun and one along the coast to Beirut, where Général Dentz's Headquarters lay.

A detailed account of the Syrian Campaign is not part of this history, except in so far as it affected General Wavell and the conduct of the war in North Africa. At this point it is sufficient to say that by the end of the first phase, which lasted until June 13th, all advances were held up and it had become very evident that the Vichy French forces were not only well entrenched and well

Map 18 *Operation Exporter*: June 1941

equipped, but that they showed not the slightest sympathy towards Gaullist or Free French ambitions. On the contrary, they greeted all attempts at propaganda or dialogue with their compatriots with contempt and abuse, the fighting between them was amongst the bitterest of the war, there were a number of violations of both the white flag and the Red Cross and the Vichy French treatment of any prisoners they took, especially British or Indian, was abominable.

But by the end of that first phase, not even Churchill expected Wavell to be paying much attention to *Exporter*. During the afternoon of June 14th, three British columns left the area of Sidi Barrani and advanced some twenty-four miles towards the Egyptian frontier.

Operation Battleaxe had begun.

The 'Tiger' convoy, by which Churchill's generosity after the loss of Cyrenaica had been best expressed, arrived at Alexandria on May 12th, and the Prime Minister's courage was rewarded by the fact that of the five fast transports in which vital cargoes travelled, only one had been lost – the *Empire Song* carrying 57 tanks and ten Hurricanes struck mines in the narrows to the south of Malta and had blown up, fortunately with no loss of life. The result was that by mid-May Wavell's armament had been theoretically increased by 135 Matildas, 82 cruisers (of which 50 – enough to re-equip one complete tank regiment – were the new Mark IV 'Crusaders'), and 21 light tanks, while the force at the command of the acting Air Officer Commander-in-Chief, Air Marshal A. W. Tedder (for Longmore was away in London at the time) had been increased by 43 Hurricanes.

There was, however, the inevitable time-gap between the arrival of the tanks and their readiness for action (a hiatus which Churchill never seemed able to understand) while they were unloaded, taken to workshops for the fitting of essential sand-filters and modifications to cooling systems, their new features studied by technicians and they could then be issued to the troops who were to use them.

They were by no means universally popular, the Mark IV Crusaders in particular showing exactly the same defects of thin armour and mechanical unreliability as their predecessors. Even after the most complete overhaul the Delta workshops could provide, a journey of thirty miles over the rough going and drifting sand was enough to put at least 10 per cent out of action. Sir David Hunt, then serving on the Staff, tells of one cavalry officer who so hated his Crusader that with the concurrence of his crew he swopped it for a 3-ton lorry on the grounds that it would go anywhere the tank could go, would not break down so often, and if hit by an anti-tank shell would suffer merely a neat and probably

inconsiderable hole in its fabric, instead of brewing up and in-
cinerating the crew.

However, most of the tanks were at last taken over by their crews
and joined the reconstituted formations of the 7th Armoured
Division – but this was by no means the same division which had
won the resounding victories leading up to Beda Fomm. For one
thing, they had been without tanks of any sort for four months, and
now at least one regiment was to be mounted in this new model
which they were seeing for the first time. Moreover, many of the
stalwarts of the division, including for instance 'Blood' Caunter,
had found other outlets for their energies and enterprise during the
interregnum, and were either no longer in Egypt or had been
promoted and appointed to duties from which they could now not
be spared. Two promising officers and some senior N.C.O.s had
joined the Long Range Desert Group and others were attached to
various new unorthodox units which were springing up like flowers
in April, though a proportion of them were to prove to be weeds.
And now Pat Hobart was no longer there to drill the remainder
quickly back into shape.

All squadrons had received their new tanks by June 9th, but at
O'Moore Creagh's urgent representations they were given another
five days for extra training before the onset of *Battleaxe* – the
operation whose declared aim was now to destroy Rommel's forces
in the frontier area and follow up as far as Tobruk, where the
garrison was to be relieved and the enemy forces defeated. The
combined forces would then sweep forward as far as the Derna–
Mechili line.

The operation was to be commanded in the field by Lieutenant-
General Sir Noel Beresford-Peirse, and he had two divisions under
his command – the 4th Indian now under Major-General Frank
Messervy (who had led Gazelle Force in Eritrea) and 7th
Armoured under Creagh. Neither of these divisions, however, was
up to full strength, each lacking one brigade.

The 4th Indian Division, which would at the outset push along the
coast through Halfaya towards Sollum and Capuzzo, consisted of
the 11th Indian Brigade with Rajputana Rifles and Mahrattas at the
foot of the Escarpment and the Camerons at the top, and the 22nd
Guards Brigade which was motorised and would advance to attack
Capuzzo and then exploit if possible up towards Bardia.

Those responsible for the numeration of the units of the 7th
Armoured Division carried out their duties with a fine disregard for
the problems of the historian. The 7th Armoured Division consisted
of two brigades, 4th Armoured and 7th Armoured. The 4th
Armoured Brigade consisted basically of two regiments (both at
Battleaxe armed with Matildas) – 4th Royal Tank Regiment and 7th

Royal Tank Regiment; 7th Armoured Brigade also consisted of two regiments – 2nd R.T.R. in a mixture of A9, A10 and A13 cruiser tanks (to which they were well accustomed although these were new ones), and 6th R.T.R. in the new Crusader tanks. The Support Group, temporarily commanded by Jock Campbell, consisted of four batteries of the Royal Horse Artillery and their old friends, 1st Battalion King's Royal Rifle Corps and 2nd Battalion The Rifle Brigade.

The duties for the 7th Armoured Division were to some extent dictated by their weapons. However indestructible the Matildas had proved to be in the past, their speed was but a trifle more than that of marching infantry, and their capability for co-operation with cruisers, the oldest of which had a speed of 15 m.p.h. while the Crusaders were reputed to be able to move at 27 m.p.h., was thus much restricted. The Matildas of 4th R.T.R. would therefore be used, at least initially, as infantry support, two troops accompanying the Rajputanas and Mahrattas along the coast road, one squadron with the Camerons in their attack on the garrison at the top of Halfaya Pass, the rest shepherding 22nd Guards Brigade on and into Capuzzo and then exploiting towards Sollum if necessary, and then up to Bardia if all went well. Point 206, which was known to be held in strength by the enemy, lay along the axis between Sidi Suleiman and Capuzzo, and the Matildas would certainly be necessary there.

The main bulk of 4th Armoured Brigade would thus be on the southern wing of the infantry advance, and available if necessary to support their brothers in the cruiser tanks of 7th Armoured Brigade, as these swung in an even wider circle to the south aiming up towards the Hafid Ridge where it was believed the bulk of Rommel's armour lay. The Support Group would string out behind the cruisers to form a shield during the battles on the coast and escarpment, against possible enemy intrusion from the direction of Sidi Omar. The main aim of the 7th Armoured Division was to bring the German armour to battle, to destroy it and then prepare to sweep westwards towards Tobruk and the second stage of the battle.

Above the advance would fly 98 Hurricanes and Tomahawks, while ranging beyond them, over and past Tobruk, 105 heavy and medium bombers would attack Rommel's supply routes and the reinforcements which he would undoubtedly move up once he realised the seriousness of the attack – all under the direction of Air Marshal Tedder who was stripping the rest of his command of every possible aircraft to give support to *Battleaxe*. Both Tedder and Beresford-Peirse would direct the operation from well to the rear – Tedder from Maaten Baggush and Beresford-Peirse from Sidi Barrani.

Both Wavell and Beresford-Peirse were pinning their hopes for the success of *Battleaxe* on the toughness and expertise of the Indian and Guards infantry, on the proven durability of the Matildas, and on the capacity of the cruisers to bring the German panzers to battle and then to defeat them.

Dawn on June 15th broke clear and fine, and all troops and vehicles were on the move. Along the top of the Escarpment, 2nd Camerons and their escort of thirteen Matildas of 4th R.T.R., with a battery of 31st Field Regiment, marched or drove stolidly forward towards their first objective, the garrison at the top of Halfaya, aware that to their right and below the lip their comrades of the 1st/6th Rajputana Rifles and 2nd/5th Mahrattas were moving parallel and level with them. The commander of the 4th R.T.R., Lieutenant-Colonel Walter O'Carroll, caught the mood of the moment exactly:

> To start with the tanks moved in double line ahead and slowly so as to make a minimum of noise; they were also ready to shake out in the event of hostile air. By 0530 there was not very much further to go before they might expect fire to open on them and they slowed down and fanned out. The guns [British] should open about 0540, and they did not wish to get mixed up in the 25-pounder concentration. The sun was rising behind and light forward was excellent. No guns sounded. The tanks crept on. At Halfaya the month before, Major Miles had found the enemy still in bed or shaving when he arrived, but they were Italians. Now it seemed almost too good to be true that the garrison should be so caught again . . . [6]

It was indeed. At 0600 when Major Miles – in the absence of the planned artillery cover, for the supporting battery had bogged down in the soft sand over which his tanks and the infantry had advanced with no trouble – gave the orders for the Matildas to fan out and lead the charge towards the top of the pass, it was the last order he was to give. Artillery fire crashed out ahead of them within which could be heard quite clearly the flat, whip-lash crack of the 88mm., and within a minute all but one of the Matildas, including Miles's, were in flames – and their reputation as Queen of the Battlefield gone for ever. The Camerons debussed, opened their ranks into artillery formation and marched steadily on between the lines of blazing tanks, praying for their own guns to open up and that the gap between themselves and their objectives would close more quickly – but long before it was below a thousand yards, German armoured cars and lorried infantry debouched from the head of the pass and charged, overrunning one company and chasing the remainder away into the heads of the wadis seaming the Escarpment, from where they could do little for the rest of the day but wait for darkness and watch the battle being fought out below them.

By 0730, the Mahrattas and Rajputanas were within three miles of the Reverend Bach's post at the bottom of the pass, and they had six Matildas of A Squadron 4th R.T.R. to lead them, and some 25-pounders in support. The Mahrattas moved along the base of the Escarpment and the Rajputanas on the slopes above, and the broken ground gave them excellent cover for the first mile. They then reached a curve in the line of approach, and as they rounded it, came under heavy fire from ahead and above which pinned them down – and the Matildas on the right flank ran into mines upon which four of them promptly blew up while the remaining two were blocked in positions from which they could do little but act as pill-boxes.

Map 19   *Operation Battleaxe*: June 15th–17th, 1941

That was virtually the end of the attacks on Halfaya Pass, and Rommel's faith in the military expertise and foresight of his remarkable cleric had been fully justified.

Further south on the upper plateau, however, matters had gone better for the central thrust. Matildas of 7th R.T.R. (4th Armoured Brigade) had by-passed Point 206 which was known to be strongly held, paused by the Wire until the motorised Guards Brigade arrived and then swept on across the frontier at a steady eight miles an hour. They reached Capuzzo just before noon, chased the garrison away into the desert and then, slightly to their surprise, found themselves the object of several well-pressed counter-attacks in which five of their Matildas were knocked out and another four damaged. But the Guards infantry came up and consolidated the position, successfully fought off a much more serious counter-attack about 1830, and the joint forces then prepared for all-round defence during the night and possible exploitation of successes gained the following day.

The news from the most southerly flank, where the cruisers of 7th Armoured Brigade had swung around to Hafid Ridge had been so good so early that the failure to capture Halfaya Pass to the north had not seemed too serious a check. The brigade had been led by the older and lighter cruisers of the 2nd R.T.R. in order that the Crusaders of the 6th R.T.R. should be held as a 'card up the sleeve' until the last possible moment, and shortly after 0900 they had arrived at what the leading squadron commander, partly blinded by the shimmering and ever-growing heat-haze, believed to be the objective.

But Hafid Ridge consisted in fact of three gentle crests and between them lay the German anti-tank guns, including four 88mms. As the A9s and A10s breasted the first rise there was a blast of fire, two violent explosions as a pair of A9s brewed up – and the rest were then retreating rapidly while their crews, especially the gunners, faced up to a very awkward fact: their only armament consisted of machine-guns and 2-pounder anti-tank guns – and however effective their high-velocity solid shot might be against armour, it was useless against gun positions or dug-in infantry which required high explosive to shift them. And the bulk of the British 25-pounders was back with the Support Group.

After consultation, two squadrons of 2nd R.T.R. put in a flank attack just before noon between the first and second ridges, swept along the gun line machine-gunning the artillerymen and their supporting infantry and reached the end of the line for the loss of only one tank; but then the commander realised the presence of more enemy positions behind the second ridge, ordered a hasty retreat away from the danger area but failed to make contact with five of his tanks (owing to shortage of radio sets the allocation had been reduced to only one per troop) – and these swept on and were never seen again.

By this time, messages were coming in from the R.A.F. that long lines of German armour were streaming towards the battle area from the west, so Brigadier Russell, commanding 7th Armoured Brigade, ordered the first wave of Crusaders to clear the enemy posts from the ridge and set the scene for the main armoured battle for which the generals had been planning. They were encouraged by reports from observers at the front that the Germans there appeared to be pulling back anyway and this would seem the ideal moment to attack – so as the lighter tanks of 2nd R.T.R. (among which was one commanded by Lieutenant Joly) drew back, the Crusaders swept forward over the first crest – to see exactly what they hoped and expected, a group of German lorries and towed guns moving up and over the crest beyond.

In less than five minutes, the Crusaders were topping the second crest to be met in their turn by a storm of fire from the waiting anti-tank guns – 88mms as well as 50mm. and 37mm. guns, all of which were quite effective at that range. In their first action, the Crusaders had thus been neatly ambushed, and within minutes eleven had been completely knocked out and six more badly damaged; and now it was seen that over thirty panzers of a battalion from the 5th Panzer Regiment were coming in from the west. Light was failing by this time and, as neither side was particularly anxious to close, a long-range battle ensued during which the surviving cruisers of 7th Armoured Brigade slowly drew back towards the frontier Wire, leaving over half of their tank strength on the field either totally wrecked or, worse still, available for repair and use against them by the indefatigable German recovery teams. The tank returns for the following morning revealed that 2nd R.T.R. had but twenty-eight tanks still fit for action, while of 6th R.T.R.'s fifty Crusaders, only twenty remained.

A significant fact about the performance of the 7th Armoured Brigade on the first day of *Battleaxe* was not discovered until afterwards; it would not have achieved what little success it did, had it not been for the violent battle being fought for most of the day around Point 206 by Matildas of A Squadron of 4th R.T.R. (whose other troops had accompanied the infantry attacks against Halfaya). They had advanced along the Wire in the early morning, then after overrunning two small German posts came up against the very well-fortified Point 206, whose anti-tank guns repeated the successes on the other parts of the battlefield by knocking out eight of the Matildas before the end of the day. Twice the post changed hands and it was not until the sixteen Matildas of B Squadron came up in the evening that Point 206 was firmly held in the British hands; but the fierce fighting which went on during the daylight hours had at least protected the inner flank of 7th Armoured Brigade's advance against the Hafid Ridge.

The details of another event of that epochal day seem not to have been fully known for many months. The Rifle Brigade history contains the following passage:

> Two years later we heard from a German officer prisoner who was an inmate of our prison cage at Hammam Lif after the German surrender in Tunisia that about twenty of our Matildas broke clean through during the fighting [presumably around Capuzzo], and advanced on a defenceless Bardia, which contained only German administrative units. There were German 88-mm. flak guns in Bardia for anti-aircraft defence of the harbour. The officer commanding them stopped a German supply column which was passing through Bardia at the time, waylaid a truck which contained 88-mm. anti-tank ammunition, lined his guns up south of the perimeter defences and gave battle to our tanks. After a short slogging match eleven tanks were left and one 88-mm. gun. This gun destroyed all the remaining tanks . . . The officer was awarded the Ritterkreuz.[7]

It has not proved possible to confirm in every detail the truth of this account, but it is certainly true that a number of Matildas were never accounted for in the final battle analysis. And what is certain is that of the hundred-odd Matildas which went into action with the 4th Armoured Brigade on the morning of June 15th, only thirty-seven were still capable of action when night fell, although the fitters would have eleven more ready by the following morning.

In all, then, by the end of the first day of *Battleaxe* British armour had been reduced to about 50 per cent of its strength, and as yet had failed to bring the main strength of the German panzers to battle.

Rommel, though obviously concerned by the loss of Capuzzo, the isolation of Major the Reverend Bach's forces at Halfaya, the known destruction of artillery and infantry positions along the Hafid Ridge and the suspected loss of Point 206, was sufficiently well informed by his intercept service of losses and problems on the British side to be able, by about midnight on June 15th, quite coolly and confidently to begin planning the battle for the following day.

He had instructed the new commander of 5th Light Division, Generalleutnant von Ravenstein, to put his leading combat group on the road from Tobruk towards Sidi Azeiz as early as the evening of June 14th, and it was a panzer battalion of this group which had arrived to the west of Hafid Ridge on the evening of the 15th and pushed the cruisers of 7th Armoured Brigade back to the Wire. Behind them, the rest of 5th Light Division was coming up and by midnight almost all had arrived at Sidi Azeiz.

Meanwhile, Neumann-Sylkow's 15th Panzer Division had remained more or less where it had been stationed in the morning, its anti-tank and artillery batteries and its infantry taking the brunt of the British attack, while the majority of its panzers – though not all – were held back on Rommel's orders to the north of the battle area. He had no intention of committing them to battle until the situation clarified. Around Capuzzo, panzers had been in the original clash and in the counter-attacks, but as their chief tactic had been to lure the British tanks on to the anti-tank batteries and not to accept action themselves unless it was forced upon them, they had not suffered many losses.

Although Rommel had started the battle with less tanks in the area than the British, and although he had meanwhile obtained an exaggerated idea of British strength, with the arrival of 5th Light and increasing knowledge of British plans for the following day he felt that prospects now favoured him. He knew, for instance, that Beresford-Peirse had ordered the 4th Indian Division both to renew its attacks on Halfaya Pass and to consolidate its hold on Capuzzo; and he was in no way disturbed when he heard that a battalion of the Scots Guards had mounted a successful night attack on the post back at Musaid. He also knew that General Messervy had been ordered to release 4th Armoured Brigade from its duties of protecting the infantry so that its Matildas could join the cruisers of 7th Armoured Brigade to fight that set tank-versus-panzer battle which the British seemed determined to bring about.

Rommel had no intention of allowing such a battle to take place, principally because he did not believe that the role of armour was to fight armour. In his opinion – shared, indeed, by the majority of the German panzer leaders – the task for armour was to find weak places in the enemy defence, which would generally be infantry positions, break through them and then attack the soft-skinned and unprotected rear echelons of the enemy supply organisation. It was the task of artillery to fight tanks, and infantry to capture artillery posts – a case almost of scissors cut paper, paper wraps stone, stone sharpens scissors.

Even without this philosophy, however, he had a more urgent task for his panzers than the destruction of the British armour – a matter which seemed to be progressing quite satisfactorily without their intervention. Bach and his men at Halfaya were trapped and running out of supplies, and the panzers of 5th Light Division must attempt to get through to them as quickly as possible by swinging down to the south from Sidi Azeiz to Sidi Omar, then east and across through Sidi Suleiman. Neumann-Sylkow's 15th Panzer Division could best help this move by a determined attack in the centre against Capuzzo, which would pin down the Guards Brigade and perhaps also the Matildas of the 4th Armoured Brigade, despite Beresford-Peirse's contrary intentions for them.

And as the British apparently intended to begin the day's fighting shortly after dawn, he would anticipate them and strike while it was still dark.

The battle in front of Capuzzo was joined by 0600 (15th Panzer had started their approach an hour before) and it developed in a way which Rommel would have regretted, for it became a copybook pattern of a well-conducted defensive. There was no need for a bait to tempt the German panzers on to the British anti-tank guns, for Rommel had in effect ordered this while Neumann-Sylkow carried it out in detail. Eighty panzers attacked Capuzzo in two columns, one on each side, and they ran into a barrage of artillery and anti-tank guns supported by the guns of Matildas held stationary in hull-down positions, which virtually made anti-tank gun-posts of them.

And owing to the strong infantry element at Capuzzo, there could be little or no possibility of retreat for the British, who thus were forced to stand and fight it out. This they did to such effect that by 1000 Neumann-Sylkow was reporting his tank strength down to but thirty tanks and the morale of his panzer crews falling fast; smoke and flame covered the battlefield and the wreck of the old Italian stone fort was ringed with burning panzers stopped in their tracks by 25-pounders brought up after the fort had been taken, or caught and penetrated in flank by the 2-pounders as they turned. All the time, machine-guns chattered and rifles cracked and German panzer crews and escorting engineers or infantry fell beneath the famous rapid fire of the British infantry. By noon, 15th Panzer Division was drawing back, counting its losses and hastily salvaging whatever they could from the maul, while the British watched and waited again and on the right even felt strong enough for the Scots Guards to move across from Musaid and take the Sollum barracks at the top of the pass.

Meanwhile, behind Capuzzo at Halfaya, the situation was reversed. Mahrattas and Rajputanas below the Escarpment and Camerons above were trying to shift Bach and his men from the vital posts they held, but like the panzers a few miles away the British infantry were trying to advance against prepared positions, manned by men who knew quite well that there was nowhere for them to retreat to – for the Guards Brigade lay between them and their support.

But to the south-west and west an entirely different battle was being fought, for here there was ground for manoeuvre. The panzers of 5th Light had begun their move down past the western edge of the Hafid Ridge at dawn, and all day the remaining cruisers of 7th Armoured Brigade side-stepped with them, at first by themselves as 4th Armoured were indeed tied down at Capuzzo and then, as the battle moved south towards Sidi Omar, aided by the infantry and guns of the Support Group columns which had been shielding the south-western flank.

There had been some unexpected and lucky successes for the British during the early part of the day – a combined charge by tanks of both 2nd and 6th R.T.R. which drove a column of enemy transport thinly escorted by panzers well out into the desert, and an attack on an unescorted column of soft-skinned transport which dispersed it and left a wide expanse of the plateau littered with wrecked and smoking lorries; but when the British cruisers tried to fight it out with the panzers, the results were rarely favourable to them.

The basic reasons for this were technical. Like the British tank school, the Germans had opted for three types of tank, one of which was little more than a light reconnaissance tank. But the other two, instead of being divided in the British way into different types to fight in different battles – in infantry battles in support or in tank battles in manoeuvre – were divided into vehicles with differing armaments to fight in the same battle. Their Panzerkampfwagen IIIs were armed with a 50mm. anti-tank gun which was in fact marginally inferior to the British 2-pounder (40mm.) but the Panzerkampfwagen IVs were armed with a 75mm. gun which could fire both high explosive and smoke at ranges of up to 3,000 yards, and the British tanks carried nothing to equal this. Moreover, the two types of panzers were trained to work together and the effect of their co-operation and armament on the cruisers of 7th Armoured Division that morning, even when the latter were covered by the 25-pounders of the Support Columns, was ominous.

When the panzers of 5th Light turned to attack a line of British cruisers and artillery, they did so at about fifteen miles per hour, and once they had closed to 3,000 yards their 75mm. guns could open fire with high explosive. This could inflict some damage on the tanks – but would annihilate the unprotected 25-pounders and their crews. As it would take the panzers six minutes to cover the 3,000 yards and the guns three minutes to limber up and get out of action, this meant in practice that the guns must cease firing and begin pulling out as soon as shell-fire began exploding around them; and it was quickly found that the 2-pounder anti-tank guns in the cruisers were only really effective against the German panzers at ranges of less than 500 yards.

British 25-pounders outrange
German 75mm. tank guns
until forced to retire

A

3,000 yds   2,500   2,000   1,500   1,000   500
                                                                          B

German Pzkw IVs' 75mm. H.E. wholly effective against   British 2-pounder tank guns firing solid shot (and
British gun crews from point A and becoming   German 50mms) only really effective against armour at
increasingly effective against British armour during the   500 yards
6 minutes it takes to reach B

Thus, when a squadron of about forty German panzers attacked a line of ten British cruisers (and by the morning of June 16th, the entire 7th Armoured Brigade had only forty-eight tanks left and the first engagements had already taken their toll), even though it was supported by a troop of four 25-pounders, the only guns which could engage the panzers before they came within 3,000 yards were those of the artillery – who would then come under H.E. fire from which they were virtually unprotected and must, in the light of simple mathematics, pull out. And from that moment until the panzers had closed to within the 500-yard range of the cruisers' 2-pounders, there was nothing the British could fire at them which could do them anything but trivial damage.

Many British tank gunners during that frustrating morning opened fire at German panzers at ranges of a thousand yards or more – a futile gesture for not only could their solid shot deliver little but a glancing blow, but in the shimmer and haze as the heat of the day increased, their comparatively rudimentary gun-sights were useless. The panzers had better armament and optical equipment, sounder engineering and therefore fewer breakdowns and, moreover, their crews had been given more time to get used to their vehicles in the conditions in which they were operating. Mr Churchill's impatience for action was wasting the fruits of his own beneficence.

Thus, as the morning wore on, the strength of 7th Armoured Brigade was whittled away and by noon when the commander of 6th R.T.R. withdrew his Crusaders to the Wire for refuelling and replenishment, he found that he had only ten runners left – and the remainder of 2nd R.T.R. were at that very moment fighting a desperate rearguard action to enable the Support Group column which had gone down to Sidi Omar the previous day to get away. By mid-afternoon both R.T.R.s were back east of the frontier, about six miles apart and with their supporting artillery further back still, the tank crews watching anxiously the massing of panzers along the Wire, totally incapable of interfering with the preparations for the next stage of the advance which was obviously imminent.

It came about 1900, just as the light was fading – in itself an indication of the high degree of German training – and as on so many occasions that day, the Crusaders had to wait under heavy fire until the approaching panzers came within effective range, watched all the time by men of their Support Group to the rear, paralysingly unable to help them:

> There we first saw that most depressing sight – the tracer of the solid shot from our 2-pounder guns describing graceful parabolas in the air and bouncing anything up to five or six hundred yards short of the enemy tanks, while the tracer from enemy weapons flew on much flatter curves and 'brewed' our tanks up one after the other. When the 7th Armoured Brigade concentrated at Bir Khireigat the next morning they had nine 'runners' left.[8]

After the first attack on the 6th R.T.R. Crusaders, the panzers had turned against the even lighter and older tanks of the 2nd R.T.R. and annihilation of the British cruisers was only averted by the onset of complete darkness. June 16th, 1941, was the day when the British tank crews first realised that their own experts on armoured warfare had been out-thought by Hitler's.

It also marked the beginning of the last twenty-four hours which Wavell was to spend on a desert battlefield, for with the perception which always took him to the place where he was most likely to be needed, he had arrived at Sidi Barrani during that afternoon to find that Beresford-Peirse was away visiting Messervy and Creagh. Despite the trend of the day's events, Beresford-Peirse had confirmed them in their orders to hold on at Capuzzo with the infantry, and to consolidate the armour of 4th and 7th Brigades the following morning for a mass onslaught against Rommel's panzers, and by evening there was perhaps a little more ground for the somewhat spurious hope that this might be achieved. There had been an unexpected easing of pressure against Capuzzo, so perhaps in the morning the Matildas might indeed be able to get away; but the lessons which had been learned that day by the tank crews had obviously not yet percolated to the higher ranks. They would take some time to do so.

Rommel had not needed to learn many lessons that day, and late in the afternoon he gave an excellent example of what his countrymen called his *Fingerspitzengefühl* and which his opponents with wry admiration and perhaps a little more elegance were to call 'The Rommel Touch'.

'It is often possible', he was to write later, 'to decide the issue of a battle merely by making an unexpected shift of one's main weight.'

This he proceeded to do. He had carefully followed the engagement between the 5th Light panzers and the 7th Armoured tanks and watched them clash west of Sidi Omar:

> The violent tank battle which ensued was soon decided in our favour and the division succeeded in fighting its way through to the area north-east of Sidi Omar and continuing its advance on Sidi Suleiman. This was the turning-point of the battle. I immediately ordered the 15th Panzer Division to disengage all its mobile forces as quickly as possible and, leaving only the essential minimum to hold the position north of Capuzzo, to go forward on the northern flank of the victorious 5th Light Division towards Sidi Suleiman. The decisive moment had come.[9]

The switch of thrust from one side of the arena to the other was made during the late afternoon and evening of June 16th, but not appreciated by the British until 0600 the following morning when the full weight of Rommel's remaining panzers – which had been on the move since 0430 – fell upon the weak and exhausted screens west of Sidi Suleiman and began inexorably to press them back towards the Escarpment and the battles around Halfaya.

Creagh was the first to realise the danger which now threatened the entire Battleaxe Force, and at 0930 sent a message to Beresford-Peirse requesting his presence for advice and instructions – a message which was promptly picked up and retailed to Rommel who was not slow to grasp its implications:

> It sounded suspiciously as though the British commander no longer felt himself capable of handling the situation. It being now obvious that in their present bewildered state the British would not start anything for the time being, I decided to pull the net tight by going on to Halfaya.[10]

As Wavell was still with Beresford-Peirse, he took over command, flew up to Halfway House in a light Magister aircraft which hugged the ground the whole way and so escaped the attention of the Luftwaffe fighters who now dominated the sky, arriving at 1145. However, before he had time to issue orders he discovered that General Messervy at Capuzzo had also realised the danger the infantry were in, and had disobeyed his orders of the night before to release the Matildas to augment the Crusaders' attack on the panzers and instructed them instead to hold the southern border of a channel leading back along the edge of the Escarpment through which the survivors of the 22nd Guards Brigade could escape as far as Halfaya at least, and accompanied by the Camerons, perhaps back even further.

It had been obvious to Wavell since the previous afternoon that tactical control of the battle had been exercised almost since the beginning through the co-operation between Creagh and Messervy, with Beresford-Peirse too far back to be in touch. Even the security between the two subordinate generals had been better than that between themselves and Western Desert Force Headquarters, for whenever they had felt the need to communicate directly they had foxed Rommel's intercept service by talking in Hindustani; and now the retreat which neither Wavell nor Beresford-Peirse had sanctioned was well under way.

'I think you were right to withdraw in the circumstances,' Wavell later told Messervy, 'but orders should have come from Western Desert Force' – a remark which underlined the hollowness of a situation in which junior officers could be right in usurping the responsibilities of their seniors.

And now the tactical advantages reverted to the British.

The Matildas came stolidly back from their positions around Capuzzo, the Crusaders fell back on their flank and Campbell's artillery from the Support Group was with them to hold the line – against panzers now with emptying fuel tanks and, more vitally, bereft of the striking power of the 88mms or even their lighter anti-tank guns. From hull-down positions the British tanks with their 2-pounders fought a six-hour battle with the 25-pounders alongside them, both elements of the defence confident at last that the other would not retire – at any rate until the rear columns of infantry scuttling back from Capuzzo and Halfaya had passed, by which time they could all go.

It was mid-afternoon before the crash of battle began dying down from the west, and 1600 before the leading panzers felt their way forward to find that there was now nothing between themselves and the delighted and triumphant men of Major Bach's force. Below them, the last of the Mahrattas and Rajputanas had gone, and as on Rommel's urgent instructions the panzers turned west and swept towards Musaid and Capuzzo it was to find that the trap was empty, the quarry escaped – and their commander furious at what he considered their ineptitude at trying to squeeze out the pocket instead of blocking off the neck..

Rommel could be as unfair to his subordinates as any other high-level commander.

On the last day of *Battleaxe*, Churchill, shaken by the accumulating evidence of the loss of what he had romantically come to look upon

as his own 'Tiger Cubs', left London and went down to his home at
Chartwell which he had shut up for the duration of the war, to roam
disconsolately through the empty rooms and the once-immaculate
gardens, now shabbier, now showing the signs of less exact attention.
It was not an atmosphere conducive to optimism, impartiality of
judgment or even of charity; and while he was there Wavell's report
on the events of the last few days arrived, opening with the chilling
sentence 'I regret to report failure of "Battleaxe".' During the next
few days, the figures of the British losses came in – losses for what
the maps showed only too clearly had been no gain at all.

XIII Corps had lost 122 officers and men killed, 588 wounded and
259 missing. The R.A.F. had lost 36 aircraft and the artillery had
lost four of their guns; but the figures which rubbed salt into
Churchill's wounds were the ones which revealed that of the
hundred-odd Matildas with which the battle had opened, 64 had
been lost together with 27 of the cruisers. He had not stripped
Britain of her defences, ignored the advice of his Chiefs of Staff and
braved the dangers of the Mediterranean passage for results such as
these. The arrival of a further cable from Wavell strengthened a
resolve already firmly in his mind:

> A. P. Wavell to Prime Minister   21st June, 1941
> Am very sorry for failure of 'Battleaxe' and loss of so many Tiger
> cubs, especially since I have realised from figures produced by
> liaison officer how short we are of requirements at home. Fear
> this failure must add much to your anxieties. I was over-optimistic
> and should have advised you that 7th Armoured Division
> required more training before going into battle. Feel I should also
> have deferred 'Exporter' till we could have put in larger force,
> but in both places I was impressed by apparent need for im-
> mediate action.[11]

The fact that both operations had been launched under strong
pressure from London was left unsaid by Wavell, and ignored by
Churchill.

The Prime Minister had decided: Wavell must go.

But how? It would be better if it could be done with only the
faintest hint of censure on Wavell's performance, for too many
people would spring to his defence asserting that he was being made
a scapegoat for the Government's own mistakes; and it would be
better still if matters could be so arranged that Wavell did not
return to London where he could well prove an embarrassment, and
if questioned by the Press or by some of Churchill's parliamentary
opponents, might give answers which would be best not heard.

The solution was, in fact, quite neat and simple. As Churchill
wished command of the armies of the Middle East to devolve upon

the present Commander-in-Chief in India, General Auchinleck,
and as Wavell had considerable experience of military service in
India, the generals could simply exchange commands; Wavell would
enjoy sitting under the pagoda tree – and he would be a long way
from London.

The cables flew between Whitehall and Cairo, Whitehall and
Delhi, Delhi and Cairo – polite, flattering, compliant; in due course
aircraft bearing the new Commander-in-Chief Middle East and his
personal staff arrived in Cairo, and after a few days of meetings and
talks, other aircraft flew in the opposite direction bearing the old
one away. The talks between the two generals had been very
friendly as they knew each other well, but undoubtedly Auchinleck
had cause for a great deal of thought on other problems than those
of pure military tactics or strategy as he took up the reins of his new
command.

As for Wavell, he had been shaving when the news of the Prime
Minister's decision was read to him by his C.o.S. on the morning of
June 22nd, and he had showed not the slightest emotion.

'The Prime Minister's quite right,' he said. 'This job needs a new
eye and a new hand.' And he went on shaving.

He made no complaint when his request for a brief period of
leave in London before taking up his new appointment was refused,
but one decision by the Chiefs of Staff caused a tightening of the lips
and an abruptness of manner which warned those who knew him to
keep away for the rest of the morning. Two days before the official
announcement of his new post, command of troops in Iraq reverted
to India and would thus still be Wavell's responsibility. Churchill
was not the only person to have salt in his wounds.

Epilogue

The Prime Minister had issued strict instructions that the exchange of Commanders-in-Chief between India and the Middle East was to remain secret until both officers had taken up their new appointments, but some five hours before Wavell learned of his removal from the theatre he had commanded for so many turbulent months, *Operation Barbarossa* had launched three vast German Army Groups across the Russian frontier in the greatest military spectacle the world had yet seen, so it is hardly surprising that Auchinleck's arrival in Cairo and Wavell's departure a few days later failed in any case to catch the world's headlines. No great controversy erupted – even in the British Parliament – when eventually the news of the exchange became general. Questions were asked, certainly; editorials appeared in due course expressing slight puzzlement and even disquiet; but it was not until many months or even years had passed that arguments developed among historians and other military analysts about the justice or otherwise of Wavell's treatment.

The first popular attempts concentrated, as usual, upon personal factors and tried to magnify their effects. Undoubtedly Wavell's relations with Churchill from almost their first meeting had left a lot to be desired; and after his reply to Churchill's demand for a board of enquiry following the evacuation of British Somaliland, ending with that cogent admonition 'A big butcher's bill is not necessarily evidence of good tactics', it is a tribute to Churchill's restraint that Wavell remained in such high office for as long as he did, reaching in the end, indeed, the topmost pinnacle of promotion.

It would seem therefore that personal spite on the part of higher authority cannot be blamed for Wavell's removal from the Middle East Command. Was he himself right, therefore, when he remarked that the job needed 'a new eye and a new hand'?

Certainly, it would not have been surprising if the enormous responsibilities which he had borne in such difficult times and circumstances had tired him, but there was little sign of this – and indeed he was to tackle times and circumstances just as difficult in his new command within a few months of taking it up. His admirers – and there are many, for his qualities of mind and spirit were great and affected everyone with whom he came into contact – claim that although the change of scene and task was perhaps beneficial, the manner of its presentation and its timing was unfair, its communication to him unnecessarily ruthless. And they point out that under Wavell's command, even though the Greek and Cretan campaigns had been disasters, those in Syria and Iraq had been successful, while the destruction of the Italian armies in Cyrenaica and Italian East Africa had been two of the most resounding victories in history.

His critics, however, claim that there is another side to that picture. The victory against Graziani's army, it can be argued, was in fact a tactical victory won by General O'Connor – almost in spite of Wavell's interference. Though O'Connor remained a friend and admirer of Wavell's for the rest of his life, he also remained convinced that if Wavell's appreciation of the achievements of the first forty-eight hours of *Operation Compass* had been that of a true military genius, so far from removing 4th Indian Division and sending it down to East Africa, he would have left it in place and thrown in the 6th Australians as reinforcement instead of replacement, at the same time organising behind the combined force the strongest support and administration echelons that could be culled from his command.

Such measures could so have accelerated the advance of Western Desert Force that Tobruk would have been theirs by Christmas, Benghasi and El Agheila by early January, and by the end of that month XIII Corps would have been in Tripoli, Rommel still in Germany and the Afrika Korps nothing but an impractical military dream. And with the whole of the North African coast from Egypt to Tunisia in British hands, East Africa could then have been left, as Churchill was later to write, 'to wither on the bough'.

As it was, Wavell threw away O'Connor's victory by stripping Cyrenaica of its most experienced formations and sending them to Greece on a mission about which his own planning staff had the gravest doubts. Francis de Guingand was later to write how he and the Director of Military Intelligence, Brigadier Shearer, had put together papers showing both that Tripoli was within the grasp of O'Connor's force, and that, in view of the known resources and methods of the German Wehrmacht, the proposed expedition to Greece held little chance of success and every prospect of disaster.

The latter paper was returned to them with the single note ' "War is an option of difficulties" – Wolfe. A.P.W.' – which, though apt, was to prove frustrating. Genius chooses the right options; and despite persistent post-war declarations, Wavell was not under overwhelming pressure from Churchill, and could have withstood Eden had he wished.

Those tantalising 'Ifs' of history . . .

*

Wavell and his personal staff arrived in Delhi in July, 1941, and had hardly time to grasp the ramifications of either the internal political situation in India or the military predicament on her borders before it became obvious that enormous dangers threatened the sub-continent from Japan.

Within days of the attack on Pearl Harbor and while the Western world was still watching with horror the astonishing explosion of Japanese military energy which was to menace the borders of India, completely contain the Dutch Eastern Empire, brush the north coast of Australia and control almost half the Pacific Ocean, Wavell had been appointed Commander-in-Chief of all Allied Forces in the area, responsible, in fact, for the A.B.D.A. area – the letters standing for American, British, Dutch and Australian.

Wavell took up the appointment on January 4th, 1942 – commenting wryly, 'I am getting used to holding babies, but this looks like being the worst behaved of all!' – and during the seven weeks that the appointment lasted he saw the complete loss of Allied air and sea supremacy, and the fall of Manila, a substantial part of the Philippines, Hong Kong and Singapore. And with the abolition of A.B.D.A. he returned to India as Commander-in-Chief, faced with the problems of checking the flood of Japanese expansion through Upper Burma towards Assam.

Needless to say, the forces with which he was expected to defend India were as exiguous and as poorly equipped as those with which he had safeguarded the Nile Delta and the Suez Canal – but this time he was opposed by an enemy as fanatical, efficient and hardy as his first desert enemy had been unenthusiastic and ill trained. It was fortunate from a defensive point of view that the battle terrain in Upper Burma is as difficult as it is, though this was not an advantage much appreciated by the men of the Fourteenth Army later in the war.

Neither did they ever appreciate the onset of the seasonal monsoons; but when the May monsoon broke in 1942 it at least eased the tasks of the two under-strength Indian divisions and one brigade, which were all Wavell could deploy to hold 1,200 miles of land frontier and sea coast threatened by the Japanese advance . . . and there was no reliable intelligence network in Burma to inform Wavell of the temporary hiatus in Japanese aggressive plans for the area. Though he could hope for the best, he had undoubtedly to plan for the worst.

On January 1st, 1943, Wavell was made Field Marshal, the third soldier to gain the rank since 1939, the others being Ironside and Dill, both of whom were then shunted out of the main stream of military endeavour into inconspicuous backwaters. Perhaps the intention in Whitehall was that throughout 1943 the India/Burma theatre should be a backwater – and from the meagre supply of reinforcements and equipment to arrive there, commensurate with the needs, such a suspicion would appear not unjustified; but the presence of the Japanese in Burma ensured that it would certainly not be a calm and peaceful backwater.

Neither did Wavell believe it should be an inactive one. Despite the enormous tasks of recruiting and building a huge Indian Army with which to augment British formations when the time came to drive the Japanese back the way they had come, there were roads to build 'across the grain' of some of the most difficult country in the world, huge advanced dumps to be assembled at such places as Imphal and Dimapur – and at least one aggressive operation to plan and mount. The attempted capture of Akyab Island and the re-occupation of Upper Arakan failed because of the same lack of adequate materials that had caused the failure of *Battleaxe*, and because at that time the Japanese soldiers were more skilled at jungle fighting than the British and Commonwealth ones; but valuable lessons were learned – for other times and other commanders.

The most significant contribution that Wavell made at that time to the eventual defeat of the Japanese could well have been the encouragement he gave to that military enigma Orde Wingate. In the same way that Wavell had encouraged the Jock Columns and the Long Range Desert Group in the Middle East, he ensured that men, materials and training facilities were made available for the Long Range Penetration Columns which were to win fame as 'Chindits'. He allowed the first expedition to go ahead despite the disruption of overall plans when Chinese support was suddenly withdrawn for a major drive towards their operational area, and then, despite the heavy casualties incurred, he kept the basic idea alive – and indeed expanded Wingate's force from one brigade to three in the face of concerted opposition from more orthodox minds.

He was recalled to London for talks in April, 1943, and his report on the failure of the Akyab and Arakan operations did nothing to improve his standing with Churchill. Nevertheless, he was invited to join the retinue accompanying the Prime Minister to the Third Washington Conference, and here Wavell attended whichever talks demanded his presence and, when asked, gave his views with his usual taciturnity; but it was evident to all that his star was hardly in the ascendant. Upon the party's return to London, he was informed of new appointments, new concepts, and new leaders to put them into operation: Lord Mountbatten was to be appointed Supreme Commander of South-East Asia Command. Wavell would become Viceroy and Governor-General of India.

So ended Wavell's military career. It can hardly be said to have ended in obscurity, for he remained Viceroy until 1947, and in forty years of military life had risen to the highest possible rank and won an earldom – not an unsuccessful life for the son of an orthodox but obscure officer of a county regiment. That his name was not to be indissolubly linked with any epoch-making and spectacular victory is perhaps unfortunate; but perhaps it was implicit in his nature.

Though neither shy nor retiring, he was undoubtedly immensely reserved and taciturn – perhaps too strongly committed to his oft-repeated aphorism: 'The herd is usually wrong.' He not only lacked the common touch – he spurned it.

But there is no doubt that in those early, exiguous days in both the Middle East and in India he was the right man in the right job. As his biographer has said: 'He was adversity's general. There was no other man.'

Appendix I:
Forces engaged in Operation Compass

British and Commonwealth Forces

Commander-in-Chief, Middle East   General Sir Archibald Wavell

WESTERN DESERT FORCE (LATER XIII CORPS)
Lieutenant-General R. N. O'Connor

Corps Troops:
    7th Royal Tank Regt (Matildas)
    1st and 104th Royal Horse Artillery
    51st Field Regt R.A.
    7th and 64th Medium Regts R.A.

7th Armoured Division – Major-General M. O'Moore Creagh

4th Armoured Brigade – Brig. J. S. L. Caunter
    7th Hussars
    2nd Royal Tank Regt
    6th Royal Tank Regt

7th Armoured Brigade – Brig. H. E. Russell
    3rd Hussars
    8th Hussars
    1st Royal Tank Regt

Support Group – Brig. W. H. E. Gott
    1st King's Royal Rifle Corps
    2nd Rifle Brigade
    1st and 4th Royal Horse Artillery

Divisional Troops:
    11th Hussars
    3rd and 106th Royal Horse Artillery
    2nd Field Squadron, Royal Engineers
    141st Field Park Troop, Royal Engineers
    No. 2 R.A.F. Armoured Car Company

4th Indian Division – Major-General N. M. de la P. Beresford-Peirse
(withdrawn December 11th)

5th Indian Infantry Brigade – Brig. W. L. Lloyd
  1st Royal Fusiliers
  3rd/1st Punjab Regt
  4th/6th Rajputana Rifles

11th Indian Infantry Brigade – Brig. R. A. Savory
  2nd Queen's Own Cameron Highlanders
  1st/6th Rajputana Rifles
  4th/7th Rajput Regt

Divisional Troops:
  Central India Horse
  1st Northumberland Fusiliers (Machine-gun Battalion)
  1st, 25th and 31st Field Regt R.A.
  3rd Royal Horse Artillery
  4th, 12th, 18th and 21st Field Company (Sappers and Miners)
  11th Field Park Company

16th British Infantry Brigade – Brig. C. E. N. Lomax (attached 4th
  Indian Division until December 11th)
  2nd Queen's Regt
  2nd Leicestershire Regt
  1st Argyll and Sutherland Highlanders

Selby Force – Brig. A. R. Selby
  3rd Coldstream Guards
  W Company Northumberland Fusiliers
  A Company 1st South Staffordshire Regt
  A Company 1st Cheshire Regt
  Detachment 1st Durham Light Infantry
  A Troop 7th Hussars
  Attached artillery

6th Australian Division – Major-General I. Mackay (joined operation after
  departure of 4th Indian Division)

16th Australian Infantry Brigade – Brig. A. S. Allen
  2nd/1st Batallion
  2nd/2nd Battalion
  2nd/3rd Battalion

17th Australian Infantry Brigade – Brig. S. G. Savige
  2nd/5th Battalion
  2nd/6th Battalion
  2nd/7th Battalion

19th Australian Infantry Brigade – Brig. H. C. H. Robertson
  2nd/4th Battalion
  2nd/8th Battalion
  2nd/11th Battalion

Divisional Troops:
  6th Cavalry Regt
  2nd/1st, 2nd/2nd and 2nd/3rd Field Regt, Royal Australian Artillery
  2nd/1st, 2nd/2nd and 2nd/8th Field Coys, Royal Australian Engineers

Italian Forces

Comandante Superiore   Maresciallo d'Armata Rodolfo Graziani

TENTH ARMY
Generale d'Armata   Gariboldi   (until November 17th, 1940)
Generale d'Armata   Berti   (until December 23rd, 1940)
Generale d'Armata   Tellera   (died of wounds February 7th, 1941)

XXI Corps – Generale di Corpo d'Armata Bergonzoli (H.Q. Bardia)
  1st Libyan Division (at Maktila)
  2nd Libyan Division (at Tummar)
  4th Blackshirt Division (at Sidi Barrani)
  Maletti Group (at Nibeiwa)
  63rd Cirene Division (at Rabia/Sofafi)
  62nd Marmarica Division (along Escarpment between Sofafi and Halfaya)
  64th Catanzaro Division (at Buq Buq)
  1st Blackshirt Division (at Bardia)
  2nd Blackshirt Division (at Bardia)
  Frontier Guard units and Fortress troops in Bardia

XXII Corps – Generale di Corpo d'Armata Petassi Mannella (H.Q. Tobruk)
  61st Sirte Division (in Tobruk)
  Fortress troops and artillery in Tobruk

XX Corps – Generale di Corpo d'Armata Cona (H.Q. Giovanni Berta)
  60th Sabratha Division (at Derna)
  27th Brescia Division (at Slonta)
  17th Pavia Division (at Cirene)
  Babini Armoured Brigade (at Mechili)

Note: Metropolitan Divisions such as Brescia and Pavia usually consisted of approximately 13,000 men; Libyan and Blackshirt Divisions of approximately 8,000.

Appendix II:
Forces engaged in Operation Battleaxe

British and Commonwealth Forces

Commander-in-Chief, Middle East   General Sir Archibald Wavell

XIII CORPS
Lieutenant-General Sir Noel M. de la P. Beresford-Peirse

7th Armoured Division – Major-General Sir Michael O'Moore Creagh

4th Armoured Brigade – Brig. A. H. Gatehouse
4th Royal Tank Regt (Matildas)
7th Royal Tank Regt (Matildas)

7th Armoured Brigade – Brig. H. E. Russell
2nd Royal Tank Regt (mixed cruisers)
6th Royal Tank Regt (Crusaders)

Support Group – Brig. J. C. Campbell
1st, 3rd, 4th and 106th Royal Horse Artillery
1st King's Royal Rifle Corps
2nd Rifle Brigade

Divisional Troops:
11th Hussars
4th Field Squadron
143rd Field Park Squadron

4th Indian Division – Major-General F. W. Messervy

11th Indian Infantry Brigade – Brig. R. A. Savory
2nd Queen's Own Cameron Highlanders
1st/6th Rajputana Rifles
2nd/5th Mahrattas

22nd Guards Brigade – Brig. I. D. Erskine
1st Buffs
2nd Scots Guards
3rd Coldstream Guards
22nd Guards Brigade Attack Company

Divisional Troops:
  Central India Horse
  25th Field Regt
  31st Field Regt
  4th, 12th, 18th and 21st Field Company (Sappers and Miners)
  11th Field Park Company

German and Italian Forces

Comandante Superiore   Generale d'Armata Italo Gariboldi

DEUTSCHES AFRIKA KORPS
Generalleutnant Erwin Rommel

Corps Troops:
  two regiments Italian artillery in Bardia
  one regiment flak (88mm.)

15th Panzer Division – Generalleutnant W. Neumann-Sylkow
  Panzer Regt 8
  Reconnaissance Battalion 33
  Battery P.A.K. (anti-tank)
  Battery flak (88mm.)
  Rifle Regt 104
    Battalion lorried infantry
    Battalion motor-cycle infantry
    Battalion foot infantry (under Major the Rev. Wilhelm Bach at
    Halfaya)
  Divisional artillery at Point 206

Trento Division
  Three infantry battalions and one artillery regiment in area Sollum–
  Musaid–Capuzzo

5th Light Division (later 21st Panzer Division) – Generalleutnant J. von
  Ravenstein
  Panzer Regt 5
  Reconnaissance Battalion 3

Notes

Unless otherwise stated, the place of publication is London.

1 The First Adversaries

1 A. P. Wavell, *Allenby: Soldier and Statesman*, Harrap 1946, p. 245.
2 John Connell, *Wavell, Scholar and Soldier*, Collins 1964, p. 22.
3 Summary of lectures to Staff College candidates, 1930–5, quoted in Connell, op. cit., pp. 161–2, 164.
4 John Masters, *Bugles and a Tiger*, Michael Joseph 1956, Ch. 2.
5 Kenneth Macksey, *Armoured Crusader: Major-General Sir Percy Hobart*, Hutchinson 1967, p. 64.
6 Ibid., pp. 111–12.
7 Quoted in Macksey, op. cit., p. 91.
8 Quoted in Macksey, op. cit., pp. 159–60.
9 Quoted in Macksey, op. cit., p. 160.
10 Quoted in Generale Giuseppe Mancinelli, 'La Preparazione dell'Italia Fascista alla Guerra', in *Storia della Seconda Guerra Mondiale*, Italian edn ed. Angelo Solmi, Rizzoli (Milan) 1967, p. 337.
11 Mancinelli, op. cit., pp. 336–7.

2 Skirmish and Circumspect Advance

1 Brigadier Dudley Clarke, *The Eleventh at War*, Michael Joseph 1952, p. 95.
2 Field Marshal Lord Wilson of Libya, *Eight Years Overseas*, Hutchinson 1950, pp. 20, 21, reproduced by permission of the Estate of the late Field Marshal Lord Wilson of Libya.
3 Quoted in Kenneth Macksey, *Armoured Crusader: Major-General Sir Percy Hobart*, Hutchinson 1967, p. 169.
4 Quoted in Macksey, op. cit., pp. 170–1.
5 Macksey, op. cit., p. 173.
6 Clarke, *The Eleventh at War*, pp. 105–6.
7 Ibid., p. 107.

3 *The Pace Quickens*

1 Quoted in John Connell, *Wavell, Scholar and Soldier*, Collins 1964, pp. 255–6.
2 Winston S. Churchill, *The Second World War, Vol. II*, Cassell 1949, p. 382.
3 Quoted in Connell, op. cit., p. 268.
4 Colonel C. A. H. M. Noble, M.C., unpublished diary.
5 Quoted in Connell, op. cit., p. 277.
6 Churchill, *Second World War*, pp. 483, 484.
7 Quoted in Connell, op. cit., p. 288.
8 Quoted in Connell, op. cit., p. 289.

4 *The 'Five-day Raid'*

1 Cyril Joly, *Take These Men*, Constable Publishers 1955, p. 50.
2 Quoted in John Connell, *Wavell, Scholar and Soldier*, Collins 1964, p. 286.
3 Lieut-Colonel G. R. Stevens, *Fourth Indian Division*, McLaren (Toronto) n.d., p. 18, reprinted by permission of the President, Chairman and Committee of the 4th Indian Division Officers' Association.
4 Joly, op. cit., p. 54.
5 Alan Moorehead, *African Trilogy*, Hamish Hamilton 1944, p. 68.
6 Joly, op. cit., pp. 61–2.
7 Stevens, op. cit., p. 23.

5 *First Battle for Tobruk*

1 Quoted in B. H. Liddell Hart, *The Tanks, Vol. Two*, Cassell 1959, p. 50.
2 General Sir Richard O'Connor, personal account of the Western Desert campaign, unpublished 1941, TS. p. 30.
3 Quoted in Liddell Hart, op. cit., pp. 52–3.
4 Quoted in Liddell Hart, op. cit., p. 53.
5 Gavin Long, *To Benghazi*, Australian War Memorial (Canberra) 1952, p. 148.
6 Ibid., p. 150.
7 Ibid., p. 177.
8 Ibid., p. 193.
9 O'Connor, op. cit., TS. pp. 49–50.
10 Ibid., TS. p. 45.
11 Ibid., TS. p. 46.
12 Ibid.
13 Quoted in Chester Wilmot, *Tobruk*, copyright © Chester Wilmot 1944, reprinted by permission of Angus and Robertson Publishers, Sydney, p. 36.
14 Quoted in Wilmot, op. cit., p. 37.
15 Quoted in Wilmot, op. cit., p. 38.
16 Long, op. cit., pp. 233–4.

17 Lieutenant Hennessy, quoted in Wilmot, op. cit., p. 44.
18 Quoted in Long, op. cit., p. 239.

6 Beda Fomm: The Narrow Victory

1 Gavin Long, *To Benghazi*, Australian War Memorial (Canberra) 1952, p. 252n.
2 Major R. H. W. S. Hastings, *The Rifle Brigade in the Second World War*, Gale and Polden (Aldershot) 1950, pp. 54–5.
3 Cyril Joly, *Take These Men*, Constable Publishers 1955, p. 74.
4 Ibid., pp. 74–5.
5 Quoted in George Forty, *Desert Rats at War*, Ian Allan 1975, p. 69, reprinted by permission of Mr A. C. Brown.
6 Quoted in Forty, op. cit., pp. 69, 70.
7 Alan Moorehead, *African Trilogy*, Hamish Hamilton 1944, pp. 106–7.
8 Joly, op. cit., pp. 86–7.

7 'In all directions . . .'

1 Major-General I. S. O. Playfair *et al.*, *History of the Second World War*, (hereafter referred to as the *Official History*), *The Mediterranean and Middle East Vol. I*, H.M.S.O. 1954, p. 396.
2 Antony Brett-James, *Ball of Fire: The Fifth Indian Division in the Second World War*, Gale and Polden (Aldershot) 1951, p. 20.
3 Lieut-Colonel G. R. Stevens, *Fourth Indian Division*, McLaren (Toronto) n.d., p. 32, reprinted by permission of the President, Chairman and Committee of the 4th Indian Division Officers' Association.
4 Ibid., p. 36.
5 John Connell, *Wavell, Scholar and Soldier*, Collins 1964, p. 382.
6 General Sir Richard O'Connor, personal account of the Western Desert campaign, part II, unpublished 1941, TS. p. 2.
7 Quoted in Connell, op. cit., p. 383.
8 The Earl of Avon, *The Eden Memoirs: The Reckoning*, Cassell 1965, p. 195.
9 W. B. Kennedy Shaw, *Long Range Desert Group*, Collins 1945, pp. 24–5.
10 Ibid., p. 37.
11 Ibid., p. 42.
12 Ibid., p. 65.

8 Enter Rommel

1 Heinz W. Schmidt, *With Rommel in the Desert*, Harrap 1951, pp. 16–17.
2 *The Rommel Papers*, ed. B. H. Liddell Hart, Collins 1953, p. 104.
3 Ibid., p. 105.
4 Quoted in John Connell, *Wavell, Scholar and Soldier*, Collins 1964, pp. 385–6.
5 Quoted in Connell, op. cit., p. 387.

6 *The Rommel Papers*, p. 107.
7 Ibid., p. 110.
8 Ibid., p. 111.
9 Ibid., p. 113.
10 Ibid.
11 Quoted in Connell, op. cit., pp. 434, 435.
12 Quoted in Connell, op. cit., p. 437.
13 Quoted in Connell, op. cit., p. 438.
14 Quoted in Connell, op. cit., p. 439.
15 Quoted in Connell, loc. cit.

9 *Battleaxe*

1 *The Rommel Papers*, ed. B. H. Liddell Hart, Collins 1953, p. 133.
2 Ibid., p. 132.
3 Ibid., p. 134.
4 Ibid., pp. 139, 140.
5 Quoted in Major-General I. S. O. Playfair *et al.*, *Official History, Vol. II*, H.M.S.O. 1956, p. 203.
6 Quoted in B. H. Liddell Hart, *The Tanks, Vol. Two*, Cassell 1959, p. 84.
7 Quoted in Major R. H. W. S. Hastings, *The Rifle Brigade in the Second World War*, Gale and Polden (Aldershot) 1950, p. 72.
8 Quoted in Hastings, op. cit., p. 73.
9 *The Rommel Papers*, p. 144.
10 Ibid., p. 145.
11 Quoted in John Connell, *Wavell, Scholar and Soldier*, Collins 1974, p. 502.

Index